PASSAGES IN
THE LIFE OF
A RADICAL

PASSAGES IN THE LIFE OF A RADICAL

SAMUEL BAMFORD

COSIMO CLASSICS
NEW YORK

Passages in the Life of a Radical
© 2005 Cosimo, Inc.

Cosimo, P.O. Box 416
Old Chelsea Station
New York, NY 10113-0416

or visit our website at:
www.cosimobooks.com

Passages in the Life of a Radical originally published by Macgibbon & Kee in 1843.

Library of Congress Cataloging-in-Publication Data
A catalog record for this book is available from the Library of Congress

Cover design by www.wiselephant.com

ISBN: 1-59605-287-2

PREFACE

'WE HAD plenty to drink. They always wanted to know why I did not drink, I told them my stomach was very bad so Bamford went and fetched me nearly a tumbler of wine, he gave a toast, which was "May the tree of liberty be planted in Hell, and may the bloody butchers of Manchester be the fruit on it", or very like that.'

This, from one of the less official of the Home Office papers relating to Bamford and the reforming movements, has a real smell of the 1819 radical atmosphere about it. It is not difficult to sense the authentic tone of the amateur informer, snivelling, righteous, mealy-mouthed. And Bamford's muddled oath conveys something of the fierce sense of injustice, the energy and fervour of the reformers. He was thirty-one years old at the time, a recognized leader of political agitation in his native Middleton, and soon to be jailed for a second time. The writer of this report, known only to the government as 'Y', had just spent the evening with Bamford and his associates in an illegal liquor shop, where the provision of pikes and other weapons was being discussed.

It was a time of violence and conspiracy. But this is something that *Passages in the Life of a Radical* is perhaps at some pains to minimize. Bamford began to write the book some twenty years later, in 1839. His aptitude for literary work had led him to London, where he had become a newspaper correspondent. In 1848 he enrolled as a special constable to help keep down the Chartists who had assembled on Kennington Common, and in 1851 found himself a comfortable post as a kind of messenger boy in Somerset House. A striking contrast with the unsettled gusto of his youth: as a boy, Bamford had learnt the weaving trade of his home town only to give it up for a seaman's life on a collier trading between Shields and London. Abandoning this too, he walked back to Manchester to become a warehouseman before settling as a weaver in Middleton, where he entered whole-heartedly into working-class political life. In those days, his enthusiasm and vigour were obviously immense. He argued forcefully and organized effectively. He knew (as the *Passages* makes abundantly clear) every public house in South Lancashire. His child was solemnly placed in his arms at his wedding ceremony. He penned effusive, if derivative, verses, and wrote hearty songs for his comrades. A true reformer, he believed himself the equal of any man: we can admire the scorn with which he treated the blustering of Nadin, the corrupt and loyalist deputy constable of Manchester, who arrested him and hoped to see him hang. Sidmouth and the Privy Council were obviously impressed by the dignity with which he faced them.

At the time of which Bamford was writing, Middleton, five miles North of Manchester, was a small weaving town of about 1,000 houses. There had been weaving in Middleton since at least the earlier part of the seventeenth century, but by the late 1770's the process was well advanced by which such small upland towns – Oldham and Rochdale were others – were largely populated by small farmers, agricultural labourers and the like, who had turned from the land to weaving.

The topographer John Aiken wrote of Middleton in 1795 that 'the farms are occupied mostly by weavers, who alternately engage themselves in the pursuits of husbandry and the more lucrative one of the shuttle'. The shuttle may well have been more lucrative: but if the cotton trade of Lancashire was indeed expanding in the years after the Napoleonic wars, yet the recessions of 1817 and 1819 were catastrophic, and especially catastrophic for the weavers. They provided the support for the reforming politicians, those who in 1817 planned the March of the Blanketeers (of which Bamford disapproved). A crowd of 12,000 assembled to hear the speeches before the march began, and, despite the peaceful dispersal and the failure of the demonstration, the authorities were sufficiently alarmed to arrest Bamford, together with many others, a fortnight later.

In the Spring and Summer of 1819, when real wages had fallen to less than half the figure of 1810, The Times' correspondent had to report that the wretchedness of the weavers 'seems to madden them against the rich, who they dangerously imagine engross the fruits of their labour'. Again, it was above all the weavers who gave their support to the initial gathering of forces leading to the meeting in Saint Peter's Fields; the names of weavers figure prominently in the requisition to the meeting.

Economic distress, then, the grinding poverty to which the operatives were subjected, was the major factor in producing the disturbances in the Manchester area in these years. It is surprising, perhaps, that Bamford's reminiscences do not make more of this. But he was interested in other things when writing the book. In many ways his primary concern was to establish an idea of the sobriety and good sense of his own political character, and it is likely that he had been much more of a militant than he would have us believe, though contemporary evidence is thin. Bamford's complete writings show him to be as much the recorder of a previous way of life as a reformer. This is important to an understanding both of his own character and of his place in working-class history. His *Early Days* (published in 1848) makes a great deal of the village wakes and festivities, the folk-lore and superstitions of his youth. By the 1820's, he claims, these were fast disappearing. But Bamford liked to retain a kind of half-belief in the local stories of boggarts, fyerin and similar creatures. Hence the story, told in jail, of the unfortunate Chirrup, and hence his fondness for recounting the fate of Archibald Hilton of Middleton, 'a decent, elderly man', spirited away after an intemperate evening, most probably by witches, and never seen or heard of again.

Bamford's interest in – and championing – of his local dialect has a similar regional feeling for a vanishing past. Many of his poems were written in dialectal form, as indeed are parts of the *Passages*, though here he makes the proper concessions to comprehensibility. Bamford still remains a major source for the study of Lancashire dialect; and surely it is the regional flavour of his autobiography, and that particular ability to deflate pretension that dialect often has, that give the work its air of honesty, of no-nonsense. His disgust at the way that he sees the affairs of parliament to be conducted is that of a Northerner as well as of a radical.

The centre of Northern radicalism was of course Manchester, and the town was famous for it. Francis Place, the radical Charing Cross tailor, looking back on the period, remarked that 'a stranger walking through their towns was "touted", i.e. hooted, and an "outcomling" was sometimes pelted with stones. "Lancashire brute" was the common and appropriate appellation. Until very lately it would have been dangerous to have assembled five hundred of them on any occasion. Bakers and butchers would at the least have been plundered.' That extraordinary eccentric and sportsman Jack Mytton had a horse called Anti-Radical whose name he always entered as Radical when racing it in the area.

But the Government thought the situation less of a joke. Spies and informers like 'Y' reported regularly, as did the magistrates, and the medieval system of maintaining law and order, which amounted to only two constables assisted by a permanent deputy constable and a few beadles, had to be bolstered by other forces. The magistrates were convinced that the meeting in Manchester would be attended by dangerous armed hordes: the manufacture and distribution of weapons had long been reported. At night, the reformers were drilling on the moors, and, as a Middleton plumber informed Sidmouth, 'they went through their exercises as with muskets'.

Dispensing with the services of the more calm and moderate General Byng, the Manchester magistrates called in the military and enrolled more than three hundred special constables. The account of the Peterloo meeting is undoubtedly the high point of Bamford's book. The meeting itself, and the intentions of the leaders, were completely peaceable. The ensuing massacre was shameful and appalling, and if the immediate horror of the event seems slightly toned down in the author's recollection, we have here an expression of what was most dignified and courageous in the reaction to the outrage.

Bamford was arrested again, as were the other leaders, and at the York trials they were found guilty on a variety of charges. His subsequent imprisonment at Lincoln marks the end of Bamford's active participation in the movements for reform. He later expressed little but contempt for such leaders as 'Orator' Hunt, and had no sympathy for their methods or their aims. His attitude to the Chartists is not one that endears.

It is easy to think of him as a turncoat: many people did. But it is more accurate to regard Bamford as one whose political day was over. He himself was aware of this: it was what gave him the urge to record the transition he had seen in Middleton from one society to another. And if he did quieten his previous activities in the interests of later respectability, he never denied or regretted them. He was right to feel the pride that is an essential part of his autobiography, a pride that prison did not break, nor the alienation of later years.

TIM HILTON

PUBLISHER'S NOTE

THIS edition omits the last five chapters of Bamford's work, as published in book form in 1844 by Messrs Simpkin, Marshall, London. These relate mainly to the author's problems in publishing the work and to the reception he thought it received once it began appearing. The author was flattered by some lordly attention and by a civil notice in the high Tory *Quarterly Review*. In the first edition of the book (published in two volumes), Chapter L is erroneously numbered twice in Volume II. For this edition, the chapters have been numbered consecutively, and in Arabic not Roman numerals.

PASSAGES IN THE LIFE OF A RADICAL

Chapter 1

THIS work will be found to contain narratives of, and observations on, some of the most remarkable and interesting events which took place in the manufacturing districts of Lancashire, and other parts of England, during the years 1816, to 1821, inclusive. It will record the proceedings of the parliamentary reformers and their opponents; and will present personal and biographical notices of active and distinguished individuals, in the ranks of reform, and elsewhere. The writer was a partaker in most of the scenes he will describe. They are vividly impressed on his memory; some of them are also interwoven with the feelings of his heart.

He undertakes not, to conduct his reader, by flowery paths, to cooling and grateful shades in summer; nor to carpeted halls, sumptuous feasts, and downy couches, in winter. The traveller with him (and he thinks the reader will not part company by the way) must e'en be content sometimes to wander, pilgrim-like as it were, through pathless and unsheltered wastes; to sojourn amid, and to converse with, the most patient and suffering of his fellow-subjects; to sit with them on their cheerless hearths; to learn the extent of their endurance from their own sad and too true narrations; to witness their fortitude; to appreciate their homely good sense, but lately understood; and then he may enquire, as doubtless he will, by what means their wrongs were produced, and for what purposes they were continued.

But the track of the journeyers will not be always wafted by sighs, nor bedewed with tears: sufficient amusement will be found by the way, to keep melancholy at a distance, unless when we wait for, and court her humanizing influence. Whether, therefore, we are amid thorny bewilderments of the world; whether amongst the thoughtless, the heartless, the proud, and the oppressive; or with the poor, looking to heaven, having looked in vain to earth for bread; everywhere, something will arise for instruction, and probably also for amusement. Even at the prison door – nay, shrink not, good reader, we must go further than even there;–in the deepest cell, with the fierce law yelling 'treason, treason, life, life,' we will endeavour to be cheerful, and to make most of the little sunshine which the mercy of heaven sheds through one's bars. So, whether in solitudes of the heart – in desolations of home happiness – in the tumult of multitudes – 'mid the jarrings of opinion – when deserted by friends – when assailed by foes – in scenes of peril – in days of trial – in solemnities of judgment – and the solitudes of prison – the writer will endeavour to dispense to his companion, a portion of that cheerful fortitude, which, in all his reverses was never long absent; and which constantly encouraged him to apply those consoling assurances, 'I will not leave thee, nor forsake thee:' 'As thy day is, so shall be thy strength.'

The writer does not pretend to make his work a strict record, but a narrative only of events, in most of which he was personally concerned. His course, he conceives to be obvious, and untrammelled by the particularities of strict chronology. Enjoying freedom and ease in his work, he trusts he will not, on that account, be less entertaining to his readers. To those whose right avocation, talent and education have made it, he leaves the task of discussing philosophically, the causes of the effects he will describe. Some fervid and superior mind will in time arise, to give the history of a great nation careering through a long war; her princes, nobles, priests, and all the wealthy of her land, dazzled by glory, and intoxicated with triumph. Suddenly their plumes are shaken by a portentous sound. It is her artizans and labourers, who struggling through adversity, and directed by an extraordinary genius, are pealing the shouts of, 'Liberty, Liberty.'

At such a period the Author proceeds.

Chapter 2

IT IS matter of history, that whilst the laurels were yet cool on the brows of our victorious soldiers on their second occupation of Paris, the elements of convulsion were at work amongst the masses of our labouring population; and that a series of disturbances commenced with the introduction of the Corn Bill in 1815, and continued, with short intervals, until the close of the year 1816. In London and Westminster riots ensued, and were continued for several days, whilst the bill was discussed; at Bridport, there were riots on account of the high price of bread; at Biddeford there were similar disturbances to prevent the exportation of grain; at Bury, by the unemployed, to destroy machinery; at Ely, not suppressed without bloodshed; at Newcastle-on-Tyne, by colliers and others; at Glasgow, where blood was shed, on account of the soup kitchens; at Preston, by unemployed weavers; at Nottingham, by Luddites, who destroyed thirty frames; at Merthyr Tydville, on a reduction of wages; at Birmingham, by the unemployed; at Walsall, by the distressed; and December 7th, 1816, at Dundee, where owing to the high price of meal, upwards of one hundred shops were plundered. At this time the writings of William Cobbett suddenly became of great authority; they were read on nearly every cottage hearth in the manufacturing districts of South Lancashire, in those of Leicester, Derby, and Nottingham; also in many of the Scottish manufacturing towns. Their influence was speedily visible; he directed his readers to the true cause of their sufferings – misgovernment; and to its proper corrective – parliamentary reform. Riots soon became scarce, and from that time they have never obtained their ancient vogue with the labourers of this country.

Let us not descend to be unjust. Let us not withhold the homage, which, with all the faults of William Cobbett, is still due to his great name.

Instead of riots and destruction of property, Hampden clubs were now established in many of our large towns, and the villages and districts around them; Cobbett's books were printed in a cheap form; the labourers read them, and thenceforward became deliberate and systematic in their proceedings. Nor were there wanting men of their own class, to encourage and direct the new converts; the Sunday Schools of the preceding thirty years, had produced many working men of sufficient talent to become readers, writers, and speakers in the village meetings for parliamentary reform; some also were found to possess a rude poetic talent, which rendered their effusions popular, and bestowed an additional charm on their assemblages, and by such various means, anxious listeners at first, and then zealous proselytes, were drawn from the cottages of quiet nooks and dingles, to the weekly readings and discussions of the Hampden clubs.

One of these clubs was established in 1816, at the small town of Middleton, near Manchester; and I, having been instrumental in its formation; a tolerable reader also, and a rather expert writer, was chosen secretary. The club prospered; the number of members increased; the funds raised by contributions of a penny a week became more than sufficient for all out goings; and taking a bold step, we soon rented a chapel which had been given up by a society of Kilhamite Methodists. This place we threw open for the religious worship of all sects and parties, and there we held our meetings on the evenings of Monday and Saturday in each week. The proceedings of our society; its place of meeting – singular as being the first place of worship occupied by reformers, (for so in those days we were termed) together with the services of religion connected with us – drew a considerable share of public attention to our transactions, and obtained for the leaders some notoriety. They, like the young aspirants of the present, and all other days, whose heads are as warm as their hearts, could sing with old John Bunyan –

> *Then fancies fly away,*
> *We fear not what men say.*

Several meetings of delegates from the surrounding districts were held at our chapel, on which occasions the leading reformers of Lancashire were generally seen together. These were John Knight, of Manchester, cotton manufacturer; William Ogden, of Manchester, letter-press printer – afterwards immortalized by Canning, as the 'revered and ruptured Ogden;' William Benbow, of Manchester, shoe maker; —— Bradbury, of Manchester, stone cutter; Charles Walker, of Ashton, weaver; Joseph Watson, of Mossley, clogger;

14

Joseph Ramsden, of Mossley, woollen weaver; William Nicholson, of Lees, letter-press printer; John Haigh, of Oldham, silk weaver; Joseph Taylor, of Oldham, hatter; John Kay, of Royton, student in surgery; Robert Pilkington, of Bury, cotton weaver; Amos Ogden, of Middleton, silk weaver; Caleb Johnson, of Middleton, cotton weaver; – and Samuel Bamford, of Middleton, silk weaver. Soon afterwards we were joined by John Johnston, of Manchester, tailor; and Joseph Mitchell, of Liverpool, draper. Such were the conditions of all whom I recollect as standing prominently forward in those days, through evil and through good report, in our district of the country. About half of them are in their graves; the remainder I hope may live to see the bread found, which so long ago they 'cast upon the waters.' Let not any man despise the humble workers of a great change: such have often been the forlorn hope of truth against error – of right against wrong. Let no christian condemn humble beginnings: such were they in life's station, who cast the seeds of living bread in the wilds of Galilee, from whence it spread to Antioch, and to proud Rome.

One of our delegate meetings deserves particular notice. It was held on Sunday, the 16th December, 1816; when it was determined to send out missionaries, to other towns and villages, particularly to Yorkshire. Pilkington, Fitton, and Benbow, were, I believe, selected to go forth on this our first mission. The experiment was considered somewhat hazardous, for at that time the great towns of Yorkshire, Halifax, Bradford, and Leeds, to which they were bound, had shown but small sympathy with the cause of reform. They went, however, and, I believe, made an impression which awakened the cause in that county. At this meeting a man of the name of William Wilson appeared as the delegate from Moston; he was known to several present, and being considered a good reformer, was chosen secretary for the occasion. He thus took copies of all the resolutions and proceedings; soon afterwards it was discovered that he was in communication with the police of Manchester. He then left the country, abandoning his wife and a young family of children; and was next heard of as a police officer at London, to which place his wife and children followed him. Whether or not he is in the present force, I have not heard; but there was recently a man of his name, whose marks were, S.38. Can this be our first traitor?

On the first of January, 1817, a meeting of delegates from twenty-one petitioning bodies, was held in our chapel, when resolutions were passed declaratory of the right of every male to vote, who paid taxes; that males of eighteen should be eligible to vote; that parliaments should be elected annually; that no placeman or pensioner should sit in parliament; that every twenty thousand inhabitants should send a member to the house of commons; and that talent, and virtue, were the only qualifications necessary. Such were the moderate views and wishes of the reformers in those days, as compared with the present: the ballot was not insisted upon as a part of reform. Concentrating our whole energy for the obtainment of annual parliaments and universal suffrage, we neither interfered with the house of lords; nor the bench of bishops; nor the working of factories; nor the corn laws; nor the payment of members; nor tithes; nor church rates; nor a score of other matters, which in these days have been pressed forward with the effect of distracting the attention, and weakening the exertions of reformers; – any one, or all of which matters would be far more likely to succeed with a house of commons elected on the suffrage we claimed, than with one returned as at present. Quoting scripture, we did, in fact say, first obtain annual parliaments, and universal suffrage, and, 'Whatsoever thou wouldest shall be added thereto.'

Some of the nostrum mongers of the present day, would have been made short work of by the reformers of that time; they would not have been tolerated for more than one speech, but handed over to the civil power. It was not until we became infested by spies, incendiaries, and their dupes – distracting, misleading, and betraying – that physical force was mentioned amongst us. After that our moral power waned; and what we gained by the accession of demagogues, we lost by their criminal violence, and the estrangement of real friends.

Chapter 3

Author's Views on Education, and Annual Parliaments

IT MAY not be amiss to state that the opinions contained in this work, whether of persons or transactions, are those of the writer at the period they refer to. Time, the ameliorator of all things, has not passed him without leaving some experience; and the lessons of that severe handmaid, making him better acquainted with mankind and himself, have somewhat matured his judgment and increased his charity; changing also, he hopes for the better, some of his views both of men and things. Hence, though elsewhere he will speak of the conduct of Henry, now lord Brougham, strongly, as he felt at the time; he would, in his present frame of mind, make large allowances in judging of the present circumstance. Our educators, are, after all, the best reformers, and are doing the best for their country, whether they intend so or not. In this respect, lord Brougham is the greatest man we have. He led popular education from the dark and narrow crib where he found it, like a young colt, saddled, and cruelly bitted by ignorance, for superstition to ride. He cut the straps from its sides, and the bridle from its jaws, and sent it forth, strong, beautiful, and free.

Still, we want something more than mere intellectuality; that is already vigorous in produce, whilst souls lie comparatively waste. The Persians of old, first taught their children to SPEAK THE TRUTH, and that was a wise beginning; but like the embalming of the Egyptians, lost to the present day. The young mothers of England, and the anxious fathers, should do more – they should give LIFE to the SOULS of their offspring, and encourage and strengthen, as well as comfort their young hearts. Their constant lesson should be, 'With thy whole soul, love and support whatsoever is right. With thy whole soul, hate and oppose whatsoever is wrong. Fear not any thing, save the contamination of sin.' The schoolmaster might then finish the intellect; and the spirit of him who said, 'Father, forgive them,' should be invoked to shed its dove-like mercy over all. Education so grounded and built upon, would bring us hearts, and brave ones too, brimful of nobleness and truth; and heads to work any thing requisite for their country. Intellect neglected may be repaired; but a soul once in ruin, nothing human can restore.

Nor would the writer at the present day be found praying for annual parliaments, though he would endeavour to attain the same end by better means.

Annual general elections, would, he is convinced, be a great political evil to the country; and reviewing all that he has seen of elections, he does say, they are generally conducted in a manner which is disgraceful to civilized society. The infamy they generate, is equalled by the bungling knavery of their management. He needs not go into their history, but he would ask a rational man to note the proceedings of one of these 'good old English' events; and then say whether it were not more like 'hell broke loose,' than any thing human. Behold the banners; hear the music; mere glare and noise; the speakers – one side yelled dumb, the other drummed deaf – good men bullied by ruffians, and spit upon by poltroons – demagogues cheered – scurrillity applauded – fraud devised and practised – truth suppressed – falsehood blazoned – friendship severed – hatred gratified – courage threatened – cowardice rewarded – vanity flattered – modesty disparaged – cupidity bribed – sobriety scoffed – gluttony indulged – conscience hushed – honour abandoned – wrong triumphant – right abashed and contemned. Who could wish for annual recurrence of these things throughout the nation? frequent enough their visitation when they can no longer be avoided. General elections annually, would be annual curses; and single borough or county elections are best let alone until there be good cause. As, in his petition to the house of commons, in 1837, the writer would pray that we might have the benefit without the disturbing force. He would say, let the house of commons, be, like that of the lords, indissoluble; – members to render an account of their conduct annually; individual members be liable to be displaced by their constituents, at any time; and elected, displaced, or retained, as private servants are, viz: as they do well their duty, or otherwise. The sense of the electors to be taken annually – by ballot in districts; all elections to be by ballot. No hustings; no nomination farce; no mob gatherings; no ruffianism; no demagogueism; no canting and deception of the multitudes; nor opportunity for the display of insolence and ignorance to win a passing clap or huzza. Many evils would be done away with; excitement would be moderated; sober-mindedness would take place of extravagance; court intrigue, or ascendancy of faction, would not have the power of dispersing the people's servants, nor of throwing the country into a ferment of brute passion, to take advantage of it.

Such plan would the writer substitute for that of annual parliaments; and so far his opinions have changed on that point. Having thus taken his ground with the reader, he may proceed.

Chapter 4

THE Hampden club, of London, of which Sir Francis Burdett was
the chairman, having issued circulars for a meeting of delegates at
the Crown and Anchor, for the purpose of discussing a bill to be
presented to the house of commons, embracing the reform we
sought, I was chosen to represent the Middleton club on that
occasion. I shall not notice the abuse which this small honour
brought upon my shoulders, further than to say, that it gave me an
unexpected insight into the weakness of some whom I had considered as the best of friends to myself and the cause. I thus early
got a dose of disgust which would have banished me from amongst
them, had I not considered that by retiring I should abandon my
duty and gratify my new enemies. I therefore took up my cross,
forgave them, and attended my appointment in London.

I had scarcely alighted from the coach at the Elephant and Castle,
ere I was accosted by Benbow, who took me to his lodgings near
Buckingham Gate, where I became comfortably settled for the
present. He had been in London some time, agitating the labouring
classes at their trades' meetings and club-houses. That night he
conducted me to the Crown and Anchor Tavern; and whilst I stood
gazing around a large hall, which seemed wonderfully grand and
silent for a tavern, a gentleman came out of a room and accosted
my companion, who increased my curiosity, and awe by pronouncing the name of Mr Hunt. He invited us within; and we there
found a small party of delegates, recently arrived, in friendly conversation with Mr Cleary, the secretary of the London club. This
was an event in my life. Of Mr Hunt I had imbibed a high opinion;
and his first appearance did not diminish my expectations. He was
gentlemanly in his manner and attire; six feet and better in height,
and extremely well formed. He was dressed in a blue lapelled coat,
light waistcoat and kerseys, and topped boots; his leg and foot were
about the firmest and neatest I ever saw. He wore his own hair; it
was in moderate quantity, and a little grey. His features were regular,
and there was a kind of youthful blandness about them which, in

amicable discussion, gave his face a most agreeable expression. His lips were delicately thin, and receding; but there was a dumb utterance about them which in all the portraits I have seen of him was never truly copied. His eyes were blue or light grey – not very clear, nor quick, but rather heavy; except as I afterwards had opportunities for observing, when he was excited in speaking; at which times they seemed to distend and protrude; and if he worked himself furious, as he sometimes would, they became blood-streaked, and almost started from their sockets. Then it was that the expression of his lip was to be observed – the kind smile was exchanged for the curl of scorn, or the curse of indignation. His voice was bellowing; his face swollen and flushed; his griped hand beat as if it were to pulverize; and his whole manner gave token of a painful energy, struggling for utterance.

Such was the appearance of Mr Hunt as I saw him that night, and on subsequent occasions. His every day manners, exhibiting the quality and operations of his mind, will, of necessity, occupy some portion of the future pages of this work. He was constantly, perhaps through good but misapplied intentions, placing himself in most arduous situations. No repose – no tranquillity for him. He was always beating against a tempest of his own or of others' creating. He had thus more to sustain than any other man of his day and station, and should be judged accordingly.

Thomas Cleary, the secretary to the Hampden club, was also in the room; he was perhaps twenty-five or twenty-six years of age, about middle stature, slightly formed, and had a warmth and alacrity in his manner which created at once respect and confidence. He was, and I have no doubt is yet, if he be living, worthy of, and enjoying the esteem of all who know him. Hunt ferociously traduced his character at a subsequent election for Westminster, but the shame recoiled on the calumniator. Afterwards he attempted to fix upon Cleary the stigma of being a Government spy, and intimated that he tried about this time, to involve some of the delegates in illegal transactions; a charge as absurd as it was false.

But to return. The day of meeting arrived; Sir Francis Burdett was in the country, and the worthy old Major Cartwright took the chair. With a picture of that venerable patriot in my recollection, let me pause, and render the tribute due to integrity and benevolence. He was far in years – I should suppose about seventy; rather above the common stature; straight for his age; thin, pale, and with an expression of countenance in which firmness and benignity were most predominant. I see him, as it were, in his long brown surtout and plain brown wig, walking up the room, and seating himself placidly in the head seat. A mild smile played on his features, as a simultaneous cheer burst from the meeting. Cobbett stood near his right hand. I had not seen him before. Had I met him anywhere save in that room and on that occasion, I should have taken him for a gentleman farming his own broad estate. He seemed to have that kind of self-possession and ease about him, together with a certain bantering jollity, which are so natural to fast-handed and well-housed lords of the soil. He was, I should suppose, not less than six feet in height; portly, with a fresh, clear, and round cheek, and a small grey eye, twinkling with good-humoured archness. He was dressed in a blue coat, yellow swansdown waistcoat, drab kersey small-clothes, and top boots. His hair was grey, and his cravat and linen were fine, and very white. In short, he was the perfect representation of what he always wished to be: an English gentleman farmer.

The proceedings of the meeting it is not requisite that I should go into; they have long been matters of record. The absence of the Baronet was the subject of much observation by the delegates; and yet, in deference to his wishes, as was understood, a resolution was introduced and supported by Cobbett, limiting the suffrage to householders. This was opposed by many, and especially by the delegates from the manufacturing district; some of whom were surprised that so important a concession should be made to the opinion of any individual. Hunt treated the idea with little respect, and I thought he felt no discomfort at obtaining a sarcastic fling or two at the Baronet. Cobbett advocated the restricted measure, scarcely in earnest, and weakly, and alleging the impracticability of universal suffrage. The discussion proceeded for some time and no one grappled the objection; until, fearing the resolution would be adopted, I in a few words explained how universal suffrage might be carried into effect, by taking the voters from the Militia list, or others made on the same plan. Hunt took up the idea, in a way which I thought rather annoyed Cobbett, who at length arose, and expressed his conviction of its practicability, giving me all the merit of his conversion. Resolutions in favour of universal suffrage and annual parliaments were thereupon carried; and soon afterwards the meeting was adjourned to the day following. Several of our country delegates were now presented to Cobbet by Benbow, who appeared to act almost as master of the ceremonies. I was not however introduced to the great man, and soon after he left the room.

On the day when parliament was opened, a number of the delegates met Hunt at the Golden Cross, Charing Cross; and from thence went with him in procession to the residence of lord Cochrane, in Palace Yard, where a large petition from Bristol, and most of those from the north of England, were placed in his lordship's hands. There had been some tumult in the morning; the Prince Regent had been insulted on his way to the house, and this part of the town was still in a degree of excitement. We were crowded around, and accompanied by a great multitude, which at intervals rent the air with shouts. Now it was that I beheld Hunt in his element. He unrolled the petition, which was many yards in length, and it was carried on the heads of the crowd, perfectly unharmed. He seemed to know almost every man of them, and his confidence in, and entire mastery over them, made him quite at ease. A louder huzza than common was music to him; and when the questions were asked eagerly, 'Who is he?' 'What are they about?' and the reply was, 'Hunt! Hunt! huzza!' his gratification was expressed by a stern smile. He might be likened to the genius of commotion, calling forth its elements, and controlling them at will. On arriving at Palace Yard, we were shewn into a room below stairs, and whilst lord Cochrane and Hunt conversed above, a slight and elegant young lady, dressed in white, and very interesting, served us with wine. She is, if I am not misinformed, now lady Dundonald. At length his lordship came to us. He was a tall young man; cordial and unaffected in his manner. He stooped a little, and had somewhat of a sailor's gait in walking; his face was rather oval; fair naturally, but now tanned and sun-freckled. His hair was sandy, his whiskers rather small, and of a deeper colour; and the expression of his countenance was calm and self-possessed. He took charge of our petitions, and being seated in an arm-chair, we lifted him up and bore him on our shoulders across Palace Yard, to the door of Westminster Hall; the old rafters of which rung with the shouts of the vast multitude outside.

Chapter 5

ABOUT this time I was formally introduced to Mr Cobbett, by Benbow. He received me in a manner which was highly gratifying to my feelings. This was at his office, or rooms, in Newcastle-street, Strand. A number of other delegates were present, but I thought Cobbett gave the preference above all, to our friend Fitton of Royton; whose sarcastic vein had particularly pleased him. Fitton had, in a speech at a public meeting, designated a certain class in Manchester, 'The Pig-tail Gentry;' a ludicrous idea certainly, and one which made Cobbett laugh till his sides shook. No man could enjoy a bit of sarcasm better than he.

A number of us went one morning to visit Sir Francis Burdett at his house in Park-place. The outside was but of ordinary appearance; and the inside was not much better, so far as we were admitted. To me it seemed like a cold, gloomy, barely furnished house; which I accounted for by supposing that it was perhaps the style of all great mansions. We were shewn into a large room, the only remarkable thing in which was a bust of John Horne Tooke. Sir Francis came to us in a loose grey vest coat, which reached far towards his ancles. He had not a cravat on his neck; his feet were in slippers; and a pair of white cotton stockings hung in wrinkles on his long spare legs, which he kept alternately throwing across his knees, and rubbing down with his hands, as if he suffered, or recently had, some pain in those limbs. He was a fine-looking man on the whole, of lofty stature, with a proud but not forbidding carriage of the head. His manner was dignified and civilly familiar; submitting to, rather than seeking conversation with men of our class. He however discussed with us some points of the intended Bill for Reform, candidly and freely; and concluded with promising to support universal suffrage, though he was not sanguine of much co-operation in the house. Under these circumstances we left Sir Francis; approving much that we found in and about him, and excusing much of what we could not approve. He was one of our idols, and we were loath to give him up.

Still I could not help my thoughts from reverting to the simple and homely welcome we received at lord Cochrane's, and contrasting it with the kind of dreary stateliness of this great mansion and its rich owner. At the former place we had a brief refection, bestowed with a grace which captivated our respect; and no health was ever drunk with more sincere goodwill than was lord Cochrane's: the little dark-haired and bright-eyed lady seemed to know it, and to be delighted that it was so. But here scarcely a servant appeared; and nothing in the shape of refreshment was seen.

On the afternoon of a Sunday, Mitchell went with me to endeavour to find a former play-fellow of mine, who was now a soldier in the Foot Guards. He had fought the campaigns of Portugal, Spain, and France; and we now found him a colour serjeant at Knightsbridge barracks. The brave fellow received us with every demonstration of friendship. I told him what business had brought us to London, and that my fellow visitor was here on the same errand. Our business made no difference with him; he brought forth his ration, and we took a hearty lunch, after which we went with him to the non-commissioned officer's room at the canteen. About half a dozen serjeants were there, to whom my friend introduced us, making known, without the least reserve, or show of it, the business we were come upon to the metropolis. That seemed not to weigh with them, and we were soon in a free conversation on the subject of parliamentary reform. When objections were stated, they listened candidly to our replies, and a good-humoured discussion, half serious, half joking, was promoted on both sides. I and Mitchell had with us, and it was entirely accidental, a few of Cobbett's Registers, and Hone's Political Pamphlets, to which we sometimes appealed, and read extracts from. The soldiers were delighted; they burst into fits of laughter; and on the copies we had, being given them, one of them read the Political Litany through, to the further great amusement of himself and the company. Thus we passed a most agreeable evening, and parted only at the last hour. Mitchell and I returned to the city; neither of us, I firmly believe, having any further thought of the circumstance, than to regret that evenings so rationally and so peaceably spent, came so seldom.

Very soon after this a law was passed, making it death to attempt to seduce a soldier from his duty. Could it possibly be, that the occurrences of this evening led to the enactment of that law?

Several times I attended meetings of Trades' clubs, and other public assemblages of the working men. They would generally be found in a large room, an elevated seat being placed for the chairman. On first opening the door, the place seemed dimmed by a suffocating vapour of tobacco, curling from the cups of long pipes, and issuing from the mouths of the smokers, in clouds of abominable odour, like nothing in the world more than one of the unclean fogs of their streets, (though the latter were certainly less offensive,) and probably less hurtful. Every man would have his half-pint of porter before him; many would be speaking at once, and the hum and confusion would be such as gave an idea of there being more talkers than thinkers – more speakers than listeners. Presently 'order' would be called, and comparative silence would ensue; a speaker, stranger or citizen, would be announced with much courtesy and compliment. 'Hear, hear, hear,' would follow, with clapping of hands, and knocking of knuckles on the tables till the half-pints danced; then a speech, with compliments to some brother orator or popular statesman; next a resolution in favour of parliamentary reform, and a speech to second it; an amendment on some minor point would follow; a seconding of that; a breach of order by some individual of warm temperament; half a dozen would rise to set him right; a dozen to put them down; and the vociferation and gesticulation would become loud and confounding. The door opens, and two persons of middle stature enter; the uproar is changed to applause, and a round of huzzas welcome the new-comers. A stranger like myself enquiring who is he? the foremost and better dressed one would be answered, 'that gentleman is Mr Watson the elder, who was lately charged with high treason, and is now under bail to answer an indictment for a misdemeanour in consequence of his connection with the late meeting at Spafields.' The person spoken of would be supposed to be about fifty years of age, with somewhat of a polish in his gait and manner, and a degree of respectability and neatness in his dress. He was educated for a genteel profession, that of a surgeon; had practised it, and had in consequence moved in a sphere more high than his present one. He had probably a better heart than head; the latter had failed to bear him up in his station, and the ardour of the former had just before hurried him into transactions, from the consequences of which he has not yet escaped. His son at this time was concealed in London, a large reward having been offered for his apprehension. The other man was Preston, a co-operator with Watson, Hooper, and others, in late riots. He was about middle age; of ordinary appearance; dressed as an operative, and walked with the help of a stick. I could not but entertain a slightful opinion of the intellect and trust-worthiness of these two men; when on a morning or two afterwards, at breakfast with me and Mitchell, they narrated with seeming pride and satisfaction, their several parts during the riots. Preston had mounted a wall of the tower, and summoned the guard to surrender. The men gazed at him – laughed; no one fired a shot – and soon after he fell down, or was pulled off by his companions, who thought (no doubt) he had acted fool long enough.

Such were two of the most influential leaders of the London operative reformers. I repeat that I thought meanly of their quali-fications for such a post. But how blind is human perception – how slow should we be to condemn! I myself was at the same moment going hand and heart with some who were as little to be depended upon as the above; and yet I could not perceive my situation. The blind were then leading the blind.

During the debate on the report of the Green Bag Committee, I obtained an order for admission to the gallery of the house of commons. I well recollect though I cannot describe, all the con-flicting emotions which arose within me as I approached that assembly, with the certainty of now seeing and hearing those whom I considered to be the authors of my country's wrongs. Curiosity certainly held its share of my feelings; but a strong dislike to the 'boroughmonger crew' and their measures held a far larger share. After a tough struggle at elbowing and pushing along a passage, up a narrow staircase, and across a room, I found myself in a small gallery, from whence I looked on a dimly lighted place below. At the head of the room, or rather den, for such it appeared to me, sat a person in a full loose robe of, I think, scarlet and white. Above his head were the royal arms, richly gilded; at his feet several men in robes and wigs were writing at a large table, on which lamps were burning, which cast a softened light on a rich ornament like a pon-derous sceptre of silver and gold, or what appeared to be so. Those persons I knew must be the speaker and the clerks of the house; and that rich ornament could be nothing else than the 'mace' – the same thing, or one in its place, to which Cromwell pointed and said, 'Take away that bauble; for shame – give way to honester men.'

On each side of this pit-looking place, leaving an open space in the centre of the floor, were some three or four hundreds of the most ordinary-looking men I had ever beheld at one view. Some were striking exceptions; several young fellows in military dresses gave relief to the sombre drapery of the others. Canning, with his smooth, bare, and capacious forehead, sat there, a spirit beaming in his looks like that of the leopard waiting to spring upon its prey. Castlereagh, with his handsome but immovable features – Burdett, with his head carried back, and held high as in defiance – and Brougham, with his Arab soul ready to rush forth and challenge war to all comers. The question was to me solemnly interesting, whilst the spectacle wrought strangely on my feelings. Our accusers were many and powerful, with words at will, and applauding listeners. Our friends were few and far between, with no applauders save their good conscience, and the blessings of the poor. What a scene was this to be enacted by the 'collective wisdom of the nation.' Some of the members stood leaning against pillars, with their hats cocked awry; some were whispering by half dozens; others were lolling upon their seats; some with arms a-kimbo, were eye-glassing across the house; some were stiffened immovably by starch, or pride, or both; one was speaking, or appeared to be so, by the motion of his arms, which he shook in token of defiance, when his voice was drowned by a howl as wild and remorseless as that from a kennel of hounds at feeding time. Now he points menacing, to the ministerial benches – now he appeals to some members on this side – then to the speaker; all in vain. At times he is heard in the pauses of that wild hubbub, but again he is borne down by the yell which awakes on all sides around him. Some talked aloud; some whinnied in mock laughter, coming, like that of the damned, from bitter hearts. Some called 'order, order,' some 'question, question;' some beat time with the heel of their boots; some snorted into their napkins; and one old gentleman in the side gallery actually coughed himself from a mock cough into a real one, and could not stop until he was almost black in the face.

And are these, thought I, the beings whose laws we must obey? This the 'most illustrious assembly of freemen in the world?' Perish freedom then, and her children too. O! for the stamp of stern old Oliver on this floor; and the clank of his scabbard, and the rush of his iron-armed band, and his voice to arise above this babel howl – 'Take away that bauble' – 'Begone; give place to honester men.'

Such was my first view of the house of commons; and such the impressions strongly forced on my feelings at the time. The speaker alluded to, was Henry Brougham. I heard at first very little of what he said, but I understood from occasional words, and the remarks of some whom I took for reporters, that he was violently attacking the ministers and their whole home policy. That he was so doing, might have been inferred from the great exertions of the ministerial party to render him inaudible, and to subdue his spirit by a bewildering and contemptuous disapprobation. But they had before them a wrong one for being silenced, either by confusion or menace. Like a brave stag, he held them at bay, and even hurled back their defiance with 'retorted scorn.' In some time his words became more audible; presently there was comparative silence, and I soon understood that he had let go the ministry, and now unaccountable as it seemed to me had made a dead set at the reformers. Oh! how he did scowl towards us – contemn and disparage our best actions and wound our dearest feelings! Now stealing near our hearts with words of wonderful power, flashing with bright wit and happy thought; anon like a reckless wizard changing pleasant sunbeams into clouds, 'rough with black winds and storms,' and vivid with the cruellest shafts. Then was he listened to as if not a pulse moved – then was he applauded to the very welkin. And he stood in the pride of his power, his foes before him subdued but spared – his friends, derided and disclaimed – and his former principles sacrificed to 'low ambition,' and the vanity of such a display as this.

I would have here essayed somewhat with respect to Canning, and the character and effects of his eloquence; but little appertaining to him remained on my mind. Every feeling was absorbed by the contemplation of that man whom I now considered to be the most perfidious of his race. I turned from the spectacle with disgust, and sought my lodgings in a kind of stupor; almost believing that I had escaped from a monstrous dream.

Such was my first view of Henry Brougham; and such the impressions I imbibed, and long entertained, of that extraordinary man. He sinned then, and has often done so since, against the best interests of his country; bowing to his own image, and sacrificing reason and principle to caprice or offended self-love. But has he not done much for mercy, and for the enlightenment of his kind? See the African dancing above his chains! Behold the mild but irresistible light which education is diffusing over the land! These are indeed blessings beyond all price – rays of unfading glory. They are lord Brougham's; and will illumine his tomb when his errors and imperfections are forgotten.

Chapter 6

Habeas Corpus Act suspended — Blanket Meeting at Manchester — March and dispersion of the Blanketeers — Treasonable Plot — Joseph Healey, the Doctor; his observations and discoveries in the welkin

SOON afterwards I left the great Babylon, heartily tired of it, and returned to Middleton, where events rapidly pressed on my attention.

On the morning of Sunday, the eighth of March, Benbow called on me at Middleton. I had lost sight of him since my return from London – the habeas corpus act was already suspended, and I supposed from some remarks of his that he had thought it best not to be so much in public at Manchester as he previously had been. He had, however taken a great share in getting up and arranging the Blanket Meeting; and now, after commending the intended proceeding, and dwelling on the good effects it would produce, he asked me to join in the meeting and expedition, and to bring as many of my neighbours as I could. I flatly refused; and stated my reasons, which will shortly appear. He enlarged his commendations – calculating with certainty, that the blanketeers would march to London, thousands in number; and that their petitions would be graciously if not with some awe, received by the Prince Regent in person. I maintained my opinions – he answered with reproaches; I treated the plan as a chimera, and held lightly the judgement of its proposers and concocters. Benbow went away in a huff; and I remained, with a lowered opinion of my former comrade.

On the night of Sunday, the ninth of March, I was requested to attend a meeting in the house of one of my neighbours, where a number of friends wished to hear my opinion with reference to the Blanket Meeting. I went to them and spoke freely in condemnation of the measure. I endeavoured to show them that the authorities of Manchester were not likely to permit their leaving the town in a body, with blankets and petitions, as they proposed; that they could not subsist on the road; that the cold and wet would kill numbers of them, who were already enfeebled by hunger and other deprivations; that soldiers always marched in divisions for the easier procurement of food and lodgings; and that an irregular multitude like themselves, could not, on an emergency, be provisioned, and quartered. That they need not expect to be welcome wherever they went, especially in such of the rotten boroughs as fell in their way, against the franchise of which they were petitioning; that the inhabitants would bolt their doors against them; and that if they took possession by force there was the law to punish them. That many persons might join their ranks who were not reformers but enemies to reform, hired perhaps to bring them and their cause into disgrace; that if these persons began to plunder on the road, the punishment and disgrace would be visited on the whole body; that they would be denounced as robbers and rebels; and the military would be brought to cut them down or take them prisoners. In conclusion, I earnestly cautioned them against having anything to do with the proposed meeting; and intimated that the parties who had got it up, were not to be depended upon – that their blind zeal over-ran every reasonable consideration; and that if they, my neighbours, took part in the meeting, they would probably repent when it was too late. Whether it was in consequence of what I said I cannot tell; but I was afterwards gratified on hearing that no person from Middleton went as a Blanketeer.

But of this meeting, which was our first great absurdity, I must write more particularly.

It was one of the bad schemes which accompanied us from London, and was the result of the intercourse of some of the deputies with the leaders of the London operatives – the Watsons, Prestons, and Hoopers. Mitchell and Benbow had cultivated a rather close acquaintance with these men, little suspecting, I have no doubt, that their new friends had already fallen under the influence of instigators who betrayed all their transaction to the government. But the London leaders, or at least, such of them as I conversed with, were, as I have shewn, men of frank character and bearing, and apparently of sincere intention; and their manner, flattering by the confidence it bestowed, naturally led to a reciprocal feeling, and to the formation of connections, the effects of which now began to appear.

Our maxim had hitherto, in all our proceedings been – 'Hold fast by the laws.' It was the maxim of Major Cartwright, our venerable political Father, and had been adhered to with a religious observance. But doctrines varying from this now began to be broached, and measures hinted, which, if not in direct contravention of the law, were but ill disguised subterfuges for evading its intentions.

The meeting took place according to appointment; but I not being there, my brief description must be taken as the account of others. The assemblage consisted almost entirely of operatives, four or five thousands in number; and was held on that piece of ground (Saint Peter's Field) which afterwards obtained so melancholy a celebrity. Many of the individuals were observed to have blankets, rugs, or large coats, rolled up and tied, knap-sack like, on their backs; some carried bundles under their arms; some had papers, supposed to be petitions rolled up; and some had stout walking sticks. The magistrates came upon the field and read the riot act, and the meeting was afterwards dispersed by the military, and special constables; and twenty-nine persons were apprehended, amongst whom were two young men, named Bagguley and Drummond, who had recently come into notice as speakers, and who being in favour of extreme measures, were much listened to, and applauded. But my warm friend, Benbow, took care not to make his appearance on that occasion.

On the riot act being read, about three hundred persons left the meeting to commence their march to London. Some of them formed a straggling line in Mosley-street, and marched along Piccadilly, being continually joined by others, until the whole body was collected, near Ardwick Green. The appearance of these misdirected people was calculated to excite, in considerate minds pity rather than resentment. Some appeared to have strength in their limbs and pleasure in their features; others already with doubt in their looks, and hesitation in their steps. A few were decently clothed, and well appointed for the journey; many were covered only by rags which admitted the cold wind, and were already damped by a gentle but chilling rain. Some appeared young, with health on their cheeks, every care behind and hope alone before; the thoughts of others were probably reverting to their homes on the hill sides, or in the sombre alleys of the town, where wives and children had resigned them for a time, in hopes of the return with plenty, and never more to part.

Here a youth was waving his hand to a damsel pale and tremulous with alarm; yonder an attenuated being, giving back, after kissing it, a poorly child to the arms of its mother – he hastens towards his comrades with willing but feeble steps, looking back on those, so poor, but oh! how dear – the child is hushed with a caress, the mother turning it gently to her cold and nurtureless bosom – nurtureless of every thing save deep and tender love. Her looks are still directed the way he goes; he has disappeared: and whilst her tears flow, the poor but cleanly mantle is drawn over the little one, and in a conflict of grief, hope, and fear, she thoughtfully wends to her obscure and cheerless abode. A body of yeomanry soon afterwards followed those simple-minded men, and took possession of the bridge at Stockport. Many then turned back to their homes; a body of them crossed the river below, and entered Cheshire; several received sabre wounds, and one man was shot dead on Lancashire hill. Of those who persisted in their march it is only necessary to say, that they arrived at nine o'clock at night in the market place at Macclesfield, being about one hundred and eighty in number. Some of them lay out all night, and took the earliest dawn to find their way home. Some were well lodged and hospitably entertained by friends; some paid for quarters, and some were quartered in prison. Few were those who marched the following morning. About a score arrived at Leek, and six only were known to pass Ashbourne bridge. And so ended the blanket expedition! 'What would you really have done,' I said to one of them, 'supposing you had got to London?' 'Done?' he replied, in surprise at the question; 'why iv wee'd nobbo gett'n to Lunnun, we shud ha'tan th' nation, an' sattl't o'th dett.' Such, and about as rational, were some of the incoherent dreams which at this time began to find favour in the eyes of the gross multitude.

But another cause was assigned for the dispersion of the blanketeers. It was said that a purse containing from thirty to fifty pounds having been made up, was given to one of the principal leaders, with instructions to proceed on the London road a day or two in advance, to procure food and lodgings for money, where they could not be had for friendship or a more urgent motive. That 'the good man,' by some mistake, got out of the right way, and wandering far into Yorkshire, he never found himself till the money was all spent; and the blanketeers, thus losing their commissary and paymaster, were broken by the same means which had dispersed more numerous armies, viz. want of necessaries; and thus 'the nation' was saved for that time. However true or otherwise this account may be, it is certain that the man suddenly disappeared (but others did the same) and was out of the way a month or two, after which he paid a visit to Middleton on his return, as he said, from Yorkshire to Manchester. He was always somewhat doubted afterwards; and his last appearance in this quarter was in the character of an adroit crimp to a fortune-promising attorney.

It was about this time, though I have not the exact date, that the first out-of-door meeting was held at Rochdale. Fitton, Knight, myself, and several other public characters were invited to attend and I did so. The day was cold and very wet; the hustings were fixed on the bare moor of Cronkeyshaw; none of the speakers save myself kept their appointment; nothing in the form of resolution or petition had been prepared, and I had to select and arrange these from an old Statesman newspaper which I found at the rendezvous, the Rose, in Yorkshire street. The town wore an appearance of alarm, and a company or two of soldiers were under arms in the main street. The meeting was however well attended, and the hearts of the people seemed to warm in proportion to the merciless cold of the wind and rain, which latter teemed upon us during the whole of the proceedings. On our return, the poor redcoats were still carrying arms, though, as one of the woollen weavers remarked, it would be to little purpose should they be wanted, 'as the water was already running over at the muzzles of their guns; 'they might squirt us,' he said, 'but could not shoot us.' On this occasion I received pay for my attendance. On our return to the Rose, besides refreshments, the committee presented me with four shillings, and I accepted the money because I thought I was entitled to it, having lost work to that value at home. But I never, except on this occasion, took money or any other remuneration, for attending reform meetings. I considered it a mean thing, though the practice was coming much into use, and several of my friends without any scruple continued to do so until 'their occupation' was gone! It was a bad practice, however, and gave rise to a set of orators who made a trade of speechifying, and the race has not become extinct. These persons began to seek engagements of the kind; some would even thrust themselves to the committees for remuneration, and generally received it. He who produced the greatest excitement, the loudest cheering, and the most violent clappings, was the best orator, and was sure to be engaged and well paid; and in order to produce those manifestations, the wildest and most extravagant rhodomantade would too often suffice. Such speakers quickly got a name; the calls on them were frequent; and they left their work or their business, for a more profitable and flattering employment; tramping from place to place hawking their new fangles, and guzzling, fattening, and replenishing themselves, at the expense of the simple and credulous multitude. Steadiness of conduct and consistency of principle were soon placed as it were at a distance from us. Our unity of action was relaxed; new speakers sprung like mushrooms about our feet; plans were broached, quite different from any that had been recognized by the Hampden Clubs; and the people, at a loss to distinguish friends from enemies, were soon prepared for the operations of informers, who, in the natural career of their business, became also promoters of secret plots and criminal measures of various descriptions. The good and fatherly maxim of the worthy old major, 'Hold fast by the laws,' was by many lost sight of.

How far the moral of these facts is applicable to the present day, will be judged by an observant public, and may perhaps not be deemed ill-timed by some of the more intelligent of those who have been found amongst the persons styled Chartists. If from the records of past errors good can be extracted for present emergencies, it will be well, and let us endeavour to do so. History is a faithful monitor, requiring only to be consulted in a truth-seeking spirit, when she will vouchsafe to become a friendly counsellor, saying to her enquirer, 'come blind one and see; come lost one, and behold thy way.' Nations may read their fate in the histories of nations; and individuals may be advised by a memoir so humble as mine.

At dusk on the evening of Tuesday, the 11th of March, the day after the blanket meeting, a man dressed much like a dyer was brought to my residence by Joseph Healey, who had found him enquiring for me in the lower part of the town. The stranger said he had something of a private and important nature to communicate, in consequence of which I and the stranger and Healey, went to the sign of the Trumpeter, where we were accommodated with a private room. The man now told us that he was deputed by some persons at Manchester, to propose that in consequence of the treatment which the blanketeers had received at the meeting and afterwards, 'a Moscow of Manchester' should take place that very night.

34

The man paused and looked at us severally. I intimated that I knew what he meant, and desired him to go on. He said it would entirely depend on the co-operation or otherwise of the country people; that other messengers had been sent to every reform society within twenty miles of the town; that if the answers were favourable to the project, the light of the conflagration was to be the signal for the country people to come in – and, in such case the Middleton people were requested to take their station on St George's field. He said the plan had been arranged by a meeting held at Manchester; that the whole force would be devided into parties, one of which was to engage the attention of the military and draw them from their barracks; another was to take possession of the barracks and secure the arms and magazine; another was to plunder and then set fire to the houses of individuals who were marked out; and a fourth was to storm the New Bailey and liberate the prisoners, particularly the blanketeers confined there. I said it was a serious thing to undertake, and that an answer could not be returned from Middleton until some friends had been consulted. On my rising to go out, the man appeared alarmed, and begged I would not betray him. I assured him he had nothing to fear, and desired him to stay with Healey until my return, which would be very soon, on which he seemed reconciled to my going. I speedily went to five of my acquaintance, chiefly members of the committee, and desired them to repair immediately to Healey's house, where business of importance would be laid before them. I then brought up the stranger and the doctor, and telling the man he might confide in us, he repeated nearly word for word what he had said at the Trumpeter. I then said I would have nothing to do with the scheme; that it was unlawful, inhuman, and cowardly. I told him he appeared to be a simple young fellow, and was probably the dupe of some designing villain. My friends agreed with my opinion both as to the proposal and the instrument who broached it: we bade him however not to mistrust us; gave him refreshment, and sent him away, more in sorrow for his peril (being persuaded he was in the hands of villains) than of resentment for the decoy he had attempted. We bade him good night, and he went his way.

The young man said his name was Sumuel Priestly; I observed that he had lost a finger from his left hand; he said he lived at Bank Top, Manchester. I afterwards made enquiries respecting him on the spot, but never could hear of such a person in the place or neighbourhood. This statement however cannot now injure him.

After he was gone we consulted about this strange message and unknown messenger. We had not heard of the plot before; and though we doubted not that it had been sanctioned, as the man stated, by the Manchester Committee, that circumstance did not increase our confidence. We had no reliance on their sagacity or their integrity as a body: men who could get up and countenance the blanket expedition had no weight with us. They were moreover reported to be under the influence of spies from the police; a suspicion which many circumstances tended to strengthen. The plot itself did the same; the unknown messenger, the precipitation, 'to be done that very night'; the population for twenty miles around an immense town to be brought upon it by midnight, and then to be divided, apportioned, and set to work by men of whom they knew nothing! The proposal was too absurd as well as iniquitous to excite anything save wonder and disgust even with simple and inexperienced ones like ourselves. Besides, would Major Cartwright have sanctioned such a measure? Certainly not. – And then we almost regretted that we had suffered the emissary to depart.

It was deemed prudent that Healey and I should on that night, sleep from home, and at some place where our stay could be proved, should anything arise to render such a step necessary; and none could tell what might be necessary, as in those days of alarm and uncertainty, no one knew what was impending. An old female reformer accordingly gave us her house and bed, and turning the key, locked us in, whilst we, in our simplicity, were quite satisfied with having taken so wise a precaution against any false evidence which might by possibility be brought to connect us with the plot of which we had been apprized. We retired to rest and lay talking this strange matter over until sleep overtook us. I was first to awake, and seeing a brightness behind the curtain, I stepped to the window, and sure enough beheld in the southern sky, a stream of light which I thought must be that of a distant fire. It was a fine crisped morning, and as I looked, a piece of a moon came wandering to the west from behind some masses of cloud. Now she would be entirely obscured; then streaks of her pale beams would be seen breaking on the edges of the vapours; then a broader gleam would come; then again it would be pale and receding: but the clouds were so connected that the fair traveller had seldom a space for shewing her unveiled horn. I saw how it was; my conflagration had dwindled to a moonbeam, and as I stood with the frost tingling at my toes 'an unlucky thought' (as we say, when excusing our own sins we impute them to a much abused sable personage) came into my head, to have a small joke at the doctor's expense; and as it was a mode of amusement to which I must confess I was rather prone, I immediately began to carry it into effect. I gave a loud cough or two; the doctor thereupon grunted and turned over in bed; when, in the very break of his sleep, I said aloud, as I crept beneath the bedclothes, 'there's a fine leet i'th' welkin, as th' witch o' Brandwood sed when the devil wur ridin' o'er Rossenda.' 'Leet,' said the doctor; 'a fine leet, weer? weer?' 'Why go to th' windo' an' look.' That instant my sanguine friend was out of bed and at the window, his head stuck behind the curtain. 'There's a great leet,' he said, 'to'rd Manchester.' 'There is indeed,' I replied, 'it's mitch but weary wark is gooin' on omung yon foke.' 'It's awful,' said the doctor; 'thei'r agate as sure as we're heer.' 'I think there's summut up,' I said. I was now snugly rolled in the clothes, and perceived at the same time that the doctor was getting into a kind of dancing shiver, and my object being to keep him in his shirt till he was cooled and undeceived, and consequently a little sprung in temper, I asked, 'dun yo really think then of th' teawn's o' foyer?' 'Foyer,' he replied; 'there's no deawt on't.' 'Con yo see th' flames doctor?' 'Nowe, I conno' see th' flames but I con see th' leet ut coms fro' em.' 'That's awful,' I ejaculated. 'Aye its awful,' he said;' come an' see for yorsel.' 'Nowe, I'd reyther not,' I answered; 'I dunno' like sich seets; it's lucky ut we're heer – they conno' say ut we'n had owt to do wi' it, at ony rate, con they doctor?' 'Nowe,' he said, they conno.' 'It keeps changin',' he said. 'Con yo' yer owt?' I asked. 'Nowe, I conno' yer nowt,' he said. I however heard his teeth hacking in his head, and stuffed the sheet into my mouth to prevent my laughter from being noticed. 'Ar yo' sure doctor?' I asked. No reply. 'Is it blazin' up?' I said. 'Blazin' be hanged!' was the answer. 'Wot dun yo' myen, doctor – is it gwon eawt then?' 'Gullook!' he said, 'it's nobbut th' moon, an' yo' knewn it oth' while.' A loud burst of laughter followed, which I enjoyed till the bed shook; my companion muttering imprecations and sundry devil's prayers against all 'moon doggs an' welkin lookers,' by which terms I knew he meant myself for one.

Chapter 7

PERSONAL liberty not being now secure from one hour to another, many of the leading reformers were induced to quit their homes, and seek concealment where they could obtain it. Those who could muster a few pounds, or who had friends to give them a frugal welcome, or who had trades with which they could travel, disappeared like swallows at the close of summer, no one knew whither. The single men stayed away altogether; the married ones would occasionally steal back at night to their wan-cheeked families, perhaps to divide with them some trifle they had saved during their absence – perhaps to obtain a change of linen or other garment for future concealment – but most of all, as would naturally be the case, to console, and be consoled by their wives and little ones. Perhaps one had found an asylum amongst kind friends, and had brought home a little hoard, the fruits of his own industry and carefulness, or of their generosity. Perhaps he had been wandering in want, not daring to make himself known, until his beard disguised him, his shoes and stockings were trampled from his feet, and his linen was in rags; when at length, worn out and reckless, he would venture home, like the wearied bird which found no place to rest. Perhaps he had been discovered to be a reform leader, and had been threatened, mayhap pursued, and like a hunted hare now returned to the place of former repose. Then he would come home stealthily under cover of darkness; his wife would rush into his arms, his little ones would be about his knees, looking silent pleasure – for they, poor things, like nestling birds, had learned to be mute in danger.

But with all precautions, it did sometimes happen, that in such moments of mournful joy the father would be seized, chained, and torn from his family before he had time to bless them or to receive their blessings and tears. Such scenes were of frequent occurrence, and have thrown a melancholy retrospection over those days. Private revenge or political differences were gratified by secret and often false information handed to the police. The country was distracted by rumours of treasonable discoveries, and apprehensions of the traitors, whose fate was generally predicted to be death or perpetual imprisonment. Bagguley, Johnson, Drummond, and Benbow, were already in prison at London; and it was frequently intimated to me, through some very kind relations in law, that I and some of my acquaintance would soon be arrested. This sort of information was always brought to Middleton by parties who, being in the manufacturing line, visited Manchester twice or thrice a week for the purpose of disposing of their goods. They appeared to be well acquainted with the movements of the police; they could tell when King's messengers arrived or departed; how many state warrants had been issued; who would be next apprehended; and such like useful and pleasant things, which they always took care to make known in such quarters as made it sure to reach those they wished to render unhappy, by anticipation of troubles they could not now avoid. And strange to say many of their predictions were verified. King's messengers did arrive: government warrants were issued; and the persons they mentioned were taken to prison. A cloud of gloom and mistrust hung over the whole country. The suspension of the Habeas Corpus Act was a measure the result of which we young reformers could not judge, save by report, and that was of a nature to cause anxiety in the most indifferent of us. The proscriptions, imprisonments, trials, and banishments of 1792, were brought to our recollections by the similarity of our situation to those of the sufferers of that period. It seemed as if the sun of freedom were gone down, and a rayless expanse of oppression had finally closed over us. Cobbett, in terror of imprisonment, had fled to America; Sir Francis Burdett had enough to do in keeping his own arms free; Lord Cochrane was threatened, but quailed not; Hunt was still somewhat turbulent, but he was powerless – for he had lost the genius of his influence when he lost Cobbett, and was now almost like Sampson shorn and blind. The worthy old Major remained at his post, brave as a lion – serene as an unconscious child; and also, in the rush and tumult of that time, almost as little noticed. Then, of our country reformers, John Knight had disappeared; Pilkington was out of the way somewhere; Bradbury had not yet been heard of; Mitchell moved in a sphere of his own, the extent of which no man knew save himself; and Kay and Fitton were seldom visible beyond the circle of their own village; whilst to complete our misfortunes, our chapel-keeper, in the very tremour of fear, turned the key upon us and declared we should no longer meet in the place.

Our Society, thus houseless, became divided and dismayed; hundreds slunk home to their looms, nor dared to come out, save like owls at nightfall, when they would perhaps steal through bye-paths or behind hedges, or down some clough, to hear the news at the next cottage. Some might be seen chatting with and making themselves agreeable to our declared enemies; but these were few, and always of the worst character. Open meetings thus being suspended, secret ones ensued; they were originated at Manchester, and assembled under various pretexts. Sometimes they were termed 'benefit societies;' sometimes 'botanical meetings;' 'meetings for the relief of the families of imprisoned reformers,' or 'of those who had fled the country'; but their real purpose divulged only to the initiated, was to carry into effect the night attack on Manchester, the attempt at which had before failed for want of arrangement and co-operation.

Chapter 8

Search for a temporary Home — Doctor Healey's Paternity — Some account of himself — A glance at the Author's Ancestry — Healey's uncle Richard, his house and Family — View from Knowe Hill

WEARIED at length with the continued alarms of my intended arrest and committal to prison, I consented to leave home for a day or two, to find some place, where, unknown, I might earn a subsistence until the cloud was blown over, and I could return in safety. Healey, who also had expectations of being wanted shortly, determined to accompany me with a like view; and so, in the thick grey morning, with light purses, and somewhat heavy hearts, we left our humble but dear homes, and struck into the open country –

> Down a quiet green lane where two rindles flow;
> Unto lands where the night-hunters stealthily go;
> Cross'd Roche's dark stream; o'er a barren heath hied;
> And up to the moorlands wild and wide.

Healey wished to see his uncle Richard, who was a farmer and publican on the moors to the N.W. of Middleton; and soon, as the sun broke out and the mist cleared, we found ourselves traversing Hopwood Ley in that direction. How delicious was the air, wafting breezy and free over the budding woods! Now sweeping up the hollows, now coming through the dew pearls and shaking the hazle bloom – now bearing towards us the bold note of the throstle – anon receding to nestle softly in the dingles with the melody of the blackbird! How happy were those simple children of nature; happy in their loves, in their rude nests; in their offspring, and in their unconsciousness of danger. The lapwing's plaintive cry as it wheeled above, was in unison with our feelings – the bird also seemed like ourselves to have no resting-place; whilst the cony, frisking before us, and disappearing, shewed us he too had a home. But the bracing air, the warm life-giving sun, the glorious beings of nature around and above us, whilst they excited our attention gradually dispelled the gloom of our feelings, and we also began to be cheerful if not happy – remembering that there is no hill without its vale, no storm without its calm, no shadow without its sun. So we went on – now climbing a hedge, now leaping a rindle, now starting a hare, or springing a woodcock, now treading a bit of swamp, now up a knoll through the gorses, then by the skirt of a meadow, and round to the hill-foot, by the music of a stream, where

> Spring moves on as glad we gaze,
> Calling the flowers wherever she strays.
> Come from the earth, ye dwellers there,
> To the blessed light, and the living air:
> For the snowdrop hath warned the drift away;
> And the crocus awaiteth your company;
> And the bud of the thorn is beginning to swell;
> And the waters have broken their bonds in the dell.
> And are not the hazle, and slender bine,
> Blending their boughs where the sun doth shine?
> And the willow is bringing its downy palm,
> Garland for days that are bright and calm;
> And the lady-flower waves on its slender stem;
> And the primrose peeps like a starry gem.'

Thus tramping o'er Spinthreeds and the Wilderness, we approached Captain Fold, the sight of which led Healey into some remarks on his father, his family, and his own early days.

He said he was born at Captain Fold, where his father lived and was a famous cow-leech, being fetched by the farmers to all parts of the country when their cattle were sick; that he also dabbled a little in medicines for the human frame, and was successful in most of the cases which he undertook – and they were such as had baffled common applications. That his father was a devout man, of the Methodist persuasion, and a firm believer in witches and witch-craft; which persuasion he also inherited. That in those days there were many sudden and uncommon disorders, which few persons understood, and fewer still could cope with. Such were often treated by his father on the 'supernatural plan,' and he was generally successful. He was almost sure to be sent for when cattle were supposed to be amiss from the influence of infernal spells; which he counteracted sometimes by other spells, drugs and herbs prepared at particular seasons, and under certain forms and ceremonials. He had also great faith in the power of faith, and the efficacy of private prayer. He died, however, leaving my companion unprovided for; and he was put apprentice to a cotton weaver at Bolton, where he learned the business, but under such oppressions and cruelties from his master and dame, as instilled into him a thorough abhorrence of tyranny. At the expiration of the term of his bondage he came to Chadderton, where he had a married sister living; and after introducing a new method of twisting-in warps, by which he saved a little money, and clothed himself respectably, he paid his addresses to his present wife and was accepted; and came to Middleton to reside with his wife and her parents. He accounted for his getting into the surgical profession, by supposing that he derived a taste for it from his father. He first began by selling simple drugs; after which he got some books, and ventured to compound and prescribe medicines. Next he succeeded in 'breathing a vein;' and lastly became a tooth drawer, and general practitioner of the surgical art; and now 'he was thankful, he needed not turn his back on any of his neighbours in the same line.' There was only one point he said, and that was the art obsteric, in which he was deficient; and he hoped to attain that yet. Such were my companion's past trials and present attainments. In sketching his father however, he omitted one remarkable circumstance, and if he knew it, honour be to his filial regard for the omission; it accords however very closely with the son's outline of the remarkable old man. It was said that so firm was his belief in the human application of divine faith, and such his assurance of being perfected in it, that he ascended the ridge of his barn in the presence of his assembled neighbours, and after praying for, and exhorting them, he, in the full expectation of being buoyed up, flung himself off, and fell souse on a dung heap below. Such a misdirection was, of course, a great handle to the ungodly; but in the old man's opinion, it was no disproof of the power of faith, but an intimation only of his own weakness and imperfections in that divine attainment.

Doctor Healey, or, 'the doctor,' as we must now call him, was about five feet six in height; thirty-two or three years of age; with rather good features; small light grey eyes; darker whiskers and hair; with a curl on his forehead, of which he was remarkably proud. He was well-set in body, but light of limb; his knees had an uncommonly supple motion, which gave them an appearance of weakness. He had an assured look; and in walking, especially when with a little 'too much wind in the sheet,' he turned his toes inward, and carried an air of bravado which was richly grotesque. In disposition he was, until afterwards corrupted, generous and confiding; credulous, proud of his person and acquirements. A book-buyer, but little of a reader; less of a thinker; and no recollector of literary matters. Hence, with an imperturbable self-complacency, he was supremely oblivious of the world, its history, manners, and concerns; except such as directly interfered with the good or evil of his own existence. At this time, his attire was scarcely more decent than my own; both were somewhat too seedy. but that was a circumstance on which a learned doctor, and a self-devoting patriot could look with indifference.

> 'Was there for honest poverty,
>   That hung his head an' a' that?
> The coward slave, we pass'd him by;
>   We durst be poor for a' that.'

His hat was somewhat napless, with sundry dinges on the crown, and up-settings and down-flappings of the brim, which shewed it to have tupped against harder substances than itself, as well as to have seen much 'winter and rough weather.' He wore a long drab top-coat, which, from its present appearance, might never have gone through the process of perching. His under-coat was of dark un-cut fustian, which by his almost incessant occupation in 'the laboratory,' preparing ointments, salves, and lotions, had become

43

smooth and shining as a duck's wing, and almost as impervious to wet; his hamsters were similar in material and condition to his coat, whilst his legs were encased in top-boots, no worse for wear, except perhaps a leaky seam or two, and a cracked upper leather. Such was one who will have frequently to make his appearance in this work. He had within him, at this time, no doubt, the germs of many faults which might not have appeared at all, had he not been thrown into connections which perverted his naturally simple, inoffensive, and even amiable nature. But of these matters we have nothing at present to say; nor would the writer, under any circumstances feel justified in acting up to the code of friendship which prevails in the higher circles of society. He would consider it base, after accepting the confidence of a fellow being, to wait his dissolution, and then, under pretence of doing justice to his memory, blazon his imperfections before the world. Oh, no! such a code will not, I hope, obtain with the chroniclers of the humble and poor. With them let friendship remain sacred; confidence unbetrayed; kindnesses remembered; and injuries forgiven, if not forgotten. Life's journey is, indeed, so bestrewn with sadness, that we are permitted to smile at the ridiculous, whether in friend or foe; and in this view, some of the most amiable men, have been the greatest promoters of mirth. Doctor Healey may occasionally help us in this way, and we will enjoy the heart-easing cheer he provides us; but with the dark side of his character, of which he had only a common human share and extent, the world has now nothing to do. We quarrelled, and our friendship was dissevered, but he speaks not from the tomb; and I write not a book to upbraid one who cannot reply.

But, the reader may say, we have only one of the travellers here; why does not the author furnish a portrait of the other? Behold him then. A young man, twenty-nine years of age; five feet ten inches in height; with long well-formed limbs, short body, very upright carriage, free motion, and active and lithe, rather than strong. His hair is of a deep dun colour; coarse, straight, and flaky; his complexion a swarthy pale; his eyes, grey, lively, and observant; his features strongly defined and irregular, like a mass of rough and smooth matters, which, having been thrown into a heap, had found their own subsidence, and presented, as it were, by accident, a profile of rude good nature, with some intelligence. His mouth is small; his lips a little prominent; his teeth white and well set; his nose rather snubby; his cheeks somewhat high; and his forehead deep and rather heavy about the eyes. His hat is not quite so broken, but quite as well worn as the doctor's; his coat of brown cloth, as yet unpatched, but wanting soon to be; his waistcoat of lighter colour, bare and decent; his hamsters of dark kerseymere, grey at the knees; and his stockings of lambs' wool, with some neat darning above the quarters of his strong nailed shoes. Such, reader, was the personal appearance of him who now endeavours to amuse thee; of the qualities of his mind and disposition, an opinion may be formed from this work.

Having crossed the river Roch, we came to the foot of Crimble, where I told Healey the story of Christian and Faithful, at the hill, Difficulty; and said I would be his Faithful, and would help him up this Difficulty. I remarked that he must have many sins to answer for, through his selling of drugs at extortionate prices, quacking a little in his practice, and sometimes drawing sound teeth when he could not find faded ones. He turned on me when we got to the level, and he breathed more freely. He bade me look towards those fields and that venerable hall which one of my ancestors lost by rebellion against a king; and he narrated a story which I had heard before, how, in the civil wars, the eldest of two brothers, held this estate of Bamford, and fought against the king, who was dethroned: and at the restoration, the elder brother fled into exile and died there, leaving his children heirs only to poverty and obscurity; meantime his younger brother, who had fought on the royal side, was put into possession of the hall and estates, and thus they descended from him, to the last of the name who held the property. Healey remarked that I indeed had not an estate to lose, but was taking a fair course for losing my head, and was already an outcast wanderer on lands belonging to my ancestors.

On coming to Bakslate Moor, Healey said the neighbourhood was formerly infested by witches. His father had often been called upon to counteract their infernal schemes. He firmly believed all this, and I did not combat his opinion: on the contrary, I said I was sure it had been a place of witches. He asked why I believed so? I bid him notice it; did it not look like a barren and withered land, full of slate pits, rushy knobs, and dry wiry grass, from which even asses turned away? Besides, I had been witched myself by one of them. Healey looked serious, and enquiringly. I assured him I had. I was so bewitched that on a Midsummer morning one of them withdrew me to a place, where I gave myself to her for life; and the charm remained so strong that I had never yet attempted to break it, nor even wished to do so. He smiled on perceiving my meaning, and said he was not alluding to the witchcraft of love.

We now began to ascend the road leading to the Moors, and a climb of about two miles brought us upon the level of the hill at Ashworth Moor; soon after which we came in sight of Learock Hoyle, in modern English, 'Lark's Hole;' a substantial hostel and farmhouse, which Healey informed me was his uncle Richard's, or Dick's, as he sometimes called him. The old man was at work in a stone quarry near the road-side; he was about sixty years of age, strong and active for his time of life, and hearty too, for he came out of the quarry, and gave us a blunt and frank welcome, and took us into the house. His wife was a remarkably clever and good-looking woman, much younger than her husband, and the very personification of a managing, self-confident, and civil landlady. Two fine thriving lasses, taking after their mother, and a son more like his father, were their stock of children. And here this family had lived many years, contented with a sufficiency of plain comforts, at a lone house on the borders of a moor. I could not but reflect on the advantages they must derive from thus enjoying life freely in a world of their own, and with a moderation which gave promise of a long continuance. They seemed but little affected by what was going on, politically, in the districts below and around them: they were clear of the anxieties and tumults of business, which were heart-rending, and distracting the inhabitants of the great towns situated within their view, and, in fact, within their hearing, (for we could distinguish the noise of the lumbering roll of the carriages, like the eternal moan of a distant sea;) and contrasting the quietness of this nest, this 'Hole of the Lark,' with the errors and terrors of scenes I had quitted, I could not but detect my yearnings for a shelter with those I loved, in some quiet nook, little known, and seldom visited.

Having rested and taken refreshment, we went strolling upon the moor, and ascended Knowe, or Knowl-hill, from whence we had an extensive prospect. In the distance on our left, were the moors towards Todmorden and Walsden; following the horizon, we next saw the ridge of Blackstone-edge, streaked with sungleams and dark shadows; then the moors of Saddleworth, particularly Oaphin with his white drifts still lingering, and Odermon with his

46

venerable relics of druidism, his 'Pots an' Pons.' The mountains of Derbyshire and Cheshire rose like a region of congealed waves; whilst Vale Royal, to the south, lay reposing in a glorious sun; and the country towards Liverpool was bounded by a bright streak, probably the Irish sea. A dim white vapour indicated the site of Preston or Blackburn; Bolton seemed near at hand, and Bury close on our right below. Manchester, Stockport, Ashton, Oldham, and Rochdale, were distinctly visible; and neither last nor least regarded, was one small speck – it was the white end of a house at Heabers, which directed our looks to the misty vapour of Middleton, rising beside dark woods from the vale in which the town is situated. That was the smoke of our own hearths, heaped by those who were thinking of us. We could almost see them: whisht! could we not hear the voices of our children? Of their mothers calling them home? And in the fond imagination we shouted their names, but there was no reply; and then, feeling we were cut off and outcast, we more sadly understood the human desolateness of Him, who said, 'The foxes have holes, and the birds of the air have nests, but the son of man hath not where to lay his head.'

But even in this wild region were objects to call us back to reality, and teach us that in every situation there is something to be thankful for, – that

There is mercy in every place –

and that a bounteous Creator is nowhere unmindful of those he has called into life. A beautiful spring of water, pure as a cup from heaven's banquet, was gently brimming over a bason of white sand and pebbles into which it arose. A sward of sweet green grass, lined the margin of a silvery band that lay glimmering and trickling on the sunny side of the hill; whilst here and there were tufts of rushes, glistering with liquid pearls. We took the water in our hands and drank 'to our families and friends;' 'to our suffering brethren everywhere;' 'to the downfall of tyranny and soon;' and 'to liberty,' with three huzzas. An old black-faced tup, lifted his horns from the heather, looked gravely at us, and giving a significant bleat, scampered off, followed by such of his acquaintance as were browsing near.

47

Chapter 9

The Valley of Holcome — Healey in Full Practice — The Woman of Musbury

ON the morning following we bid our worthy host and his family good-bye, and after taking the way towards Edenfield a short distance, we struck into a deep stony road on our left, and descended to the valley of Holcome. We had counted our stock of money after turning out, and found it to be greatly diminished; for as uncle Richard refused pay for our board and lodging, we had spent in liquor more freely than we otherwise should have done, and our finances were now exceedingly light. Our intention was to enter Bolton that night, where Healey had a brother possessed of property, who he thought would either assist him with a little money, or find him a retreat for a short time, whilst I could easily get a loom in some of the neighbouring villages. But this plan was afterwards abandoned, as will shortly be seen.

After traversing this beautiful valley for some distance, we entered a public-house and took seats in the kitchen. A stumpy rosy-cheeked lass, with cherry ripe lips, and arms as red as apples, served us with ale; after which a decent elderly dame came in and told her to 'goo an' get sum moor o' that stuff for Mary tooth wur no betther.' I nudged the doctor, who immediately took the hint, and informed the dame, with his best grace, that if any of the family were ill of the tooth-ache, he could either cure it, or take out the tooth. She said her daughter had got it very bad and was in another room. Healey said he was a surgeon, and would extract it if she liked. 'Well really,' said she, with surprise, looking at his unctuous clothes, 'yo may be a docthur, but yo look'n more like a kawve-lad.' Healey seemed offended, and I assured the dame that he was 'as regular a bred surgeon as ever wur born ov a woman' – and in confirmation, Healey pulled out a case of lancets and his tooth-drawing instrument. At this moment a young woman entered the room, with her face rolled in flannel, and one cheek puffed and swollen. Her mother told her what Healey said, and being in extreme anguish, she suffered him to examine her mouth, after which he assured her it would be a mere flea bite, and he could have the tooth out in 'no time,' and at last she consented to have it drawn. I never liked to hear the crash of bones pulled out of living flesh, and so I walked into the yard, but had not been there a minute, ere a piercing scream called me in again, and I beheld the young woman on the floor, sputtering blood; and the doctor also on the floor near the fire, and literally swamped in a pool of cream, the mug of which lay in fragments beside him. I saw there was no murder in the case, and if my life had been at stake, I could not have refrained from loud and hearty laughter. I assisted the young woman to rise, but my mirth was abated when on spitting out, two teeth instead of one, dropped into her lap. The doctor, meantime, had got up and begun to wipe the fluid from his face and clothes; he was quite silent and looked very rueful. The old woman now came into the place, and with her two men, one of whom we soon understood to be a constable, and the other an overseer. 'These ar um,' she said, yo seen what havock theyn made; an iv yo hadno comn they met ha' kilt us for owt I kno'. That little devil pretended to be a docthur, an' put a pair o' pincers into th' wenches meawth, an' has very nee poo'd her yed off; an' th' tothers no better nor him. Beside, theyn brokken my mug an' shed my kryem.' 'An' look at theese,' said the patient, casting an enraged glance at the doctor; 'hee's poo'd two teeth eawt istid o' one.' The doctor begged to be heard; the constable said he 'had bin sworn at Howkham Kwort, an' munt doo his duty; an' iv thur wur a charge he munt take us afore a magistrate'. The overseer said, 'that wur reet, ackwordin to Burn's justice.' I did not relish the idea of going before a magistrate just at that time, lest something might escape as to who we were and what had brought us into that part; so I said, I and my friend were quite ready to go with the gentlemen anywhere, to have this misfortune explained; but as they appeared to be men of good understanding and respectable manners, and seemed to know something of law, I thought the matter might as well be talked over a little, and if a glass of something to drink were added, it would not, at any rate, make matters worse than they were. This was declared to be very reasonable by all parties, and accordingly we adjourned with the officers to another room, and were soon afterwards joined by two persons apparently farmers; and a jug of warm ale with some grattered ginger in, and I think, also a dash of the first syllabled liquid, being placed on the table, with tobacco and pipes, we drew round the fire. Healey now requested that the young woman might be called, and she making her appearance, he very submissively requested to see the teeth; they were produced, and he then wished to examine her mouth without his instruments, which was also conceded after some persuasion, when he cleverly slipped one of the teeth, a sound one into the orifice from which it had been taken; gently compressed the gum to make it close up; and ordering a squib of rum, with directions to keep it in her mouth a minute, and then put it out, he declared she was as well as ever. The patient did as she was bid, only instead of putting out the rum, she swallowed it, and then said she thought she was better. This made Healey proud as chanticleer, and taking a hearty draught of the ale, he said he would not stand in second place to any doctor they could produce in the whole country. The overseer was next instituted chairman, and the dame of the house was called, asked what was her charge; she said as her daughter was better, she would only charge five shillin' for 'th' mug breakin' an' kryem sheedin', an' if that wur sattl't o' wud be reet.' The doctor said he thought the case was a very hard one, for he had done his patient a great service at the risk of his limbs almost. The young woman, he said, was in a most favourable position for the operation; the extractors were fixed, and he was bringing out the tooth very nicely, when she screamed, threw up her foot, with which she took him in the ribs, and sent him to the other end of the room, where he alighted slap against the wall, and falling on the mug, broke it, and was at the same time seriously bruised himself. The young woman was asked if that was true? she replied, she believed it was; and the company then agreed, that as there was no charge except for damage, the patient had best pay half-a-crown for tooth-drawing, and the doctor three shillings for the mug and cream. The doctor heard the decision with a kind of inward groan, for nothing hurt his feelings more than paying money when he should be receiving it. He however threw down one of the few sixpences which he had left, and the old woman took it in settlement of the damage. This matter being adjusted, we were partaking another pot, when a man came in from Bolton, and in conversing said the radicals were in great alarm there, it being reported that King's officers had arrived from London for the purpose of arresting some of the leaders, and that the police were very sharp on the lookout for them. This information was not lost by us, and we exchanged significant glances without being observed.

We were talking on various matters, when the door was opened, and a personally fine looking woman with an infant at the breast, advanced timidly, and said she wished to speak to the overseer. Her outer garments were of very homely material, being seemingly cotton fents dyed blue, but neatly fitting her person, and very clean. She had a pair of light clogs on her feet, and her stockings were, I could perceive, well darned above the buckles. Her petticoat and bedgown, were of the same blue cotton, and the latter was open at the bosom, where a fine boy lay smiling at his pap. Her apron was striped calico; and her head gear consisted of a striped napkin, apparently also a fent, over a mob cap, very white; from beneath which a lock of black hair had escaped, and hung as if in contrast with a bosom of as pure white as ever appertained to human nature. Her features also were handsome; her cheeks were faintly tinged on a very pale ground. Her mouth was somewhat wan; she seemed rather exhausted; and as she stood, the tears came into her dark and modest eyes. 'Weer dusto com fro,' asked the overseer; 'an' wot dusto want? theawrt a new un at ony rate,' he continued. She said she came from Musbury, and wanted relief for her husband, herself and two children, besides the infant. 'An 'wot dun yo doo for a livin?' interrogated the overseer. They wove calico, she said, when they could get work and were able; but the children at home were ill of the measles; the shopkeeper had refused them any more credit, and her husban' had 'wurched for 'em till he fell off his looms, and wur beginnin' oth' feyver th' docthur said so.' 'Hang thoose docthurs,' said the overseer, 'why conno they let foke dee when thur time comes.' 'I hope he'll no' dee yet' said the poor woman, tears streaming in plenty. 'I think he'd com reawnd iv yod nobbut let us have a trifle o' summut to carry on wi'; an' iv yo win (intreatingly) I'll hie me whom, an' I'll put th' chylt i'th' keyther an' set at yon wark, an' I'll finish it mysel; an' we'n not trouble yo ogen unless we'en sum new misfortin'.' The overseer asked the farmers, who it appeared were rate-payers, what they thought of the case; and the result was, that he gave her two shillings, and promised to call and see the family. But she must tell her husband he must not begin of the fever. 'Its o'idlety, idlety; an' iv th' paupers o'th' taewn yerd at he geet owt wi' bein ill o'th' feyver, theyd' o' begin.' 'Nowe, nowe, theyd'n ha no feyvers i' their teawnship.' She took the money, curtseyed, and thanked the overseer and rate-payers. One of them said she had been 'a decent wench;' he knew her father in better days, and offered her a glass of the warm ale, which she put to her lips, and swallowed a small quantity. Her cheeks turned deathly pale; she put out her hand as if her sight was gone; her grasp relaxed; the child dropped on Healey's knee, and I caught the fainting woman in my arms. 'Hoos clem'd to dyeth,' said one of the rate-payers. 'Hoos as dyed as a dur nail,' said the other. 'I didno' deny her relief,' said the overseer. The doctor handed the child to the landlady, and called for some brandy, which was brought, together with a sharp smelling bottle which was applied, but there was not any perceptible breathing; and she shrunk down seated upon the floor, I kneeling and still keeping her in a leaning posture.

And, shall I be ashamed to say, that whilst I thus held her, tears escaped, and chased down a furrow already made by care on that cold and pale brow? Oh, no! could I have withheld my deepest sympathy from that beauteous mother, my sister in humanity, perishing thus for want of food, my heart must have turned to stone. Healey chafed her temples with the liquor, sprinkled her face with water, opened her hands, and tried to get a drop of liquid into her mouth, but her teeth were set. 'Poor thing,' said the doctor, 'she must have been very ill.' 'Hoos dun for i' this ward,' said one of the men. 'I relieft hur,' said the overseer, 'for I seed hoo'r none o' eawr reggilur paupers.' 'We shan ha' to have an inquest,' said the constable. 'Moor expence, an' moor,' said the overseer; 'but they conno say 'at I neglected 'em, con they.' Whilst these observations and many others were passing, the features of the sufferer became less rigid; the jaw relaxed; a drop of brandy and water was administered; a slight tinge of pink appeared on her cheeks; the chafings and smellings were continued; a sigh after some time escaped, and in a minute or two those dark fringed eyes unclosed; she looked inquiringly around, and soon appeared to comprehend her situation. In a short time she was restored; her child was again pressed to her bosom; the two shillings were made up to five; she took a cup of warm tea with the family; and in another hour she was slowly wending up the hill towards Musbury.

Chapter 10

Bury — A Night Hag — The Hush Shop

IT was dark when we entered the neat country town of Bury; for after what we heard of the state of things at Bolton, we deemed it best to avoid that neighbourhood; probably also we were influenced by a natural leaning towards home; and, in consequence, though scarcely determined, we were travelling thitherward ere we had agreed so to end our journey. After the departure of the woman we consented to another libation with our new acquaintance, and our stay was prolonged at some risk, as questions were asked, and suppositions expressed, which required more caution than it was agreeable to maintain. My little comrade also was in his own estimation become a very big man, and a most important personage. The liquor was getting into his head, and he shewed his wonted inclination for 'sprozing,' the best exemplification of which, is that of a turkey-cock spreading his feathers. It was at the sacrifice of a considerable share of vanity, that he was restrained from telling the constable and overseer who and what he was; his great abilities, which he would have proved by singing and recitations, (in both of which, he murdered every thing he uttered;) and his great practice, and the cures he had effected. I therefore got him away decently; and our next halting place was 'The Grey Mare,' a public-house opposite the church in the aforementioned market town. We were both hungry, not having tasted food since morning; we bought a steak which we wished to have cooked at this house, but were informed it could not be done; 'they had something else to do than to cook steaks on Saturday nights.' The place indeed was full of customers, apparently country people, come to the town to make their markets, so we went on to the next house, where our meat was cooked, and we washed it down with a jug of pretty good ale. There was here also, much company; and we learned from their conversation that several persons had been arrested the day before for high treason at Manchester, and that two of them were named Ogden and Johnson. This was no very encouraging news to us; nor were our feelings tranquillized when soon after a respectable-looking, rather elderly man came into the room, and surveying the company

53

round, went away without saying a word. We soon learned that he was the deputy-constable of the town, and this incident hastened our departure.

The night was cloudy and overcast, but the glare of the shops threw a good light into the street, which was well filled with market people. We were anxious to get out of the way, and resolved to take the field road, as being most calculated to favour escape if we should be pursued, as well as to prevent pursuit. We accordingly enquired the way to 'Gig Bridge,' and following our directions, we found ourselves, after a short walk, on the bank of an apparently deep stream, which we knew must be the Roch; and following its course we were soon on a narrow wooden bridge, which we passed, without any of that unpleasant motion which had obtained for it the reputation of a dangerous passage. The clouds, now, instead of blowing off, as we had thought they would, became more thick and the night darker. We knew little of the way; Healey not a foot of it, and I had only a slight notion of its general direction. At the worst, however, we could take the hunter's road till we came to a house. The path led us between a high bank on our right, and what, in the darkness, seemed to be a deep and tangled wood on our left. Proceeding cautiously, for the road was crooked and uneven, we came to the verge of the wood, where two roads lay before us; and we were considering which to take, when the light of a lanthorn flashed close upon us, and we asked the person who bore it, (a woman) where the two roads led to ? She was low in stature, with an old red cloak thrown over her shoulders, and a handkerchief, tied hood-like, around her head and face. She held the light up to Healey as he stood next to her, and looked at him stedfastly, and I had an opportunity for observing that she was considerably aged. Some thin locks of grey hair were streaming in the wind and flapping across her face; her eyebrows were expansive and grey; and her two quick dark eyes, set in wrinkles, seemed peculiarly brilliant for her age. Her face was furrowed and brown; her features had been regular, perhaps handsome, but now appeared careworn and anxious; and her teeth were still even and white. She evidently had not been a marketing, as she had not either bundle or basket, but held a stick, on which she leaned, on one hand, and the lanthorn in the other. 'Good mother,' said Healey, 'weer dun theese two roads lyed too ?' 'To mony places i' this ward,' she replied, 'an' mayhap some ith' tother. This,' pointing to the left, 'lyeds to th' Frogg-hole, an'

54

Yep-fowd, an' Yeddy-hill, on th' Top o' Yep; an' that,' pointing to the one before us, 'lyeds to th' Hollins, an' th' Cathole, an' th' Castle, an' Thurston-fowd. But weer dun yo' want to goo too,' she asked, 'o'er sitch a wilderin counthry, an' sitch o' neet as this?' We said we were strangers, but if we could find Whittle or Bowlee we should be right. 'Follow me then,' she said; and immediately stepped out at a pace which we little expected. Healey followed close after the lanthorn, now making an observation more free than wise; now asking questions, some of which must have sounded mysteriously to our guide. 'Yore no meety good uns, I dare say,' she muttered. 'Yore as like excisemen, as owt 'at I ever seed.' Healey seemed wishful to humour the supposition, and asked if there were any hush-shops in that part of the country? She turned round, thrust the light's full glare close to his face, and with a furious voice and gesture, said – 'hush, foo; keep the secret; iv I dunno' tel the theaw winno' know.' That moment lanthorn and lanthorn bearer disappeared, and the next there was a crash and a plash! Healey had fallen through a hedge, down a steep bank, and into the channel of a brook. I should have followed him, but saved myself from going over by clasping a young tree, by which I held; whilst, stooping down, I got hold of my companion, and he was again safely landed.

After some puffing and gasping, and sundry emphatic wishes bestowed on 'the owd hag,' as Healey called our late guide, I reminded him that he had brought it upon himself by pretending to be an exciseman, and pressing unpleasant questions about the neighbourhood. 'Where was the owd limb?' he asked. Had she sunk into th' earth, or flown into th' air? 'Hoo went in a flash as quick as gun-shot, lanthorn, leet, an' o', an' nobody should make him believe 'at hoo wur owt elze but an arrant witch.' I said it was a strange occurrence, and not to be exactly accounted for at that time; but it was of no use standing there – we must move in some direction, or we should not get home before daylight. So we groped about, and at last perceived a tree which lay across the gully, over which we stepped, holding by the branches, and soon had footing on a rising ground and an open field, over which we were directing our course, when our attention was excited by a laugh of almost unearthly tone, which came like a jeering yell upon the wind; and looking towards our right, we perceived below us at some distance, a light, dancing as it were, and moving at a rapid pace through the profound darkness. 'There gwos yon beldame, an' crone, an' hoo devil, on' bowt an' sowd infernal as hoo is,' said Healey. The laugh was renewed, but sounded fainter, and almost like a scream of pain; and the next moment the light began to descend, and suddenly disappeared as if sunk into the earth. An exclamation of horror and surprise escaped my companion; and we continued over an uneven country; now by the roar of waters and weirs, now across dingles, levels, and swamps; until at length espying a glimmer which was stationary, we concluded it must come from a house, and hastening forwards, we soon heard noises of song, laughter, and revelry; and finding they proceeded from a human habitation which we thought must be a tavern, we opened the door and entered without ceremony.

Chapter 11

An Interior — A Reception — A Battle — An Operation in Surgery — Home

THE building was thatched, and consisted of several rooms on the ground floor, two of which were occupied by company. The room into which we entered was a square one, with a good fire of turf and wood burning opposite the door. On the centre of the floor stood a kind of low table, formed of an inner door which had been lifted from its hinges, and placed on bricks and logs of wood to serve as a table, and on it two candles in clay sockets were burning. About a dozen pots, of nearly all sorts and shapes, were upon the table; each pot containing ale, or what appeared to be so. The room was dimmed by tobacco smoke; but we could discern not fewer than some eight or ten men, seated in various parts of it, some on stools, some on piled bricks, some on logs of wood; whilst others occupied empty firkins, mugs capsized, or any other article affording a seat. The company was not less dissimilar in appearance, though all seemed of the labouring class. Some were farm servants, some factory workers, and some were weavers; there were also one or two, who we found were poor men, but not workers at any branch, being known sots, bullies, and occasionally thieves. The other room was occupied by customers much the same as these; but the blows on their table, and the tremendous cursings, told us they were at high words about a game at cards. On our entering, all eyes were directed towards us, and the hum of their voices was hushed to silence. 'Well, what dun yo' want,' said a brawny dark-bearded fellow, turning towards us with a most unwelcoming look. I informed him we had lost our way, and merely called to enquire about it; but, as we were in the house, we would taste his ale if he had no particular objection. 'Wot are yo', an' weer dun yo come fro,' was demanded sternly; several of the company rising and repeating the questions. I said that if it was of consequence to the master or mistress of the place, they should know before we went away. If we drank their ale, we would satisfy them for it, and whether we had any or not, there would not be any harm done, we supposed.

'Mother! come heer;' shouted the dark man from the stair's foot; when, who should make her appearance but the same old woman who about an hour before had vanished so unaccountably. 'Excise-men!' 'Informers!' she screamed, at the top of a thrilling voice; and at that moment, each man of the company was on his feet; hands were clutching at our throats, and a prospect of certain manglement or murder, stared from those ferocious countenances. A crash in the next room, and a smashing of pots was heard; and whilst we were, vainly, as it seemed, endeavouring to evade our fate, a stout, low-built man, rather decently clad, and with a weaver's green apron twisted around his middle, rushed into the room; said he knew us both, well – that we were neither excisemen nor informers – and that he would pledge his life for us. The company then fell back; candles were brought – a circle was formed around us, gazing in curiosity and doubt – and at last we were permitted to sit down, and partake of the ale. The old woman however, persisted that we were excisemen, or sent by the excise; and narrated what Healey had asked, and how she slipped the light under her cloak at a sudden turn of the road, leaving Healey to walk into the ditch, and his comrade after him. This caused a loud laugh at our expense; and it was repeated, when we admitted that it was true except in one particular. Our friend, the poacher, for such he was, meantime had taken the dark-bearded youth, the son, aside, and explained our names and condition to him, he whispered to his mother, and a word was passed round, which caused an entire change of manner to us by the whole company. I felt a curiosity to observe human nature in such a place, and being now readily supplied with ale, I took my pipe, and listened with some interest to the conversation;

whilst Healey made himself agreeable by singing, in his best manner,

> *'The deil cam fiddlin' thro' the toon,*
> *An' danc'd awa wi' th' exciseman.'*

We had not, however, been at peace long, ere the carders in the next room again quarrelled, and proceeded to that length, that a battle was determined upon. Lights, of candles and pitch-rope, and bog-pine, were procured, and the combatants stripped, and accompanied by every man, went into a small plot of ground behind the house. The combatants were our friend the poacher, and another man, younger and heavier, who chiefly earned his living by dog breaking, and under-strapping to gamekeepers and their masters. Betwixt the men there had been an unfriendly feeling for some time, and now, over this potent ale, for it was good, though new, their hostility was again excited, and probably decided. The ring was formed with as much silence as possible. The men stripped to their waists, and then kneeled down and tied their shoes fast on their feet. They then dogged for the first grip, much as game cocks do for the first fly; and after about a minute so spent, they rushed together and grappled, and in a moment the dog-man gave the poacher a heavy kick on the knee, and was at the same time thrown violently on the ground, on his back, his antagonist alighting on him like 'a bag of bones.' It was now a ground fight for some time, and exhibited all the feats of a Lancashire battle, which I take to have been derived from a very remote date, long before the 'Art of Self-defence,' or indeed, almost any other art, was known in these islands. There was not, however, any of that gouging of the eyes; or biting the flesh; or tearing, or lacerating other parts, which are so often imputed to Lancashire fighters, by Cockney sportsmen and others, who know little about them. It was all fair play, though certainly of a rough sort, and as thorough a thing of the kind as I had ever seen. Doggy, after gaining breath, tried to turn on his belly, which Poacher aimed to prevent, pressing the wind out of him by his weight upon the chest as he lay across him, and, at times throttling him until his eyes stared as if they were looking into another world. In one of those suffocating agonies, Doggy flung round one leg, and locked it in one of his opponent's, and in a moment they were twisted together like the knot of a boa constrictor; and the next, Doggy turned on his belly, and got upon his knees. There was a loud shout, and much cursing and swearing;

and several bets were offered and taken as to the issue of the contest. Poacher now laid all the weight he could on Doggy's head and neck, to prevent him from getting upright. He grasped him below the arms, and kept clutching his throat; and the latter, for want of breath, to carry on with, kept tearing his hands from their gripe: both snorted like porpoises, and it began to appear that our friend Poacher was the worst for wind. Some heavy kicking now ensued, until the white bones were seen grinning through the gashes in their legs, and their stockings were soaked in blood. Poacher was evidently a brave man, though now coming second; in one of his struggles, Doggy freed himself, and rushed on Poacher with a kick that made the crew set their teeth, and look for splintered bones: and Poacher stood it though he felt it. There was another clutch, and a sudden fling, in which Poacher was uppermost, and Doggy falling with his neck doubled under, he rolled over, and lay without breath or motion, black in the face, and with blood oozing from his ears and nostrils. All said he was killed; and that opinion probably softened the shout of triumph which was set up by those who had won their bets. The doctor, who had been trodden out of the ring during the battle, was now loudly called for; and at length, with that air of important gravity so habitual to the 'profession,' he approached along an avenue made through these wildlings, and kneeling by the man on one side, Poacher being on the other, holding a pitch torch, in great concernment, he felt for a pulse – declared there was none – and, binding the arm, he pulled out a lancet, and opened a vein cleverly, the blood, as if still in battle, dashing hot and red in Poacher's face – a circumstance, which made some laugh, and others look grave, it being taken by them as a dying accusation of murder. The man bled freely, the blood trickling into a dark red sud on the trodden grass. Poacher presented a picture of horror and misery. After the accident he stepped aside, and putting on his shirt, returned to the ring, where he took his station as before described, looking with intense anxiety on the livid features of his prostrate foe. He had wiped the blood from his own eyes with his knuckles; and the ghastly white of those cavities, contrasting with the gore on his cheek and beard, now parched and glittering in the torch-light, gave him an appearance of more than mortal horror and despair. The arm being bound up, Doggy was conveyed into the house and laid on the table, a turf or two being placed under his head, by way of pillow. He had, to the great joy of Poacher, begun to breathe during the bleeding, and now appeared in a sound sleep, and the doctor assured the Poacher he would come round in a short time; he had only been a little 'stunished,' which had 'brought on a fainting fit,' and he would soon be better. Poacher was most grateful for the information; he declared he would never fight again, and swore the doctor was the finest man in all England; and that if one hare only was living on lord Suffield's grounds, he should have it for his stew-pot next Sunday. The doctor enjoyed his triumph; he drank to the company all round, not omitting the wounded man, who remained motionless and prostrate. Some of them said his neck was awry, and the doctor examining him more minutely, bathed his head in cold water; after which, adjusting the neck, he got two staves of a butter tub, and placing one on each side, resting on the shoulders, and jutting above the head, he tied them firmly but gently, with a couple of red cotton hanks, and the man soon after opening his eyes, though scarcely sensible, he was conveyed home on the shoulders of his party. The doctor then dressed Poacher's wounds; we soon after left the place, guided into the road by Poacher, who was going that way, and arrived at Middleton without further adventure.

And, shall we part here friend, reader? On my very threshhold shall we part? Nay: come in from the frozen rain, and from the night wind, which is blowing the clouds into sheets like torn sails before a gale. Now down a step or two. – 'Tis better to keep low in the world than to climb only to fall. It is dark, save when the clouds break into white scud above; and silent, except the snort of the wind, and the rattling of hail, and the eaves of dropping rain. Come in! – A glimmer shews that the place is inhabited; that the nest has not been rifled whilst the old bird was away. Now shalt thou see what a miser a poor man can be in his heart's treasury. A second door opens, and a flash of light shews we are in a weaving room, clean and flagged, and in which are two looms with silken work of green and gold. A young woman, of short stature, fair, round, and fresh as Hebe; with light brown hair escaping in ringlets from the sides of her clean cap, and with a thoughtful and meditative look, sits darning beside a good fire, which sheds warmth upon the clean swept hearth and gives light throughout the room, or rather cell. A fine little girl, seven years of age, with a sensible and affectionate expression of countenance, is reading in a low tone to her mother.

'And he opened his mouth and taught them, saying, Blessed are the poor in spirit; for theirs' is the kingdom of heaven. Blessed are they that mourn; for they shall be comforted. Blessed are the meek; for they shall inherit the earth. Blessed are they which do hunger and thirst after righteousness; for they shall be filled. Blessed are the merciful; for they shall obtain mercy. Blessed are the pure in heart; for they shall see God. Blessed are the peacemakers; for they shall be called the children of God. Blessed are they which are persecuted for righteousness sake; for theirs is the kingdom of heaven. Blessed are ye when men shall revile you, and persecute you, and shall say all manner of evil against you for my sake.'

Observe the room and its furniture. A humble but cleanly bed, screened by a dark old fashioned curtain, stands on our left. At the foot of the bed is a window closed from the looks of all street passers. Next are some chairs, and a round table of mahogany; then another chair, and next it a long table, scoured very white. Above that is a looking glass with a picture on each side, of the resurrection and ascension on glass, 'copied from Rubens.' A well-stocked shelf of crockery ware is the next object, and in a nook near it are a black oak carved chair or two, with a curious desk, or box to match; and lastly, above the fire-place, are hung a rusty basket hilted sword, an old fusee, and a leathern cap. Such are the appearance and furniture of that humble abode. – But my wife!

> *She look'd; she redden'd like the rose;*
> *Syne, pale as ony lily.*

Ah! did they hear the throb of my heart, when they sprung to embrace me? my little love child to my knees, and my wife to my bosom.

Such were the treasures I had hoarded in that lowly cell. Treasures, that, with contentment, would have made into a palace

> *the lowest shed*
> *That ever rose on England's plain.*

They had been at prayers, and were reading the Testament before retiring to rest. And now, as they a hundred times caressed me, they found that indeed, 'Blessed are they that mourn, for they shall be comforted.'

Chapter 12

A Midnight Visitant — A Secret Meeting — A Plot — Oliver, the Spy — His first Essay in the Way of Business

ABOUT the middle of the night, on the night after my return home, we were awoke by a gentle knocking at our outer door, I arose and asked who was there? A voice replied, 'a friend;' and I opened the door, and a man walked in, muffled up to the eyes. I asked him who he was; when, half laughing, in his natural voice, he said, 'don't you know me?' and I then recognized him as my most intimate acquaintance and co-delegate at London. He said he had particular reasons for coming disguised, and at that unseasonable hour, and that he wished to see me and some half-dozen of our most trusty reformers in the morning, at the house of a friend whom he named, residing at Stannicliffe, a short distance from Middleton. I promised to attend him as desired, and he departed. At the time appointed, myself and several others went to the house, and being shewn into a private room with our visitant, he commenced by entering into details of his private business transactions, from which it appeared that he was greatly embarrassed, and knew not how to extricate himself. He had been to various places; at home he durst not remain; and had last come from London, where he had been in communication with some of the best friends to reform, who, with himself, had come to a determination to strike a decisive blow at once. He then detailed a plan which, if acted upon with energy, would, be said, effect all that was required. Some ten or a dozen of our best men were to provide themselves with arms, and march to London, where they would be joined by others, and, at a time agreed upon, the united body were to rush upon the ministers at a cabinet council, or a dinner, and assassinate the whole of them. All London would then rise; the population would subdue all before it; the country would be our own, and a new government would be established. Our arms were to consist of a stout walking staff, with a socket at one end for the reception of a dagger, which, he said, 'may be easily made from the blade of a common knife, such as this,' (taking one from the table.) Pistols might also be carried by those who could procure them. When asked how the money for the journey was to be raised, he pulled a gold watch from his pocket, and said, if no other means were left, he would dispose of that to raise money. This would not do: it was rather too bare a trap. Besides, it was far wide of our code of reform, and we declined having anything to do with it. We also endeavoured to dissuade him from lending himself to such projects; and we left him without making any impression upon him.

The fact was, this unfortunate person, in the confidence of an unsuspecting mind, as I believe, had during one of his visits to London, formed a connection with Oliver, the spy – which connection, during several succeeding months, gave a new impulse to secret meetings and plots in various parts of Lancashire, Yorkshire, and Derbyshire; and ended in the tragedy of Brandreth, Ludlam, and Turner, at Derby. This was probably Oliver's first demonstration on his 'professional tour': it failed – but from that very week, private meetings, for highly criminal purposes, again commenced. Agents came from Manchester, and glided through the country, depositing their poison wherever they could. Meetings were held at Blackley; two or three at Middleton; one or two at Chadderton; the same at Failsworth; and again at Manchester – where some fools and their deluders, having been collected, a partial explosion took place, of which further notice will occur shortly.

Let us not, however, in recounting these transactions, lay blame where it ought not to be. Let us not confound the blind instrument, with the intelligent agent who directed it. If the individual before alluded to, our mysterious visitant, erred greatly in these matters, he suffered for his error. A leading provincial journalist, with much apparent truth, afterwards stigmatized him as 'a spy;' the sore obloquy stuck to him long, and whether it has yet been entirely removed, admits of doubt. But, had he been a spy, he would not have been left to struggle with poverty and disgrace in England, but would have been removed, and provided for, as Oliver was. HAD HE BEEN A SPY HE WOULD HAVE BETRAYED THOSE WHO NEVER WERE BETRAYED. We may allow that he was credulous and inconsiderate, and consequently unfit to be a leader in those or any other times; but this is far short of an admission that he was a co-villain with Oliver. He was an egregious dupe no doubt, but, he was not a spy.

If it be asked, why did not you, as consistent and honest reformers, denounce this plot to the government at once, as, in obedience to the laws, you ought to have done? My reply is, because we were persuaded the government knew of it already; that, consequently, if attempted it would fail; and lastly, because we had accepted the man's confidence, and he had placed his safety in our hands. This last dilemma may serve to caution others, how they accept responsibilities which may lead to criminality or dishonour.

Chapter 13

Treasonable Meetings at Ardwick Bridge — Apprehension of the Delegates — Arrest of the Author — Occurrences at Royton, Oldham, and Manchester

I HAD reprehended the doctor freely for attending one or two of the private meetings before alluded to, and he had avoided my company during nearly a fortnight, when, on the morning of Saturday, the twenty-ninth of March, he suddenly made his appearance at my residence, and with a woeful look asked if I had heard of the arrest of the delegates at a private meeting, at Ardwick Bridge, the night previous. I said I had heard of the transaction; it was only what I had been expecting, and I had offended him by speaking my opinion. He said he wished I would go to his house for a short consultation; I went, and found there one William Elson, who had been connected with one or two of these meetings. They wished for my advice as to what was best to be done under the circumstances.

Amongst the persons arrested was John Lancashire, a Middleton man, who had been delegated from a meeting at which both of my friends, as I understood, had attended. I blamed them for having anything to do with private meetings, and advised them, they having committed themselves, to leave home for a time, as I had not a doubt the police were in possession of their names and would be after them. Elson, I said might go anywhere, as he was not much known: Healey I advised to go to his brother at Bolton, and get some money, and keep out of sight entirely, until something further was known. His best way would be to avoid Manchester, and go over Kersal moor, and Agecroft bridge; and as I had a relation in that quarter who wished to see me, I would keep him company as far as Agecroft. My advice was adopted; Elson went to prepare for his flight, and Healey commenced doing the same. I was now informed that Lancashire had a pike concealed in his house, and I went thither and got that destroyed. On my return, instead of finding Healey ready, he was busy combing his hair, and adjusting his neckcloth. I urged him to get away if he valued his life; and after some further delay, I saw him fairly on the road, and then went to prepare myself, and in a few minutes I set out after him. We had appointed to meet at Rhodes, Healey taking a circuitous road over Bowlee, whilst I went a nearer, but still indirect way through Alkrington wood.

I was walking towards the church-yard at my usual leisurely, but rather swift pace, quite satisfied that Healey was out of all danger of being captured, and without the remotest idea of any peril to myself, when a voice hallooed, and looking back I beheld Joseph Scott, the deputy-constable of Middleton, hastening towards me. I concluded instantly that he wanted me; and disdaining the thought of flying, I returned and met him, and he took hold of me, saying, I was the King's prisoner. I asked him what for? and he said I should see presently; and we had not gone many yards on our return, when we were met by Mr Nadin, the deputy constable of Manchester, and about six or eight police officers, all well armed with staves, pistols, and blunderbusses: two of these took hold of me, and the whole party marched back to the doctor's house.

Here they handcuffed me; and whilst they searched for the doctor, my wife in great distress rushed into the room, and desired to know what I had done amiss, that I should be treated in that manner. One of the men had threatened to shoot her at the door, but she rushed past him, and now, whilst she clung to me distracted and terrified, another would have rudely forced her away, but was rebuked by his superior, which saved him from punishment, and the party probably from the unpleasantness of a street battle with my neighbours. A crowd had collected in front of the house; and when we came out, and were proceeding down the street, there was a shout, and a piece of brick passed near the head of Mr Nadin, who, probably apprehensive, and not without reason, of a volley, snatched a blunderbuss from one of the men, and facing about swore dreadfully that he would fire amongst the crowd if another stone was thrown. I turned round, and begged they would not commit any violence, for I was willing to suffer for the cause I had espoused. Either from the threat, or my wish, or both, my neighbours paused;

and I was conducted to the Assheton's Arms public-house, at the lower end of the town. We stopped here some time, and I had an opportunity for observing the person of my principal captor, Mr Nadin. He was, I should suppose, about six feet one inch in height, with an uncommon breadth and solidity of frame. He was also as well, as he was strongly built; upright in gait, and active in motion. His head was full sized, his complexion sallow, his hair dark and slightly grey; his features were broad and non-intellectual, his voice loud, his language coarse and illiterate, and his manner rude and overbearing to equals or inferiors. He was represented as being exceedingly crafty in his business, and somewhat unfeeling withal; but I never heard, and certainly never knew, that he maltreated his prisoners. At times he would indulge in a little raillery with them, possibly from a reason of his own, but I never was led to suppose that he threw away a word of condolement on those occasions. He was certainly a somewhat remarkable person in uncommon times, and acting in an arduous situation. He shewed, however, that he had the homely tact to take care of his own interests. He housed a good harvest whilst his sun was up; and retired to spend his evening in ease and plenty on a farm of his own within the borders of Cheshire. I shall have to recur to him frequently in the course of this work. At present such was he, who with firm step, but uneasy bearing, paced the floor of the parlour at the Assheton's Arms Inn. His men were all about the house, and some of them would frequently step in and communicate something to him, and orders and observations passed, which were unintelligible to me. I was seated at the further end of the room, near a table. On another table near to which he passed and repassed, were a couple of blunderbusses and some pistols, and also a jug of ale and some glasses, one of which he filled and gave to me. 'Yor a set o' roof devils,' he said, 'i' this Middleton, but we mun ha' sum moor on yo' afore lung.' 'We are pretty fair for that,' I replied, 'but,' looking through the window, and seeing the people collecting, 'I wudno' advise yo' (I said,) to walk me eawt oth' teawn, as yo' did'n hitherto; iv yo' dun, there will be some yeds brokken.' 'Dunno' consarn thesel' obeawt that,' he replied with a knowing look; 'theaw'l see heaw ween orthert that, ofore lung'; – and whilst we talked, a coach, escorted by a party of dragoons, drove up to the door – I was handed in, with Mr Nadin, and one of his men, and we drove at a rapid pace towards Chadderton; I chanting to myself,

Farewell ! ye honey-winged gales;
Farewell ! ye sloping hills and dales;
Ye waving woods that sweep the sky;
Ye daisy'd meadows that lowly lie.
No more, to pluck your sweets I rove,
My fond arm locked round my love;
I now must bid a long adieu,
To Midia's lonely bowers and you.

On arriving at the Red Rose, at Chadderton, the coach stopped, and some of the men having entered the house, returned and informed Mr Nadin, that 'he was not at home, but his wife expected him soon, as he was only gone to Manchester.' This was one of the houses at which private meetings had been held, and the person alluded to, was Mr Edward O'Connor, who, for having unwittingly permitted such a meeting, was involved in this affair, as will shortly appear. On the road towards Chadderton Hall I advised my conductor to draw up and return to Manchester; assuring him, he would not capture any more of my batch that day, and in confirmation, I pointed to Chadderton Heights, and the neighbouring country, over which scores of people were running like hunters, as if to meet the coach near Royton: all the country was up, I said, and every one whom he might want, would be apprized of his coming. He growled a deep oath, saying he had never seen anything like that before: the officer commanding the dragoons, who rode by the coach door, observed that he had seen something like it in Ireland, but never anywhere else.

Passing Street-bridge, and Royley, we entered the village of Royton, the streets of which were deserted, and the doors shut. We soon returned to Royley, and the constables made a dash into a house in search of a man named Mellor, but he was not there. A crowd was collected near the carriage, and as I was expecting to move on, the door was suddenly opened, and a long, thin, barrel of a human body, was thrust into the coach, head first – a couple of stilt-like legs being doubled up after it. 'Lock 'em together,' said Mr Nadin, and it was no sooner said than done. This person had met some of the runners in a back court or alley, and threatened to beat in their brains with a walling hammer which he had in his hand.

George Howarth, for that was the name of my new companion,

was a decent, labouring, married man, of Royton, and was about six feet four inches in height. He said he thought it a very hard case – 'he cudno' tell wot he'd dun amiss.' Mr Nadin said he'd know 'wot he'd done amiss' before he was much older.

'Why bless your life, Mesthur Nadin,' said George, 'yore a graidley felley for owt 'at I kno' to th' contrary; an' I never sed nowt ogen yo' i' my lyve.'

'Aye, an' I'll make thee into a graidley felley too, afore I ha' dun wi' the. Theaw'rt a moderate length to begin wi', but theaw'll be lunger afore theaw comes back to Reighton: ween ha' thee hang'd,' said our keeper.

'Nay, Mesthur Nadin,' said George, 'dunno' say so: they axt wot I had i' mi' hont, an' I shode 'em: it wur nobbut a bit ov a walling hommer 'at I'd bin a borroin'.'

'Aye,' said Mr Nadin, 'an' theaw sed theawd knock their brains eawt wi' it. But ween larn thee, an' o' yo' Jacobins, heaw yo' threaten to kill th' King's officers: theaw'll be hang'd as sure as theaw sits theer.' George seemed thoughtful upon this.– He looked at the shackles, and at me; and soon after, we drew up at the Spread Eagle public house, in Manchester-street, Oldham.

The soldiers were here regaled with bread, cheese, and ale. The street was filled with a great concourse of people, and some of the military kept guard whilst the others refreshed. George and I, were seated on a form at the back of the room: the policemen took other seats, and Mr Nadin and the officer placed themselves at a table, on which were set forth some nice ham, and bread and cheese, and a flagon or two of ale. They had all cut, and drank, and helped themselves without ceremony; and, observing George give a most wolfish look towards the victuals, I asked him if he could like some ? had he not breakfasted ? He said he had not; he was just going to breakfast when he happened to call for that unlucky walling hammer.

'Captain,' I said, addressing the officer of dragoons, 'are your prisoners to remain without food ?'

'Oh, certainly not,' he replied, 'Come up and take what you choose.' George and I, then advanced, and each got a decent wedge of cheese with bread to it, and a quart of ale was also set before us.

It would have created an appetite in a satiated alderman, had he seen, as I did, the healthful gusto with which my companion disposed of huge and sundry uncut lumps of bread and cheese; his nether jaw paused not, except when he sucked down a stream of ale, after which it churned again as vigorously as that of a wild boar. I too paid no small compliment to the savoury viands, but was a small epicure beside my companion, who never ceased until both our rations were devoured, after which he finished with the last draught of ale, and soon after, the whole party set off towards Manchester.

The coach stopped at Hollinwood, whilst search was made for a man named Wilson, who, however was not captured. George and I were left in the coach alone, but guarded, and I took the opportunity to dispel any concern he might entertain on the subject of hanging; telling him, if there was any preference in that line, I should obtain the favour before him.

A stream of people followed the coach and dragoons through the streets of Manchester; and on approaching the Exchange, down Market-street, the 'Merchant Princes' crowded the steps, and welcomed the poor caption with loud huzzas!

Chapter 14

The Bridge of Tears — The Tribulatory — A Groupe — A Dungeon — An Old Acquaintance — New Comrades

READER! Hath it ever been thy fortune, or misfortune, to pass from Bridge-street, in Manchester, to New Bailey-street, in Salford? Hath business, or pleasure, or curiosity, or charity towards an afflicted prisoner, or mercy, or a yearning love for some of thine own in trouble, or interest, or duty, ever led thee that way? If so, thou hast passed a very plain bridge, with high parapets of a dull red stone, and spanning, with two arches, a rather broad stream, which here flows turpid, black, and deep, betwixt the said towns. That, reader, is 'THE BRIDGE OF TEARS.' Venice hath her 'BRIDGE OF SIGHS;' Manchester its 'BRIDGE OF TEARS;' and this is it. Not that tears have been more prevalent here than sighs, but that enow of the former have been here shed, to baptize it indelibly as, 'The Bridge of Tears.' Yes – sprinkled with scalding drops, wrung from human misery, the responses at that baptism were groans of afflicted souls in broken hearts; the high priestess, Justice, sometimes deaf as well as blind, performing the lavation, from her scales, where life was weighed by law, and heart's blood by hoarded gain; and the sponsors being Fear, and Hate, and Penitence, and blighted Hope!

Who, that recurs to recollections during forty years, and cannot enumerate tragedies enacted herabouts, and calamities witnessed which have called forth tears enow to have washed those channels with their stream? Do we not still hear, as it were, the appalling cry, when, during a great flood, a scaffold, on which nine human beings stood, broke down, and they were swept away, whilst hundreds of their fellow townsmen and relatives stretched forth their hands, and implored God and man to save them, but in vain? Who hath so soon forgotten the thirty-four fine fellows, who perished at the launch of a boat? and that still hears not the shout of horror which arose off this bridge at the dreadful sight? the heart broken moans of wives and children, fathers and mothers, brothers and sisters, as they came, distracted and weeping, to bestow an embrace which could not be returned?

And thou, too, poor, and beautiful, and innocent, Lavinia Robinson; what heart but responds to thy affliction! It was midnight, and there came a deep moan, that told of grief not to be comforted; of a wounded spirit which could not be borne. Soft, but hasty footsteps approached; and again, tones were heard almost too plaintive for human woe. Then there was a pause, and a plunge, and a choking, bubbling scream; and all was silent around that Bridge of Tears!

How many hundreds of human beings have crossed this bridge, conscious they were never to return? What strings of victims have been dragged over it? – some in the serenity of innocence, some in the consciousness of habitual guilt, and others in a bowed and contrite spirit; but each followed by weeping friends, who still loved, when all the world besides was hostile or indifferent to their fate! Aye, times have been, when life was paltered to petty law; and the gallows was rigged for a fraud on a bank, or a theft from a warehouse, or a potato scramble, when children were perishing at home for want of food.

And now a sad spectacle occurs to my recollection. It was a fine sunny forenoon, and the church bells were tolling funereally, and Bridge-street was so crowded, that you might have walked on human heads. All eyes were turned towards this Bridge of Tears, and what came there? Ah! men on horseback, with scarlet liveries, and white wands; and trumpeters richly invested, who sent forth a note of wail that might have won pity from a heart of stone. Next came halberdiers, and javelin men; and then a horseman, of lofty, but gentle bearing, who, as he rode, turned, and cast a kind look towards one who followed, sitting high in a chair of shame, placed in a cart. And who is he? that youth so heart-broken and hopeless, that draws tears from all eyes? at whose approach all heads are bared, all expressions are hushed, save sobs and prayers? For though he was but, 'a poor Irish lad,' they said 'he was very comely,' and 'it was a great pitty,' and 'hard that he could not be spared,' and then, 'might God support and comfort him!' High he sate, with his back to the horses, his whole person exposed, his feet and well-formed limbs being incased in white trowsers, stockings, and pumps, as if he were going to a bridal. His vest also was light coloured, and a short jacket displayed his square and elegant bust; his shirt was open at the collar, and his brown hair was parted gracefully on his forehead, and hung upon his shoulders. Despair, and grief beyond utterance, were stamped on his countenance, mingled with a resig-nation which said, 'Father, not my will, but thine be done. Receive my spirit.' He seemed faint at times, and his colour changed, and he tasted an orange, listening anon to the consolations of religion. Tears would gush down his cheeks, and as he stooped to wipe them with his handkerchief he was somewhat withheld by the cords which bound him to that seat of shame. A coffin, a ladder, and a rope, were in the cart below him; whilst, by its side walked a dogged-looking fellow, whose eyes were perhaps the only ones unmoistened that day. This was indeed, a passage of tears; and a day of sadness, and of contemplation on the mysteries of life, and death; with the consolement, at last, that, now, 'his troubles were ended,' and 'all tears were wiped from his eyes.'

Such was the spectacle of that 'poor Irish lad,' George Russel, who was hanged on Newton Heath, for – stealing a piece of fustian! or, as the old ballad had it.

> *To rob the croft,*
> *I did intend,*
> *Of Master Sharrock's,*
> *At Mill-gate end.*

Far be it from my wish, friend reader, to palliate wrong of any degree; but let us hope, and, if necessary entreat, that all waste of life, like this, may have now passed for ever from England. That all useless inflictions may be ameliorated; and that henceforth Justice may be enthroned with Equity and Mercy; for without these she is but a sanguinary executioner.

Now, reader, what do we next approach? A building of sombre appearance; with flanking towers, and shot-holes, and iron spikes jutting above high walls; and ponderous black fetters, hung above the barred window, and grated portal. That, reader, is the Golgotha, the living sepulchre of those victims I have described. It is commonly called 'The New Bailey,' but that being a term of obsolete meaning, I shall take the freedom to coin an expressive one, and call it 'The Tribulatory.'

The coach drove up to those cage-looking gates; the people, by hundreds, were trodden back by the dragoons; the gates flew open, as if saying, 'Come! Come!' to victims for a feast; and I and George entered, and were immediately conducted into an interior court-yard, where a number of gentlemen, and several military officers stood to receive us; and my fellow prisoner being taken away, I was left in the midst of a circle formed by these new observers. The late Rev. W. R. Hay, and the late Mr Norris, both magistrates, were there. The late Colonel Teasdale, of the First Dragoon Guards, then a major, I believe, scanned me from top to toe; and, perhaps, piqued at my cool reserve, a young officer of the same regiment, very laddish, and with limbs long enough for windmill arms, stepped a foot, and said, 'You look very fierce this morning,' to which I quietly replied, ''tis well *you* cannot.' A person, whom I took to be the Boroughreeve of Manchester, for the time, uttered a small impertinence, which I answered by a look; and Messrs Hay and Norris coming up, the former, after a civil recognition, told me that I was arrested on suspicion of high treason, and would be imme-diately sent to London for examination by the Secretary of State, under whose warrant I was a prisoner. I thanked the magistrates for their information, and said I was willing to be examined any-where; but not having a change of linen, could I not write to my wife for some? Mr Hay said I might, and they would take care it was sent; but I must leave the letter unsealed, as it must be ex-amined before it was forwarded, and when the things arrived there, they would give instructions to have them transmitted to London. With this arrangement I was satisfied, and thanked the magistrates for their kindness, I bowed to them, and was conducted into the governor's office, where I wrote home to the above effect, and also encouraged my wife and child to be of good cheer, for I was unconscious of any crime, and hoped soon to be with them again. A turnkey then led me up a winding stone stair, very clean, and sanded with white sand; at the top was a long arched gallery, also well limed and clean; and here, opening a strong nailed door, he motioned me to step inside, which I did, when, swinging the door to with a bang that sounded through the corridor, he turned the key, and I was left alone.

My cell was the first on the second floor, on the left side of the governor's office, and I thought they had shut me in there to have a quick eye and ear upon me. The dungeon was as compact as if cut from solid rock; and the floors and wall, like all that I had seen, were unexceptionable with regard to cleanliness. It was of an oblong form, probably about nine feet in length, by five in width; the door was at one end, and a window of a half circle in form, was at the other: it was unglazed, but by a careful forethought against any accidental tumbling out, by sleep walkers, or others, it was provided with a cross net work of massy iron bars. There were also a couple of wooden shutters inside, which the occupant might close when he had no wish for the free winds to come with their visits of mock condolement, or to catch a glimpse of the moon and her glorious children, to remind him of someone at home, and her clustering brood around her. On each side of the cell, close to the wall, stood a narrow bed on cross legs; and beneath the window was a stone ledge, which might serve for a seat, or a step to get up to the window shutters.

I had been in this place some time, and was pacing backwards and forwards to preserve warmth, when a noise in the yard excited my curiosity, and getting up to the iron bars of the window, I was astonished and concerned on beholding there my neighbour, the doctor, stalking, or rather staggering along the flags below, with all the dignity he could assume. With his hands resting upon his hips, his legs extended to a straddle, and an air of authority, he shouted to some persons who were laughing at him – 'Bring me that bundle I say; I am a reformer, and such will I live and die. My name is Doctor Healey, and I will never flinch, so help me God! I say, bring hither that bundle.' I could not contain any longer; flinging myself on one of the beds I gave way to a hearty burst of laughter, and soon afterwards heard them conduct his majesty into one of the lock-ups.

I now expected every moment being called out for my journey, and begun to wish it, as I had become very cold. Four o'clock arrived, and I heard the turnkeys locking the prisoners in their cells for the night; and, soon after, four young lads were put into the cell in which I was. They asked me what I was there for; and having satisfied them, they shewed not any reservations in letting me know they had each been convicted of felony. – They were good tempered lads, and appeared to be naturally well disposed; one of them gave up his share of bed to me, for which I divided amongst them my supper of bread and cheese; and after having sung a number of flash songs, and exchanged enquiries with their acquaintance in other cells, they betook themselves to repose, and I did the same as well as my situation and excited mind permitted.

Chapter 15

Companions for a Journey — Comfortable Equipments — How the Doctor had been overtaken and Captured — Stockport — Disley — Derby — Leicester

AT five o'clock on Sunday morning I heard the welcome rattling of keys, and soon after I was taken into the yard, where to my surprise, I found, besides Healey, John Lancashire, a weaver, from Middleton; Joseph Sellers, a cutler and grinder, from Manchester; Nathan Hulton, a bleacher, I think, from New Mills, in Derbyshire; John Roberts, a cooper, from Manchester; Robert Ridings, a weaver, from Failsworth; and Edward O'Connor, publican, of the Red Rose, at Chadderton. I had expected being conducted to London alone, and certainly was not prepared for a mix-up with these men, whom I knew were part of those taken at the plot meeting at Ardwick. Being here, however, and without the power to extricate myself, I resolved to make the best of my situation, and soon recalled my wonted cheerfulness. Healey was as grim as a sweep: he had been tumbling in a dirty smoky lock-up all night, and was now ready to perform 'The Moor of Venice.' I shook my head, and, in order to rouse him, said he was a fine fellow to bring himself into that place. He turned quickly, as I expected, and said, 'What did I think of myself? Was not I in as great a hobble as he was?' which retort turned the laugh against me as I intended, and put us all in good humour; and the doctor then went to a water tap and washed his face.

Having been arranged in two parties, of four and four, we were heavily ironed by the legs. Mr Nadin, who superintended the operation, ordered out body and neck collars, and armlets, with chains; but Mr George Williams, and Mr Stephen Dykes, King's messengers, into whose custody we were transferred, objected to the use of those irons, and they were put in the boot of the coach, which awaited us at the gates. Besides the messengers we were accompanied by Joseph Mills, and James Platt, both officers of the Manchester police. The messengers then formally took us into custody in the King's name, and gave us to understand, that if we conducted ourselves with propriety on the road, every indulgence would be extended to us. We assured them we would try to deserve their kindness; and, congratulating each other on our removal from a place to which, above all others, we had a dislike, we mounted the coach, and left The Tributatory at six o'clock, on the morning of Sunday, the 30th of March, 1817.

And now, whilst we traverse the dull streets, void of inhabitants, save watchmen retiring from their beats: drowsy topers staggering home, with bleared eyes, torn clothes, and empty pockets; and here and there, a sprightly maid on hands and knees, cleaning steps and door plates; – let us recur to the doctor, and give an account of his apprehension, as I had learned it from him whilst we were being ironed.

On leaving home, he took with him, besides his top-coat, a bundle of clothes, his tooth-drawing and bleeding instruments, and a Barclay's Dictionary, in quarto; intending to raise money on the latter, if no other means presented itself. The Middleton constables after seeing me safely lodged at the Assheton's Arms, got a hint about the doctor, and set out after him at full speed, but without cry. The little man had stepped into a shop in Simister-lane, in hopes of selling his dictionary, which, after some time lost in conversation, was declined; and he was returning down the lane, when a woman called him into a house to draw a tooth. He gladly accepted the invitation, performed the operation cleverly, pocketed his fee, and was coming away to join me, but was too late. The constables got a view of him, and, encumbered as he was, with top-coat, bundle, and dictionary, it would have been useless attempting to run, so he resigned himself to his fate, and was taken in great triumph to the Royal Oak public house, at top of Bowlee. There were about half a dozen constables and helpers; and now, having made good their capture, they sat down, determined to enjoy themselves after their morning's exertions. A plentiful ale posset was first despatched, after which there came hot and cold ale, and lastly, some potent glasses; many of which were paid for by farmers and others, who knowing the doctor, came to see him, and bid him good-bye. Of all these things the doctor partook to his wish, which was not a small one according to his size; one of the farmers also bought his dictionary, and the little man was, in a short time, as happy as a king, and for anything he seemed to know to the contrary, as potent. An hour or two were passed in jocular entertainment – the doctor spouted and sung for them as was his wont – and a verse of a fine old song, on a genial subject, made his captors almost as jovial as himself.

> '*I love no roast but a nut brown toast,*
>   *Or a crab laid on the fire;*
> *But little bread will do my stead –*
>   *Much bread I nought desire.*
> *No frost, no snow, no wind I trow,*
>   *Could hurt me if it would;*
> *I am so wrapp't, and thoroughly lapp't,*
>   *Of this jolly good ale, and old.*
> *Back and side, go bare, go bare;*
>   *Both foot and hand go cold;*
> *But belly, God send thee good ale enough,*
>   *Whether it be new or old.*'

From this last place they adjourned to the Black Boy in Old Millgate, where the party dined, and the doctor again went through his performances, to the great amusement of a room full of country and towns-people, who were glad to obtain admission by feeing the waiters. He was next taken to the Police Office; his presence at which place was said to have given the chief of the police great satisfaction; and shortly after he made his appearance at The Tribulatory, as before described.

And now let us proceed on our journey:

Our appearance at Stockport, where the horses were changed,

seemed to excite much interest and attention, and we learned from the observations of several of the town's-people, that we were known as 'The Manchester Rebels.' At Disley we breakfasted; and the doctor so much enjoyed it, that he said, if that was being a state prisoner, he wished he had been one five years before – an expression, which, coupled with the hearty compliment we all paid to the viands, probably impressed our conductors with the belief that we had been most cruelly famished ere we became prisoners. At Derby, we had just got seated comfortably at dinner, when our Jehu came in, whip in hand, saying, as usual, 'Coach, gentlemen; coach, coach.' Mr Williams told him to go back, and when we were ready we would let him know; he seemed not to comprehend this, and shewed an air, until he was bid, peremptorily, to walk out; the coach he was informed was ours, and must wait for us and not we for it. The vehicle had been especially hired for the journey.

We had by this time so won the good opinion of the King's messengers, that they did me the honour to say privately, the irons should be taken off, and we should travel the remainder of the journey as common passengers, if I would give my word for the sure conveyance of the party. I said I could not do that: three of the men only were personally known to me; a fourth I knew only by name, and the others I had never seen before that morning. Besides, their conduct towards us had been so kind, that I should be extremely sorry if they incurred any blame, by endeavouring to render us comfortable: we could do as we were, the conveyance which carried us carried our chains also. On emerging from the court-yard into the street, we found that a considerable crowd had collected, many being persons of respectable appearance. They gazed with a strong curiosity; several lent us a hand to mount; the coach dashed forward, and as we waved a farewell we received their cheers in return.

Nothing requiring notice occurred until we arrived at Leicester, where we stopped at the head inn. The landlord supposing probably that we were transported felons, shewed us into a tap-room; ejecting a number of coach cads, stable helpers and others, to make way for us. He refused to find a better room, and was impertinent and rude towards the King's messengers, until they exhibited their badges of office, informed him who and what they were, and demanded, at his peril for refusing, the best accomodation the house afforded. The master then became a most obsequious servant, shewed us into a large and elegantly furnished room; and in a very short time set before us a good warm supper. The windows here looked into the street, and they were presently darkened by curious gazers, who climbed up the shutters to get a peep at us, and hung to one another like bees swarming about a hive. Before we left this house we were each presented with a night-cap; and, on remounting the coach, several gentlemen, whom we understood to be magistrates, handed us a glass of wine each, with which we drank their good healths, and drove off.

Chapter 16

A Night Journey: its Objects and Reminiscences — Music and Poetry — Redbury — Chatterton: His 'Elinoure and Juga,' — London — Bow Street

THE night was gleamy and star-light; and as the coach dashed forward we soon entered upon what seemed a pretty rural country. Now we passed a large substantial-looking farm house, with its homestead; now a loving couple were overtaken walking arm in arm by some deep and bowered lane; next the mirth of home-wending youths would be heard; or mayhap the strains of a devout hymn from some chapel comers. Anon, a white cottage would lend us a blink from its cheerful hearth. Ah! what a paradise seems the lowliest shed, when viewed from the vista of a prison-door – how enviable appear the humblest mortals that walk abroad of their own free-will – and what a dove-nest is that, where a fair hand is seen closing the white chamber curtains for the night! Yes, it is at such moments, and under impressions produced by such objects, that we can best appreciate the blessing of the poorest hearth – of the humblest home; in which, as I have before intimated, if there be contentment, happiness will surely abide. Wise indeed is he, and wealthy beyond all riches, who enjoys with a thankful heart, the blessings, few though they be, which he finds bestowed on his humble estate; remembering gratefully, that 'better is a dinner of herbs, with love, than a stalled ox, and hatred therewith.' But we seldom find out these things until it be too late: we count not our jewels perhaps, until the dearest are lost.

Our party of four was now inside the coach, and we began to sing. Ridings, who understood music, gave one or two pieces with a pathos and solemnity which I never heard expressed before.

Glory to thee, my God, this night,

brought the singing parties of our own homes to our recollection; and we all participated in the emotions of our amiable and talented musician. O'Connor sometimes laughed, sometimes cried like a child; at last he broke out into that mournful lament,

> *'Where is my cabin-door fast by the wild wood?*
> *Sisters and sire, did ye weep for its fall?*
> *Where is the mother, that look'd on my childhood?*
> *And where is my bosom-friend, dearer than all?*
> *Oh! my sad soul, long abandon'd by pleasure,*
> *Why didst thou dote on a fast-fading treasure?*
> *Tears, like the rain-drop may fall without measure,*
> *But, rapture and beauty, they cannot recall.'*

To which, we all responded as chorus:

> *'Where is my cabin-door, fast by the wild wood?'*

Morning at length broke, and as we approached the dark woods and green meadows of Woburn, I gave my

SERENADE

> *The grey dawn of morning is spreading on high;*
> *And Venus is glowing so bright in the sky;*
> *The cattle are lowing, the tender lambs bleat;*
> *Arise, dearest Mary, before it be late.*
>
> *The sweet-scented blossom is cover'd with dew;*
> *The flowers of the field are perfumed anew;*
> *The blithe birds are singing on ev'ry green tree;*
> *Arise, dearest Mary, and come unto me.*
>
> *Thy breath is more sweet than the breeze of the morn;*
> *The lily's pure white doth thy bosom adorn;*
> *Thy look is as bright as the beaming of day;*
> *Oh! come dearest maid, to thy true love away.*

79

Lancashire also sung a sweet and simple melody, to words somewhat like the following.

> '*I wonder why my love is cold,*
>   *Whilst I so kind would be?*
> *I would give hoards of countless gold,*
>   *To win thine heart from thee.*
> *To win thy love, my beauteous maid,*
>   *And find it ever true:*
> *One thousand jewels, too, were thine,*
>   *That flash like sun-bright dew.*'

We breakfasted at Redburn, a small village, which takes its name from a clear, sedgy stream, immortalized by the unfortunate Chatterton; and said, with much probability of truth, to have been reddened with blood at the great battle of St Albans.

> *Onne Ruddeborne bank, twa pynynge maydens sate,*
> *Their tears fast dryppeynge to the waterr cleere,*
> *Ech one bementyng for her absent mate,*
> *Who atte St Albonns shook the morthrynge speare,*
> *The nottebrown Ellynor to Juga fayre.*

> '*Champyons whose bloud wylle wythe thie waterrs flowe,*
> *And Rudborne streeme, be Rudborne streeme indeede.*'

At this place we breakfasted, washed, and made ourselves as decent as we could, preparatory to our entrance into London. O'Connor's legs were swelled, and the chains gave him much pain. A few miles short of London, the coach stopped at a road-side public-house, where, whilst taking a little porter, my companions had an opportunity for conferring, without the immediate presence of our conductors. I then found they were afraid of each other, and that they expected nothing less than a trial, and a conviction on the evidence of some one or two of the party. I endeavoured to unite them; and persuaded them to say as little as possible when examined by the secretary of state; and at length they agreed to say, that the meetings they had attended were to raise subscriptions for the families of prisoners, and of those who had left the country in consequence of the suspension act. This they were to admit and abide by; and each pledged himself to be faithful to the agreement, and then we all went on again with confidence and satisfaction.

We arrived in London about twelve o'clock, and were immediately conveyed to Bow-street, which was filled with people before we could be got off the coach. We were placed in a decent room, our irons were immediately removed, and most of us wrote home to our families. A gentleman named Capper was introduced, and I thought he seemed to scrutinize us very much. Sir Nathaniel Conant, an elderly and respectable-looking gentleman, also came in, and informed us that Lord Sidmouth could not see us that day, and that we should be well provided for at a house in the neighbourhood. Soon afterwards we were conducted in couples to a room prepared at the Brown Bear public house, opposite; where, after supper, the doctor amused ourselves and keepers (who were eight or ten police officers) with several recitations in his most florid style. Messrs Williams and Dykes came and brought with them a friend, and they each seemed much entertained. Mr Perry, one of the chief officers at Bow-street, afterwards entered, and apologized for having to submit us to what might be a small inconvenience. It was customary, he said, to secure prisoners during the night by a chain, and he hoped we should take it as a mere matter of form; we expressed our readiness to submit to whatever restraint might be deemed necessary. Small chains being produced, myself, Lancashire, and Healey, were fastened together, and the other five were in like manner secured, after which we continued our amusements during an hour or two, and then went to rest on beds in the same room, still secured by chains to the bed posts, and to each other.

On the following morning our kind conductors, the messengers, again came to see us, and furnished some of the party with clean linen; other articles of dress were not withheld to such as wanted them most. John Lancashire and the doctor were completely changed in appearance, and came forth dapper, smart young fellows. To all, except myself and O'Connor, something was furnished: we were probably excepted, not because our apparel was better than that of the others, but because it was in a more careful condition, and we had also put on clean linen before we left home. The kindness of Messrs Williams and Dykes, made, I am sure, a strongly grateful impression on the minds of the whole of their prisoners; and I may also add, that the demeanour of the Bow-street officers, was, without exception, such as might be expected from men who knew their duty, and had the full power to perform it. It presented a striking contrast to the conduct which was at that time generally practised by men of the same station at Manchester.

Chapter 17

ABOUT four o'clock, P.M. we were conveyed in four coaches to the secretary of state's office at Whitehall. On our arrival we were divided into two parties of four, and four; and each party was placed in a separate room. A gentleman now appeared, who asked severally, our names and occupations, which he wrote in a book, and then retired. In a short time another person came and called my name, and I rose and followed him along a darkish passage. I must confess that this part of the proceedings gave rise to some feelings of incertitude and curiosity, and brought to my recollection some matters which I had read when a boy, about the inquisition in Spain. My conductor knocked at a door, and was told to go in, which he did; and delivered me to an elderly gentleman, whom I recognized as Sir Nathaniel Conant. He asked my christian and surname, which were given: he then advanced to another door, and desiring me to follow him, he opened it, and bowing to a number of gentlemen seated at a long table covered with green cloth, he repeated my name, and took his place near my left hand. The room was a large one, and grandly furnished, according to my notions of such matters. Two large windows with green blinds, and rich curtains, opened upon a richer curtain of nature, some trees, which were in beautiful leaf. The chimney-piece was of carved marble, and on the table were many books; and several persons sat there assiduously writing, whilst others fixed attentive looks upon me. I was motioned to advance to the bottom of the table, and did so: and the gentleman who sat at the head of the table, said I was brought there by virtue of a warrant issued by him, in consequence of my being suspected of High Treason – that I should not be examined at that time, but must be committed to close confinement until that day sen'night, when I should again be brought up for examination. Meantime, if I had anything to say on my own behalf, or any request to make, I was at liberty to do so; but I must observe, they did not require me to say anything.

The person who addressed me, was a tall, square, and bony figure, upwards of fifty years of age, I should suppose; and with thin, and rather grey hair: his forehead was broad and prominent, and from their cavernous orbits looked mild and intelligent eyes. His manner was affable, and much more encouraging to freedom of speech than I had expected. On his left sat a gentleman whom I never made out; and next him again was Sir Samuel Shepherd, the attorney general, I think, for the time; who frequently made use of an ear trumpet. On Lord Sidmouth's right, for such was the gentleman who had been speaking to me, sat a good-looking person in a plum-coloured coat, with a gold ring on the small finger of his left hand, on which he sometimes leaned his head as he eyed me over: This was Lord Castlereagh.

'My Lord,' I said, addressing the president; 'having been brought from home without a change of linen, I wish to be informed how I shall be provided for in that respect until I can be supplied from home.' The council conferred a short time, and Lord Sidmouth said I should be supplied with whatever was necessary. I next asked, should I be allowed freely to correspond with my wife and child, inform them of my situation, and to receive their letters, provided such letters did not contain political information?

'You will be allowed to communicate with your family,' said his lordship; 'but I trust you will see the necessity of confining yourself to matters of a domestic nature. You will always write in the presence of a person who will examine your letters; you will therefore do well to be guarded in your correspondence, as nothing of an improper tendency will be suffered to pass. I speak this for your own good.'

'Could I be permitted to have pen, ink, and paper, in prison?' I asked; 'and could I be allowed to keep a small day-book, or journal, for my amusement?'

'It is an indulgence,' was the reply, 'which has never been granted to any state prisoner; and as I do not see any reason for departing from the established rule, I should feel it my painful duty to refuse it.'

I said I had heard that the suspension act contained a clause securing to state prisoners the right of sending petitions to parliament; and I wished to be informed if there were such a clause?

His lordship said the suspension act did not contain any such clause, but the power to petition would be allowed by His Majesty's ministers, and I should have that liberty whenever I thought proper to use it. I bowed, and retired.

The other prisoners were then severally called in, and informed of the cause of their arrest, in the same terms that I had been; and that they would be again examined on that day sen'night. All of them afterwards declared they had not made any statement or disclosure of any description; but that, according to the agreement mentioned, they had remained silent as to the purpose of their meetings. One characteristic incident was however said to have occurred before the privy council. On the doctor being asked how he spelled his surname? he answered in broad Lancashire; 'haitch, hay, haa, l, hay, y:' (H, e, a, l, e, y,) but the pronunciation of the e, and a, being different in London, there was some boggling about reducing the name to writing, and a pen and paper were handed to him. The doctor knew that his *forte* lay not in feats of penmanship any more than in spelling; and to obviate any small embarrassment on that account, he pulled out an old pocket book, and took from it one of his prescription labels, on which the figures of a pestle and mortar were imposed from a rudely engraved plate; and these words, 'JOSEPH HEALEY, SURGEON, MIDDLETON. PLASE TAKE —— TABLE SPOONFULS OF THIS MIXTURE EACH —— HOURS.' This he handed to Lord Sidmouth, who, as may be supposed received it graciously, looked it carefully over, smiled, and read it again; and passed it round the council table. Presently they were all tittering, and the doctor stood quite delighted at finding them such a set of merry gentlemen. The fact was, the first blank had been originally filled with a figure of two: 'Plase take 2 Table Spoonfuls,' &c.; but some mischievous wag had inserted two cyphers after the figure, and made it read '200 Table Spoonfuls of this mixture each 2 hours.' However it was, the doctor certainly imbibed a favourable opinion of the council; the circumstance was supposed to have transpired from his own lips; and I certainly had seen such a card in his possession before he went to London, but I never saw it afterwards.

In the same vehicles which brought us to the Home-Office, we were next taken to the prison at Coldbathfields, and placed in the inner lodge until a ward could be got ready for our occupation. O'Connor, who was unwell, and whose legs were swollen and painful from the gout and his chains, was taken from us and put into a sick ward; as was also Robert Ridings, who was likewise in delicate health: and who being already incipiently consumptive, died soon after his return, from colds as he thought, taken during his journey homewards.

Whilst we were in the lodge, Evans the younger, one of the London Reformers – who as well as his father was confined in this prison under the suspension act – came to the gate to speak with a friend. Samuel Drummond also, who has been mentioned as being apprehended at the Blanket Meeting, was walking in a court yard, seemingly in good health and spirits.

When our place was ready, a turnkey conducted the six of us who remained together, through a number of winding passages to a flagged yard, into which opened a good room, or cell, about ten yards in length, and three in width. On each side of the room were three beds, placed in what might be termed wooden troughs; at the head of the room a good fire was burning; and we found a stock of coal and wood to recruit it at our pleasure. There were also a number of chairs, a table, candles, and other requisites; so that, had it not been for the grating at the window above the door, and the arched roof, bound by strong bars of iron, we might have fancied ourselves to be in a comfortable barrack. After surveying the place thoroughly, and striking the walls to ascertain if they were hollow, we stirred up the fire, drew our seats to the hearth, and spent the evening in conversing about our families and friends, until the hour of rest; when we concluded by singing 'The Union Hymn,' which I led for that purpose.

THE UNION HYMN

Ye Bards of Britain, strike the lyre,
  And sing the Happy Union;
In strains of patriotic fire,
  Oh! sing the happy union;
Not distant is the welcome day,
When woe, and want, and tyranny,
Shall from our Isle be swept away:
The grand epoch of liberty
  Awaits a faithful union.

Oh! worthy is the glorious cause,
  Ye patriots of the union;

85

Our fathers' rights, our fathers' laws,
  Await a faithful union.
A crouching dastard, sure is he,
Who would not strive for liberty;
And die, to make Old England free
From all her load of tyranny;
  Up ! brave men of the union.

Our little ones shall learn to bless
  Their fathers of the union.
And every mother shall caress,
  Her hero of the union.
Our plains with plenty shall be crown'd;
The sword shall till the fruitful ground;
The spear shall prune our trees around;
And joy shall everywhere abound,
  To bless a nation's union.

Then Britain's Prince shall truly reign;
  His subjects will defend him;
And, free'd from loath'd corruption's train,
  Bright honour shall attend him.
Whilst foreign despots evermore,
Shall venerate Old Albion's shore;
And war, with all its crime and gore,
Forgotten, and for ever o'er;
  Shall crown a nation's union.

And now, whilst my fellow-prisoners are sleeping – some probably agonized by visions of the scaffold and block; others again winging their souls homeward in sweet dreams – let us, my reader, discuss the spirit of the foregone Hymn. If thou sayest it is inconsistent with the advice to contentment, which I have already given, I reply, that a spirit of humble satisfaction with the good things a man hath – a full appreciation of the blessings he enjoys – is not by any means incompatible with fair means, and honourable wishes for the obtainment of other good things which he hath not. That there is a time and a means for all rightfully obtainable things; and that the industrious and patient man will sooner arrive at his ends by a beaten and legalized path though he advances slowly, than will he, who breaking down all barriers, is himself broken down, as he must be, unless the nation become his pioneer. – That the industrious and poor man, best serves his country by doing his duty to his family at home. – That he best amends his country, by giving it good children; and if he have not any, by setting a good example himself. – That he best governs, by obeying the laws; and by ruling in love and mercy his own little kingdom at home. – That his best reform, is that which corrects irregularities on his own hearth. – That his best meetings, are those with his own family, by his own fireside. – That his best resolutions, are those which he carries into effect for his own amendment, and that of his household – That his best speeches are those which promote 'Peace on earth, and good-will towards mankind.' – That his best petitions are those of a contrite heart, addressed to THE KING OF HEAVEN, by whom 'they will not be despised;' and those to the governors of the earth, for the peaceable obtainment of ameliorations for his brother man. – And, that his best means for such obtainment, is the cultivation of good feelings in the hearts, and of good sense in the heads of those around him. – That his best riches is contentment. – That his best love is that which comforts his family. – That his best instruction is that which humanizes and ennobles their hearts. – And, that his best religion is that which leads him to 'Do justice, to love mercy, and to walk humbly with his God.' – Would he triumph? let him learn to endure. – Would he be a hero? let him subdue himself. – Would he govern? let him first obey.

Should my reader, as I may almost expect, especially if he be a young and sanguine politician, feel as if I were presuming too much, let me remind him that at the time I am writing of I was in my thirtieth year; at my present writing, in my fifty-third, (well and hearty and free of wind and limb, thank God) he may then perhaps allow that a close and somewhat severe experience of twenty-five years, (say from 1815) entitles a man to have an opinion of his own, and to express it – if not, he has lived to very little purpose, either for himself, or his fellow-beings. May I not then say in the language of the Royal Bard of Israel – 'Wisdom is the principal thing, there-fore get wisdom, and with all thy getting, get understanding. Exalt her, and she shall promote thee; she shall bring thee to honour when thou dost embrace her. She shall give to thine head an ornament of grace; a crown of glory shall she deliver to thee.'

Chapter 18

ON the morning following, we were aroused from sleep by a loud report of fire-arms; and soon afterwards the door of our room was opened, and a turnkey saluted us with a 'good morning,' and a 'hope that we had slept well': we thanked him, assured him we had, and he left us. We now rose, and put the place in order; washed ourselves, and took a survey of our department and its premises. The door opened into a flagged yard, about twelve yards in length, by nine in width, and to which we descended by a couple of steps. On the right, and the front of the door, the yard was bounded by high and strong palisades; beyond which was a large garden, bounded again by a lofty wall, above which we could see upper windows of buildings. On our left we were separated from another yard by a wall about nine feet high; abutting upon it were a sewer, a water tap, and other conveniences. A door was fixed in one corner of the wall, and near it was a second door, which led into the passages of the prison; whilst above our heads, and along our front, appeared the windows, strongly barred, of numerous cells, and the thorough-fares communicating with them. Such was our position in this place; on viewing which as a prison, we saw nothing to complain about.

At breakfast time the turnkey again made his appearance, with another man, who took from a basket six loaves of bread, of nearly a pound each; a pipkin containing two pounds of butter; a jar, with two pounds of sugar; a canister, with one pound of tea; six cups and basins, salt, plates, dishes, half a dozen knives and forks, a kettle, a pan, and other articles to complete a kitchen service – to which were added, a wash-basin, soap, and clean towel – so that we began to look a little homely; and soon having the kettle boiling we sat down to a comfortable cup of tea, wishing that those at home, and all others who deserved it, might have as good a breakfast as ourselves. At noon we dined on a quarter of pork, with potatoes and other vegetables; to dilute which each man was allowed a pot of porter, and pipes and tobacco were added. Our supper was tea and cold meat; and thus, so far as diet was concerned, we lived more like gentlemen than prisoners. I recollect, however, one of the party shaking his head at what appeared to us profusion, and observing, that he did not think any better of his own case for all that; for, said he, it's always the way here, when they intend to hang 'em, they let 'em have whatever they choose to eat or drink – only they *will* hang 'em at last. This remark made an impression on some of my companions; and most of them seemed to be of opinion that all this kindness would prove only precursory to some terrible act of severity. And the idea was strengthened, when, a few days after, on some of us requesting to have books to read, a bible, a prayer book, some tracts, and 'sermons for persons under sentence of death,' were put into our hands.

But long before this, one of our men had made a most interesting discovery. He came in with surprize and joy in his countenance, and said, 'there were women in the next yard.' Another followed saying, there were women indeed! The question was asked, what sort ? and we all ran to ascertain that point according to our several tastes. The oldest man amongst us was speaking to one of them through the key-hole; and he had already commenced a negociation for a kind of 'friendly compact,' which was soon agreed upon, and ratified by both parties, by mutual congratulations, and good wishes expressed through the key-hole. They were, if I recollect aright, just the same number of women as we were of men – six; and they readily undertook to assist us in every possible way within their power. They were to wash and darn whatever small articles we had that required it, and to do all our needlework generally; besides which, they were to obtain and transmit to us, all the information they could respecting ourselves, and to be faithful and secret in their communications. They vowed, indeed, to be true friends! and we never had cause to doubt their word. On our part, we promised to keep faithfully their secret information, and to render them whatever services lay in our power; and we also kept our compact. The signal when either party was wanted was to throw a piece of blue slate (of which several pieces lay in the yard) over the wall, when the other party was to repair to the key-hole and receive the communication. Poor things! tears came into their eyes when we spoke to them in words of confidence and kindness; and they wept bitterly when we touched, as we were almost compelled to do, a more tender chord – when we asked about their former condition in life, and enquired respecting their fathers, and mothers, their husbands, or their children. Some of our men almost promised to love them, (a word of strange power over the heart of woman,) and we could see a faint, hopeless smile, when the head was turned aside, as if to look back on some recollections of former days.

One alone was of matronly age; the others varied, I should think from twenty to thirty. Two had infants at the breast, and all of them were widows or married women. Two had lost their husbands, who were officers, in the service of their country; and the husband of a third, also in a military capacity, was absent on a foreign station. One or two had been seduced and deserted; and more than that number had disgusted their connections, by becoming intemperate, after which they descended to poverty, crime, and disgrace. All had been condemned to death, or to long terms of transportation; and they severally acknowledged that they narrowly escaped the fulfilment of their sentence, only by urgent, and powerful interest of most respectable connections. None of them were less than good-looking; some were more than that; and two were remarkably fine women, for we could see their form and stature as they paced the yard at a distance from the door. One of the young ones was a little dimpled cherry-looking thing; but the melancholy of her eye was strangely at variance with the rosy health of her cheek. One of them would tell of her poor old father in the country – of his ancient mansion, and the servants he had around him; another thanked God, that her mother had, by death, escaped the affliction of seeing her disgrace; and another would talk of what her husband, (her Henry, I think she called him,) would do when he came home – how he would after all, forgive her, 'knowing it was distress,' and get her liberated, and how they would be happy again, and she virtuous and ever affectionate. Poor things! with such bright hopes and illusions they would amuse themselves; and they seemed consoled when we talked with them of such matters, and thereby helped them to relief by floods of tears.

We too had our illusions – our thoughts of home, and our hopes, as well as our fears. But our case at present wore a worse aspect than theirs; their periods of imprisonment were definite, and some of them soon to expire, whilst ours were all uncertainty. They knew the worst; we knew nothing, save that we were in the power of those we had made our enemies. Besides, they shook their heads, and sighed when we talked about going home soon, and leaving them. They had heard us termed, 'the Lancashire rebels;' and that we were to be tried for High Treason, and the case was expected to go hard against us.

I may, perhaps I ought to say, that their demeanour justified us in crediting their account of themselves. They were very friendly, but nothing more; they never so far as I could learn, gave encouragement to improper freedoms of speech; nor do I believe that any of our men greatly offended in that respect.

After our first dinner, we had a decent surplus of meat and vegetables left. One asked, 'what shall be done with these?' another said, 'it would never do to send them back; if we did, we should have so much less the day following.' 'Cut it up for the women,' said a third, and it was done; and we made them up as nice a little dinner as we could. The meat, excellent pork, was reduced to slices, and put on a flat dish; the vegetables and bread, and all our other little trifles, were similarly disposed on another dish; the slate, the ever welcome messenger, was then thrown over the wall, and they were presently at the door. 'Will you do us another favour?' asked our spokesman. 'With pleasure,' was the reply. 'Look down then, and accept a trifle from our table.' A space below the table admitted this; there was a scream of delight, and a 'hush, hush;' and the dishes were hurried away, emptied, washed, and returned in like manner, with ten thousand thanks for our remembrance of them. How indeed could we have forgotten them – the poor, lost, cut-off, and world-despised beings? After tea we did the same; we gave them plentifully of our stock – our tea, our sugar, and our butter – bread they had; they told us they secreted our gifts until they were locked up in their house, and the turnkeys had retired for the night, when they set on a pan, brought their stores from their hiding place, and had a feast that might have comforted a Queen.

The day following we did the same, (and continued it.) We cut them up the remainder of a leg of mutton, weighing thirteen pounds and a half – with carrots, parsnips, and other condiments. They informed us, that there was astonishment in the governor's kitchen, when the platters with the clean bones only were returned. It was no wonder, the domestics said, 'that the people of Lancashire rebelled, if they were all starved, as they were sure they must have been, from the enormous quantities of meat we devoured.'

Chapter 19

The Author's Advice — Adopted and Acted upon — Second Examination before the Privy Council — Visitation of the Magistrates' Committee

AFTER we had finished our first dinner, and had got seated with our pipes, and allowance of porter, we set about making regulations amongst ourselves; the principal of which was, that each was to become rooms-man for the day, in turn, and, as such, servant to the others. The reader will recollect that our party now consisted of James Sellers, Joseph Healey, John Lancashire, Nathan Hulton, John Roberts, and myself. I now addressed them, saying I had a matter of some consequence to mention, and hoped they would consider it seriously, and act in their best discretion. I said they well knew that, though I had been arrested and confined with them, (providentially, it almost appeared to me) I had not, at any time, been connected with their secret meetings; and, that both Lancashire and Healey could testify, that I had always condemned such meetings – my maxim being, 'Hold fast by the law.' That consequently, I considered myself in small jeopardy compared with themselves, unless suborned and false witnesses were brought against me; which however, the government could doubtless procure if it chose. I therefore viewed myself as standing on much better ground than I did them; they having been apprehended in the act of carrying on a secret meeting for unlawful purposes. That such difference however, now I was with them, should not prevent me from doing my best to render them a service, and with that view, giving them my best advice. They should remark, I said, that, either through the interposition of Providence, or the fatuity of the government, they were, (O'Connor and Ridings excepted, neither of whom were deeply versed in their private transactions) all together in one place. That hitherto, as I understood from their conversations, none of them had been questioned by the Privy Council; and that consequently, no admissions or declarations had been made to that body. They all solemnly declared, nothing had escaped from their lips. Then, I continued, 'the piecrust is yet whole, and you may keep it so.' I proposed that every day after dinner they should appoint a chairman, who should put such questions to them as he considered the Privy Council were likely to do at their next examination, supposing some one of their body to have given secret information. That their replies should be deliberated upon, and determined accordingly; and those replies should be committed to memory, and, in substance, strictly adhered to at their next interview with the ministers. That they would consequently all give the same account; all be of one party, and of one mind; and that if government brought them to trial, it would have to unmask its spies and informers, instead of making them fall by their mutual contradictions, mistrusts, and jealousies, which as it seemed to me, the government would prefer doing.

They all declared it was the best of advice; and it was adopted with acclamation. I would have retired, but they would not suffer me, and insisted that I should become their questioner. I complied at length – put them through a catechising according to my poor ability – and established a set of replies, such as I thought would either answer or ward off any question they were likely to encounter. The basis of the old tale was adopted – Their meetings were to devise relief to persons who had fled from the suspension act, and to their families in their absence. This was to be the skeleton; we stuffed and padded it in our own way, and threw over it a cloak of plausibility, which we thought the devil himself could not penetrate. And so we continued day by day, catechising and drilling, until my fellows would, I believe, have stood before old Rhadamanthus without quail or fear.

We now began to be much better satisfied with ourselves and each other; those thoughtful and suspicious looks which had hitherto indicated fear and mistrust were no longer observable. Our time passed more agreeably; and, striving to amuse each other, we had no lack of songs, hymns, and love and family tales, with scraps of plots and insurrections, and droll blunders, which sometimes caused roars of laughter.

About this time we discovered we had some little attendants upon us which we were extremely desirous to get rid of; how, or where we picked them up, we could not tell; but every man was infested, and we made it known to our attendant, who informed the governor, Mr Atkins. A more thorough or speedy removal could not have been effected anywhere; that worthy and humane gentleman immediately caused all our bedding to be taken out, our room to be cleansed, new and clean bedding to be supplied, all our linen to be changed, and our other clothes to be carefully examined; and we felt no more of that nuisance.

On the ninth of April we were conveyed in coaches, as before, to the Home Office, at Whitehall. But let me apprize the reader, that, not having the means for writing, and not being able to commit every particular to memory, I cannot pretend to furnish a verbatim report of my examinations, and shall only give the substance of what passed on those occasions.

I was introduced to the Council with the previous formalities, and by the same person, Sir Nathaniel Conant. Lord Sidmouth repeated what he had said on my first examination, viz.: that I was arrested on suspicion of High Treason, and that they were willing to hear what I had to say in reply. I said I was not conscious of having deserved suspicion of treasonable practices, as, instead of being a promoter of violence and disturbance, I had always been a friend to peace and order; and, with that purpose, had used my little influence to the utmost amongst my neighbours. That if his lordship was as well acquainted with the situation of the working people as I was, and of the conduct which I had pursued amongst them, he would see the justice, as well as the policy of restoring me to my family. I acknowledged I was a Parliamentary Reformer, and always should be so, until that measure was obtained – that no circumstance or situation whatever could induce me to disavow my opinions – nay, I considered it as the pride and glory of my life to have, in some degree, merited the name of a Reformer; but I never advocated its obtainment by violence. – That I had trusted, and endeavoured to inspire my neighbours with the like confidence, that when our grievances and sufferings were properly made known to Parliament, attention would be paid to them, – that we had petitioned, but were not listened to. That I could not tell how to account for this neglect, save by crediting the existence of corruption in the Honourable House; but still I would not recommend its removal by violent means. That I firmly believed Reform would ultimately take place; circumstances occurring in their own due time, which would induce His Majesty's Ministers and Parliament to take the measure into consideration. That I had always been an enemy to private meetings – had deprecated them as much as possible, believing that Reform did not require privacy; and, finally, that, in my opinion, nothing save reform could preserve the country from revolution. No questions were asked, and I was reconducted, as before.

When the other prisoners had been severally introduced, we were conveyed to our old quarters; and the day following James Sellers was taken from our party, and put, as we understood, into the deputy governor's house.

In the course of this week we were visited by the magistrates appointed to examine the prison. I was rooms-man for the day, and was stripped, with sleeves rolled up, and washing some pots which had been used at our mess when the gentlemen entered the room, preceded by Mr Beckett, the deputy governor of the prison. They bade us 'good morning,' and asked if we were comfortable. We answered in the affirmative; at which they expressed satisfaction. One of them, an elderly gentleman, (Mr Sketchly, I believe,) asked Mr Beckett, 'which is Bamford?' and Mr Beckett pointed me out.

The gentleman was pleased to compliment me, and said he understood I was a poet.

I thanked him for his favourable opinion, – but disclaimed being a poet; I was only a country rhymester, I said – just capable of throwing a few doggerel verses together.

He asked how I received my education, as he understood I was but a poor man?

I said I did not pretend to much education – my father did, however, send me to school, where I was taught to read; I first begun to write at a Sunday school, kept by the Methodists, and I afterwards went to other schools; but what little information I was possessed of had been chiefly acquired by my own reading and study.

He said he was sorry to see us in our present situation; it was a pity men should be so deluded.

I replied, that we did not consider ourselves to be deluded men; I, at any rate, did not suppose myself to be one. – I had not done anything to repent of: I had not said anything that I would not repeat again under the circumstances.

How was it possible, he asked, that we could be dissatisfied with the taxes – poor people paid no taxes; how could taxation operate on them?

I said, 'suppose a tax were laid upon land, or on the landlord – as his leases expired, the rents of his farms were advanced to meet the tax, and the farmer was obliged, in order to meet the advance, to lay an additional charge on the produce of the farm, The shopkeeper who purchased from the farmer then advanced to his customer, and the poor man being a customer as well as others, paid the advanced price for so much as he consumed; and that was the way in which taxation operated on the poor.'

To this there was no reply; and soon after our visitors took their departure.

Bad as our case was (and we supposed we should have a long imprisonment of some years at least,) there were others in this place, besides our women friends, whom we could pity. For two hours every forenoon, a low dark complexioned man, with somewhat of a military carriage, took his walk to and fro under the garden wall, at the greatest allowable distance from, but parallel with our yard. He was an object of interest to us, and we often bowed to him, which he always politely returned. He had been, we were informed, a long time in this prison, and likely to remain much longer, being entirely at the disposal of the Secretary of State. He had once or twice annoyed the Prince Regent, by obtaining access to his presence, and demanding payment of a large sum of money which he asserted the Prince owed him, he being 'The King of Denmark.' He had been imprisoned before for such annoyances; and soon after his liberation he went again, and attempted to ride into the palace of Carlton House, for the purpose of obtaining 'his money' from 'his cousin,' the Regent of England. He was said to be perfectly sane in all matters except these, viz.: that he was the King of Denmark, and that our King owed him a great sum of money. The elder Evans, one of the London prisoners, a wordy and intemperate man, was also allowed his stated walks in the garden, but he never ventured to exchange a word with us.

On Tuesday, the sixteenth of April, we were again taken to the Home Office. John Roberts was called in first, Hulton second, Healey third, and myself the fourth, when Lord Sidmouth thus addressed me:—

'Mr Bamford, the persons who have been examined to day are committed to prison, from whence they will not be liberated, except by a due course of law. From the information received respecting you, His Majesty's Ministers would not be justified in adopting the same course towards you; you will therefore be brought up for another examination, which will take place this day week.' I then retired.

The day following, Roberts, Hulton, and the doctor, were taken out of our ward and sent to different prisons. Roberts, with John Bagguley, before mentioned as an orator at the Blanket Meeting, were consigned to Gloucester Jail. Hulton and Sellers were sent to Exeter; whilst John Johnstone of Manchester, also before mentioned, Samuel Drummond, of the same place, and our friend the doctor, were conveyed to Dorchester.

The day after their departure, George Plant, of Blakeley, William Kent, of Chadderton, and James Leach, of Spotland, who were apprehended at the Plot Meeting at Ardwick, and had remained in the New Bailey since, arrived in London; and after passing in review before the Privy Council, as we had done, were brought to this general *depot* for all dangerous and suspected characters. Kent, who had a lame arm, was placed in the hospital; Leach was put in the outer yard; and Plant was locked up with Lancashire and myself. As soon as our mutual surprize had subsided, and some enquiries were answered, we made Plant acquainted with the plea which the other prisoners had acted upon; we fully explained every thing to him, and he readily undertook to tread most faithfully in our footsteps. We were now only uneasy least Kent and Leach, to whom we had no hopes of access or communication, should give a different account of the private meetings when brought up again, as they were to be. It would seem, however, as if there was a Providence on the side of these deluded men. The same afternoon, as I was walking in the yard, I heard a cough, and looking up to the window of one of the passages, which opened towards our premises, I saw Kent standing, and immediately made him acquainted with the account the others had given to the Privy Council – told him Plant was already initiated, and would act accordingly, and he must do the same, or all would come out against them; and he promised he would. He also said he could see Leach and speak to him, and would make him acquainted with the course he was to pursue. The day after, he appeared at the window again, and told us he had spoken to Leach, and all would be right at the next examination; and now we were perfectly satisfied.

I think it was the day after this, that Plant, Kent, and Leach, were formally examined at the Home Office; after which Kent and Lancashire were sent to Chelmsford Jail, and I and Plant were left in my old domicile.

Our poor neighbours over the wall had now made up their minds to resign us entirely; they thought the worst, the penal danger was

over, and that long imprisonment, as in their case, would be substituted for the sterner inflictions of the law. There were both
pleasure and regret at their communications; pleasure that our lives
were comparatively out of danger, and regret that they should
lose our company, as it were, and with it the few comforts we had
bestowed. I could not promise any good fortune for myself, for I was
entirely dark as to my future destination; but I tried to cheer them,
by saying, that however long I might remain, they should always
share my tea and coffee, and have a good slice or two of my dish.
The poor women expressed their gratitude in the warmest terms.

My present comrade was, I should suppose, about twenty-five
years of age; he was a weaver, and had left a wife, and one or two
young children, at Crab-lane-head, in Blakeley, near Manchester.
He was fully as tall as myself; thin, very pale, with black hair, black
eyes, thick lips, big white teeth, a kind of stiffness, and a stoop in
the shoulders. He was indeed, in person, rather an oddity; but I
believe, as simple and innocent intentioned a man as could be produced. He related some curious particulars of the conduct adopted
towards him by the Police of Manchester, during his detention at
the New Bailey.

He said that Joseph Platt, one of the police beadles, who had
formerly known him, and whose parents were then neighbours to
Plant, came to him one night in his cell, and after reminding him of
old acquaintance, and expressing much friendship towards him,
said he had obtained permission to make a proposal, and it would
be his fault if he did not take advantage of it for his own good. Two
of the persons already sent to London, he continued, had offered,
on condition that their lives were spared, to disclose the whole of
the Manchester plot, and to give details of the proceedings of the
conspirators at their several meetings. These discoveries, he said,
would place all the rest in jeopardy; and they might think well, if
they got off with transportation for life. He added, that, knowing
Plant, and having a great respect for him, and a kind feeling towards
his family, he had, as a great favour, obtained permission from the
magistrates to mention the thing to him; and to say, that if he,
(Plant) would come forward, and give a statement of all he knew
about the conspiracy, he should have the first chance of becoming
King's evidence, and of thereby saving his life, procuring his freedom at any rate, and very likely of getting something handsome in
the way of a provision afterwards.

George assured me, that his only reply to this, (which was re-peated on a second visit) was, that 'he knew nothing, and could not, therefore, tell any thing;' that such had been his constant answer; that he never in the least varied it; and that at length, his friend Platt gave him up, and resigned him, as he said, to the scaffold, or to perpetual chains abroad.

If such was his answer to Platt, (and I never had any reason for doubting it) he certainly gave the true one. He had never been at a plot-meeting before the one at Ardwick; and the proceedings at that had scarcely commenced when the police arrived, and took the whole party into custody.

Chapter 20

The Botanist — The Bird Catcher — and, The Lover — Their Agreement

AND now, reader, the natural current of my story leads us from this prison (where one's heart already pants to return) to the deep woods, sombre shades, and bare wilds of Lancashire; to speculations and ceremonials founded on superstitions of the rural population; and to beings and appearances, a thorough belief in which does even in the present day retain its place amongst the undeniable evidences narrated by the dwellers of the glens and moorlands of the county. At the time I am writing of, such opinions were still more prevalent than at present; when I was a child, a disbelief of them was looked on as an almost impious exception; they are now quickly departing from amongst us, and in another twenty years will probably be entirely ranked amongst the obsolete superstitions of a benighted age.

But, to be more explicit; know that my friend Plant was a firm believer in ghosts, witches, and hobgoblins; in the virtues of herbs under certain planetary influences; and in the occult mysteries of Culpepper and Sibley. He was entirely self-taught; had been a great reader, – knew something of arithmetic, – was a botanist, – and a dreary minded wanderer in lonely dells, on moors and heaths; searching after herbs of surpassing virtue, of mysterious growth and concealment, and of wonderful and unaccountable power.

How a man of his tastes and pursuits, became induced to resign them for the culture of unpoetic politics, it might perhaps be interesting to enquire. Possibly he was drawn into the vortex by the force of example amongst his numerous class. Possibly, being a knowledge seeker, he might wish to learn something of the new doctrine, – the great political 'Heal-all.' Possibly his little learning was flattered, and latent ambition urged him to seek distinction; or, assigning higher motives, he might really wish to render a service to his country. However it was, he proved unfortunate; his first experiment in the political line was also his last.

One night after we were locked up, having drawn near the fire and lighted our pipes, we entered as usual into conversation, which he soon led to his favourite subject, botany. We discussed the occult virtues of herbs, and the connection with the spiritual and planetary worlds, – in which he believed as firmly as in his own existence. I did not dispute with him, but was rather an enquirer and a listener; and as he narrated, in perfect assurance of their realities, the visionary experiments he had made – and their strange and fearful results, I enjoyed the illusions of the superstitions of my childhood which now recurred, as it were, like a tide after a long ebb, with double force. I felt interested – encouraged him to continue – and he finished by recounting an attempt in which he was once concerned, to take and carry off 'Saint John's Fearn seed.'

He said that in one of his, 'Yarbin Eawts,' as he termed his rambles after herbs, he was in Guestless, or more properly, Griselhurst Wood, in Birkle, when a storm induced him to seek shelter in a cottage which he had observed at no great distance from the wood side. He was made welcome, and pulled off his coat and hung it to dry before the fire, which the good woman improved by adding coal and root stocks to the blazing heap. She was a widow about middle age, and had an only child, a son, a decent looking youth, who sat mending her clogs beneath the window. He might be from eighteen to twenty years of age; very fair for a country lad, with light red, or 'goween-coloured,' hair; tall, and of a thoughtful way of speaking. The room was barely furnished but clean, and the articles were well arranged. There was a bread-flake covered with oat cakes; a bit of nice bacon; part of a sack of potatoes; and 'a drink mug,' reaming with ale; and he was given to understand that 'decent, honest foke' were sometimes accommodated there both with meat and drink; that, in short, it was a 'hush shop.' He accordingly ordered a jug of ale, and cut a rasher of bacon, which he was roasting on a fork, when the door opened, and a short, broad-set, and dark-visaged man entered, carrying two cages, with each a gorse-cock, a pot with some bird-lime and water, and a number of limed twigs.

'Hallo, Chirrup,' said the young man; 'I thowt if th' storm didno' send thee fro' th' hill side, summut wud be op.'

'Why, indeed, it's likely to be a weet afternoon; an' th' brids are o' away to th' covers; an' th' twigs are weet an' winno howd iv owt coom; an' th' wynt makes sitch a din, at no gorse-cock can be yerd ogen it; an' I've had quite enoof for to-day, for I've seen that at I shall never forget to th' last day o' my life.'

'Wot wor it, Chirrup?' said the young man, laying down the clog, and looking earnestly at the bird catcher, for such he was.

'Bangle, my lad, it wur th' bonnyist brid at ever flew o' wings.'

'Well then, it wur nother gorse-cock, ouzle, nor dunnock, at any rate; an' yo'd no coers to catch it wi. But wot wur it like; wot kullur wur it.'

'It wur as fair a gowden yallo as ever glizzent; wi' white wings o'th' untherside.'

'That wur indeed a strange brid,' said Bangle; 'but wot mickle wur it? and wot wor it like i' shap?'

'It wur as like an ouzle as owt as ever theaw seed i' thelyve, o' but th' kuller;' said Chirrup.

'An' weer did it come fro'? an' wot becoom on it?' enquired the earnest Bangle.

'I seed it fost üt top ov a stone wall; it wur plumin its wings i'th' sun-leet, an' it lookt like a thing o' livin gowd: it made my heart jump. An' then it coom nar th' cages, an' then nar th' twigs; an' I thowt if ever mon won heaven, I should get that brid; an' I lee beind th' rush hoyle, panting till I could yer my heart thump, – that bonny innocent brid, – I thowt it wur mine; an' thur coom a glor o' lett at made o' dazzle agen; an' thoose white wings flash'd, an' away it went i'th' glizzen, an' th' thunner-din, o'er th' moor.'

'An' weer wurto when theaw seed it?' enquired Bangle.

'I wurno far off Owd Birkle; an' just oppo' th' edge o'th' Wilder Moor.'

'Aye, there's bonny brids bin seen i' Owd Birkle afore,' said the youth, flushing red, and then pale as a sheet. 'But the bonnyist it seems hasno' bin taen yet.'

'Nowe, I wish it wur;' interrupted Chirrup; 'I'd giv o'th' cocks an' linnits at ever I cag'd, for yon beauty at I've seen an' lost to-day.'

'Happen not lost,' observed Plant, 'while there's life there's hope.'

'Thank yo' for that,' said the youth Bangle; 'while there's life, there's hope; aye, while there's life, there's hope.'

'Did I not olis tell the so,' said his mother, looking significantly at Plant and Chirrup. 'One on yo wants a brid, an' one a bride; but faint heart never won fair lady; an' lyen i' rush hoyles till th' bally warches 'll never catch yallo' wagtails.'

'It wur as much a wagtail as theaw'rt a dagtail,' said Chirrup, 'an' theaw'd be pottert iv ony body co'd the so.'

'Wagtail or not,' said the woman, 'it wur a brid o' some sense; for it chose to fly wi' th' thunner devils sooner nor tarry wi' thy daubing lime twigs. I howd it *wit* good ut ony rate. As for that gawmblin o' mine,' she continued, 'he met ha' had his coo-dove lung sin, iv he'd nobbut ha' follod th' advice o'Limping Billy at Ratliffe. His feyther, dyed an' gwon as he is, wudno ha' ston sighen' an' yammerin' as this dus; he coom a kworten i'th' owd way, lung dree miles fro' Affeside, an' iv th' dur wurno oppent when he coom, he'd ha' punst it oppen. He didno come glooring at th' chimney reech an' then maunder back again.'

The rain having set in dree, and several jugs of ale having been emptied, a free discourse ensued between Plant, Chirrup, and young Bangle, in which the woman occasionally took a part; and it was soon explained to Plant, for Chirrup seemed to have known some of the circumstances before, that the youth was love-smitten, and almost hopelessly so; the object of his passion being a young beauty residing in the house of her father, who held a small milk farm on the hill side, not far from Old Birkle. The lad was of an ardent temperament, but bashful, as the truest lovers often are. His modest approaches had not been noticed by the adored one; and, as she had danced with another youth at Bury fair, he imagined she was irrecoverably lost to him, and the persuasion had almost driven him melancholy. Doctors had been applied to, but he was no better; philters and charms had been tried to bring down the cold-hearted maid, but all in vain, –

He sought her at the dawn of day;
He sought her at the noonin';
He sought her when the evenin' gray
Had brought the hollow moon in.

He call'd her on the darkest night,
With wizard spells to bind her;
And when the stars arose in light,
He wandered forth to find her.

At length sorcerers and fortune-tellers were thought of, and Limping Billy, a noted seer, residing at Radcliffe Bridge, having lastly been consulted, said the lad had no chance of gaining power over the damsel, unless he could take Saint John's Fearn seed; and if he but secured three grains of that, he might bring to him whatever he wished, that walked, flew, or swam.

'Iv that's so,' said Chirrup, on hearing the last, 'I'd goo to th' seet o' devil-dom to win yon brid.'

'I'd good to th' smell on't to win mine,' said young Bangle.

'An' I'd go to th' leet on't,' said Plant, who had been listening with much interest to the conversation, and who had for years been wishful to engage companions for trial of that mysterious experiment. He then opened to them his lore in botany; telling them of wonderful herbs and sympathies and cures, and concluded by saying that he knew where the finest clump of fern in the country grew; and offered to conduct them to it at the proper time, viz: on the eve of Saint John the Baptist. It was agreed: and meantime Chirrup was to get particular instructions from Limping Billy for taking it; and so, night approaching, and the rain having abated, the three separated, and Plant and Chirrup went to their several homes.

Chapter 21

Boggart, or Feyrin-ho — Feyrin ho Kloof — Saint John's Fearn

ON the left hand, reader, as thou goest towards Manchester, ascending from Blackley, is a rather deep valley, green swarded, and embowered in plantations and older woods. A driving path which thou enterest by a white gate hung on whale-jaw posts,[1] leads down through a grove of young trees, by a modern and substantial farm house, with green shutters, sashed windows, and flowers peeping from the sills. A mantle of ivy climbs the wall, a garden is in front, and an orchard, redolent of bloom, and fruit in season, nods on the hill-top above. Here, at the time Plant was speaking of, stood a very ancient house, built partly of old fashioned bricks, and partly of a timber frame, filled with raddlings and daub, (wicker work, plastered with clay.) It was a lone and desolate-looking house indeed; misty and fearful, even at noon-day. It was known as 'Boggart-ho,' or 'Fyrin-ho;' and the gorge in which it is situated, was, and still is known, as 'Boggart,' or 'Fyrin-ho' Kloof,' 'the glen of the hall of spirits.' Such a place might we suppose, had Milton in contemplation when he wrote the passage of his inimitable poem.

> *Tells how the drudging goblin sweat,*
> *To earn his cream-bowl, duly set,*
> *When, in one night, ere glimpse of morn,*
> *His shadowy flail had thrash'd the corn*
> *Which ten day-labourers could not end;*
> *Then lies him down, the lubber fiend;*
> *And, stretch'd out, all the chimney's length,*
> *Basks at the fire, his hairy strength;*
> *And cropful, out of door he flings,*
> *Ere the first cock his matin sings.*

By the side of the house, and through the whole length of the valley, wends a sickly, tan-coloured rindle; which, issuing from the great White Moss, comes down, tinged with the colour of its parent swamp. Opposite the modern house, a forbidden road cuts through the plantation on the right, towards Moston-lane. Another path leads behind the house, up precipitous banks, and through close bowers, to Booth Hall; and a third, the main one, proceeds along the kloof, by the side of the stream, and under sun-screening woods, until it forks into two roads: one a cattle track, to 'The Bell,' in Moston; and the other a winding and precipitous foot-path, to a farm house at 'Wood-end;' where it gains the broad upland, and emerges into unshaded day.

[1] Those somewhat remarkable posts have been removed of late years, and stout pillars of stone occupy their places.

About half way up this kloof is an open cleared space of green and short sward: it is probably two hundred yards in length, by sixty in width; and passing along it from Blackley, a group of fine oaks appear on a slight eminence, a little to the left. This part of the grove, was, at the time we are concerned with, much more crowded with underwood than at present.[1] The bushes were then close and strong; fine sprouts of 'yerth groon' hazel and ash, were common as nuts; whilst a thick bush of bramble, wild rose, and holly, gave the spot the appearance of a place inclosed and set apart for mysterious concealment. Intermingled with these almost impervious barriers, were tufts of tall green fern, curling and bending gracefully; and a little separate from them, and nearer the old oaks, might be observed a few fern clumps of a singular appearance; of a paler green than the others, – with a flatter, and a broader leaf, – sticking up, rigid and expanded, like something stark with mute terror. These were 'Saint John's Fearn;' and the finest of them was the one selected by Plant for the experiment now to be described.

Chapter 22

The Eve of Saint John — The Meeting — The Midnight Scene — Taking of the Fern — Fates of Chirrup, Bangle, and Plant

A LITTLE before midnight on the eve of Saint John, Plant, Chirrup, and Bangle, were at the whale-jaw gate, before mentioned; and having slightly scanned each other, they proceeded, without speaking, until they had crossed the brook at a stepping-place, opposite the old Fyrin-ho'. The first word spoken was, 'What hast thou?'

'Mine is breawn an' roof,'

said Plant, exhibiting a brown earthen dish. 'What hast thou?' he then asked.

'Mine is breet enough,'

[1] Those oaks have been felled, and the kloof is now comparatively denuded of timber; the underwood on the left side is also nearly swept away. Sad inroads on the ominous gloom of the place.

said Chirrup, shewing a pewter platter; and continued, 'What hast thou?'

> '*Teed wi' web an' woof,*
> *Mine is deep enough,*'

said Bangle, displaying a musty, dun skull, with the cap sawn off above the eyes, and left flapping like a lid, by a piece of tanned scalp, which still adhered. The interior cavities had also been stuffed with moss and lined with clay, kneaded with blood from human veins; and the youth had secured the skull to his shoulders by a twine of three strands, of unbleached flax, – of undyed wool, – and of woman's hair; from which also depended a raven black tress, which a wily crone had procured from the maid he sought to obtain.

> '*That will do,*'

said a voice, in a half whisper, from one of the low bushes they were passing. Plant and Chirrup paused; but Bangle, who had evidently his heart on the accomplishment of the undertaking, said, 'Forward, – if we turn now a spirit hath spoken, we are lost – Come on,' and they went forward.

A silence, like that of death, was around them as they entered on the open platting. Nothing moved either in tree or brake. Through a space in the foliage the stars were seen pale in heaven; and a crooked moon hung in a bit of blue, amid motionless clouds. All was still and breathless, as if earth, heaven, and the elements, were aghast. Anything would have been preferable to that unnatural stillness and silence – the hoot of the night owl – the larum of the pit sparrow – the moan of the wind – the toll of a death bell – or the howl of a ban-dog – would, inasmuch as they are things of this world, have been welcome sounds amid that horrid pause. But no sound came – no object moved.

Gasping, and with cold sweat oozing on his brow, Plant recollected that they were to shake the fern with a forked rod of witch hazle, and by no means must touch it with their hands; and he asked in a whisper if the others had brought one? Both said they had forgotten, and Chirrup said they had better never have come; but Plant drew his knife, and stepping into a moonlighted bush, soon returned with what was wanted, and they went forward.

The green knowe – the old oaks – the encircled space – and the fearn – were now approached: the latter stiff and erect in a gleamy light.

'Is it deep neet?' said Bangle.

'It is,' said Plant.

> *'The star that bids the shepherd fold,*
> *Now the top of heaven doth hold.'*

And they drew near. All was still, and motionless.

Plant knelt on one knee, and held his dish under the fearn.

Chirrup held his broad plate next below, and

Bangle knelt, and rested the kull directly under both, on the green sod; the lid being up.

Plant said,

> *'Good Saint John, this seed we crave,*
> *We have dared; shall we have?*

A voice responded:

> *'Now the moon is downward starting,*
> *Moon and stars are all departing;*
> *Quick, quick; shake, shake;*
> *He whose heart shall soonest break,*
> *Let him take.'*

They looked, and perceived by a glance, that a venerable form, in a loose robe was near them.

Darkness came down like a swoop. The fearn was shaken, the upper dish flew into pieces, – the pewter one melted, – the skull emitted a cry, and eyes glared in its sockets; – lights broke, – beautiful children were seen walking in their holiday clothes, – and graceful female forms sung mournful and enchanting airs.

The men stood terrified and fascinated; and Bangle, gazing, bade 'God bless 'em.' A crash followed, as if the whole of the timber in the kloof was being splintered and torn up, – strange and horrid forms appeared from the thickets, – the men ran as if sped on the wind, – they separated and lost each other. Plant ran towards the old house, and there, leaping the brook, he cast a glance behind him, and saw terrific shapes, some beastly, some part human, and some hellish, gnashing their teeth, and howling and uttering the most fearful and mournful tones, as if wishful to follow him, but unable to do so.

In an agony of terror he arrived at home, not knowing how he got there. He was, during several days, in a state bordering on unconsciousness; and when he recovered he learned that Chirrup was found on the White Moss, raving mad, and chasing the wild birds. As for poor Bangle, he found his way home over hedge and ditch; running with supernatural and fearful speed, – the skull's eyes glaring at his back, and the nether jaw grinning and jabbering frightful and unintelligible sounds. He had preserved the seed however, and having taken it from the skull, he buried the latter at the cross road from whence he had taken it. He then carried the spell out, and his proud love stood one night by his bed-side in tears. But he had done too much for human nature, – in three months after she followed his corpse, a real mourner, to the grave!

Such was the description my fellow-prisoner gave of what occurred in the only trial he ever made with Saint John's Fearn seed. He was full of old and quaint narratives, and of superstitious lore, and often would beguile time by recounting them. Poor fellow! a mysterious fate hung over him also. After his return from London, which was in a few days, he seemed to have become disgusted by the levity of his young and handsome, but thoughtless wife. In a short time he suddenly disappeared from the country, and has not been heard of since.

Chapter 23

Author's Fourth Appearance before the Privy Council — A Mother's Lamentation for her Child — A Pair of Cockneys — Fifth Attendance before the Privy Council, and Author's Discharge

IT was, I think, on the 23rd of April, that I was taken to the Home Office with George Plant, for my fourth examination.

Having been introduced in the customary way, Lord Sidmouth said,

Mr Bamford; the information which we expected to have received respecting you, is not yet arrived; therefore you will be remanded for another examination, which will take place next week.

To which I replied,

My Lord; if you think proper to wait for information which will establish a charge of high treason against me, your Lordship may wait for ever, as I am certain that no such information will arrive. I also went on to state, that my conduct had been quite opposed to treason, – that I had certainly done all which lay in my power to promote the cause of Parliamentary Reform, but I had always acted openly, and I trusted legally, – that I did not think his Majesty's ministers were fully acquainted with the state of the country, and the condition of the people; nor did I perceive how they could be, considering the partial source from whence their information must be derived – that the gentry, or what were called the higher classes, were too proud, or too indifferent, to examine minutely, the abodes of the poor and distressed; and that the interests of many, as well as their want of accurate knowledge, tended to elicit from them distorted or partial statements of fact. The poor, I said, would be content, could they only procure the common necessaries of life by hard labour, but they could not even do that; and if ministers were thoroughly acquainted with the distress of the people, they would be almost surprised that the country was not a scene of confusion and horror, instead of being as it was, peaceable, though discontented. I said more than this, to the same purport; but the above are the principal heads on which I touched. The council, as they always did, listened to me with patience and attention; and whatever I said was written down by gentlemen who appeared to be clerks or secretaries. I was then reconducted, and I and Plant were lodged in our old quarters; and the day following he was discharged, and I was left alone.

One evening, as I was pacing my yard thoughtfully, and somewhat touched by that 'hope deferred which maketh the heart sick,' I was startled, astonished, and affected, by a sudden burst of the most mournful and woe-fraught cries that ever struck my ear, or moved my heart. At first it was a wild and agonized scream, intense and full, as if the soul was coming forth in unspeakable woe. It was a long time ere I could distinguish words amid that pity-moving cry; at length I heard a name, and words of endearment. 'My Ann,' – 'my love,' – 'my child.' It was the name of my own child; and I must leave to parents, who have known separation from their homes and their offspring, the task of appreciating my feelings, whilst, transfixed and listening, I caught the name of one so dear, accompanied by the most heart-broken lament that I had ever heard from human suffering. 'My Ann!' – 'my love!' – 'my child!' – 'my beauty!' 'my lost love!' – and so she continued, raising and lowering her voice in an almost musical though entirely unartificial cadence, and in the simplest utterance of soul affliction. The mourner was a female convict; and the tidings had been brought to her in her cell that her child was dead.

Poor thing! – I then felt that others might be more unhappy than myself, – that I had still something to be thankful for, – that I had yet a dove-nest in reserve, – at least I so hoped, – to which I could return after the present storm had blown over; and I retired to my ward for the night, contented with my lot, and entirely cured of the melancholy of 'hope deferred.' But the tones of that poor woman still rung in my ears; and I either dreamt of, or heard her cries, mingled with the night-wind, and resounding through the corridors of the prison.

Whilst thus alone, I endeavoured at times to amuse myself by writing verses; and not having pen and ink, I scored them on a flag in the yard with the stump of a tobacco pipe. In this manner was produced 'An Eclogue,' celebrating the doctor's visit and mine to Knowl-hill, as previously recorded.

> *O'er the dark heath, and over wintry Knowl,*
> *The evening sun, shone out his fainting ray;*
> *The wonted winds on other hills did howl,*
> *And left soft breezes whispering wantonly.*
> *Wide, o'er the moorland, bleating flocks did stray;*
> *And vernal spring again returning smil'd;*
> *When, by the rindle, gliding swift away,*
> *Two strangers stepping wearily and toil'd,*
> *Sought the lone summit of the barren wild.*

I also frequently chatted with my neighbours over the wall; and took care to supply them with the requisites for a good cup of tea, and whilst I remained, they wanted not for anything which my stores could afford.

In the course of a few days an old coal meter and his son, both of whom were committed for some harsh chastisement of a neighbour's child, were placed in my ward; and though they had no politics about them, they contributed to render the days less irksome by their conversation and manners, which were of the most perfect Cockney cast. They started back and stood wide agape when I opened upon them in broad Lancashire; the old man put on his spectacles, and peered at me as if I were uttering barbarous Russ, or a Lappish incantation. On the other hand, they confounded me with their v's and w's; and I soon discovered that one half of their nouns were of no known language, or even dialect; but were mere slang terms, used by classes (workmen, thieves, or prostitutes, as the case might be) and arbitrary in the localties where they had obtained currency. The speech of a born and resident Cockney, is probably never two years the same. New incidents and objects are continually giving rise to new ideas and expressions; every genius, and there are some droll ones, carries his lexicon at his tongue's end; and if he be assured and flippant, as he probably will be, he will certainly obtain utterers for his coinage; and the more grotesque and un-English it is, the better will be its acceptance. The talent, we must allow, of some great national writers has recently done much towards rendering the slang of one class general, if not permanent; but at the time I am writing of, no attempt had been made to produce a book of the terms; they had not, except perhaps a few dashes by Fielding, been introduced by genius to the press, and consequently they were only a confused and undefined mass of jargon.

On the 29th of April I was again introduced to the Privy Council, Lord Sidmouth said, 'Mr Bamford, I hope you are now before me for the last time. – You will be discharged on conditions which will be read over to you; the same conditions which others of your fellow prisoners who have been discharged, have accepted. I assure you I feel great pleasure in thus restoring you to your family.'

I said, I hoped nothing would be proposed to me which was at variance with my political principles, as I could not consent to forego any rights to which, as an Englishman, I was entitled. His Lordship could not desire me to give up the only right I had exercised; namely, the right of petition.

His Lordship said; 'Nothing will be proposed to you, which an honest and a good man need object to. We are not averse to the subject petitioning for a redress of grievances; it is the manner in which that right has been exercised which we condemn; a right may be exercised in such a way that it becomes a wrong, and then we must object to it. Mr Bamford; there are three things which I would have you to impress seriously on your mind. The first is, that the present distress of the country arises from unavoidable circumstances; – the second that his majesty's ministers will do all they can to alleviate such distress; – and, thirdly, – no violence, of whatever description, will be tolerated, but it will be put down with a very strong hand. I wish you well; I assure you I wish you well;

and I hope this is the last time I shall ever see you on an occasion like the present.'

I sincerely thanked his Lordship for his good wishes and condescension, and expressed my gratitude for the kindness I had experienced whilst his Lordship's prisoner; and having asked, and very obligingly obtained permission to have my liberty the following morning, until the coach started, I bowed to his Lordship and the Council, and retired.

I was next conducted to the private office of Sir Nathaniel Conant, which was in a lower room in the same building, where, in the presence of Sir Nathaniel and a clerk, I gave my personal bond in the sum of a hundred pounds, to be levied on my goods and chattels, 'if, within twelve months from that day, I appeared in his majesty's court of justice at Westminster.'

Chapter 24

Further Kindness from the King's Messengers — A Glimpse at the 'Infernals' — Departure from Prison — Arrival at Home

I MUST own that I did not clearly comprehend the meaning of this bond. I could not guess at the reason why I was not to 'appear in his majesty's court of justice at Westminster,' as well as any other British subject; and I could only account for the exception, by supposing it was the common form, – a mere official ceremony: indeed Sir Nathaniel intimated as much, and Lord Sidmouth had said, it was only what the others had agreed to. I afterwards however, had reason to suppose, that it was intended to deter me, should I become so disposed, from commencing an action in the above court for false imprisonment, which I could have done, the indemnity bill not having then passed. I should imagine, however, that my bond could hardly have kept me out of court, unless the law could be made to commit *felo de se*; unless it could be made to forbid a subject from claiming the law. But these questions I must leave to those who are learned in such matters.

On returning from Sir Nathaniel's office to the messengers' room, I was warmly congratulated by Mr Williams, one of the kind messengers who brought myself and companions from Manchester. He cautioned me in a friendly manner as to my future interference in politics, and concluded by inviting me to his house the morning following; and soon after, I stepped into the coach, and was conducted to my old quarters for the night.

After breakfast on the succeeding morn, I collected every article I had left, in the provision and grocery line, and conveyed them under the door, to the women; and bidding them farewell, I told them to keep up their spirits, and mind their good resolutions; and with a thousand thanks, and their best wishes, I left them, and the old coal meter and his son, and passed into the inner yard of the prison. Here I encountered my fellow captive, James Leach, from Rochdale. He was much affected, and expressed great anxiety as to the duration of his imprisonment, and whether it were likely to end in a capital charge, or be merely detention as a state prisoner. I consoled him as well as I could, – and told him, I now thought it would be imprisonment only, and that not of long duration. He sat down on a stone, and shed tears. I was grieved to see him so much depressed, and did all in my power to cheer him; promising also to go over and see his mother and other relatives, and inform them of his actual condition and future prospects; and so I left him.

On arriving at the outer gates, I found one of the turnkeys smartly dressed, and ready to accompany and conduct me; for I was a stranger to the town, and could not, therefore, have readily found my way; neither was I to be lost sight of, until carried off by the coach. He first took me to Mr Williams's, I think, in Jermyn-street. We were received with much kindness; and after partaking a lunch, that gentleman made me a handsome present of clothes. He also consigned to my care as a present from Mr Dykes, his fellow-messenger, a stock of clothes for the doctor, and some money for his wife; and I must say, that the kindness of these two gentlemen to myself, and to my less fortunate comrades, was such as will, whilst we live, deserve our warmest gratitude.

My conductor, as may be supposed, was rather well acquainted with the town, and with those descriptions of its residents who were most frequently under the cognizance of the police. He asked if I should like, before I quitted London, to look into one or two of the 'flash cribs,' 'shades,' and 'infernals,' as he called them? and I assented. He led me then through lanes and alleys, and sombre courts, where our fellow-beings, both male and female, young and old, appeared in squalid misery; and where a disgusting odour came reeking from the doors and windows of every habitation. I mentally ejaculated,

> *Oh! let me live afar from scenes like these,*
> *Where the winds bend the giant armed trees;*
> *Bask on my own dear banks of new-blown flowers,*
> *When thirsty sol has supp'd the morning showers.*

The dens we visited, were indeed horrid and murky shades. But it was morning, and the thieves and their 'pals' as he termed the repulsive females seemed drowsy and almost as blind as owls in sunshine. He showed me some characters who had already figured conspicuously at the Old Bailey; and one or two he pointed out who were to be had up again in a short time.

These revelations, the objects they distinguished, and the mode of life they illustrated, were almost wonders to me and my conductor seemed to enjoy my surprise. I could almost write a book on the scenes and characters I noticed in the course of two hours. But such a production is the less necessary, inasmuch as a clever writer of the present day has, in his life and adventures of a famous housebreaker, disclosed quite as much as it is either requisite or agreeable to know of such characters and their modes of life.

After visiting many other places, and gratifying my curiosity as well as the time would permit, I returned to the prison and dined. After again seeing James Leach, and bidding him good-bye, I took leave of Mr Adkins, the governor, and of Mr Beckett, the deputy governor, whose behaviour to me had been uniformly kind; and leaving the prison with my morning's conductor, I mounted the coach, at 'The Peacock,' Islington, and quitting London, I arrived at home on the morning of the second of May.

Chapter 25

Offices of Friendship — Home Blessings — Why not contented — Want of
Advisers — A Simile

HAVING taken an early opportunity for delivering to Healey's wife the presents for her husband and herself, I afterwards in conformity with my promise to James Leach, visited his mother, and other relatives at Spotland bridge, near Riochdale. To these poor, but industrious and respectable people, I gave a faithful account of the situation in which I had left him; told them all about our imprisonment, and the treatment we had experienced; and concluded with as consoling a prospect for the future, as I thought the facts justified. I felt great pleasure in this latter part of my mission, because I wished to soothe the old woman's uneasiness on account of her son; and I came away with the agreeable assurance, that I had contributed to make this family happier than I found it.

I now went to work, my wife weaving beside me, and my little girl, now become doubly dear, attending school or going short errands for her mother. Why was I not content? – why was not my soul filled and thankful? – what would I more? – what could mortal enjoy beyond a sufficiency to satisfy hunger and thirst, – apparel, to make him warm and decent, – a home for shelter and repose, – and the society of those he loved? All these I had, and still was craving, – craving for something for 'the nation,' – for some good for every person – forgetting all the time to appreciate, and to husband the blessings I had on every side around me; and, like some honest enthusiasts of the present day, supervising the affairs of the nation to the great neglect of my own, – of my

Hours more dear than drops of gold.

But it was not with us then, as it is now: and we have that excuse to plead. We had none to direct or oppose us, except a strong-handed government, whose politics were as much hated as their power was dreaded. We had not any of our own rank with whom to advise for the better, – no man of other days who had gone through the ordeal of experience; and whose judgment might have directed our self-devotion, and have instructed us that, before the reform we sought, could be obtained and profited by, there must be another, a deeper reform, – emerging from our hearts, and first blessing our households, by the production of every good we could possibly accomplish in our humble spheres, – informing us also, and confirming it by all history, that, governments might change from the despotic to the anarchical, when, as surely as death, would come the despotic again; and that no redemption for the masses could exist, save one that should arise from their own virtue and knowledge, – that king tyranny, and mob tyranny (the worst of all) might alternately bear sway; and that no barrier could be effectually interposed, save the self-knowledge, and self-control of a reformed people.

But, as I said, we had none such to advise. Our worthy old major was to us a political reformer only; not a moral one. His councils were good so far as they went, but they did not go to the root-end of radicalism. He seemed to have forgotten in the simplicity of a guileless heart, good old man as he was, that the people themselves wanted reforming, – that they were ignorant and corrupt; and, that the source must be purified before a pure and free government could be maintained.

In the absence therefore, of such wholesome monition – in the ardour also, and levity of youth, – and impelled by a sincere and disinterested wish to deserve the gratitude of my working fellow-countrymen; it is scarcely to be wondered at, that I soon forgot whatever merely prudential reflections my better sense had whispered to me whilst in durance; and that with a strong, though discreetly tempered zeal, I determined to go forward in the cause of parliamentary reform.

And so, as it were, like another Crusoe, I lay with my little boat in still water, waiting for the first breeze to carry me again to the billows.

Chapter 26

Private Meetings and Plots in Yorkshire — Thomas Bacon — Author's Caution to Him — Its Rejection — Bacon's Betrayal and Fate — Brandreth, Turner, and Ludlam executed — Oliver, the Spy

SOON after my return, I found that a secret influence had been at work during my absence, exciting to, and carrying on, private meetings, and suspicious intrigues in our neighbourhood; and that one of my neighbours in particular, whom I wished better, had been so deluded as to give his attendance at one or two meetings of a suspicious character which had been held in Yorkshire. I became aware also, though my information was not very distinct, that my old acquaintance Joseph Mitchell, and another person, a stranger whom I did not know, were the chief movers in these proceedings, –

that the stranger had made frequent enquiries after me since my return, – and that I might expect to hear shortly, of a decisive blow being struck for 'the liberties of the country.'

I treated these reports with contempt or reprehension, as might be requisite at the time. The enunciation of Mitchell's name certainly did not awaken confidence on my part: nor did the intelligence that he was moving about with a well-dressed, and apparently affluent stranger, at all tend to repress certain forebodings which had begun to arise in my mind.

One day, when I was at work, a message was sent requesting me to step over to the Dog and Partridge public house, which was opposite to where I lived. I went, and found an aged grey-headed man, stooping beneath probably seventy years; his venerable locks, hanging to his shoulders, and having in one hand a stick, and on the other arm a basket containing rolls of worsted and woollen yarn, and small articles of hosiery which he seemed to have for sale. On looking at him more steadfastly, I recognised him as my old co-delegate to London, from the town of Derby, Thomas Bacon, and I shook him heartily by the hand and sat down beside him.

With him was a tall decent-looking young man, much like a town's weaver; wearing a blue coat, and with a clean white apron wrapped about his waist. After a civil salutation to him also, I addressed friend Bacon, and asked what particular business might have brought him to our part of the country, so far from his residence? With a smile, he pointed to his wares; but almost immediately gave me to understand that he carried them only as a disguise to his real business.

He said a delegate meeting was to be held in Yorkshire, which would cause a finishing blow to be levelled at the boroughmongers, as I should shortly hear; and, that a man from Middleton, whose name he gave, and who had attended several previous meetings, was particularly wanted on the present occasion; and he concluded by asking me to direct him to that man.

I paused, as if striving to recollect the person, – repeating the name, and considering meantime, what might be the consequences to my neighbour, if I sent the unconscious emissary to his house; and I finished by declaring there was no such man; and that the name must be a fictitious one. I then took the opportunity to caution my old friend against forming connections so liable to abuse, and so dangerous and unwise, as well as hurtful to the country, directed, as they were, against a strong government, and for the overthrow, by force, of a national order of things.

The old man seemed struck by what I said about the delegate from Middleton having given a false name; but he huff'd at my advice, and said I should, not withstanding there might be a traitor or two, soon learn something which I at present little understood.

I reminded him that I had but just returned from a government prison : and told him that from what I had observed, or been able to gather in various ways, I was sure no force would avail in overturning the present state of things, – that I believed ministers had eyes to see and ears to hear, and tongues to whisper whatever occurred; and that he might depend on it, neither he nor any persons with whom he might be connected, could take one step beyond the pale of the law, without being instantly in the gripe of the executive. I entreated him to consider these things, – to pause, and not be led away and lead others at his time of life.

He drank his beer rather hastily, – took up his basket, – thanked me for my good wishes, – but declined my advice, saying he was 'too old a politician to be counselled by one so young as myself;' and so, motioning his companion, they both went down the street, and to my satisfaction, took the road back towards Manchester.

Reader, this pertinacious old man was, in a few weeks after, arraigned for high treason at Derby; and pleading guilty, was with fourteen others, transported for life : whilst the young man, who was one of the Turners, was hung and beheaded, with the equally unfortunate Brandreth and Ludlam.

The stranger whom Joseph Mitchell had so assiduously introduced amongst the discontented classes of Lancashire, Yorkshire, and Derbyshire, first inveigled them into treasonable associations, – then to armed insurrections – he got them to arm as has been done in the present day; and then betrayed them. How one, if not more, of my neighbours at Middleton escaped, has just been shown. I thought it no dishonour to deny a person and a name, when apprized that their discovery would probably lead to the ruin of the parties I sought after, if not of many others.

That stranger, – that betrayer, reader, was OLIVER THE SPY.

Chapter 27

IT may perhaps not be amiss to refer to a few of the more prominent national events which occurred in the year 1817, after my liberation from prison.

On June the 13th, the Habeas Corpus Act was further suspended.

On the 16th, Sir Francis Burdett's motion relative to the conduct of Oliver the Spy, who had consummated his villanies, and had been accidentally unmasked, was made the House of Commons.

On the 4th of October, there were great disturbances at Worcester.

On the 18th, Jeremiah Brandreth was tried, and found guilty of high treason, – and, on the 22nd was sentenced, with Turner and Ludlam, to be executed.

On the 5th of November, the Princess Charlotte died, lamented by the whole nation; and, it was expected, that now the hand of death had struck within the Prince Regent's threshold, his heart would be moved, and he would respite the prisoners under sentence at Derby; especially when he considered, that they had been instigated to crime, by a government agent, – Oliver, the Spy. But, his heart was untouched; and the day after that on which his daughter expired, they were brought forth and executed!!!

On the 28th of January, 1818, a bill was introduced into parliament, to restore the Habeas Corpus act; and, on the 10th of March, an indemnity bill passed.

By this time all the state prisoners had been released, and had arrived at home. My friend Healey returned quite an altered man; instead of being flattish in front, and somewhat gaunt looking, he came home plump and round, and genteelly dressed; with one or two large boxes, a rather heavy purse, and his finger bedizened by a broad gold ring, which he said he had received for an 'extraordinary operation on the teeth of a great lady of Devonshire.'

James Leach also arrived in Middleton about the same time, on his way home. I went to see him at the public-house where he stopped, and found him also much altered in outward appearance and manner. Instead of the simple-minded and soft-hearted lad I had left at Coldbath-fields, I now found a person smartly attired, and with some cash in his pockets. I perceived also, that he affected superiority, and was somewhat distant, and that my neighbours took notice of this. But, as I despised all affectation, and not the less because he displayed it, and as I cared nothing about his motives for coolness, I did not trouble him with any questions on either subject, but merely remarked them, and he went his way.

I found afterwards, that this young man and his relatives had been secretly propagating reports that I had acted as a spy for the government, – that I had become that being most abhorrent to my soul; and had in fact, purchased my own liberation from prison, by betraying this James Leach, and my companions.

This was a sore blow to my feelings, – heavier from not being expected, and coupled as it was, with deep ingratitude. I had the consolation however, to know that I had not deserved this at their hands, – that I had merited the very reverse of detraction, – and that their best good offices would not have been more than equivalent to the entire good faith with which I had served them in their hour of humbled sorrow. But, why should I expect them, or their like, to reciprocate with me? Because I judged of them as was then my wont with respect to nearly all mankind – that their sentiments were as disinterested as my own, – and that they were worthy of friendship because they stood in need of it. When however, I found out my error, the pride of an indignant though wounded spirit was my solace, and I looked with serene contempt above the calumny and the calumniators, leaving to time the obliteration of the injury, and the infliction of shame on my detractors.

The principal of these is now reputed to be wealthy. With the aid of political friends, he entered the provision line, soon after his return from prison. He has maintained *his* distance and *his* superiority ever since, and he is welcome to both, and his riches to boot. He has, however, never yet found an opportunity to acknowledge the service I formerly rendered him; and it was not, until one of the late elections for Rochdale, that I obtained distinct evidence of the part he had been playing, though I knew as much; I then however sent for him into a public company, where his words were repeated to his face, and, not being able to deny them, or to prove any thing against me, he acknowledged the latter, and so I left him, and have ever since held him at *his* distance, and in *his* unenviable superiority.

Healey also scarcely acted the part of a friend in these matters. He heard the slanders, and conveyed them to me by hints and half-sentences, – a line of conduct which I should not now tolerate for one moment, – but he never spoke out candidly, nor disclosed his authors. He however had his reward. I did that for him which I would have done at the time for the other, or for any friend in need. He became ill of the typhus fever, and when he sent for me, he was fast sinking under the worst symptoms of the disorder. He took medicines, but they seemed of no avail, and he expressed his belief that he should die. May I be forgiven, for I swore he should not! and I got a large tub in which I placed him, and his wife filled it nearly to the brim with water as hot as he could bear. I washed and laved him all over; and then lifted him out, and rubbed him with a cloth till his skin burned, and then I put him into bed, and covered him well up; he fell into a sound sleep, and awoke streaming with perspiration, and from that time he began to get better.

One other instance of that kind of friendship which I now began to suspect was more common in the world than I had previously supposed, and then I shall have done, for the present, with these kind of disfigurements.

A few weeks before I was apprehended, our friend, John Knight, of Manchester, (for my wife and myself, considered all persons as friends, who came to our house as reformers) called at Middleton, on his way into Yorkshire, or from Yorkshire, and took tea with us. My wife, who never deemed any trouble too great, if bestowed for 'the cause,' made as much ado of the old man as if he were her father; and we were both pleased to observe that our venerable, but physically hearty guest, enjoyed his repast to perfection. We then spent an hour or two with some neighbours, and our friend went on his journey.

On the Friday, or Saturday after my arrest, my wife went to Manchester, for the purpose of hearing whatever tidings might have arrived, of myself, or fellow-prisoners; and with this view, she directed her steps to the house of our friend Knight, who then lived in Hanover-street. She thought that, at any rate, she might derive some consolation from his experience; some relief from that wearisome uncertainty, which oppresses, without nerving the mind to endure. The morning was fine, and she left home without either cloak or umbrella, and with a light cotton shawl only thrown over her shoulders. But before she got to Manchester, the sky became gloomy, and there came on a storm of wind and cold rain, and her clothes were presently wet through. In this condition, and that inclement weather, she knocked at the door, and felt relieved for the moment, when, as it tardily opened, our old friend's visage appeared betwixt the door and the door-post. He did not ask her to step in, but his leaden and immoveable features were welcome, though the dull eyes were fixed uninvitingly upon her. She then told him who she was, and said she wished to know whether he had heard anything of the prisoners at London, of whom her husband, she reminded him, was one? He received her name with an 'ho,' and a nod, – still holding the door as if a thief stood outside. He said he had not heard anything, but at 'old Drummond's, in Hunter's-lane,' she would probably hear some information. The wind and rain came down, if possible more fiercely than before. She pulled her shawl about her, and burst into tears, and when she looked again, our venerable friend had disappeared, and the door was closed in her face.

At Drummond's, not one of which family had ever seen her before, her reception was quite different. She no sooner mentioned my name, by which alone I was known to them, than they took her into a room where was a good fire; – took off her wet shawl and outer garments, and gave her dry hose and shoes, – and set before her refreshments, and pressed her to partake of them with that real good feeling which always produces good manners. In short, they conferred on her, all that kindness which might have been expected from him who had so unnaturally closed his door against her. They gave her also some encouraging accounts from London, where their son (Samuel) was, as well as myself, a prisoner; and she returned home in much better spirits than she came.

Reader! shall I tell thee, 'Old Drummond, the Reed-maker, in Hunter's-lane,' was an Irishman, and that is saying enough for him. John Knight, I believe, first drew breath amongst the hills of the West Riding of Yorkshire, but that must not suffice. Whilst we applaud the simple and touching hospitality of the former, and through him, do homage to the characteristic of his generous nation, we must not suffer the repulsive insensibility of the latter, to disparage his better-hearted countrymen in our estimation. Few are the Yorkshiremen, I am convinced, who would have done as John Knight did.

Chapter 28

WITH the restoration of the Habeas Corpus Act, the agitation for reform was renewed. A public meeting on the subject, was held at Westminster, on the twenty-eighth of March; and in June, Sir Francis Burdett's motion for reform was negatived in the House of Commons.

Numerous meetings followed in various parts of the country; and Lancashire, and the Stockport borders of Cheshire, were not the last to be concerned in public demonstrations for reform. At one of these meetings, which took place at Lydgate, in Saddleworth, and at which Bagguley, – Drummond, – Fitton, – Haigh, – and others, were the principal speakers; I, in the course of an address, insisted on the right, and the propriety also, of females who were present at such assemblages, voting by show of hand, for, or against the resolutions. This was a new idea; and the women, who attended numerously on that bleak ridge, were mightily pleased with it, – and the men being nothing dissentient, – when the resolution was put, the women held up their hands, amid much laughter; and ever from that time, females voted with the men at the radical meetings. I was not then aware, that the new impulse thus given to political movement, would in a short time be applied to charitable and religious purposes. But it was so; our females voted at every subsequent meetings; it became the practice, – female political unions were formed, with their chair-women, committees, and other officials; and from us, the practice was soon borrowed, very judiciously no doubt, and applied in a greater or less degree, to the promotion of religious and charitable institutions.

But, had I been allowed my own way, all the borrowing would not have been on one side. I often said to my companions; 'observe our neighbours, the Church-folks, – the Methodists, – and the Ranters, – what charms they add to their religious assemblages by the introduction of vocal music. Why has such an important lesson remained unobserved by us? Why should not we add music, and heart-inspiring song to our meetings? and then I wrote my

'Lancashire Hymn,' to one of the finest trumpet strains I ever heard.

> Great God, who did of old inspire
>   The patriot's ardent heart,
> And fill'd him with a warm desire
>   To die, or do his part;
> Oh! let our shouts be heard by Thee,
> Genius great of liberty.
>
> When fell oppression, o'er the land
>   Hung like a darksome day;
> And crush'd beneath a tyrant's hand,
>   The groaning people lay;
> The patriot band, impell'd by Thee,
> Nobly strove for liberty.
>
> And shall we tamely, now forgo
>   The rights for which they bled?
> And crouch beneath a minion's blow,
>   And basely bow the head?
> Ah! no; it cannot, cannot be;
> Death for us, or liberty!
>
> Have we not heard the infant's cry,
>   And mark'd the mother's tear?
> That look, which told us mournfully
>   That woe and want were there?
> And shall they ever weep again,
> And shall their pleadings be in vain?
>
> By the dear blood of Hampden, shed
>   In freedom's noble strife!
> By gallant Sydney's gory head!
>   By all that's dear to life!
> They shall not supplicate in vain;
> No longer will we bear the chain.
>
> Souls of our mighty sires! behold
>   This band of brothers join.
> Oh: never, never be it told,
>   That we disgrace your line;

> *If England wills the glorious deed,*
> *We'll have another Runnimede.*

These verses were intended to have been sung at a meeting of perhaps two thousand people, which about this time was held at Middleton; but, unfortunately for their purpose, and not less injudiciously, they were first submitted to John Knight, and one or two others, whose insusceptibility could not find any charms in music, and to whom no sounds were so fascinating as their own voices uttering interminable harangues. The proposal to sing was by these persons condemned as 'an innovation,' and the idea of introducing music at our meetings, was abandoned.

Methinks I now observe my elderly reader, first secure his spectacles, and then shaking his head, say, 'Ah! he is wide at sea again; with a strong mast, a heavy sail, and not so much as the breadth of a duck's foot for oar or rudder, – What next ? – Doth he founder head down, or again break ashore ? – Let us see.'

About this time a public meeting for reform was held at Birch, near Middleton, which was worthy of notice for one incident. It was moved and seconded, that petitions to the Lords and Commons should be presented in the usual manner; when, William Benbow, who had lately returned from prison, made his way through the crowd, and mounting the waggon, urged the people, in a violent and irrational address, to march to London, and, 'present their petitions at the point of the sword and pike.' He was loudly cheered, with expressions such as, 'Aye, that's the way,' – 'Go on Benbow,' – 'That's the man for us.' At that same time he was pondering on a retreat from the country; of that country which he was endeavouring to distract by a course of violence. That very week or the week following, he sailed from Liverpool to join Cobbett in America.

When I afterwards met some of his applauders, and asked them what they thought of the man who could urge them to rush on destruction, and then hasten out of the way? they shook with indignation.

And now, having, as it were, disposed of some of the minor passages of my political life, I address myself to the description of more serious transactions; and gradually approach that current of circumstances, which led to a catastrophe, – a vortex, – in which we were inextricably involved, – submerged, – and, for the time, apparently lost.

Already, methinks I hear the cries of our multitudes, and feel the tremor of the earth beneath their footsteps. The air is agitated by a sound like the roar of vast waters; and the earth shakes as if floods were coming from their abyss. But why hasten to contemplate, before its date, a spectacle so awful, – so distressing? 'Sufficient for the day is the evil thereof.' That picture shall therefore remain veiled for the present, whilst I direct the attention of my reader to the chief personage in the drama about to be enacted, and to some circumstances preliminary to the great event.

And may the spirit of all truth, – insensible to fear, – uninfluenced by partiality or prejudice, – and, superior to resentment, – correct my heart, and guide my discretion, whilst I portray scenes, and record transactions which now crowd to my recollection.

Chapter 29

Arrival of Henry Hunt in Manchester, January, 1819 — He is assaulted at the Theatre — His intimation to the Author — The Picked Ten — The Play House — Interview with Nadin — Play abandoned — Carousal — Return

Thou raised'st thy voice, and the people awaking,
  Beheld the foul source of corruption displayed.
And loyal stupidity, quickly forsaking,
  They found themselves plunder'd, oppressed, and betrayed;
Then, loud as the storm in its fury out-rushing,
  The shouts of the thousands for freedom arose;
And liberty only, shall sooth them to hushing,
  And liberty only, shall lull to repose.

SUCH were the sentiments with which Henry Hunt was received at Manchester, in January, 1819. In a day or two afterwards, he was assaulted, and mal-treated at the Theatre, by some military officers, and residents of the town; because, as they alleged, he hissed when 'God save the King' was called for.

The same week a letter was put into my hands at Middleton, from Mr Hunt, requesting me to call upon him at the Spread Eagle, the day following.

I attended according to his request, and he informed me that on a certain night thereafter, he would again visit the theatre; and that, the attendance of myself and some ten or a dozen of stout fellows in the pit, and near to the Fountain-street entrance, would be agreeable to him and his Manchester friends. I undertook to come with the requisite force, and he promised to furnish tickets for our entrance.

About five o'clock on the afternoon of the day appointed, – it was, I think, on the Monday following, – a gang of ten rough-looking country fellows attracted some notice as they passed through several of the streets of Manchester. Their appearance was somewhat remarkable, even for countrymen. Their dress was of the readiest, fit for 'donning or doffing,' their hats were mostly beyond damage by warfare, – their shirt collars, clean and white, were thrown open, – some wore their breeches unbuttoned at the knees, as the Irish do, – some tramped in heavy clogs, rimmed with iron, – others wore strong shoes, with clinker nails grinning like a rasp of shark's teeth; all bore stout cudgels of greater length or weight; – some carried blackthorn, – some hazel, – and others again had taken a fancy to that portable and effective cudgel, the green English holly. Their bearing was not less striking, – they were all young men, – tall, gaunt, and square-built, – long-legged, free-limbed, and lithe as stag-hounds; and as they went, tramp, tramp, along the flags, people looked, startled, and looked again; whilst the observed ones, nothing noticing, went onwards like men who knew their work, and were both able and willing to perform it. In this manner, they proceeded the whole length of Long Mill-gate, – across the Old Church Yard, – up Hunter's-lane, and Cannon-street, – across High-street, and to the Robin Hood public house, in Church-street.

This party consisted of myself, and nine picked men of my acquaintance, from Middleton. Our business was to attend the play, – to protect Mr Hunt if requisite, and to retaliate with punishment, any insult that might be offered to him, or any of his friends. In this business however, we did not expect to stand alone, nor were we disappointed.

Before six o'clock we were at the pit-door; it was a cool, and rather wet evening; no other persons were on the flags at that time; and as we stood there, chatting, laughing, and sometimes dancing a rough step, we began to attract notice, – for it was no common thing to see half a score of working men at the pit entrance of the play-house, –

and presently individuals, and then small groups joined us, some as enquirers, others as listeners, some as observers, and some, as we soon found, with pretty much the same intentions as ourselves. These latter were chiefly Irish, – bricklayers, tailors, and town's weavers; and they were not lacking of instruments of force any more than ourselves. As the moon rose, we frequently got a peep at the black knobs of their shillelahs sticking above their coats, and when the press became great, we could hear them grunting to each other, 'arrah honey, but its mighty hard ribs you've got stuck there in your side.' And then there would arise a loud and hearty laugh; a regular, 'Ahh! ahh! haa!'

Other subjects also occurred for remarks. We perceived that several rather respectable looking townsmen had joined our company unnoticed by us; one or two seemed very attentive listeners, and others would be discreet but pertinacious questioners. As

'I think I've seen you before somewhere,' (addressing an individual) 'don't you come from such a place?'

'Nowe, I come fro' th' Soont-hole.' 'Soont-hole? – where's that?'

'It's i' Castleton!' 'Hum! I never heard of it before.' –

'Wot never yerd o'th' Soont-hole?' (Laughter again.) 'You seem merry!' –

'Why not? foke shud be merry 'at com'n to th' play.' 'They should, unless it be a tragedy.'

'A thrageddy? that's a skrikin' piece I reckon.' 'It is; such as Romeo, or Macbeth, or Hamlet.'

'An' wot are us to ha to-neet? dun yo' kno'?' 'I dont; I have not seen a bill.'

'Then I'll tell yo.' – We'en ha' one o' yur thrageddies, an' it shall be, "King Henry." ' (another loud laugh.)

'You are a joking set; do you all come from one place? all from Castleton?' 'Nowe, this tother chap ses he comes fro' th' Katty Green.'

'Aye! Katty Green.' 'That's near Oldham, isn't it?' 'Nowe, it's i'th' Yettons.'

'An' I come fro' th' Slaunches,' a third would say; 'an' me fro' Hee Doldrum,' continued another; and I fro' th' Tunchil; and I fro' Sholver-moor; and so they went on, concluding by another 'loud laugh' in which our friendly Paddies would join in their way, and soon after the interrogator would be missing.

The street, from York-street, to the end of the Theatre, was by this time almost filled by a crowd; and huzzas, or hisses, (though the latter were very rare,) were set up on the outskirts, as fresh bodies of working men arrived. It was considerably past seven o'clock: there was no appearance of the doors being opened, and several persons had been heard to say there would not be any performance. In a short time the rumour became more confident, that the doors would not be opened, still, no one stirred from his post, and I and my party, with our Irish around us, kept the pit door. The people began to get impatient, and one or two young fellows, brave with wine, were roughly handled for 'experimenting.' A messenger at length arrived with authority to say, 'there would not be any play, and the people might as well disperse and go home.' We called him to us, and he came, and repeated his message. I asked him for his authority? and he said Mr Ward the manager had sent him. I asked if I could see Mr Ward myself? He said I could, and offered to conduct me to him, and I gave my stick to a comrade, and followed the man into the rear of the Theatre, where he opened a door and ushered me into a room in which were a number of respectably dressed persons; one of whom advancing, addressed me with

'Bamford! wot the d—— art thou doing here?'

'Hallo; friend Nadin, – is that you?' was my reply. It was Mr Nadin, the deputy constable who spoke.

'Me? – aye its me! – but wot the d——l dus theaw want i'th' teawn at this time o'th' neet?'

'I'm come to th' play, th' same as yo' ar', I suppose. – But I want neaw to see Mr Ward, th' manager.' Several persons spoke, and, I think they said, he was in conversation with the head constables.

'Wot mun theaw want to see a play for?' said Mr Nadin.

'Oh! I'm rayther curious to see one; I untherstond it's to be a good un to-neet.'

'I kno' thee of owd; – I've seen the afore at Middleton, – Theaw may go wom, – Theaw'll see no play here.'

'I'll see one iv there is ony to be seen, or I'll ston at yon' dur till twelve o'clock. – That yo' may depend on, Jozif.'

'Who ar' yon gang 'at theaw has wi' the'?' he said.

'Oh! they're a set o' lads fro' different heawses obeawt, – they'n tell yo' if yo'n ax' 'em.'

'Well they'nd better pack off, an' thee wi' 'em, for by —— if there's any damage done, I'll look afther yo'. Theaw may tell 'em, they'n ha' no play to-neet.'

'Then nobody will,' said I, as I went out, and shut the door after me.

I had scarcely got to my former station, when a coach drove into the street, and on its being ascertained that it contained Hunt, Thomas Chapman, and other friends, a loud huzza burst from the dense multitude, mingled with a few hisses; but the minority were quickly silenced.

Hunt then mounted the box, and addressing the people, stated that the manager had written to him, saying there would not be any performance that night, and requesting (I think) that he would come up and try to get the people to disperse, and go home. He next entered on some general topics, and with singular bad taste, to say the least of it, (for his impetuosity over-ran his judgment,) he said, 'the authorities only wanted a pretext to let the bloody butchers of Waterloo, loose upon the people;' and concluded by advising them to retire to their homes peaceably. We then gave three cheers; the carriage disappeared, and the street was soon deserted. Our party went to the Robin Hood, where we were joined by a score or two of others, and we set to, and caroused until midnight, and then returned home.

It was a fortunate circumstance, that whilst we were making merry, not a whisper escaped to us, of another outrage and insult which was then being perpetrated on our friend and guest. A party of 'gentlemen,' so styled, forced themselves into his private room at the Spread Eagle, and about a dozen of them, bravely, and magnanimously, offered battle to three or four. They were a set of 'lucky dogs.' Had they been taken by us in the fact, there would have been a sore and pitiable account of them in the morning. But fate ordained otherwise; they escaped, and we,

Whilst echoes were ringing
Went laughing and singing
To the merry green woods again.

130

Chapter 30

AMONGST the meetings for reform held in the early part of the summer of 1819, were the one which took place on Spafields, London, at which Mr Hunt was chairman; and another held at Birmingham, at which Major Cartwright and Sir Charles Wolsely were elected to act as legislatorial attornies for that town, in parliament.

It would seem that these movements in the country, induced our friends at Manchester to adopt a course similar to that at Birmingham, and it was accordingly arranged that a meeting for that purpose should be held on St Peter's Field, on the 9th of August. But the object of that meeting having been declared illegal by the authorities, it was countermanded, and another was appointed to be held on the 16th of the same month.

It was deemed expedient that this meeting should be as morally effective as possible, and, that it should exhibit a spectacle such as had never before been witnessed in England. We had frequently been taunted by the press, with our ragged, dirty appearance, at these assemblages; with the confusion of our proceedings, and the mob-like crowds in which our numbers were mustered; and we determined that, for once at least, these reflections should not be deserved, – that we would disarm the bitterness of our political opponents by a display of cleanliness, sobriety, and decorum, such as we never before had exhibited. In short, we would deserve their respect by shewing that we respected ourselves, and knew how to exercise our rights of meeting, as it were well Englishmen always should do, – in a spirit of sober thoughtfulness; respectful, at the same time, to the opinions of others.

'CLEANLINESS,' 'SOBRIETY,' 'ORDER,' were the first injunctions issued by the committees; to which, on the suggestion of Mr Hunt, was subsequently added that of, 'PEACE.' The fulfilment of the two first was left to the good sense of those who intended to join our procession to this 'grand meetings'; the observance of the third and of the last injunctions, – ORDER, PEACE, – were provided

for by general regulations. Order in our movements was obtained by drilling; and peace, on our parts, was secured, by a prohibition of all weapons of offence or defence; and by the strictest discipline, of silence, steadiness, and obedience to the directions of the conductors. Thus our arrangements, by constant practice, and an alert willingness, were soon rendered perfect, and ten thousand men moved with the regularity of ten score.

These drillings were also, to our sedentary weavers and spinners, periods of healthful exercise and enjoyment. Our drill masters were generally old soldiers of the line, or of militia, or local militia regiments; they put the lads through their facings in quick time, and soon learned them to march with a steadiness and regularity which would not have disgraced a regiment on parade. When dusk came, and we could no longer see to work, we jumped from our looms, and rushed to the sweet cool air of the fields, or the waste lands, or the green lane-sides. We mustered, we fell into rank, we faced, marched, halted, faced about, countermarched, halted again, dressed, and wheeled in quick succession, and without confusion; or, in the grey of a fine Sunday morn, we would saunter through the mists, fragrant with the night odour of flowers, and of new hay, and ascending the Tandle Hills, salute the broad sun, as he climbed from behind the high moors of Saddleworth; when,

> Lo! what a world is before us spread,
> From the fringed dell, to the mountain head;
> From the spangled turf whereon we stand,
> To the bend of heaven, and the verge of land.
> Like an ocean-bed, 'tis wide, 'tis deep;
> To the right, to the left, green hills do sweep;
> And Blackstone-edge in his sunless pride,
> Doth York from Lancaster divide;
> Whilst on to the south, if away we bear,
> Oh! what shall bar our vision there?
> Nought, save the blending of earth and sky,
> Dim and afar, as eternity.

Maidens would sometimes come with their milk-cans, from the farms of Hools-wood, or Gerrard-hey, or the fold near us; and we would sit and take delicious draughts, new from the churn, for which we paid the girls in money, whilst a favoured youth or so, might be permitted to add something more, a tender word or a

salute, when blushing and laughing, away would the nymphs run, for a fresh supply to carry home.

Next would follow a long drill, in squads; and so expert were the youths, that they would form a line, and march down the face, or up the steep, or along the sides of the Rush-penny; and suddenly halting, would dress in an instant, in a manner which called forth the praises of the old campaigners. Then, when they broke for a little rest, would follow a jumping match, or a race, or a friendly wrestle, or a roll down the hill, amid the laughter of others sitting in the sun. Some would be squatted on the lee of a bush of gorse or tall fern; some reading, some conversing, in earnest discussion on the state of trade, or national affairs, or on their own privations, or those of their neighbours, – for few secrets were kept of those matters, – some would be seen smoking their pipes kindled by burning-glasses; and so till the bugle sounded to drill, and after that, away to breakfast.

Such was one of our drilling parties. There was not any arms, – no use for any, – no pretence for any; – nor would they have been permitted. Some of the elderly men, the old soldiers, or those who came to watch, might bring a walking staff; or a young fellow might pull a stake from a hedge, in going to drill, or in returning home; but assuredly, we had nothing like arms about us. There were no armed meetings. – there were no midnight drillings. Why should we seek to conceal what we had no hesitation in performing in broad day? There was not anything of the sort. – No arming, – no concealed meetings. Such as I have described, were all our drillings, about which so much was afterwards said. We obtained by them all we sought, or thought of, – an expertness and order whilst moving in bodies; and there was no hyperbole in the statement which a magistrate afterwards made on oath, that 'the party with the blue and green banners came upon the field in beautiful order!' adding, I think, that 'not until then did he become alarmed.'

Some extravagancies; some acts, and some speeches, better let alone, certainly did take place. When the men clapped their hands in 'standing at ease,' some would jokingly say, it was 'firing,' whilst those who were sent to observe us, (and probably we were seldom unattended by such,) and who knew little about military motions, would take the joke as a reality, and report accordingly; whence probably, it would be surmised that we had arms, and that our drillings were only preparatory to their more effective use.

Chapter 31

Papers relative to the Internal State of the Country: presented to both Houses
of Parliament, by the Prince Regent

BUT, extracts from 'Papers relative to the internal state of the
country,' which were laid before parliament in November, 1819,
will explain all that is requisite to be known of our proceedings, and
of the views of the authorities thereupon.

New Bailey Court House, 1st July, 1819.

MY LORD,

As magistrates of this district, we feel ourselves called upon to
communicate to your Lordship, our impressions upon the present
state of affairs within the reach of our observation. We are far
from wishing to yield to unnecessary alarm: but when we entertain serious apprehensions, we cannot refrain from making them
known to your Lordship.

We feel a difficulty in stating to your Lordship, any specific
facts upon which legal responsibility will attach to any particular
individuals at present; but, upon the general view of the subject,
we cannot have a doubt that some alarming insurrection is in
contemplation.

Of the deep distresses of the manufacturing classes of this extensive population, your Lordship is fully apprised, and the dis-
affected and ill-disposed lose no opportunity of instilling the
worst principles into the unhappy sufferers in these times, attrib-
uting their calamities not to any event which cannot be controlled,
but to the general measures of Government and Parliament; and
when the people are oppressed with hunger, we do not wonder at
their giving ear to any doctrines which they are told will redress
their grievances.

Although we cannot but applaud the hitherto peaceable demeanour of many of the labouring classes, yet we do not calculate
upon their remaining unmoved. Urged on by the harangues of a
few desperate demagogues, we anticipate at no distant period, a
general rising; AND POSSESSING NO POWER TO PREVENT
THE MEETINGS WHICH ARE WEEKLY HELD, we, as magis-

trates, are at a loss how to stem the influence of the dangerous and seditious doctrines which are continually disseminated. To these meetings and the unbounded liberty of the press, we refer the principal weight of the evil which we apprehend.

We believe, on Monday next, a meeting will be held at Blackburn, and on the following Monday, at Manchester, at both of which Sir Charles Wolsely is to preside. AS THE LAW NOW STANDS WE CANNOT INTERFERE WITH THESE MEETINGS, NOTWITHSTANDING OUR DECIDED CONVICTION OF THEIR MISCHIEF AND DANGER. We are most anxious to do every thing in our power to preserve the peace of the country, but UPON THIS MOST IMPORTANT POINT WE ARE UNARMED.

We have the honour to be,
Your Lordship's most faithful and obdt. Servants,

J. SILVESTER,   C. W. ETHELSTON,
R. WRIGHT,   J. NORRIS.
W. MARRIOTT,

Lord Viscount Sidmouth.

———

Manchester Police Office, July 16, 1819

At a meeting of the Committee 'To Strengthen the Civil Power,'

JOHN BRADSHAW, ESQ., in the Chair.

The following Resolutions were passed unanimously:—

THAT Government having signified their approbation of an Armed Association, an offer be immediately made by this Committee, through the medium of the Lord Lieutenant of this county, of an Armed Association in aid of the civil power, and for the protection of the towns of Manchester and Salford, and their immediate neighbourhood; and that Government be requested for the present to furnish Arms and Accountrements for one thousand men.

That this Committee do not conceive that any uniform will be necessary for such Armed Association.

That it is on every account desirable that the least possible sacrifice of time should be required in drilling, as it is considered only necessary that the most simple parts of military discipline should be required by such Association.

That a deputation, consisting of Mr. Norris, the resident magistrate, and Mr Moor, the first constable of Manchester, do immediately wait upon the Lord Lieutenant of the county, to communicate the foregoing resolutions, and to take his opinion thereupon.

John Bradshaw, Chairman.

Manchester, August 5th, 1819.

MY LORD,

HEREWITH I transmit your Lordship two Hand-bills published here, by which you will find that the meeting for Monday is put off. This I believe will be a great disappointment to the neighbouring towns, which have provided numbers of Flags and Caps of Liberty for the ensuing occasion. The drilling parties increase VERY EXTENSIVELY, and unless some mode be devised of putting this system down, it promises to become a most formidable engine of rebellion. I expect the operation of the Watch and Ward Act will have great effect in this instance.

I have the honour to be, my Lord,
Your Lordship's faithful and humble Servant,
Lord Viscount Sidmouth.   J. Norris.

The information of Arthur Taylor, of Great Bolton, warper.

Who saith, That he went by the direction of the magistrates, to Cockey Moor on Saturday evening, to observe the persons that were suspected to be drilling or training and exercising there: that it was about a quarter past eight in the evening, when informant got to the moor; there were about one hundred persons drilling. The prisoner George Greenhalgh was giving the word of command to about thirty-six men; they were in open column, told off in three or four divisions when informant got to them. They had been marching in files when informant first saw them. George Greenhalgh ordered them to form the line; they then advanced in line, and they did many other manoeuvres, George Greenhalgh giving the word of command. Informant was close to them. There were two other divisions on the moor, exercising under the command of other persons; these two other divisions had each about the same number of men as that under George Greenhalgh: that informant, with several others, apprehended George Greenhalgh that night: that informant, on Greenhalgh being apprehended, asked him if he had been in the army, he said, 'yes, a little, he had been in the Bury volunteers.' Informant asked him, what they were drilling for, and he replied, only to go to the meeting at Manchester on Monday, so that they might march to the band.

Sworn before, { Ra. Fletcher.   Arthur Taylor.
               { Jas. Watkins.

———

The Examination of *B. C.* taken upon Oath at Rochdale, in the County of Lancaster, the 9th Day of August, 1819, before us, John Beswick and John Crossley, Esquires, two of his Majesty's Justices of the Peace in and for the said County;

Who says, That yesterday morning I left my residence at High Crompton, between the hours of four and five, and proceeded to a place in Thornham, called Tandle Hill; that, on my arrival at this place, a large concourse of persons had assembled, to the number of two or three thousand; that of this number there were upwards of seven hundred who were drilling in companies, by marching both in slow, quick, and double quick time, and in every other respect went through the usual evolutions of a regiment; that each company might contain from fifty to sixty men, and were commanded by a person in the character of a captain, that when they were ordered to fire, it was immediately followed by a clap of hands throughout the line; that out of the number who were met, I knew a few persons who resided in Crompton, and its neighbourhood; but, of the men who were acting as drill serjeants, or officers of companies, I know nothing; yet, from my knowledge of military discipline, I am satisfied they were persons capable of organizing a regiment; that, whilst I was on the ground, I heard persons say, that they (meaning the parties in drill) were fit to contend with any regular troops, only that they wanted arms; and in the evening of yesterday, a man told me who had been at Tandle Hill, and who said he had been drilled that day, that a similar meeting would take place next Sunday, but that would be the last; that the persons remained on the ground until about seven o'clock, having been there upwards of three hours, and the whole of this time was devoted to drilling.

Sworn before { John Beswick, John Crossley. }   B.C.

———

Manchester, August 12th, 1819.

MY LORD,

HEREWITH I have the honour to transmit your Lordship certain depositions, as well respecting the situation in which certain parts of this town have been during the last week, as respecting the practice of drilling, which has so extensively taken place in this and the surrounding neigbourhood. Many more are in existence and may be added to the number, but I apprehend those which I now send will be sufficient to assure your Lordship of this alarming practice. THEY AFFECT TO SAY, THAT IT IS FOR THE PURPOSE OF APPEARING AT MANCHESTER IN BETTER ORDER, &c. on Monday next; but military discipline was not requisite for this purpose, and a more alarming object is so palpable, that it is impossible not to feel a moral conviction that insurrection and rebellion is their ulterior object.

Lord Viscount Sidmouth.   J. Norris.

F. G. maketh oath and saith, That on Thursday night, the fifth of August, he went to a field in the township of Failsworth, belonging to Robert Bury, where he saw about ninety persons, divided into four divisions and a small division which they called the awkward squad; that there was a man to give the word of command; that deponent heard them commanded to march to the right and left, to wheel, fire, &c. that the men had no fire-arms, but when the word 'fire' was given they clapped their hands together; and after they had done exercising, they formed a circle round their commander, who told them, that the intended meeting was put off, on account of their paper being illegal, but that would give them more time to drill: he then said they must have a colour, and that they must subscribe; that the man then took off his hat, and gathered round from some a penny, and from others a halfpenny each; that there were a quantity of women in the field, and the leader of the men called to them to come into the ring, and said they must subscribe also, and that he wanted twelve young ladies to carry their colours, for he was certain if there was a regiment of soldiers drawn up to oppose them they could not find in their hearts to hurt them: and their leader proposed, that as Bury, the owner of the field, had given them leave to drill in it three weeks, he should have the honour of their marching out of it: that the persons assembled did not offer to molest deponent, but damned him for being backward in falling in.

G. H. and H. I. having respectfully read over the affidavit of F. G. severally make oath that the same is true.

Sworn at Manchester aforesaid, the seventh day of August, 1819, before me, one of His Majesty's Justices of the Peace for the county of Lancaster,	Signed, F. G. G. H. H. I.

J. Norris.

———

Lancashire, to wit.

I. K. says, That on Sunday morning last, about five o'clock, in company with * * * he went to Thornham or Tandle Hills, near Middleton, and there saw two or three thousand men, and a number of them exercising in military order; – they had no arms; but he heard distinctly the words of command 'Quick march,' and 'Double quick march.' Deponent particularly noticed one company of about one hundred, march in wings under their leader, and advance also in wings; that the right wing advanced first, and the words of command, 'Fire, front rank kneeling,' and when the word of command 'Fire' was given, they clapped their hands; the leader then advanced the left wing in the same order as the right, and ordered them to fire; this was repeated several times. Deponent and Mr * * * being informed they were to assemble at Slattocks in Thornham, near Middleton aforesaid, they repaired thither, and Deponent and Mr * * * placed themselves by the roadside, in order to ascertain their numbers, when they passed Deponent and Mr * * * marching in military order four deep, when they counted seven hundred men.

Sworn before me at Salford, this tenth day of August, 1819. J. Norris.   I. K.

The Information of Samuel Fletcher, of Little Lever, collier, taken the same day:

Who saith, That on Saturday last informant was on Cockey Moor, about seven o'clock in the evening, and informant observed many persons on the Moor; there might be about two hundred; they were drilling in a military way, in different squads, and obeying the words of command given by different drillmasters; that informant saw them drilling for about two hours; that, about one or two o'clock in the morning, George Greenhalgh, one of the persons now in custody, was in the room at Starling, with several other persons also taken into custody; there were many persons in the room, and in the course of conversation, George Greenhalgh said, That the meaning of their drilling was, that they might come to that perfection, so that they might join their friends and neighbours, in Bury and the neighbourhood, and form themselves into a body at Bury, and march in order with music to the Manchester meeting; he also said, that the meeting would have been on Monday next, (this day) but it was considered to be illegal, and of course it was postponed until the Monday following, and now a requisition to the Borough reeve and Constables of Manchester was signed by more than two thousand inhabitants. Informant asked him, 'what the meaning of such a meeting could be?' George Greenhalgh said, the meaning of such a meeting was, that the country should be properly represented. Informant said, he thought the country was represented; and George Greenhalgh replied, 'No, there was Manchester, Bolton, Bury, and many other towns, that were not represented at all, and it was meant that they should be.'

Sworn before { Ra. Fletcher, Jas. Watkins.   Sam. Fletcher.

———

The Examination of John Hargreaves, of Tottington, weaver, taken the same day;

Saith, That I was not on Cockey Moor on Saturday evening last, nor was ever at any meeting but one, and that was on Monday last, and then I gave the word of command to a small party. I was in the military service thirty-six years ago; I was at the siege of Gibraltar. On Monday last, when I took the command of a small party, there were other parties on the Moor, but I do not know any one that commanded besides me; they were in divisions, and the divisions were at some distance from each other. I have heard that the parties that were drilling were to meet at Bury this day, to go to the meeting at Manchester.

Taken before { Ra. Fletcher   The ╳ Mark of
             { Jas. Watkins.   John Hargreaves.

———

Numerous other depositions appear in the papers, as to drillings, at Failsworth, Cockey Moor, Bury, Oldham, and other places; but these exhibit a fair selection of the whole of the representations made to the magistrates, and by them sent to the Home Office. An attentive perusal of them will, I think, convince the reader that my account of our drillings and their motive, is correct.

Chapter 32

Interview with Mr Hunt — Assault on James Murrey and others, at the White Moss — Meeting at the Police Office, Manchester

ON the afternoon of Friday, the thirteenth of August, I saw Mr Hunt, at the residence of Mr Johnson, at Smedley. Tuke, the painter, was amending Mr Hunt's portrait, which indeed it wanted. In the course of conversation, Mr Hunt expressed himself as apprehensive lest the people from the country should bring arms to the meeting on the following Monday; and he desired me to caution those from Middleton against so doing. He also shewed me a letter on a placard, addressed to 'The Reformers of Manchester and its Neighbourhood,' wherein he entreated them to come to the meeting 'armed only with a self-approving conscience.' He said that if the soldiers did attack the people, and take their caps of liberty and their banners, still, he hoped, they would proceed to the meeting, and not commit any violence.

I must own that this was new, and somewhat unpalatable advice to me. I had not the most remote wish to attack either person or property, but I had always supposed, that Englishmen, whether individually or in bodies, were justifiable by law in repelling an attack when in the King's peace, as I certainly calculated we should be, whilst in attendance at a legally constituted assemblage. My crude notions, which wonderfully coincided with those of the magistrates before quoted, led me to opine that we had a right to go to this place; and that consequently, there would not be any protection in law, to those who might choose to interrupt us in our right. I was almost certain there could be no harm whatever in taking a score or two of cudgels, just to keep the specials at a respectful distance from our line. But this was not permitted.

Still I scarcely liked the idea of walking my neighbours into a crowd, both personally and politically adverse to us; and without means to awe them, or to defend ourselves. Was it not a fact that a numerous body of men had been sworn in to act as special constables? – was not an armed association formed at Manchester? and had not weapons been liberally distributed? and what could we do, if attacked by those men, with nothing to defend ourselves? But Mr Hunt combated these notions. 'Were there not the laws of the country to protect us? would not their authority be upheld by those sworn to administer them? – and then, was it likely at all, that magistrates would permit a peaceable and legal assemblage to be interfered with? – If we were in the right, were they not our guardians? – If wrong, could they not send us home by reading the riot act? – Assuredly, whilst we respected the law, all would be well on our side.'

But, on the Sunday morning, a circumstance occurred which is probably eradicated from the minds of the magistrates and our opponents generally, whatever sentiments of indulgence they might have hitherto retained towards us. It is set forth in the following document, which is also extracted from the before-mentioned papers.

But, I should state, that, at that time, my wife, myself, and child, were in the habit of sleeping at the house of my wife's uncle and aunt Buckley, who lived within a few yards of our residence; and being an elderly couple, without children, and in delicate health, availed themselves particularly during fits of sickness, of our willingness to render them assistance. This was one of those periods; and we had slept at this house a week or two, when, on the morning of Sunday, the 15th of August, on going into the street, I found several neighbours in deep conversation, and soon learned that two men who had approached a party of drillers on the White Moss, had been severely beaten; and that one of them, whose name was Murrey, and who came from Manchester, had been conveyed in a shocking condition to a house in Middleton, and from thence in a coach to Manchester; and that he was not expected to recover. I was concerned on hearing this; not only because I disapproved of the violence which had been committed, but because I saw the advantage it would give our enemies against us, should the least irregularity occur in our proceedings on the following day. It was however past, and so far irremediable, and all we could do was to exhibit the greater coolness and steadiness in whatever situation we might be placed. It was certainly a misfortune; and nothing remained but to make the best of it.

The following document is the one before referred to.

Examination of James Murrey, of No. 2, Withy Grove, Manchester, Confectioner, who, on his Oath, saith, that on Sunday last, the 15th instant, he was at White Moss, near Middleton, about five miles from Manchester, between three and four o'clock in the morning, and saw there assembled between 14 and 1500 men, the greatest number of whom were formed in two bodies, in the form of solid squares; the remainder were in small parties of between twenty and thirty each: there were about thirty such parties, each under the direction of a person acting as a drill serjeant, and were going through military movements; that Examinant went amongst them, and immediately one of the drill serjeants asked him to fall in. He said he thought he should soon, or gave some such answer: he then began to move away: upon which, some persons who were drilling, cried out 'Spies.' This Examinant, and William Shawcross, and Thomas Rymer and his son, (all of whom had accompanied this Examinant from Manchester,) continued to retire; the body of men then cried out, 'Mill them.' 'Murder them.' Near one hundred men then pursued this Examinant and his companions; they overtook them near a lane-end, at the edge of the moss, and began to pelt them with clods of earth, – they at last came up to the Examinant, and his companions, and beat them very severely – Examinant begged they would not murder him; but the general cry was, damn him, kill him – murder him.' – Examinant said, 'you treat ME very differently to what nations treat each other's prisoners when THEY are at war. Suppose that I am an enemy, you ought to treat me as a prisoner;' they said, 'how will you treat us, if you take us prisoners when we come to Manchester?'

Examinant knew at the time that a meeting was appointed for the next day, (Monday) at Manchester.

The men kept beating Examinant all the time; at last, they debated among themselves whether they would kill Examinant or forgive him, and they determined to forgive him provided he would go down upon his knees and beg pardon to them, and swear never to be a King's man again, or to mention the name of a King. Examinant complied to save his life, they standing over him with sticks as he apprehended to murder him, provided he had objected. They afterwards went away. Examinant was not previously acquainted with any of the persons assembled that he saw, but is certain that he should know again two of those who beat him.

The greatest part of the number assembled had stout sticks, from three to four feet long.

In consequence of the ill-treatment received by Examinant as above, he was confined to his bed for three days.

Sworn at Manchester before me,   }   James Murrey.
this 21st day of August, 1819.   }
         Ra. Fletcher.

Some years afterwards, a young man named Robert Lancashire, informed me that the detection of, and assault on these parties happened as follows.

He said he was coming from his work at Manchester, late on Saturday night, when he fell into company with some men whom he did not know, but who proved to be Murrey and his companions. The men began to converse with him, chiefly on the state of the country, and as he was of a communicative turn, they questioned him about the drilling parties, and particularly those which were said to frequent the White Moss; and he told them all he knew about such parties. The people at the White Lion at Blackley, were up, and they all went into the house and had something to drink, during which he promised to shew the men into the road leading to the Moss. He also heard them use expressions to each other, which convinced him they were sent by the police to watch the drillers; and as they were going to take advantage of others, he determined to do the same by them. He accordingly put them into a road which led to the Moss, and afterwards taking a shorter way over the fields, he apprized the drillers of the sort of persons who were coming, and the consequence was, that they were set upon and beaten as described by James Murrey.

This circumstance, as before intimated, was unfortunate to us. On the return of Murrey and his companions to Manchester they were visited by some of the authorities, to whom their statements were given. A special meeting was held at the police office the same forenoon; and it is probable that, at that meeting, it was determined to return a full measure of severity to us on the following day, should any circumstance arise to sanction such a proceeding.

Chapter 33

Meeting at Langley Dingle — Morning of the 16th of August — Arrangements at Middleton — Address by the Author — Arrival of the Rochdale People — Procession towards Manchester

THE same forenoon we had a meeting in Langley Dingle, a pleasant and retired spot, where was a sheltered bank sloping towards the sun, with plenty of bushes and dry grass, and a rindle tumbling at our feet. Here, whilst some were sitting, some lying, and some pacing to and fro', we discussed and arranged our plans for the succeeding day.

All allowed that the occurrence at the White Moss was an un-favourable one; and I, now more than ever, impressed with the belief that we should meet with opposition of some sort, proposed that a party of men with stout cudgels should be appointed to take care of the colours, in order, that at all events, they might be pre-served. This was discussed at some length, but the more confiding views of my neighbours, together with Mr Hunt's admonition pre-vailing, my suggestion was over-ruled, and we shortly after sep-arated.

I may say, that with myself, the preservation of our colours, under any circumstances was a point of honour, worth any sacrifice. Fortunately, more placid views than mine prevailed; and if an aspect of entire confidence could have disarmed party feeling, it would have been done the following morning. But such is seldom the case; and it was not so in the present instance, as will soon appear.

By eight o'clock on the morning of Monday, the 16th of August, 1819, the whole town of Middleton might be said to be on the alert; some to go to the meeting, and others to see the procession; the like of which for such a purpose, had never before taken place, in that neighbourhood.

First were selected twelve of the most comely and decent-looking youths, who were placed in two rows of six each, with each a branch of laurel held presented in his hand, as a token of amity and peace, – then followed the men of several districts in fives, – then the band of music, an excellent one, – then the colours; a blue one of silk, with inscriptions in golden letters, 'UNITY AND STRENGTH.' 'LIBERTY AND FRATERNITY.' A green one of silk, with golden letters, 'PARLIAMENTS ANNUAL.' 'SUFFRAGE UNIVERSAL'; and betwixt them on a staff, a handsome cap of crimson velvet, with a tuft of laurel, and the cap tastefully braided with the word, LIBERTAS, in front. Next were placed the remainder of the men of the districts in fives, – the districts being as follows. Middleton proper, or that part of the town next to the Church, – Back-o'th'-Brow, – Barrowfields, – Boarshaw, – Stakehill and Thornham, – Hopwood, – Heabers – Birch, – Bowlee, – Heatons, – Rhodes, – Blackley, – Alkrington, – Little Park, – Tonge, – Parkfield, – Wood-street, and Middleton Wood. Some hundreds also joined us from Heywood.

Every hundred men had a leader, who was distinguished by a sprig of laurel in his hat; others similarly distinguished, were appointed over these, and the whole were to obey the directions of a principal conductor, who took his place at the head of the column, with a bugleman to sound his orders. Such were our dispositions on the ground at Barrowfields. At the sound of the bugle, not less than three thousand men formed a hollow square, with probably as many people around them, and an impressive silence having been obtained, I reminded them, that they were going to attend the most important meeting that had ever been held for Parliamentary Reform, and I hoped their conduct would be marked by a steadiness and seriousness befitting the occasion, and such as would cast shame upon their enemies, who had always represented the reformers as a mob-like rabble: but they would see they were not so that day. I requested they would not leave their ranks, nor shew carelessness, nor inattention to the order of their leaders; but that they would walk comfortably and agreeably together. Not to offer any insult or provocation by word or deed; nor to notice any persons who might do the same by them, but to keep such persons as quiet as possible; for if they begun to retaliate, the least disturbance might serve as a pretext for dispersing the meeting. If the peace officers should come to arrest myself or any other person, they were not to offer any resistance, but suffer them to execute their office peaceably. When at the meeting, they were to keep themselves as select as possible, with their banners in the centre, so that if individuals straggled, or got away from the main body, they would know where to find them again by seeing their banners; and when the meeting was dissolved, they were to get close around their banners and leave the town as soon as possible, lest, should they stay drinking, or loitering about the streets, their enemies should take advantage, and send some of them to the New Bailey. I also said, that in conformity with a rule of the committee, no sticks, nor weapons of any description, would be allowed to be carried in the ranks; and those who had such, were requested to put them aside, or leave them with some friend until their return. In consequence of this order, many sticks were left behind; and a few only, of the oldest and most infirm amongst us, were allowed to carry their walking staves. I may say with truth, that we presented a most respectable assemblage of labouring men; all were decently, though humbly attired; and I noticed not even one, who did not exhibit a white Sundays' shirt, a neck-cloth, and other apparel in the same clean, though homely condition.

My address was received with cheers, it was heartily and unanimously assented to, – we opened into column, – the music struck up, – the banners flashed in the sun-light, – other music was heard, – it was that of the Rochdale party coming to join us, – we met; and a shout from ten thousand startled the echoes of the woods and dingles. Then all was quiet save the breath of music; and with intent seriousness, we went on.

Our whole column, with the Rochdale people, would probably consist of six thousand men. At our head were a hundred or two of women, mostly young wives, and mine own was amongst them. – A hundred or two of our handsomest girls, – sweethearts to the lads who were with us, – danced to the music, or sung snatches of popular songs: a score or two of children were sent back, though some went forward; whilst, on each side of our line walked some thousands of stragglers. And thus, accompanied by our friends, and our dearest and most tender connections, we went slowly towards Manchester.

Chapter 34

Blackley — Harperhey — Hunt at Smedley — Personal Incident — Newtown — Progress to St Peter's Field — Our Situation there

AT Blackley, the accession to our ranks, and the crowd in the road had become much greater. At Harperhey, we halted, whilst the band and those who thought proper, refreshed with a cup of prime ale from Sam Ogden's tap. When the bugle sounded, every man took his place, and we advanced.

From all that I had heard of the disposition of the authorities, I had scarcely expected that we should be allowed to enter Manchester in a body. I had thought it not improbable that they, or some of them, would meet us, with a civil and military escort; would read the riot act, if they thought proper, and warn us from proceeding, and that we should then have nothing to do but turn back and hold a meeting in our town. I had even fancied that they would most likely stop us at the then toll-gate, where the roads forked towards Collyhurst and Newtown; but when I saw both those roads open, with only a horseman or two prancing before us, I began to think that I had over-estimated the forethought of the authorities; and I felt somewhat assured that we should be allowed to enter the town quietly, when, of course, all probability of interruption would be at an end.

We had got a good length on the higher road towards Collyhurst, when a messenger arrived from Mr Hunt, with a request that we would return, and come the lower road; and lead up his procession into Manchester. I at first, determined not to comply: I did not like to entangle ourselves, and the great mass now with us, in the long hollow road through Newtown; where, whatever happened, it would be difficult to advance, or retreat, or disperse; and I kept moving on. But a second messenger arrived, and there was a cry of

148

'Newtown,' 'Newtown;' and so I gave the word, 'left shoulders forward,' and running at the charge step, we soon gained the other road, and administered to the vanity of our 'great leader,' by heading his procession from Smedley Cottage.

A circumstance interesting to myself now occurred. On the bank of an open field on our left, I perceived a gentleman observing us attentively. He beckoned me, and I went to him. He was one of my late employers, Mr Hole, of the firm of Hole, Wilkinson, and Gartside, of Peel-street, and one of the heads of the town. He took my hand, and rather concernedly, but kindly, said he hoped no harm was intended by all those people who were coming in. I said 'I would pledge my life for their entire peaceableness'. I asked him to notice them, 'did they look like persons wishing to outrage the law? were they not, on the contrary, evidently heads of decent working families? or members of such families?' 'No, no,' I said, 'my dear sir, and old respected master, if any wrong or violence take place, they will be committed by men of a different stamp from these.' He said he was very glad to hear me say so; he was happy he had seen me, and gratified by the manner in which I had expressed myself. I asked, did he think we should be interrupted at the meeting? he said he did not believe we should; 'then,' I replied, 'all will be well;' and shaking hands, with mutual good wishes, I left him, and took my station as before.

At Newtown we were welcomed with open arms by the poor Irish weavers, who came out in their best drapery, and uttered blessings and words of endearment, many of which were not understood by our rural patriots. Some of them danced, and others stood with clasped hands and tearful eyes, adoring almost, that banner whose colour was their national one, and the emblem of their green island home. We thanked them by the band striking up, 'Saint Patrick's day in the morning;' they were electrified; and we passed on, leaving those warm-hearted suburbans capering and whooping like mad.

Having squeezed ourselves through the gully of a road below St Michael's Church, we traversed Blackley-street, and Miller's lane; and went along Swan-street, and Oldham-street; frequently hailed in our progress by the cheers of the townspeople. We learned that other parties were on the field before us, and that the Lees and Saddleworth Union had been led by Doctor Healey, walking before a pitch-black flag, with staring white letters, forming the words, 'Equal Representation or death.' – 'Love,' – two hands joined, and a heart; all in white paint, and presenting one of the most sepulchral looking objects that could be contrived. The idea of my diminutive friend leading a funeral procession of his own patients, such it appeared to me, was calculated to force a smile even at that thoughtful moment.

We now perceived we had lost the tail of our train, and understood that we had come the wrong way, and should have led down Shudehill, and along Hanging Ditch, the Market-place, and Deansgate; which route Hunt and his party had taken. I must own, I was not displeased at this separation. I was of opinion that we had rendered homage quite sufficient to the mere vanity of self-exhibition; too much of which I now thought, was apparent.

Having crossed Piccadilly, we went down Mosley-street, then almost entirely inhabited by wealthy families. We took the left side of St. Peter's Church; and at this angle, we wheeled quickly and steadily into Peter-street, and soon approached a wide unbuilt space, occupied by an immense multitude, which opened and received us with loud cheers. We walked into that chasm of human beings, and took our station from the hustings across the causeway of Peter-street; and so remained, undistinguishable from without, but still forming an almost unbroken line, with our colours in the centre.

My wife I had not seen for some time; but when last I caught a glimpse of her, she was with some decent married females; and thinking the party quite safe in their own discretion, I felt not much uneasiness on their account, and so had greater liberty in attending to the business of the meeting.

Our colours had at first been handed to the hustings; our music was already playing there. I ascended the hustings, and found them occupied by a number of men of whom I knew nothing. I desired them to get down, and to clear the boards for the speakers who were coming, and would shortly be there. I found it impossible to get them to quit; they knew not me; and they intimated that they would neither comply with my wishes on that point, nor any other persons. I therefore struck our colours from where they had been fastened, and ordered them and the music back to the centre of our body; and then taking a survey of the meeting, which I found to be of tremendous magnitude, I came down and went with the colours.

Successive parties kept arriving on the ground, and we became deeper inclosed, until we occupied about the centre of that vast multitude.

Chapter 35

IN about half an hour after our arrival at the meeting, the sounds of music, and reiterated shouts, proclaimed the near approach of Mr Hunt and his party; and in a minute or two they were seen coming from towards Deansgate, preceded by a band of music, and several flags. On the driving seat of a barouche sat a neatly dressed female, supporting a small flag, on which were some emblematical drawings, and an inscription. Within the carriage were Mr Hunt who stood up, Mr Johnson, of Smedley Cottage; Mr Moorhouse of Stockport; Mr Carlile of London; Mr John Knight of Manchester; and Mr Saxton, a sub-editor of the Manchester Observer Newspaper. Their approach was hailed by one universal shout from probably eighty thousand persons. They threaded their way slowly past us, and through the crowd, which Hunt eyed, I thought with almost as much of astonishment as satisfaction. This spectacle could not be otherwise in his view, than solemnly impressive. Such a mass of human beings he had never beheld till then. His responsibility must weigh on his mind. Their power for good or evil was irresistible, and who should direct that power? Himself alone who had called it forth. The task was great, and not without its peril. The meeting was indeed a tremendous one. He mounted the hustings; the music ceased; Mr Johnson proposed that Mr Hunt should take the chair; it was seconded, and carried by acclamation; and Mr Hunt, stepping towards the front of the stage, took off his white hat, and addressed the people.

Whilst he was doing so, I proposed to an acquaintance, that, as the speeches and resolutions were not likely to contain anything new to us, and as we could see them in the papers, we should retire awhile, and get some refreshment, of which I stood in much need, being in not very robust health. He assented, and we had got to nearly the outside of the crowd, when a noise and strange murmur arose towards the church. Some persons said it was the Blackburn people coming; and I stood on tip-toe, and looked in the direction whence the noise proceeded, and saw a party of cavalry in blue and white uniform, come trotting sword in hand, round the corner of a garden-wall, and to the front of a row of new houses, where they reined up in a line.

'The soldiers are here,' I said, 'we must go back and see what this means.' 'Oh,' some one made reply, 'they are only come to be ready if there should be any disturbance in the meeting.' 'Well, let us go back,' I said, and we forced our way towards the colours.

On the cavalry drawing up they were received with a shout, of good will, as I understood it. They shouted again, waving their sabres over their heads; and then, slackening rein, and striking spur into their steeds, they dashed forward, and began cutting the people.

'Stand fast,' I said, 'they are riding upon us, stand fast.' And there was a general cry in our quarter of 'Stand fast.' The cavalry were in confusion: they evidently could not, with all the weight of man and horse, penetrate that compact mass of human beings; and their sabres were plied to hew a way through naked held-up hands, and defenceless heads; and then chopped limbs, and wound-gaping skulls were seen; and groans and cries were mingled with the din of that horrid confusion. 'Ah! ah!' 'for shame! for shame!' was shouted. Then, 'Break! break! they are killing them in front, and they cannot get away'; and there was a general cry of 'break! break.' For a moment the crowd held back as in a pause; then was a rush, heavy and resistless as a headlong sea; and a sound like low thunder, with screams, prayers, and imprecations from the crowd-moiled, and sabre-doomed, who could not escape.

By this time Hunt and his companions had disappeared from the hustings, and some of the yeomanry, perhaps less sanguinarily disposed than others, were busied in cutting down the flag-staves, and demolishing the flags at the hustings.

On the breaking of the crowd, the yeomanry wheeled; and dashing wherever there was an opening, they followed, pressing and wounding. Many females appeared as the crowd opened; and striplings or mere youths also were found. Their cries were piteous and heart-rending; and would, one might have supposed, have disarmed any human resentment: but here, their appeals were vain. Women, – white-vested maids, and tender youths, were indiscriminately sabred or trampled; and we have reason for believing, that few were the instances in which that forbearance was vouchsafed, which they so earnestly implored.

In ten minutes from the commencement of the havock, the field was an open and almost deserted space. The sun looked down through a sultry and motionless air. The curtains and blinds of the windows within view were all closed. A gentleman or two might occasionally be seen looking out from one of the new houses before-mentioned, near the door of which, a group of persons, (special constables) were collected, and apparently in conversation; others were assisting the wounded, or carrying off the dead. The hustings remained, with a few broken and hewed flag-staves erect, and a torn and gashed banner or two dropping; whilst over the whole field, were strewed caps, bonnets, hats, shawls, and shoes, and other parts of male and female dress; trampled, torn, and bloody. The yeomanry had dismounted, – some were easing their horses' girths, others adjusting their accoutrements; and some were wiping their sabres. Several mounds of human beings still remained where they had fallen, crushed down, and smothered. Some of these still groaning, – others with staring eyes, were gasping for breath, and others would never breathe more. All was silent save those low sounds, and the occasional snorting and pawing of steeds. Persons might sometimes be noticed peeping from attics and over the tall ridgings of houses, but they quickly withdrew, as if fearful of being observed, or unable to sustain the full gaze, of a scene so hideous and abhorrent.

Chapter 36

Other Military and Civil Preparations on the Field — Incidents of the dispersion — Author's Escape — Visit to Smedley Cottage — Harperhey — Return Home

BESIDES the Manchester yeomanry, who as I have already shewn, did 'the duty of the day,' there came upon the ground soon after the attack, the 15th hussars, and the Cheshire yeomanry; and the latter, as if emulous of the Manchester corps, intercepted the flying masses, and inflicted some severe sabre wounds. The hussars, we have reason for supposing, gave but few wounds, and I am not aware that it has been shewn, that one of those brave soldiers dishonoured his sword by using the edge of it. In addition to the cavalry, a strong body of the 88th foot, was stationed at the lower corner of Dickinson-street: with their bayonets at the charge, they wounded several persons, and greatly impeded the escape of the fugitives by that out-let. Almost simultaneously with the hussars, four pieces of horse artillery appeared from Deansgate, and about two hundred special constables were also in attendance; so that, force for a thorough massacre was ready, had it been wanted.

On the first rush of the crowd, I called to our men to break their flag-staves, and secure their banners, but probably I was not heard, or understood, all being then, inextricable confusion. He with the blue banner, saved it, – the cap of liberty was dropped and left behind – indeed woe to him who stooped, he would never have risen again – and, Thomas Redford, who carried the green banner, held it aloft until the staff was cut in his hand, and his shoulder was divided by the sabre of one of the Manchester yeomanry.

A number of our people, were driven to some timber which lay at the foot of the wall of the Quakers' meeting house. Being pressed by the yeomanry, a number sprung over the balks and defended themselves with stones which they found there. It was not without difficulty, and after several were wounded, that they were driven out. A heroine, a young married woman of our party, with her face all bloody, her hair streaming about her, her bonnet hanging by the string, and her apron weighted with stones, kept her assailant at bay until she fell backwards and was near being taken; but she got away covered with severe bruises. It was near this place and about this time, that one of the yeomanry was dangerously wounded, and unhorsed, by a blow from the fragment of a brick; and it was supposed to have been flung by this woman.

On the first advance of the yeomanry, one of the horses, plunging at the crowd, sent its fore-feet into the head of our big drum, which was left near the hustings, and was irrecoverable. Thus booted on both legs at once, the horse rolled over, and the drum was kicked to pieces in the melee. For my own part I had the good fortune to escape without injury, though it was more than I expected. I was carried, I may say almost literally, to the lower end of the Quakers' meeting house, the further wall of which, screened us from observa-tion and pursuit, and afforded access to some open streets. In my retreat from the field, a well-dressed woman dropped on her knees a little on my left: I put out my hand to pluck her up, but she missed it, and I left her. I could not stop; and God knows what became of her. Two of the yeomanry were next in our way, and I expected a broken head, having laurel in my hat, but one was striking on one side, and the other on the other, and at that moment, I stepped betwixt them and escaped.

After quitting the field, I first found myself in King-street, and passing into Market-street, and High-street, I more leisurely pursued my way, taking care, lest some official should notice me, to remove the laurel from the outside to the inside of my hat. I was now unhappy on account of my wife, and I blamed myself greatly, for consenting to her coming at all; I learned however, when in Saint George's Road, that she was well, and was on the way towards home; and that satisfied me for the time.

Having met with an old neighbour, we agreed to go round past Smedley cottage, to learn what intelligence had arrived there. We descended the hill at Collyhurst, and on arriving at the bottom, we espied a party of cavalry, whom from their dress, I took to be of the Manchester yeomanry, riding along the road we had quitted, towards Harperhey. One of them wore a broad green band, or sash, across his shoulder and breast; I thought from its appearance, it was a fragment of our green banner, and I was not mistaken. They were traversing the suburbs to reconnoitre, and to pick up any person they could identify, (myself for instance, had I then been in their way); and the inglorious exhibition of the torn banner, was permitted for the gratification of the vanity of the captor. This party rode forwards a short distance, and then returned, without making any prisoners from our party.

At Smedley cottage we found Mrs Johnson, her two children, (I think two) her maid servant, and Mr Hunt's groom, who had just come from the town, and had brought the information that Mr Hunt, Mr Johnson, Knight, Moorhouse, and several others, were prisoners in the New Bailey. I was touched by the lady's situation, though she bore the trial better than I could have expected. We gave her some particulars of the meeting, to which she listened with a manner mournfully thoughtful; occasionally shedding tears, and her features pale and calm as marble. She spoke not much: she was evidently too full to hold discourse, and so, with good wishes, and consoling hopes, we took our departure.

We now called at Harperhey, and found at the public-house, and in the road there, a great number of the Middleton and Rochdale people, who had come from the meeting. My first enquiry was for my wife, on whose account I now began to be downright miserable. I asked many about her, but could not hear any tidings, and I turned back towards Manchester, with a resolution to have vengeance if any harm had befallen her. But I had not gone far, ere I espied her at a distance, hastening towards me; we met, and our first emotions were those of thankfulness to God for our preservation. She had been in greater peril and distress of mind, if possible, than myself: the former she escaped in a remarkable manner, and through the intervention of special constables, – to whom let us award their due – She afterwards heard, first that I was killed, – next, that I was wounded, and in the Infirmary, – then, that I was a prisoner, – and lastly that she would find me on the road home. Her anxiety being now removed by the assurance of my safety, she hastened forward to console our child. I rejoined my comrades, and forming about a thousand of them into file, we set off to the sound of fife and drum, with our only banner waving, and in that form we re-entered the town of Middleton.

The banner was exhibited from a window of the Suffield's Arms public-house. The cap of liberty was restored to us by a young man from Chadderton, who had picked it up on the outskirts of the field; and now we spent the evening in recapitulating the events of the day, and in brooding over a spirit of vengeance towards the authors of our humiliation, and our wrong.

Chapter 37

Author's Observations at Manchester — Redford and his Mother — Lunch at the Temple — Arming at Middleton

THOMAS REDFORD, who as before stated, had been wounded, was going to Manchester the following morning to visit his old mother, and I chose to go with him. At the house of an acquaintance of his, where we first called, we found means to procure a disguise for me, as I was desirous to move about without exciting particular notice. My hat was accordingly changed for an old slouched felt; my lapelled coat for an ancient-looking long-waisted surtout, with broad metal buttons; a handkerchief was tied over my mouth, a stick was in my hand, and a wig concealed my hair; and so attired, I walked slowly forth, a tall, pale, and feeble, elderly man, – indifferent health had then rendered me pale. I passed many persons, some of the police, who in my ordinary dress would have known me, but they all seemed quite engaged and in a hurry; and so, confident in my disguise, I made my observations at leisure.

All seemed in a state of confusion; the streets were patrolled by military, police, and special constables: the shops were closed and silent; the warehouses were shut up and padlocked; the Exchange was deserted; the artillery was ready; and it was reported that thousands of pikemen were on the way to Manchester, from Oldham, Middleton, and other surrounding districts. I entered public-houses, called for my squib of cordial, and listened, saying nothing. I overheard the groups in the streets, and the general opinion was that the authorities were stunned, and at a loss how to proceed; that many of the wealthy class blamed them, as well for the severity with which they had acted, as for the jeopardy in which they had placed the lives and property of the townspeople; whilst, all the working population were athirst for revenge, and only awaited the coming of the country folks to attempt a sweeping havock.

Some proposals which I heard assented to, filled me with horror. The immolation of a selected number of the guilty ones might have been discussed before God and man, but what these men sought would not do; and I retired, and put off my dress, more thoughtful than when I took it up.

I found Redford's mother bathing his wound with warm milk and water, and to please her, he said it was easier. It was a clean gash of about six inches in length and quite through the shoulder blade. She yearned, and wept afresh when she saw the severed bone gaping in the wound. She asked who did it? and Tom mentioned a person; he said he knew him well; and she, sobbing, said she also knew him, and his father and mother before him; and she prayed God not to visit that sin on the head of him who did it, but to change his heart and bring him to repentance. That prayer had well-nigh touched my heart also, but Tom rapped out one of another sort, to which I incontinently, as may be supposed, added my 'Amen.'

The wound having been linted, and bound with sticking plaster, Tom put on his clothes, the slash in his coat having been sewed, and the blood sponged off by a young woman. His mother then, with many prayers and much good advice, resigned him, as she said, 'to the guidance of God, through a wild and weary world.'

We called at Smedley cottage, but nothing had been heard of the prisoners since the day preceding.

On arriving at the head of the lane, before descending past Smedley hall, we met two men with a covered basket, and they asked us to go with them. They both knew me, and one of them I knew well: he was a staunch radical, and an influential one as I supposed; his name was Chadwick, and he was a shawl weaver, latterly of Stockport. They had got a good lump of a nice leg of roasted veal, and some ham to match it, and were going to the Temple bowling green to meet some friends, and to discuss their grievances and their viands over a bottle or two of porter. They had taken the meat from a public dinner table in George Leigh-street, the day before. A feast had been provided by the reformers, for the evening's solacement. After the catastrophe, anything, it would seem, was law that could be done, and a band of hungry constables and police, hastened to seize the meat; but the reformers hearing of their intention, removed some of the best joints, and left them to devour the remainder, which they did on the spot, and never paid for it. Such was the account these friends gave of their lunch, and their motive for coming out of town.

We went with them, and met some half dozen others; and a discussion ensued on the state of affairs, and the course that should be taken by the reformers. At last it was agreed to hold a larger meeting the day following on the Tandle Hills, and with mutual pledges to be punctual we separated.

I found when I got home, that there had been a general ferment in the town. Many of the young men had been preparing arms, and seeking out articles to convert into such. Some had been grinding scythes, others old hatchets, others screw-drivers, rusty swords, pikels, and mop-nails: anything which could be made to cut or stab was pronounced fit for service. But no plan was defined, – nothing was arranged, – and the arms were afterwards reserved for any event that might occur.

Chapter 38

THE day following, I attended on the hills with a trusty friend.
Notices had been sent to Oldham, Rochdale, Bury, and some other
places, but at the time appointed no one appeared. We waited for
hours, until the afternoon waned, but no one came; and then we
went down to Royton, to ascertain the disposition of the reformers
of that place. Some had been severely wounded, but most of the
people were carousing, and there did not appear to be any disposition to retaliate the outrage we had suffered, by force and arms.
I called on William Fitton, but he gave no encouragement to such
an idea. I went to John Kay, in Royley-lane, but he was as usual,
imperturbably placid. He was one of the least impassioned men I
ever knew.

After introducing the cause of my visit I asked his opinion, and
in order to obtain it frankly, I spoke the more so. 'If the people were
ever to rise and smite their enemies, was not that the time? Was
every enormity to be endured, and this after all? Were we still to lie
down like whipped hounds, whom nothing could arouse to resistance? Were there not times and seasons, and circumstances, under
which the common rules of wisdom became folly, prudence became
cowardice, and submission became criminal? and was not the
present one of those times and seasons?' It was astonishing that
men could eat and sleep; that, 'the voice of their brothers' blood,
crying from the ground, did not make them miserable.'

'It does make them miserable,' said this philosopher, – for he was
one, if ever such existed in humble life, and we are taught to believe
as much. – 'It does make them miserable; and, on account of this
affair neither you nor I are happy; but our oppressors are wretched.
We, according to the impulse of our nature, wish to avenge that
outrage. Let us be quiet, it is already in the course of avengement.
Those men would, even now, shrink out of existence, if they were
only assured of getting to heaven quietly. They are already invoking
that obliviousness which will never come to their relief.'

'Again. – If the people took vengeance into their own hands, where would they begin? where would they end? Would they de-nounce all Manchester and the whole country?' 'No! no! the authors and perpetrators only.' 'But how could they be got at? would we descend to assassination?' 'No! no!' 'To indiscriminate massacre, like that we had witnessed?' 'Oh! no! no!' 'Could we march against an army?' 'We had no thought of doing so, we had no thought of anything save avenging, in some way, our slain and imprisoned fellow-beings.' 'Then,' he said, 'we had best remain as we were; we should hear of a sensation in many parts, which would forward our cause, but the least outrage on ours would only streng-then the aggressors, and create that plea of justification which alone could mitigate their remorse.' They would exclaim, – 'See, these are the men who came with peace on their lips; behold now the violence of their hearts, – what would they not have done, had we not put them down, – and so, claiming merit for what they had done, they would next arraign their captives, our friends, and have them executed.'

Such was the substance of the arguments of our friend John Kay. His reasons had at all times some weight with me: on this occasion they were conclusive.

Several persons from Middleton came to me whilst at Royton. They said that a number of men representing themselves as depu-ties, had arrived, and were at the Suffield's Arms. On going there I found persons from Manchester, Rochdale, and Blackburn. My heart recoiled from one of the former. He was one of those whose atrocious conversation the day before, had filled me with disgust.

I told them briefly, that I would not take any part in a delegate meeting to discuss the taking up of arms. That I saw not any prospect of succeeding, and if I did, they were not the men with whom I could act. I had sent for men whom I knew, but they came not; strangers came whose faces I had never seen before, and I would not act with such; neither was it to be expected that I should. I then recapitulated the arguments of my friend John Kay, and advised them to return from whence they came, and they soon after did so. The day following, there was another attempt to get up a delegate meeting – the Manchester people seemed determined to have one – but it met with the same fate, and the men, about half a dozen in number, separated without doing any business.

Some days after, I was informed of the arrest of Joseph Healey, at Lees. I began to expect something of the sort myself, and told our constable that if he got a warrant, and would let me know, I would go with him any day, or night, to Manchester, and there should be no fuss; no one should be the wiser. He said he would take that course, should he have a warrant; and I attended to my business as usual.

Chapter 39

Narrative of my Wife's attendance at the Meeting — Of some Scenes she witnessed, and some circumstances which befel her

As a narrative collateral with these passages, the account given by my dear wife, of her attendance at the meeting on Saint Peter's Field, and of some incidents which befel her, may not be devoid of interest to the reader, and certainly will not be out of place, if introduced here. She says:

I was determined to go to the meeting, and should have followed, even if my husband had refused his consent to my going with the procession. From what I, in common with others, had heard the week previous, 'that if the country people went with their caps of liberty, and their banners, and music, the soldiers would be brought to them', I was uneasy, and felt persuaded, in my own mind, that something would be the matter, and I had best go with my husband, and be near him; and if I only saw him I should be more content than in staying at home. I accordingly, he having consented after much persuasion, gave my little girl something to please her, and promising more on my return, I left her with a careful neighbour woman, and joined some other married females at the head of the procession.

Every time I went aside to look at my husband, and that was often, an ominous impression smote my heart. He looked very serious, I thought, and I felt a foreboding of something evil to befal us that day.

I was dressed plainly as a countrywoman, in my second best attire. My companions were also neatly dressed as the wives of working men; I had seen Mr Hunt before that time; they had not, and some of them were quite eager to obtain good places, that they might see and hear one of whom so much had been reported.

In going down Mosley-street, I lost sight of my husband. Mrs Yates, who had hold of my arm, would keep hurrying forward to get a good place, and when the crowd opened for the Middleton procession, Mrs Yates and myself, and some others of the women, went close to the hustings, quite glad that we had obtained such a situation for seeing and hearing all. My husband got on the stage, but when afterwards I saw him leap down, and lost sight of him, I began to be unhappy.

The crowd seemed to have increased very much, for we became insufferably pressed. We were surrounded by men who were strangers; we were almost suffocated, and to me the heat was quite sickening; but Mrs Yates, being taller than myself, supported it better.

I felt I could not bear this long, and I became alarmed. I reflected that if there was any more pressure I must faint, and then what would become of me? and I begged of the men to open a way and let me go out, but they would not move. Every moment I became worse, and I told some other men then, who stood in a row, that I was sick, and begged they would let me pass them, and they immediately made a way, and I went down a long passage betwixt two ranks of these men, many of them saying, 'make way, she's sick, she's sick, let her go out,' and I passed quite out of the crowd, and turning to my right, I got on some high ground, on which stood a row of houses – This was Windmill-street.

I thought if I could get to stand at the door of one of those houses, I should have a good view of the meeting, and should perhaps see my husband again; and I kept going further down the row, until I saw a door open, and I stepped within it, the people of the house making no objections.

By this time Mr Hunt was on the hustings, addressing the people. In a minute or two some soldiers came riding up. The good folks of the house, and some who seemed to be visitors, said, 'the soldiers were only come to keep order; they would not meddle with the people'; but I was alarmed. The people shouted, and then the soldiers shouted, waving their swords. Then they rode amongst the people, and there was a great outcry, and a moment after, a man passed without hat, and wiping the blood off his head with his hand, and it ran down his arm in a great stream.

The meeting was all in a tumult; there were dreadful cries; the soldiers kept riding amongst the people, and striking with their swords. I became faint, and turning from the door, I went unobserved down some steps into a cellared passage; and hoping to escape from the horrid noise, and to be concealed, I crept into a vault, and sat down, faint and terrified, on some fire-wood.

The cries of the multitude outside, still continued, and the people of the house, up stairs, kept bewailing most pitifully. They could see all the dreadful work through the window, and their exclamations were so distressing, that I put my fingers in my ears to prevent my hearing more; and on removing them, I understood that a young man had just been brought past, wounded. The front door of the passage before-mentioned, soon after opened, and a number of men entered, carrying the body of a decent, middle-aged woman, who had been killed. I thought they were going to put her beside me, and was about to scream, but they took her forward, and deposited her in some premises at the back of the house.

I had sat in my hiding place some time, and the tumult seemed abated, when a young girl, one of the family, came into the vault, and suddenly crouching, she bumped against my knee, and starting up, and seeing another dead woman, as she probably thought, she ran up stairs quite terrified, and told her mother. The good woman, Mrs Jones, came down with the girl and several others, and having ascertained that I was living, but sadly distressed, she spoke very kindly, and assisted me to a chair in her front room. She offered me refreshment, and would have made tea, but I declined it. I was too unhappy to take anything except a little water. I could not restrain my feelings, but kept moaning and exclaiming, 'My lad;' – 'My poor lad!' They asked if I was married? and I said I was, and had lost my husband in the crowd, and was afraid he was killed. Those good people did all they could to comfort me. They asked where I came from, and my husband's name? and I told them I came from Middleton, but evaded mentioning his name, lest, on account of his being a leader, I should be put in prison; for though they had behaved most kindly, I doubted whether they would continue to do so, if they knew whose wife I was.

I now became wishful to go, and Mrs Jones called a special constable, and requested he would see me into Market-street, from whence I could find my way. The man very civilly took my arm, and led me over the now almost deserted field. I durst not look aside, lest I should encounter some frightful object, and particularly that which I most dreaded to see, the corpse of my husband, being almost assured he was dead or wounded. I only looked up once, and then saw a great number of horses at rest, and their riders dismounted. I durst scarcely open my eyes; and hurrying with the constable over that dreaded place, we were soon in Market-street, where thanking my conductor for his civility, he returned, and I hastened towards Shudehill, where I met one of our people, who had heard that my husband was killed. Afterwards I was informed that he was in the Infirmary: another said he was in prison; and then I heard that he was gone home; and soon after I had the pleasure of again rejoining him at Harperhey, for which mercy, I sincerely returned thanks to God.

The following list of those wounded and badly bruised, who went with the Middleton party, will conclude, for the present, my notice of the Manchester meeting. It is as follows, viz:—

David Turner, John Fallows, Charles Partington, and Ann Heywood, of Birch, near Middleton. Fallows was cut in the head, and Ann Heywood on the arm; they were afterwards married.

Ellen Evans, and Ellen Walker, of Blackley.

Abel Ashworth, of Church-stile, Rochdale.

James Weir, and James Smith, of Gravel-hole, in Thornham; the latter bruised on the right leg and arm; and badly cut on the hip.

Ann Hilton, of Little Green, near Middleton; cut on the head.

Thomas Barlow, of Little Heaton.

Thomas Kershaw, of Lowerplace, Rochdale.

Thomas Redford, of Middleton; wounded as before mentioned.

William Taylor, of Boardman-lane; badly cut on the head, and was for a considerable time a patient in the infirmary.

Ann Collinge, of Bowlee, near Middleton; very much crushed and bruised.

William Butterworth, of Stake-hill, in Thornham; badly cut on the upper arm; and, John Rhodes, of Three-pits. He was in a weakly state of health when he attended the meeting. He never looked up after, and died in the course of some weeks. His death was said to have been caused by the injuries he received, but a coroner's inquest negatived that; if inquests at that time might be considered of authority.

Total: – Bruised, and wounded by sabre cuts! Eleven men: Five women.

Chapter 40

Author's Second Arrest on a Charge of High Treason

ABOUT two o'clock on the morning of Thursday, the twenty-sixth of August; that is, on the tenth morning after the fatal meeting, I was awoke by footsteps in the street opposite my residence. Presently they increased in number, and came nearer, and from the manner in which they collected, and approached the place, I was convinced a sore trial was at hand for the little woman who lay asleep on my arm, and I felt more concern on her account than on my own. But I may as well narrate the event in verse at once.

> *They came at night, and did surround*
> *My humble dwelling whilst I slept;*
> *And I awoke, and heard a sound*
> *Of feet, as if they softly crept;*
> *And then, a firmer foot there stept,*
> *And then, I heard a number more;*
> *As if a marching pace they kept;*
> *I guessed there might be a score, –*
> *And then they knocked at my door.*
>
> *Awake! my love! I softly said,*
> *Awake! the enemy is near.*
> *Come; kiss me; be not thou afraid,*
> *A wife of mine should never fear.*
> *Arise, and dress yourself, my dear;*
> *These fellows brook but short delays.*
> *Here is your petticoat; and here*
> *Your kirtle, handkerchief, and stays;*
> *For me, love, I can abide their gaze.*

Bang! Bang! came the blows on the door. 'Hallo! who's makin that din at this time o' neet?'

My wife was crying, and all in a tremor, but I cheered her, and told her to be quick, and I would keep them in talk whilst I put on a few things of my own.

'Open the door,' said a voice, authoritatively.

'Open the door' – imitating the voice, – 'an hooa arto, at I should oppen my dur to thee? Theawrt sum drunken eawl or other, or elze theaw wud no' come i' that way.'

'Open the door, or I'll break it,' said the same person.

'Break it wilto? An hooa art theaw ot tawks o' breakin into foke's heawses ot dyed oth neet? Theaw'd better not break it, unless theaws an eyyron pot o' the' yed.'

There was another bang, and a stout push at the door, but they might as well have shoved against the Rock o' Gibraltar: the door had been firmly propped to prevent a too sudden surprise.

'Will you open the door, man?' said another voice.

'Well, but hooa ar yo' an wot dun yo' want? for thurs moor nor won, I yer.'

'We are constables, and we want you,' was the reply.

'Oh! that's a different thing quite: iv yoar constables yo' shan com in by o' myens. Why didno yo' tel me so at forst?'

By this time, both my wife and myself were decently attired; and advancing to the door, I took away the prop, and shot the bar, and bid them come in; and not soil the silk work in the looms.

A crowd of men entered; it was quite dark, but I learned from the sound of gun-stocks on the floor, that we had soldiers. My wife was terrified and clung to me. I told her to get a light, and she went towards the door for that purpose, but shrunk back on running against a musket as she groped her way: the constables also repulsed her. They said she must not go out; they would get a light themselves; and in a short time, Joseph Platt, one of my former conductors to London, appeared with a candle.

I now perceived that my visitors were a strong posse of police; some soldiers of the 32nd regiment; Mr Nadin, the deputy constable of Manchester; and several officers of infantry and hussars. These seemed interested by the proceedings, and were attentive observers of what took place. The military force consisted of a company of foot, and as I afterwards learned, a troop of hussars. The officers were no doubt surprised, that such a parade should have been deemed requisite for the apprehension of a poor weaver in his cellar.

'Well Mr Nadin,' I said, laying aside my vernacular, and speaking common English – 'and what may be your pleasure with me now?'

He informed in his usual dogged way, striving to be civil, that he had a warrant against me for high treason.

I said if that was the case, I was ready to accompany him; but he would never convict me, and if he did, my blood would kill him. He and his assistants then commenced searching the place, for arms, as I thought, on which I ridiculed their simplicity, saying, 'And do you think I should keep my depot here?' One of the men laid hold of a sugar cane, and asked what that was? I said he might surely see it was a pike shaft, but the head I had removed to another place. I had been expecting them, I said, seven or eight days, and, of course, had made the place as clear as I could for their reception.

They examined a small recess, which served as both cupboard and larder, but.

> No beef was found, nor any beer:
> No crusted wines the soul to cheer.

The drawers were rummaged; my oaken box was explored; a shawl was spread on the floor, and all my books and papers were bundled into it; there was not however, anything of consequence; some poems in manuscript, had been deposited elsewhere. I took up some of my printed poems, 'The Weaver Boy,' and would have presented a copy to each of the officers, but Nadin would not permit me; he took the books and threw them on the heap, and I thought the officers seemed displeased. He then bade one of his men to handcuff me. 'Nay, Mr Nadin,' I said, 'can this be necessary; I give you my word of honour not to attempt an escape.' With a profound oath he bade the man do his duty, and I was chained.

The order was then given to move: my wife burst into tears – I tried to console her – said I should soon be with her again; and bestowing a kiss for my dear child when she came in the morning – I ascended into the street, and shouted, 'Hunt and liberty.' 'Hunt and liberty,' responded my brave little help-mate, whose spirit was now roused. One of the policemen, with a pistol in his hand, swearing a deep oath, said he would blow out her brains if she shouted again. 'Blow away,' was the reply; 'Hunt and liberty.' 'Hunt for ever.'

Nothing further was said. The soldiers shouldered arms, and the word 'March' being given, the prisoner and his escort tramped down the street.

'I thought you very foolish,' said a young hussar officer, in a friendly tone, at my left elbow. 'Why so,' I asked; but before he could reply, he was interrupted, and I had not an opportunity for speaking to him again: I supposed he meant something about the books. 'Well, but how is this?' I said to Mr Nadin. 'You know I am not in the habit of walking on these excursions; I must have a coach.' And scarcely had we gone many yards, ere we came to a coach with the door open, the steps down, and a file of hussars on each side of the road. I stepped into the vehicle, followed by Nadin, one of his men, and a boy: the door was closed and we drove off, accompanied by the trample of horses, and the clatter of arms.

With reference to this transaction, the London Times Newspaper – whose information would seem to have been derived from some one upon the spot – said 'The party sent to arrest him, consisted of a troop of horse, a detachment of infantry, and a posse of constables. To such a formidable force, no resistance was offered, nor was there any apparent inclination to resist. The alleged traitor was called up from his bed about four o'clock in the morning, when he little expected to be honoured by such visitors; but he manifested no symptoms of confusion, displeasure, or alarm. He was even good humoured and jocose with the officers, inspiring them at the same time, with a high idea of his talent, coolness, and presence of mind. He first asked why he had been so waited upon? and was told by Nadin, that he had a warrant to arrest him. "On what charge," he rejoined. "On charge of having committed a capital felony." "Ah," he replied, "you will never convict me; my blood would poison you, man; it is as black as a bull's blood." Seeing the officers search the house for pikes, or pike-heads, he remarked upon their suspicious simplicity, saying, "and do you think that I would keep them here?" '

As if this were too good a thing to be given unmutilated, to one of my station, the same paper, as a kind of qualifier, says in another place. 'BAMFORD THE REFORMIST! – This individual, who is now in confinement, charged with seditious practises, was formerly an actor of very considerable repute, at Liverpool and other places, and was then in flourishing circumstances. He has since, we understand, procured a scanty subsistence by writing comic songs, and occasionally *jeux d'esprit*, and by trifling benefactions from actors who had formerly known him.'

This, I need not inform my Lancashire readers, was as unfounded, as it was absurd. A hand-loom weaver metamorphosed into 'an actor of considerable repute,?' and then, 'living by writing comic songs, and jeux d'esprit;'? and by 'trifling benefactions from actors.'? – That would indeed have been worse than weaving.

Who ever heard of a play actor becoming a patriot? the one all reality, the other all imitation, – the one a reflector only; the other the thing reflected. The writer of that paragraph knew but little of human nature.

Chapter 41

Consolatory assurances by the way — Incident at Harperhey — How quartered there — Police Office — New Bailey again

As we were ascending the brow at Alkrington, I remarked that it would seem as if Mr Nadin and myself were destined to be fellow-travellers; this was the second trip I had taken with him.

It was, he said; but we should not travel often.

How so? What did he mean?

It was my last journey with him, probably.

Did he think so?

Yes. – He was nearly certain I should never return from whence I was going!

Indeed! Why not? What was to be done with me then?

'Thou'll be hanged,' he said.

'Hanged! shall I?'

'Aye! thou'll be hanged at this hurry! Thou'll never come back alive!'

Might there not be a small mis-reckoning in that hanging matter? I said.

No! Speaking seriously, he did not think there would.

Well! I was not of his opinion. He would find himself mistaken ere long.

Did I expect to get off then?

I had no doubt about it.

And if I did, he would give me credit for greater cleverness than he thought I possessed, or ever should.

He had been in the fish market at Manchester, of course? He had.

And had seen live snigs there? He had.

And had seen them glide out of the rude grasp of the fish-women? He had seen that.

'Well!' I said; 'I am like one of those snigs. I shall slip through your hands this time, whether you will or not: and I hope to do more.' What was that?

'To assist in bringing to condign punishment some dozen or so, of your Manchester magistrates, and yeomanry.'

Psha! I need not speculate on such an event. This would be my last journey up that hill.

The coach stopped at Sam Ogden's at Harperhey. Nadin got out, and left me, the man, and the boy, guarded by the hussars. After sitting some time the foot soldiers came up: a person or two dressed as gentlemen also appeared; one of them said, 'where is the villain?' The door was opened and I was asked to step out. I did so, and in passing forward to the lobby, a blow, or severe push in my neck, nearly flung me on my face. I turned, and saw Mr Thomas Andrew, of Harperhey, in an attitude of menace! I shall not repeat the terms in which I addressed him; but I told him that no man, much less a gentleman, would descend to outrage a person in chains – that he had disgraced himself – and that it was well for him, – a circumstance he no doubt had calculated on, – that my hands were confined. The lobby was filled with soldiers and police, and some one said, 'no one should touch the prisoner.' Probably it was one of the military who knew not that this person was brother to the head constable of Manchester.

I was next shewn into the kitchen, and took my seat in an old armed chair, in the farther corner near the fire place. On each side of me was seated a policeman with a pistol in his hand. The Infantry piled arms in two or three stacks, and the hussars came in, in turn, whilst others remained on guard. Half a dozen tables were quickly surrounded, and as soon plentifully supplied with oat cake, cheese, and ale; to which the men set with right good will. I told them to make play, and spare nothing, and if no one else would pay the shot I would. They laughed, – said I was a hearty fellow, – and they wished they might take such a one every night. Of course, I and my two policemen replenished to our liking; but our ale was eight-penny, and of a prime tap.

The large bread-flake in the kitchen was speedily unthatched, and about half of a large old cheese disappeared. Pipes were then lighted, – more ale was brought, and being willing to improve our acquaintance, I sung, in my way, that fine old piece known as 'General Wolf's Song.'

Why, soldiers, why –
Should we be melancholy, boys?
Why, soldiers, why?
Whose business 'tis to die.
What! sighing, fie!
Kill care, drink on, be jovial, boys,

'Tis he, you, or I.
Cold, hot, wet, or dry,
We're always found to follow, boys,
And scorn to fly.

'Tis but in vain –
I mean not to upbraid you, boys, –
'Tis but in vain,
For soldiers to complain.
Should next campaign,
Send us to Him who made us, boys,
We're free from pain.
And if we remain,
A bottle and kind landlady
Cures all again.'

The jugs were again replenished; the soldiers were becoming good company; and I said if they were all of my mind, we would not march so long as old Sam would chalk up, either for King George or myself. The soldiers asked me to drink with them, – I did so, and gave them a toast. Soon after I was sent for into the bar parlour, and there found the military officers; Mr Nadin, Mr Jonathan Andrew the head constable of Manchester, and his brother. Speaking to the officers, I said they would excuse me; but there was a person in that room, to whom no deference whatever would be shewn by me, and therefore I should take the liberty to be seated. A few questions were asked; some conversation of no consequence passed; and it seemed to me, as if I were sent for, more for the purpose of observation than any other thing. At length I was re-conducted, and the ale being finished, – of which my especial guards had freely partaken, – the word to fall in was given, and in a short time we were clattering through the drowsy streets of Manchester. I was first taken to the police office, in King-street, and from thence to the prison in Salford. The turnkey appeared, in temper crusty, and half awake, – the door opened, and banged to behind me, – and the next moment I was ushered into one of the lockups.

Chapter 42

A Lockup Cell — Its Inmates — Colloquy — A Simile — Cruelty of the confinement of Wild Animals — A Quotation from Scripture

A CLOSE, warm air, tainted with an abominable odour, was the first thing that saluted my senses on entering this wretched place. It was a small cell, perhaps four or five yards in length, by two or three in width, and probably as lofty as it was long. Opposite the door was an aperture to let in a stinted quantity of air; on two sides of the room were two benches fastened to the wall; in the centre was a stove with a fire in; and at a corner on the right, was a convenience from which emanated the disagreeableness first mentioned. Two or three fellows were stretched on the benches; one was doubled up in a corner, and one lay coiled up like a dog, on the floor before the stove: one of them opened it, flung in some slack, and stirred it, and a light flashed out that shewed every corner of that noisome crib, and the persons I was now associated with.

'In the name of the devil,' demanded he who stood with what served as a fire-poker in his hand; 'what comes here?'

'He's e'en a lang un like teseln;' said another, a Yorkshireman.

'A flash cove,' said a third; 'he's a smart shirt on!'

'He's a fence, or a devout smasher,' exclaimed another; 'Come friend, let's have a word of exhortation.'

'Nay,' said one, 'that leathern skull cap looks too priggish. That'll pray none: he'll rap out, when he's been afore the beak.'

'Come friend, let's be knowing what thou'rt here for,' said he with the poker, 'we jolly boys, who give life to these palace halls, keep no secrets.'

'Then, let me know my company,' I said; 'what art thou here for?'

'Knives and forks, – third appearance, – I'm lagg'd this time.'

'And what art thou down for?' addressing another.

'Oh! mine is only bail, or good behaviour. I knocked a fancy pal down, and thrashed her bully.'

'And what art thou for?' I asked a third; 'Mutton,' he said, 'a leg of mutton, but it was all a mistake.'

'Who'll believe it,'' exclaimed he in the corner; 'thou was near being lagg'd last time, and thou goes it now, old boy: we'll both sail together; then it'll be

> '*Suppose the duke be short of men,*
> *What would old England say?*
> *They'd wish they had those lads again,*
> *They'd sent to Botany Bay.*'

He who sung this catch, was accused, he said, 'of grabbing a purse;' but, it was all a mistake, as Bill there said, about the mutton; only who'd believe it, when they couldn't find the other man as did it.'

'My case then, is worse than any of yours,' I said.

'Ah! ah! flimsies;' was the remark. – 'Notes, man, don't you know the proper names of notes? you've been in the note business, I suppose?'

'Oh no, nothing of that sort.'

'A little in the crack line, perhaps?' – 'House-breaking,' said another.

'No, not that!'

'Not on the road, surely? – not in the collecting way?

> *With your loaded pop in hand.*'

'No, not an highwayman, either,' if that is what you mean?'

'What the devil are you? – have you robb'd a church, and kill'd a man?'

'Worse than either, as the law says.'

'What have you done?' several now asked in surprise.

'My crime is honoured, if it succeed, and the most dreadfully punished if it fail. Hanging, drawing, and quartering is my doom, I understand.'

'Oh! high treason; aye, high treason; are you one of those Peter's-field pikemen then?'

'That is what they say.'

One of them now produced an old stump pipe, another some tobacco; they smoked round; their conversation turned on their own affairs; and becoming drowsy, I stretched myself on one of the benches, and was soon asleep.

When I awoke, a peep of dull light was gleaming through the lofty and grated aperture. My companions were, some huddled in drowsiness; others pacing backwards and forwards wearily, breathing the muddled and tainted air; aye, as wearily as do those unfortunate fishes, which, by human pride, – the most cruel and heartless of all insanities – are doomed to paddle around glass vials, through thick and sickening water, as an ornament to parlour windows; or for the amusement of the lady and her visitors, and the improvement of the young 'prodigies' in the study of natural history.

I admire not that philosophy which would go in a coach to see Africa in the next field; nor that religion which requires the wonders of other lands to direct it to 'nature's God,' – which crieth, 'bring hither all things, that *I* may learn to adore the Creator;' – nor that civilization which is for ever catching, and caging, and immuring, and tormenting God's noble creatures; and robbing them of their inheritance in the wilds of air, earth, and ocean, for the gratification of a selfish and indolent curiosity – for the promotion of a knowledge which availeth little, and is obtained at the expense of humanity. On behalf of the majestic lion – of the huge and stately elephant – of the powerful and terrific tiger – of the beautiful leopard – of the lonely ostrich – of the wind-footed antelope – I would say, 'Get from thy couch, lazy and voluptuous man. Wouldst thou learn a new language of wonder, come to our rocks and solitudes, and behold us in the full attributes with which thy Maker and ours hath invested us. Why wouldst thou ensnare us from these which are ours? Thou art more cruel than we. We prey only to satisfy the cravings of nature; thou inflictest worse than death – a hopeless prison, and, hunger never satisfied. The loathed spider is more merciful; he destroys life to sustain it; but thou sustainest it in torture.'

Or, falling on a theme of deeper interest – coming nearer home, – which in all our reflections we should never forget – might I not, – addressing some philosophical devotees, ask, 'Doth not our land exhibit wonders, and beauties, and fearful things too, worthy of all your superfluous astonishment, admiration, and awe? Why stretch ye forth your hands to other regions, bringing hither multitudes of beings to gratify an insensate curiosity – a frivolous taste? are there not beings here who want catching and caging? Do not

Wild human bears on slaughter bent,
And ravening wolves surround?

Are there no hooded snakes, whose fangs are juicy with poison? – no constrictors, who crush their lambs every day? – no hyenas, with laughter on their lips, and cruelty at their hearts? – no jackals, lurching down noble game? – no crocodiles, sobbing for lack of blood? – Or, dropping metaphor, which else were carried to the end of Buffon's index, – might not an enlightened philosophy discover that something was wanting by, and for, the fellow-habitants of our own country; for the regulation of this great Zoologia of ours?

Have we not strong ones that should be enfeebled? and feeble ones that should be supported? Assured ones that should be abashed? and modest ones that should be assured? Mourners that should be comforted? and joyous ones that should be made to sorrow? Hungered ones that should be fed? and pampered ones that should be made to hunger? Lost ones that should be found? and forward ones that should be forgotten? Naked ones that should be clothed? and adorned ones that should be despoiled? Wicked ones that should be punished? and righteous ones that should be rewarded? And above all, are there not ignorant ones that should be instructed? and learned ones that have yet to learn?

'Is not this the fast that I have chosen? to loose the bands of wickedness, to undo the heavy burdens, and to let the oppressed go free; and that ye break every yoke?

'Is it not to deal thy bread to the hungry? and that thou bring the poor that are cast out, to thy house? when thou seest the naked, that thou cover him; and that thou hide not thyself from thine own flesh.

'Then shall thy light break forth as the morning, and thine health shall spring forth speedily; and thy righteousness shall go before thee; the glory of the Lord shall be thy reward.

'Then shalt thou call, and the Lord shall answer: thou shalt cry, and he shall say, – Here I am. – If thou take away from the midst of thee the yoke; the putting forth of the finger; and speaking vanity.

'And if thou draw out thy soul to the hungry, and satisfy the afflicted soul; then shall thy light rise in obscurity, and thy darkness be as the noon day.

'And the Lord shall guide thee continually, and satisfy thy soul in drought, and make fat thy bones: and thou shalt be like a watered garden, and like a spring of water, whose waters fail not.

'And they that shall be of thee, shall build the old waste places; thou shalt raise up the foundations of many generations; and thou shalt be called, The repairer of the breach: The restorer of paths to dwell in.'

Chapter 43

Author Remanded — His Prison — A kind Turnkey — A Fellow Prisoner —
The two Wives

TOWARDS noon we were called out of this odious place, and taken into the court above, for examination, or rather recognition, before the magistrates. My companions were placed in the box commonly allotted to the jury, whilst I was seated at a small desk near the dock, generally occupied by the governor, or an assistant.

The magistrate on this occasion, was Mr Norris.

The felony cases were first disposed of, and it went hard against some of my late fellows. One man was afterwards committed for trial, for drilling, and several were required to find bail, or sureties, for assaults and other minor offences.

My case, Mr Norris said, was a most serious one; the charge against me was nothing less than that of high treason. The evidence would not be gone into at present, and I should be brought up for a future examination.

I asked, might I be allowed to put a question or two?

Certainly!

I wished to know who was my accuser? and on what information I had been deprived of my liberty?

Mr Norris said that would be made known to me in due time.

I said Mr Nadin had seized a number of papers and political tracts at my house, and I begged to know who held them? and from whom they would be recoverable?

Mr Norris said, the constable who seized them would be responsible: they might become necessary to the ends of justice.

That did not satisfy me, I replied. It was possible that other papers might be introduced amongst them, and I wished them to be sealed up, and deposited with a party beyond all suspicion.

I was told to be silent: if I uttered any more impertinence, I should be committed.

I said I understood I was committed.

No; I was remanded, and would be brought up on a future day, for final examination.

The Turnkey then tipped me on the shoulder, and I followed him.

My prison was now a pleasant one, compared with the cell I had quitted. To be sure, except my bed, every thing around, beneath, and above, was of iron or stone, – and those are cold comforts – yet on the whole I was agreeably disappointed in the change which had taken place. The walls were very white; the floors were well stoned; my bed seemed very clean; and there was a free current of air, as good as any gentleman in the neighbourhood breathed; and, contrasting this place with the lockup, I thought I could not wish a better if I were a king. I had also a long airy passage to walk in during the day; and there, pacing backwards and forwards, – sometimes studying, some times whistling, and sometimes singing – I contrived to pass the hours much more pleasantly than if I had been locked up with my cell companions. A thinking mind tranquillized by fortitude – with some book reminiscences, – especially poetic ones – and some cheerful thoughts of the world outside, need not, – indeed never will – give itself up to unavailing regrets because the earthly form which it directs has become circumscribed in its whereabouts. Nature, seeking its ever destined change, through life to death, and through death to another life, must necessarily become aware of the drag on existence which a prison imposes: it cannot be insensible to that, and it will doubtless wish it were removed, but a mind thus constituted need not descend to frivolous complaints.

I might perhaps have some gifts and resources not common to others; and if I had, I made good use of them in my solitary hours; and grateful for their bestowal, I derived solacements commensurate with their exercise.

> *And why indeed! should I repine?*
> *The crown, as well as cross is mine;*
> *   And if the crown I claim,*
> *It must not be, when comes the day*
> *Which dealeth out adversity,*
> *   That I should shun the same.*

True, my bedstead was of iron, and there were other requisites which 'gentlemen' prisoners of latter days are given to make a cry about. But what were these to me? – things not worth a thought – mere accidents of my situation.

> *I would not change my iron bed,*
> *For all the downy couches, spread*
> *Around corruption's throne.*

What would have become of the immortality of the gallant Sydney – he who thumbed the cold iron that was to behead him – had he complained of bone, and hearts ache too, because his bed was laid on an iron slab? such puerilities were reserved for 'gentlemen patriots' of the present day. That lion never would have been heard yelping like a cur, however he were encaged.

I happened to have a kind turnkey here: I think he had formerly known me: he was a Rochdale man, and his name was Grindrod. He found that I was unwell, having a cough, and fulness of the chest; and instead of the prison gruel, he brought me up a basin of warm tea or coffee morning and evening, from his own table; my dinners were of the prison allowance. Once or twice also, my fellow-prisoner, James Moorhouse, sent me a little fruit which I was allowed to receive. My kind jailer never hinted at remuneration, and it was not without difficulty, that on my going away I prevailed on him, to accept a small gratuity as an acknowledgment of my gratitude.

One day, as I was walking in the passage, I was astonished by the appearance of Mr Johnson at one of the end doors. He had prevailed on a person who was going through the prison, oiling and examining the locks, to let us have a moment's conversation. I told him I had visited his family – how I found them – and as many other particulars as I could compress into a few words, and we parted. Subsequently we had another chat, but nothing occurred which would interest the reader.

On the morning of our final examination, which was Friday the 27th of August, my wife and Joseph Healey's wife came to the prison to see us, if they might be allowed. Mr Andrews the late deputy constable of Bury, with whom I previously had some acquaintance was at that time connected with the Manchester police, and was on that day in attendance at the New Bailey on business. He saw the two women standing in the crowd outside the gates, and beckoning my wife, asked her if she was come to see me? She said she wished to do so, and her companion, who was Healey's wife, wished also to see her husband. He accordingly took them into a room up stairs, where there was a comfortable fire, seats, and a table. A number of soldiers' wives were about their business, and foot soldiers were walking sentry. Amongst those of the soldiers who passed to and fro' was John Hall, a Middleton man, formerly a neighbour of ours, and then, a private in the 31st regiment of foot. He conversed with them a short time and left them, and soon after re-appeared, and set before them a dinner of excellent steak and porter, which was very acceptable at the time. They were however, not the less unable to account for this, as the table was set out in a style which could not be within the means of a private soldier; but John said nothing: he refused to receive any gratuity, and having removed the things, he went about his business. They were afterwards ushered into the public court, but it was so crowded as to be insufferable, and after exchanging a few looks and mute gestures with I and Healey, who were in the dock, they were glad to escape from the crowd, and await our disposal in the room they had quitted.

The following account of our examination, abridged and corrected from the report of 'THE TIMES' Newspaper, of the 30th August, will be interesting to the reader. It cannot have been read, or if read, it cannot well have been remembered, by many under whose notice I hope this book will pass. To them, it will therefore be new matter, and its perusal will display a striking passage in the history of those days.

Chapter 44

Examination of Henry Hunt, and others, confined on a Charge of High Treason — The Suspension of that Charge, and their Committal for a Misdemeanour

"THIS being understood for nearly a week to be the day on which the determination of government, regarding the charge against Mr Hunt and his fellow-prisoners should be announced to them from the bench, and their final examination be entered upon, a considerable crowd collected near the New Bailey, as early as ten o'clock. About eleven, those who had any particular favour with the officers, or who came to give evidence were admitted into the court.

In a short time the seats round the table usually occupied by the attornies, the jury box, the stair-case leading to the gallery, and every part of the hall convenient for hearing or seeing the prisoners were crammed to excess. Meanwhile the crowds collected without, and filled the whole space between the bridge, the prison, the governor's house, and the river. A strong party of soldiers had previously been admitted into prison, and a guard appointed outside. It being the custom to exclude the multitude, who usually occupy the body of the court behind the bar, till the magistrates have taken their seats on the bench, there was a great pressure towards the gate for admission as soon as it should be opened. The civil power thinking they saw some tendency to tumult in the immense body that surrounded the doors, requested as we understood, that the military might be at their post, ready to afford assistance in case of danger. Accordingly, some of the officers of the hussars, of the 31st, and 88th, who had taken places in the jury box, eager to hear the examination of persons who have of late commanded so much of their attention, were called out, and ordered on more active duty. The shouts of the multitudes were sometimes heard in court, but from the very efficient force ready to repress any riot, no impression of danger was felt. The magistrates, we believe had assembled about eleven, but they did not take their seats on the bench until upwards of two hours afterwards. In the interval they were employed in taking depositions, or procuring the signatures of the witnesses to depositions already taken. Mr Pearson, the solicitor for the prisoners, had taken his station under the dock, with a law book under his arm, but was not known or recognized by those around him, till called out of court at half-past twelve, by Mr Norris, the stipendiary magistrate of Manchester. His white hat then excited a laugh, that being considered here as the badge of the radicals. Sir Charles Wolseley, we were told, was in court, but we did not recognize him. At a quarter past one, the magistrates entered the court, and an agitation of interest and curiosity took place. Only six magistrates occupied the bench. They were Mr Norris (chairman), William Hulton, Ralph Wright, William Marriott, Thomas William Tatton, Esqrs, and the Rev. C. W. Ethelstone. The solicitor for the crown, Mr Bouchier, took his place at the table immediately below the chairman. Mr Pearson, the prisoners' solicitor, was now accommodated with a place at the table, near his clients. The chairman, as soon as the magistrates were seated, ordered the gates to be opened, and a great rush of people into the hall immediately took place; but, happily, no one, as far as we have heard was injured by the pressure. The prisoners were then ordered to be brought up, and soon appeared in the dock. Mr Hunt appeared first, and the rest in succession, till the space allotted them was crowded. Their names were called over and answered to in the following order: – Henry Hunt, Joseph Johnson, John Thacker Saxton, John Knight, James Moorhouse, Samuel Bamford, Joseph Healey, George Swift, Thomas Jones, Robert Wilde, and Elizabeth Gaunt. Moorhouse, entering the dock, and standing in front refused to doff the reform badge – the white hat – to the magistrates, proclaiming (when desired to uncover) in a tone of real effrontery, or assumed indignation, that, 'men who had so misconducted themselves, had forfeited all title to deference or respect, and that they should meet with none from him.' An officer by his side soon settled that point of etiquette, by removing the obnoxious head-piece. Hunt's deportment was extremely courteous. We never saw him, apparently, in better health or spirits. His propriety of demeanour, his perfectly unembarrassed manner, the decency of his dress, and the whole of his external appearance, formed a strange contrast with that of his fellow-prisoners. Elizabeth Gaunt, whom it was a disgrace to have kept for twelve days in solitary confinement, and brought up in the state in which she was, could not be at first seen, having been accommodated with a chair behind her male companions. She answered to her name but feebly, being unable to speak out from a tendency to faint, in consequence of the barbarous manner in which she had been cut and trampled on the field. Hunt, on his name being called, courteously bowed and said, 'Here.' Being pressed in the dock, and hearing some noise behind, he turned and surveyed the crowd with the utmost apparent composure and good humour. His time, however, for speaking and acting now commenced. The chairman thus addressed the prisoners – 'Henry Hunt, and you severally whose names have been read over, you have been remanded on a charge of high treason.' Here there was so much noise from the agitation of the crowd behind the dock, the living mass not having yet gained the consistency at which, on occasions like this, it is usually silent, that the magistrate could not be heard. Mr Hunt, with some vehemence, interrupted him, saying, 'I cannot hear; you must command silence so as to be heard. There was more order at the meeting the other day.' The chairman called out 'order, order,' Mr Hunt – 'I must beg to hear; the matter seriously concerns us; you must be heard by us.' A short pause ensued; when comparative silence being obtained, the chairman again commenced his address to the following purport.

'Henry Hunt, Joseph Johnson, and you all severally, whose names have been read over, when you were last called into this court, you were remanded on a charge of high treason; on remanding you, you were informed that the whole of the evidence had been sent to London, to be laid before the law officers of the crown, and in the meantime you were to be detained. It was not until this morning that a communication was made from government, stating that the law officers of the crown had, for the present, abandoned the higher charge. That communication was not made to me; yet there is a gentleman present, (Mr Bouchier) who has come with orders to proceed on a less charge. The charge of high treason is not yet abandoned, but government now proceeds against you for a minor offence.'

Mr Hunt. – Is the charge of murder then abandoned? I understood from a magistrate, that I was remanded until a coroner's inquest had sat on a charge of murder, as well as treason.

Mr Hulton from the bench, said, – I did not tell you so.

Moorhouse – This then turns out to be a farce.

Mr Norris. – James Moorhouse, I shall feel it my duty to remand you, unless you conduct yourself properly.

Mr Milne, the clerk to the magistrates, then called over the names of the witnesses whose written depositions he held. The prisoners were requested to attend to the depositions, and told they had an opportunity of questioning the witnesses concerning them. On putting the book into the hand of the first, Hunt desired he might be examined alone, and the rest ordered to leave the court. Mr Bouchier did not object to this.

The first witness whose deposition was to be read was John Shawcross, clerk to the police. Mr Hunt asked his name; and demanded that he should be examined in open court, before he heard his deposition read. The magistrates overruled this demand, and the deposition was read. The witness deposed to having purchased at the Observer office on the 31st of July last a newspaper called the Observer, containing the notice of the first intended meeting on the 9th of August. The advertisement for the second meeting on the 16th, was also put in and read. The witness then produced the prohibition of the first meeting, which closed his evidence.

Mr Hunt asked if he had now the liberty of examining the witness?

Chairman. – Yes, certainly.

Mr Hunt, to the witness. – Where is your residence?

Witness – No. 4, Blossom-street, Salford.

Mr Hunt. – What is your profession, sir?

Witness. – I am clerk to the police office.

Mr Hunt. – Have you any other employment?

Witness. – Yes.

Mr Hunt. – You purchased these papers, did you?

Witness. – Yes.

Mr Hunt. – Do you know who inserted the advertisements you have deposed to, in these papers?

The chairman interfered, and said, that was not evidence.

Mr Hunt. – Who urged you to purchase the papers?

The chairman again interfered, and told the witness not to answer the question.

Mr Hunt. – Then am I to understand that the witness is not allowed to answer the question?

The chairman. – The court does not think it relevant; and will not allow the witness to answer it.

Mr Hunt. – You purchased the second paper on the 14th of August?

The witness was not allowed to answer the question.

Mr Hunt. – Your name is on each of the papers, Who directed you to put your name there?

The court again interfered, and would not allow the witness to answer the question.

Mr Johnson, one of the prisoners. – Do you take in those papers regularly, or did you purchase these for any particular purpose?

The witness was not allowed to answer the question, the Bench declaring through its chairman, that it was sufficient for him to state that he had purchased them, and marked them with his name.

Chapter 45

THE deposition of Matthew Cowper, was then read at the table. He stated the nature of the meeting; gave a history of the proceedings; and produced his notes of the commencement of a speech purporting to have been delivered by Mr Hunt at the meeting. Witness also deposed that he attended on the field at twelve at noon; that by that time half of the assemblage had collected; that most of the persons who composed it, carried large sticks, more like flails than walking sticks; that they advanced in military array, with flags and music; that one of the flags had upon it 'No Corn Laws,' and, on the other side a bloody dagger. The flags were in all sixteen, and there were five caps of liberty.

Witness examined by Mr Hunt. – Where do you reside, sir ?

Witness. – In Manchester.

Mr Hunt. – Would you favour me with your particular address ?

The bench, through its chairman again interfered, and would not allow the witness to answer the question. It was sufficient for the witness to declare he lived in Manchester.

Mr Hunt. – I demand as an act of justice, to know the residence of this man. It will be observed that he is a very material witness, and that his evidence may deeply affect us all. I am entitled to know where to find him, that if, after the trial in question, it shall be found there was no ground for this charge, I may have my remedy against him by a prosecution for perjury, or some other redress. I demand therefore, as a right, to know his residence. (Mr Hunt uttered this with considerable violence of voice and gesture.)

The magistrates consulted a minute, and then through their chairman, decided against complying with the demand. The chairman said there was no occasion for Mr Hunt to use intimidating language: it was not necessary to reiterate the word 'demand,' to obtain that justice to which every British subject was entitled, and which might be obtained by a simple request. He further stated, that he did not think it was treating the court with sufficient respect, to talk of demanding, as there was no disposition to refuse what was right, and no chance of obtaining what was wrong, by the use of strong terms. – The request of the prisoner would go as far as his demand. The court had considered the nature of the question put to the witness, and did not think it necessary that he should give his particular address: the description that he lived in Manchester and was an accountant, was quite sufficient.

Mr Hunt begged leave to reply to the observations of the chairman.

Chairman. – The court will not be replied to.

Mr Hunt. – I was merely about to state, that I had no intention of offering any insult to the court.

Chairman. – The court takes it for granted that you did not, and requires not any apology.

Mr Hunt. – I offered no insult to the court: when the witness refused to answer the question, I appealed to the court, and requested that he might be ordered to answer. I put this question in the shape of a demand, because I will not accept of anything as a favour. Addressing himself to the witness. – Now, of what profession are you?

Witness. – I am called an accountant.

Mr Hunt. – Is that your only occupation?

Chairman. – Don't answer that question.

Mr Hunt. – Were you a special constable, on Monday, the 16th, at the meeting?

Chairman. – Don't answer that question.

Mr Hunt, with great vehemence and apparent surprise. – Not answer that question? Have you any other employment than that of an accountant? Are you not sometimes employed as a short hand writer?

Witness. – I sometimes take reports of speeches.

Mr Hunt. – For the public newspapers, or for your own private amusement?

Chairman. – Don't answer that question.

Mr Hunt. – Then you say that you took my speech on the day of the meeting: did you take it in short hand, or otherwise?

Witness. – I took extracts from it on the ground and afterwards wrote it out at length. I only took the leading words. I do not mean to swear to all the words.

Mr Hunt. – Are you sure you did not misplace the words, putting some which you had in one sentence, into another?

Witness replied in the negative.

Mr Hunt. – How did you make out the remainder of the sentence from those extracts and leading words of yours?

I filled it up from memory.

When did you write out this speech from memory?

In the evening.

At what time was it delivered?

About one o'clock.

At what hour then, did you reduce your short notes into long sentences?

About five o'clock at night.

Be so good as to state how you were employed in the interval?

The chairman would not allow the witness to answer the question.

Mr Hunt remarked with considerable asperity on this interference, saying, it was important that an answer should be obtained. The witness had stated that a very considerable interval had intervened between the delivery of the speech, and the preparation of his version of it; and that in the meantime he had entrusted a considerable part of it to his memory. The retentiveness of his memory would, of course, be affected by the importance of the other events in which he had been engaged, and therefore it was but just that he should state how he had been employed.

The court over-ruled this demand.

Mr Hunt to witness. – You state that you saw certain flags and colours, and that there was one of them with a bloody dagger; now what else was there besides the bloody dagger?

The witness said he observed nothing else.

Mr Hunt. – Did you not observe a figure of justice, with the scales in one hand, and a dagger, which you call a bloody dagger, in the other?

Witness replied in the negative.

Mr Hunt. – Will you swear there was nothing else.

Witness said he could not swear there was nothing else.

Mr Hunt. – You said you saw military array; what do you mean by military array?

Witness. – I mean people marching in regular order, as regiments march.

Have you no benefit societies in Manchester? Have you not orange clubs?

The court interfered, and said these questions were quite irrelevant. Mr Hunt contended that they were quite to his purpose, for when the witness spoke of regular order being military array, it was proper to call to his mind instances in which the former might occur without the latter. Then addressing himself to the witness, he asked,

Did you ever see benefit clubs, marching with music and banners ?
The witness said he had.

Have you not seen them marching in regular order ?

The court interfered, and declared the question irrelevant. The chairman said that in interrupting the prisoner in these various questions, he and the other gentlemen acted on their best discretion. – Mr Hunt to the witness. You said that the sticks you saw in the hands of the persons who came to the meeting were more like threshing flails than walking sticks; pray what do you mean by a flail ? and what is the difference between it and a walking stick ?

The chairman prevented the witness from answering the question ?

Mr Hunt. – I was anxious to obtain an answer, because had I been allowed to go on, I should have drawn from the witness that there was nothing more common to the country people, than to use their old flails for walking sticks. – Addressing the witness. – Pray how were these sticks held ?

They were shouldered like muskets.

Many other questions were put by Mr Hunt to this witness, but nothing very important was elicited.

Chapter 46

Proceedings continued — Deposition and Examination of Richard Owen

THE deposition of Richard Owen, a pawnbroker, was read. He deposed to the military array in which different parties advanced to the meeting; to having seen Mr Hunt in the cart; to having heard a command given by one person in the cart, 'league together, and keep their enemies out;' and to several other circumstances.

Mr Hunt. – Where did you make this deposition ?
Witness. – On the field.
The clerk corrected the witness, and was supported by the

chairman, who said the witness could not have sworn it on the field. Mr Hunt objected, in an animated manner, to this interference, and said, 'I want the answer from the witness himself, and not from you. You are interfering to correct him, and to set him right in a matter which he had already sworn.'

The chairman explained, that the witness must have misapprehended the question.

Mr Hunt declared that it was most indecent in the clerk to interfere.

The chairman said it was well done on the part of the clerk.

Mr Hunt bowed, and continued the examination. – You said you made this deposition on the field?

Witness. – Yes; I made the first part of it on the field: I swore on the field, that I saw you come upon it in a carriage.

Did you not swear to seeing something more than me entering the field in a carriage?

I swore the town was in alarm, and that the meeting ought to be put a stop to.

Mr Hunt. – You did not swear to the whole of this deposition, then?

The magistrates interfered, and said it was not at all necessary for the witness to say when the deposition was first sworn, as it was supposed to be sworn to now.

Mr Hunt commenced a reply, when the chairman interrupted him, by telling him that the court would not hear anything more upon the question; and directing that the deposition should be read over a second time.

Mr Hunt strongly objected to the refreshing of the witness's memory by hearing his deposition read a second time.

Chairman. – The court intended it as a favour to you.

Mr Hunt. – Oh, my memory is very good; I seldom find that it fails me. I beg on the present occasion I may not be indulged. – To the witness. – Did you not say that the men came in military array, in your first deposition?

Witness. – No, I did not observe it.

You were so much alarmed then, that you did not state it to the magistrates?

The court again interfered.

Mr Hunt. – When did it occur to you to state these facts on oath?

The witness, of his own accord, refused to answer to the question.

Mr Hunt appealed to the bench, saying, 'Here is a witness who refuses to answer a material question; what shall I do with him?'

The court decided that the witness was not bound to answer the question. Mr Hunt on this, as he had done on several other occasions, requested Mr Pearson, his solicitor, to mark down what had occurred. – To the witness. – Did you see me in the cart?

The witness would not answer the question?

Mr Hunt again begged Mr Pearson to note down, that it had been ruled by the magistrates, that a witness was not bound to give his residence, to furnish a knowledge of where he could be found, in case a prosecution for perjury was instituted against him, founded on the evidence to which he had sworn. – To the witness, – What do you mean by military array?

I mean marching order, with flags flying, and music playing.

How? does one man marching after another make military array? Did these people observe the lock-step?

Witness said he did not know what the lock-step was.

Mr Hunt. – What did you consider the dreadful part of the array?

The witness was desired not to answer the question, the chairman observing that it was not necessary to be so particular now. All that the magistrates wanted, was to know whether there were grounds for committal. Such an examination might be entered upon at his trial, if he thought it conducive to his interest. 'Then,' said Mr Hunt, with great readiness, 'I am to understand that my trial is decided upon, and that I may be committed without further examination or evidence.' – To the witness. – Were you alarmed at the meeting?

Witness said he was.

Were other persons alarmed? Yes. – Would you mention who they were?

The witness was not allowed to answer the question.

Mr Hunt. – Had those imaginary soldiers any muskets.

No; but they had things nearly as large as muskets.

What did they do with them?

Witness said he did not observe them do anything particular.

Mr Hunt. – Did they shoulder their clubs?

No; I observed no shouldering.

Mr Hunt. – Mark that, Mr Pearson? it is very important.

John Thacker Saxton asked the witness if he should know the man who desired the multitude to 'keep their enemies out?'

The witness said he should not.

Saxton. – When was it? Was it before Mr Hunt came to the field that you heard that?

Witness. – It was before he came.

One of the prisoners asked if the witness observed Mr Hunt speak to any of the parties who, as he said, were walking in military array?

The witness said he did not.

Chapter 47

Proceedings continued — Depositions and Examinations of James Platt, Robert Derbyshire the younger, and John Barlow — Some particulars respecting Elizabeth Gaunt

THE deposition of James Platt was next read. It related to the military array; to the presence of Joseph Healey with a party going to the meeting; and to Samuel Bamford being on the hustings.

Examined by Mr Hunt. – What are you?

Witness. – A constable and beadle.

Do you earn your livelihood in that way?

I do.

Did you observe any clubs shouldered at the meeting?

No, I observed none.

Did you observe any insult offered to any person by the marching parties?

No, I neither saw nor heard of any.

Healey put an immaterial question which the magistrates would not allow the witness to answer.

Bamford asked several questions of some importance as regarded himself. Did you see me upon the hustings? Yes, was the reply.

Did you not see me anywhere else? Witness said he did not.

The deposition of Robert Derbyshire, the younger, was read. He deposed to having seen George Swift, active in arranging the crowd: and also, that Robert Wylde was on the hustings.

Mr Hunt. – Are you a constable? Did you see the people advancing in military array?

Witness said he saw them coming, but he did not notice their array.

Mr Hunt. – Did you run to the magistrates, and express alarm at the state of the meeting?

No; I had seen similar meetings before.

George Swift. – You say you heard me address the meeting; what did I say?

Witness. – You said, 'Fall back, league firm together, and keep your enemies off.'

Mr Hunt. – Did you see the yeomanry cavalry come in at this time?

The witness was told not to answer the question.

Moorhouse. – Did you see me on the hustings?

The witness said he did.

John Barlow, another witness, deposed to having seen Elizabeth Gaunt upon the carriage.

The prisoner came, or was rather carried from behind the other prisoners, to the front of the dock to be identified. She looked pale, emaciated, and almost fainting from weakness, in consequence of the wounds which she had received at the meeting, and her subsequent solitary confinement. Being unable to support herself, the magistrates ordered a chair to be brought: had she been sent to Lancaster to stand her trial, it is very probable she would not have survived the journey. On a proposition being made to alter the deposition of the witness against her in the court; Mr Hunt strongly objected to it, and when the clerk was proceeding with the alteration, Mr Hunt assured him he would call him as a witness.

Mr Milne, the clerk. – You had better not, Mr Hunt. I shall be against you.

Mr Hunt, in a very significant tone. – I have no doubt of that, Mr Clerk; mark down his words, Mr Pearson. Addressing the witness, Barlow. – When did you sign that deposition? This forenoon.

Did you know you were signing a deposition? I did.

Who wrote it?

The witness was told not to answer the question.

Mr Hunt. – Did you see Mrs Gaunt commit any offence?

Witness. – No, I only took her out of the carriage; she was then fainting.

Mr Hunt. – Did you not think it your duty to protect a defenceless woman? How could you allow her to be treated in the cruel manner she was?

Witness. – Other constables came and took her from me.

The prisoner then gave her own statement. She said that she was amongst the crowd at the meeting; that in the confusion someone put her into Mr Hunt's carriage, but she did not know who it was that put her there. She had no right to be in the coach, but was put in by two persons for safety; that she fainted away, and when she came to herself she found she had been wounded; that she threw herself into a private house and remained there some time, and might have got away had she chosen, or had she apprehended that she had committed anything illegal.

The solicitor for the crown said, that as the evidence was very slight against the prisoner, he would not press for her prosecution.

The chairman announced this to the prisoner, and stated that as the prosecutor determined not to bring any evidence against her, the court had great pleasure in ordering her immediate discharge.

Mr Hunt, with great emphasis, and apparent astonishment, – Discharged for want of evidence, after twelve days solitary confinement!

Chairman. – That will be enquired into hereafter, Mr Hunt.

Mr Hunt desired to know whom he was to consider as the prosecutor? The chairman replied, 'The crown.' 'What,' said Mr Hunt, 'the crown in person?' The chairman said, 'the solicitor for the treasurer is here to prosecute in the name of the king.'

Mr Hunt, addressing the solicitor for the treasury, – 'Your name, sir?' The solicitor for the treasury, – 'Bouchier.'

Mr Hunt. – I must know the name of the prosecutor, in order that I may bring my action in case it shall be found that I have suffered eleven days confinement, without having committed any offence. I cannot under such circumstances, prosecute the king.

The chairman. – Mr Bouchier has been sent here by the crown. I understand that the several witnesses who have deposed against you, are responsible for the facts to which they have deposed. The king's name is rightly, and ordinarily used in such prosecutions.

Mr Hunt. – I always thought that there must be some prosecutor, although the prosecution stood in the king's name.

The chairman. – The crown prosecutes; if there be any particular prosecutor, it must be the attorney-general.

Then addressing the prisoners, he asked them whether they had anything to say in their defence.

Chapter 48

HUNT, then adressing the bench, spoke to the following effect:— 'I know that I am now addressing the same magistrates who took the first depositions, and issued the warrants against me; but after that evidence, and the amended evidence has been read, it is for them, sitting in the situation which they now occupy, to administer justice. I hope, and do not doubt, they will dismiss from their minds all prejudice, and act upon the evidence. They had heard the various depositions which had just been read, and the answers of the witnesses who had been subjected to examination in open court. It would be observed, that they all agreed in certain points, but differed very materially in others; and that when examined regarding the import of words, their meaning was far from being precise or clear. Some witnesses say that those bodies which came from the country came in military array, but they could not explain what they meant by military array; they could not state whether they marched in slow or quick time, or whether they possessed the characteristic of a military march. Some say they came with sticks. One says they were so far in military array as to have clubs at their left breasts, similar to muskets; another witness as positively denied his observation of the circumstance; but all agree that none of them did any act to intimidate or offend. Can the magistrates say we should be committed on such evidence for a misdemeanour, after eleven days' solitary confinement? Is not this a sufficient punishment for any offence that we may have committed? They should consider, that the eyes of all England were fixed upon this matter, and waited with anxiety its termination. It had gone far enough, and ought here to end.'

'I cannot forget, he said, that I expected to stand here to-day on that most serious charge: it has, however, been abandoned, and I submit to you, whether there be any tittle of evidence to support the charge of conspiracy. Many of these prisoners, who are accused of having joined with me, I never saw till I saw them in this box. I admit that many of them, as well as myself, attended at the meeting for the purpose of taking part in its proceedings. I admit that I attended it to conduct those proceedings, believing that they were perfectly legal. I considered myself then as performing a necessary but a painful duty. I had before carried applications made at similar meetings to the secretary of state, for the purpose of being laid before his Royal Highness. To some of these applications I had an answer from the Prince Regent himself through the medium of his ministers, and to none of them was it objected that the meeting was illegal at which it was voted. One of these applications was the very paper which was to have been submitted to the meeting of the 16th. I did not attempt to follow, nor was it the opinion of those who took part in the proceedings of the meeting, that we ought to attempt to follow the example set by Birmingham, in the election of a representative. I had written to Mr Johnson to this effect long before the intended meeting was prohibited in Manchester: the Royal Proclamation had declared it illegal, and though I did not think it illegal, I thought it a foolish and absurd scheme. It was my opinion, that to follow such an example at such a time, would have been unjust to the people of Manchester – that an election should not have been proceeded in till its inhabitants had three month's notice. I had declared that I would not have put such a question as chairman, long before the first meeting was prohibited.'

'The resolutions which were intended to be voted at the meeting of the 16th, would have removed all doubt on this subject: they, indeed, I have been told, have been lost in the confusion which ensued: but the most respectable persons can be brought forward, who will prove that it was intended first to pass a strong vote of censure, for refusing to present the petitions of Manchester and Stockport; and then to make a solemn appeal to his Royal Highness the Prince Regent on the distressed state of the country, and on the necessity of immediately reviving the connection between the people and the throne. I cannot trust my feelings with the description of what occurred afterwards in the dispersion of the meeting: it would be much better if the transactions of that day were for ever buried in oblivion, and blotted from the history of our country. But I ask you, will you commit upon such evidence as that which you have heard? The country is at present in a state of great agitation; and will you, by protracting this prosecution, throw down the apple of continual discord?'

Here the court interrupted the speaker, and the chairman addressing him, said, 'Your language is now improper. No threat or intimidation ought to be held out. We have only to attend to our duty, and leave the care of the country to higher orders. If the country were in ten-fold the agitation which you have described, I and my brethren on the bench would do our duty.'

Mr Hunt, in continuation, said, 'This intimation shall not be thrown away upon me; I did not mean to intimidate you; I did not mean to ask for anything as a boon; I demand only justice, and would not accept a favour. I must say I suffered much bodily pain from the blows from the batoons of the constables, and the sabres of the yeomanry. They are visible. I scorned to tell the doctor of it. My health certainly has been preserved, instead of being injured, by my apprehension and confinement: the exertions I should have made, and the anxiety I should have felt, to conduct the proceedings, and to preserve the order of that meeting, would have affected me for years. Since my confinement I have slept on a bed which I would not have put under my servants: but I thank God, – said he with great fervour – that I have slept soundly; and if I have suffered any thing, it has been from commiserating the state of my fellow-prisoners, and from the recollection of those poor mangled creatures who have been put to death. When I mention the accommodation, I have nothing to say against the gaoler.'

Moorhouse. – As the law presumes persons innocent until convicted, I beg to say we ought to be used as well as possible, whilst we are kept here.

Chairman. – You may all of you have bail.

The magistrates then withdrew. Mr Bouchier was shortly afterwards going towards the magistrates' room. Mr Hunt said to him, 'I hope you are not going to the magistrates unless my solicitor goes.' The solicitor said, No. Ah! rejoined Mr Hunt significantly, you have been there already.

On the return of the magistrates, Mr Norris said, – 'Henry Hunt, and you all. We sent for Mr Bouchier, in order that we might again carefully peruse the depositions. It is a most painful duty for me to commit you for a conspiracy. We can however, lay our hands on our hearts and say, We have done our duty. As to the charge of conspiracy, though you might not all have been together previous to the meeting, yet in the eye of the law all those who commit separate acts tending to one illegal object are guilty of that crime. Coupling the two meetings together: taking into consideration the manner in which the last was assembled, with such insignia and in such a manner, with the black flag; the bloody dagger; with 'equal representation or death.'

Mr Hunt. – No one has said the black flag had a bloody dagger.

Chairman. – 'They came in a threatening manner; they came under the banners of death, thereby shewing they meant to overturn the government. There could not be any free discussion where that flag was unfurled. The charge now is, 'that of having conspired to alter the laws by force and threats.' It is an illegal proceeding, and is sufficiently made out, and we are called upon imperatively to commit you for trial by a proper jury. It is now our painful duty to commit you to Lancaster Castle. On account of the seriousness of the charge, we shall require you, Henry Hunt and Joseph Johnson, to give bail, yourselves in one thousand pounds, and two sureties in five hundred each; and all the others, themselves in five hundred pounds, and two sureties in two hundred and fifty each.

The prisoners then left the bar. Johnson and Moorhouse immediately procured bail and were liberated. Johnson was attended towards his residence by an immense multitude, shouting and applauding. Moorhouse was equally the object of popular favour; he was accompanied likewise through the market-place. Hunt complained, when asked by the magistrates in court whether he had provided bail? that he was not allowed to be visited by a respectable solicitor in the town, whom he had sent for, some days before. The chairman said he would now be sent for if Mr Hunt desired it. 'No, no,' said Mr Hunt, pointing to Mr Pearson, 'here is now my solicitor.'

From the bar I was conducted to the yard of my former cell, where I was joined by several of the other prisoners, and we were taking what should have been our dinners, when an order suddenly came that we were to prepare to set off for Lancaster Castle. Our meal was soon despatched, and we quickly bundled up our few things. We were then taken to the turnkey's lodge, and each hand-chained, after which we were placed on a four-horse coach, in the inside of which were Mr Hunt, Mr Knight, Saxton, and Nadin. The outside party consisted of myself, Swift, Wilde, Healey, and Jones, with a number of constables armed with pistols; we were also escorted by a strong detachment of hussars, and thus, amid the huzzas of an immense multitude, we drove off;

Humming perhaps, the burden of a song,

'*Heigh now ! for John-o' Gaunt's old dungeon strong.*'

Chapter 49

Sketch of the Journey — Hunt and his Party Prisoners in Lancaster Castle

PROCEEDING at a rapid pace, we soon left the dim atmosphere, and crowded streets of Manchester and Salford behind. The populous thoroughfares of Pendleton were next traversed, and a pleasant ride of twelve miles brought us to the large town of Bolton, where we changed horses, amid a throng of people, which the hussars found some difficulty in keeping at a distance. But their expressions of sympathy and good-will were not to be restrained, and the loud shouts of, 'Hunt for ever;' 'Never mind 'em, lads;' 'Down with the tyrants;' and a general huzza, with waving of hats and handkerchiefs, and clapping of hands, when we drove off, added to the cheerfulness of our party.

Soon after leaving Bolton, darkness came on, and we had scarcely cleared the moors of Horwich, when the coachman, who knew not the way, drove upon a piece of new road, and endeavouring to extricate himself, the coach began to heel on one side, and we should have gone over, constables, prisoners, and all, had not the pole broken, on which the horses were steadied, and we dismounted, and being most carefully looked to by the constables and soldiers, we walked down to the village of Lower Darwin, and were all snugly counted into a public-house there. The poor Jehu whose mistake had led to the misadventure, then got a large dividend of devils' blessings from our conducting constable.

At this place Mr Hunt refused to partake of any vinous or fermented liquor, and out of compliment to him, most of us did the same. Saxton, however, whose fiery visage told of the indulgence he loved, took brandy and water, and candidly declared that he would not attempt to carry into effect Mr Hunt's rule of temperance. He would attend a meeting at any time, he said; or make a speech, or move, or second a resolution for parliamentary reform; but a resolution for a personal reform in the matter of a little cordial, he neither could nor would entertain. A discussion ensued which caused some laughter, in which Mr Hunt joined; and having sat about an hour, the pole was repaired, and we drove into Blackburn, where we left the coach, the driver, and the hussars, and went on with a fresh vehicle and guards.

At Preston we stopped at the head inn, and took supper in a large room, to the lower end of which a number of respectable-looking persons were admitted. These genteel visitors, seemed not to have the smallest idea that their presence might be disagreeable to men in our situation; and that a plea of curiosity was likely to seem but an ungracious excuse for coming to view us as they would wild beasts, 'at feeding time.' The streets here, as at every other town where we stopped, were crowded, and we set off amid loud cheers.

Morning broke betwixt Garstang and Lancaster, and the first challenge of 'John-O'Gaunt's tower,' as it stood out before us in the mild sun-light, excited our attention. It looked indeed like the stern and lordly keep of an old baron, and a small exercise of imagination was sufficient to place in our mind's eye, its powerful chieftain, waiting in helmet, cuirass and glaive, beneath its portcullis.

We passed quickly along the streets of the town, – the hussars came trotting dusty and choked, and weary behind us, – it was about five o'clock, – few people were stirring, – and the clatter of our cavalcade aroused many from their peaceful slumbers. We dismounted at the foot of the castle steep, and walked up accompanied by our guards, and took our station beneath the arch of the grim old gate, the boldness and strength of its masonry attracting our admiration. A blow from the ponderous knocker made the place resound, and in a few minutes the wicket was opened, and we were prisoners in Lancaster Castle.

Chapter 50

Retrospection — Mistakes of Radicals not avoided by Chartists — Self Reform should precede all others — A virtuous and enlightened people are free — Address to Workmen and Chartists

AND now friend reader, since thou hast accompanied me to this my fourth place of confinement, instead of contemplating the repulsive walls, and the dungeon towers, and the massive keep, for which there may be time hereafter, let us, from the eminence of this

Wide water'd shore,

mentally cast back our eyes and survey the course by which we have arrived at so undesirable a place. And in doing this, let us not be blind to our own faults, but be simply just towards ourselves as we have been to others. Let us not spare ourselves the humiliation of blame when deserved, though it do humble our self-esteem; though we have to declare, 'this hand hath offended.'

In our progress now retrospectively scanned, how great was the portion, as we perceive, of folly which accompanied our good intentions? Groping in a mental and political twilight, we stumbled from error to error, the dim-eyed calling on the blind to follow; we fell as a natural consequence, and, a happy circumstance would it have been, had our fall served in these later times as a warning to others, but it has not.

'For a nation to be free, it is sufficient that she wills it,' and we may add that, a nation cannot be free, unless she does will it. We thought the will to be free already existed, – foolish thought – we looked for fruit ere the bloom was come forth; we expected will when there was no mind to produce it, to sustain it; for rational will is the result of mind, not of passion; and that mind did not then exist, nor does it now.

The agitators of the present day, Radicals I may not call them, have suffered greater humiliations than we did. With the example of our disasters before them, they have not avoided one evil which we encountered, nor produced one additional good. On both occasions there was too much of the 'sounding brass and tinkling cymbal,' but latterly it has been varied by dark counsels and criminal instigations from their own authorized ones. Then followed delegations, and the silly egotism of portraits, and mock-solemn conventions, and formal self-displaying orations, and words and phrases bandied beyond all human entertainment. Next came multitudes deserted of leaders, – who stood at a safe distance, – and they drove before them a cloud and a whirlwind of terror and confusion, through which were seen flashes, and conflagrations, and blood-streaks; and when it had passed, all had vanished, and there remained dungeons, beside whose open gates were weeping wives and children, and prisoners, some victims to their own folly, and some to the wickedness of others, were marching in, chained by scores.

Oh no! the still small voice of reason has not been listened to now, more than it was formerly. It speaks a language too pure, too un-assuming, too disinterested, for any human crowds that have yet appeared. It requires great sacrifices for the obtainment of great results, – a stripping of all vanity, – an abandonment of all self, – and a cleansing from all lucre. Its appeal could be understood by rare minds only, and they have not been found.

That divine monitor would caution us against the continuance in a course of folly hurtful to ourselves and others. She would have done with the repetition of mendicant harangues for the sake of lucre, – she would not have any spending of children's bread-money, in the purchase of guns, daggers, pikes, and pitch-torches, – she would not rest satisfied with outward and visible signs, nor con-fide in the assemblage of crowds, nor the passing of resolutions, nor the clapping of hands, nor waving of handkerchiefs, nor collections of money, nor the flaunting of banners, nor great dinners, nor pro-cessions, nor 'Soirees.' Turning away she would denounce them as 'vanities of vanity;' and the least of all that men could do, calculated to

Kindle souls, within degraded flesh.

Nor would she, incendiary-like, be found giving the advice to cease working, nor ordering the collection of myriads to deliberate, so that deliberation was impossible. She would not infringe on the rights of others, by, overawing the timid, disturbing the peaceful, and denouncing the upright, for refusing to go with our 'multitudes to do evil.' No! justice walks with reason, and she cuts both ways; she will not endure oppression under any guise.

Mildly and persuasively as a mother entreating, would reason lead us to self-examination, self-control, and self-amendment, as the basis for all public reform. Canst thou not control thyself, and wouldest thou govern a household? Canst thou not govern a house-hold, and yet wouldest thou direct a nation? Come to thine own bosom and home, and there commence a reform, and let it be imme-diate and effectual. One evening spent in the acquirement of useful knowledge, – in rational conversation, – in the promotion of kindly feelings, – in the restraints of sobriety, – in the comforting of families, – in the blessings of children, and the improvement of their hearts and understandings, – in the devisements of cheerful economy and industry, – in the feeling of mercy towards all God's creatures, and of love of all goodness, for his sake; one evening so spent, were to thyself and thy country, worth more than all thou hast seen, heard, or done, at Radical or Chartist meetings, since sun-light or torch-light first illuminated them.

Instead of wishing to create sudden changes, and to overthrow institutions it were better that ignorance alone, the fruitful mother of arrogance and hard-heartedness, were pulled down. The masses should be elevated; instruction becoming the hand-maid of God's grace; for it would be his work after all. Whatsoever was offensive to right feeling, or opposed to the well-being of mankind, would then disappear and become absorbed in the great up-rising of mind. Many who are now but as atoms in the dust, would then become exhalted; many would become nobles, in the truest sense; many would be masters, not so much of others as of themselves; and, affectingly sublime would be the spectacle of that new dominion of light and peace; the aurora of that great day, when, 'the lion shall lie down with the lamb.'

A virtuous and enlightened people could not be enslaved. Having conquered themselves, where should they find oppression to conquer?

[1]Turn then ye working men, ye Chartists, turn from the precipice whither you have been led blindfold, by men worse than blind. Tear off your bandages, – look around, and retrace your steps. Be not ashamed to do so; 'tis creditable to renounce error. Come back with lightened hearts to your own fire-sides, as yet undarkened by crime. Endearments are still awaiting you, – know their value, – husband the few comforts yet remaining to yourselves and families, – buy food, – clothing, – such as you may, – not arms; – those will be at hand when wanted, – when nothing else will suffice, – and, do not forget, that he is the best reformer amongst you, who, in pro-portion to his means, best nurtures his family, and instructs his children!

In such a course you would become superior to your oppressors, – to all oppression. You would have the sympathy of the good of all

---

[1] Extracted from *La Lyonnaise*, by Beranger, rendered into English verse by the Author of this volume; inscribed to Ebenezer Elliott, and addressed to 'The Hand-loom Weavers of Lancashire, and the persons styled Chartists' previous to the wickedly devised, and foolishly attempted 'National Holiday' of the latter, in 1839.

classes, – of all mankind on your side, and you would assuredly triumph. But, one day of outrage would cover you with horror, – all would be against you, and the freedom which is now brightening in your horizon, would be darkened during another twenty years.

'Away then with the pike and dagger ere you become brigands and outlaws! Turn from those who have hallooed you on to havock! Let your dream of rapine be dispelled, and the proud ones of the land shall soon know, that you are more nobly proud than themselves.'

'It is true, the middle and upper ranks have scarcely been just towards you; they have not cultivated that friendship of which you are susceptible, and more worthy than they. Had they done so, you would not have been in the hands you now are. But you can look above this misdirected pride and pity it. The rich have been as unfortunate in their ignorance of your worth, as you have in the absence of their friendship. All ranks have been in error, as it respects their relative obligations, and prejudice has kept them strangers and apart. But the delusion is passing away, like darkness before the sun, and knowledge, against which, gold is powerless, comes like the spreading day, raising the children of toil, and making their sweat-drops more honourable than pearls!'

Chapter 51

First impressions on entering Lancaster Castle — Debtors Yard and Debtors — The Round Tower and its Inmates — Another Prison Ward — Comfortable Anticipations — A Sleeping Cell — Author's horrible sensations on being locked in — Henry Hunt and John Knight, Bailed

OUR arrival seemed scarcely to have been expected so early as it took place, for, it was not until we had waited some time between the inner and outer gates that a young man, whom we afterwards found was the governor's son, made his appearance without coat, and with other indications of a hurried dressing. Having perused the documents presented by Nadin, and cast a hasty but observant glance at his prisoners, he conducted us into the debtors yard, where we were greeted with a shout and many good wishes, and shaking of hands by some debtors who were abroad. A very brief reconnoitre was sufficient for the settlement of any doubts as to the place being a most excellent one for safe detention. All around were high and frowning barriers of masonry, and we felt as completely shut in from the world, as if we were at the bottom of a great well, where neither force, nor art, nor supplication, were of any avail. On our right were high and smooth walls, capped by moveable spikes, threatening impalement to any wight, whom a desperate good fortune enabled to ascend there. At regular distances were strong prison towers containing sleeping cells; a little more in our front stood the huge gloomy mass, known as, 'John O'Gaunt's tower,' which looked like a pile hewn square from the solid rock. At the top of the yard, and on our left, were the habitations of the debtors, with their small windows all looking down into the great well; whilst, from the casements, and crib-looking loop-holes, some of the poor fellows stood clapping hands, and waving night caps, as if they really thought that a welcome to such a place must be as gratifying as to any other, and that a welcome was a compliment anywhere.

We were conducted from hence to the first criminal ward on our right, the tower of which is, I believe, called the round tower. Here we found several prisoners, and amongst them an attorney from Manchester, and his clerk, who had each been sentenced to three years imprisonment, for falsely swearing to a debt against my former fellow-prisoner, Joseph Sellers. Their time was nearly out, but the old attorney was apparently hastening fast to another world. He lay in one corner, on the floor doubled up, and in dreadful agonies from pains in his bowels and limbs; the latter caused by rheumatism. This place was very inconvenient, cold, and comfortless. A continued draught of wind brought the smoke down the chimney, and we were all coughing and nearly blinded. Soon after we were removed into the next ward but one, towards the round-house, and there we were comparatively at home, having a much better day-room and yard, and besides those amendments, we were all together, without any admixture with other prisoners, and were consequently at liberty to converse freely amongst ourselves.

There were a good kettle and pan in the day-room, and good water in a pump in the yard: we went into the town for other kitchen requisites, as plates, knives, forks, and such articles; also for bread and butter; (until our prison allowance was given us) tea, coffee and other grocery and huxtery matters, and having a fire in the place, we soon contrived to make a good breakfast, and were quite merry over it. At dinner we fared no worse; we sent out for whatever we wanted, ale and liquors excepted; the prison allowance of vegetables and soup, were in part used by us, and the remainder we gave to a felon, who was allowed to come in and clear our day-room and cells very morning. The day passed off pretty agreeably, but towards evening Hunt gave way to fits of impatience because no one appeared to bail him. He in particular inveighed against Johnson, for having, as he said, invited him down to Manchester, got him into that trouble, and then abandoned him. Sooner, he said, than he would have done as Johnson had done by him – sooner than he would have walked home at liberty, and left his friend and guest in prison, he would have had his arm torn from his body. Mr Hunt generally made use of the strongest terms he could at the moment command, and to those of us who had frequently been in his company, exhibitions of violent feeling were by no means new. He had not the candour to reflect that Mr Johnson could not better serve us than by first securing his own liberty, as a means towards furthering ours; which in this case I believe he did.

Night came, and the rattle of keys informed us that we were about being introduced to our sleeping berths. We had our choice, and Mr Hunt took the cell next the door. I, at his desire, went to the next, as he said he could call to me if he should be unwell, and John Knight went into the third; the others of our party were lodged in the cells above. During the day, which turned out rather fine and clear, I had imbibed a favourable opinion of this prison. The day-room and yard were clean and airy, and whilst the attendant was sweeping out the cells and making the beds, I had gone in, and found them with their doors all open, lighted with the forenoon sun, and as white and sweet as a constant application of quick lime could make them. The cells were perhaps eight feet in width, by ten or twelve in length, and seven or eight upwards. Over a very strong door of wood – I think with clamped nails – was a square aperture for the admission of air; on the other side the door was the passage – beyond it again was a massive iron grating, and the entrance to the passage was also secured by another door, of, I think, iron. At the head of the cell was an iron slab, full of perforations, and resting on projections from the wall; a sack with straw in, a couple of blankets or so, and a good horse-rug, made up our bed, and the whole being apparently clean, I promised myself a sleep as sound as a king could enjoy in his cups. A capital prison, thought I, and a strong one too, and though it kept one from rambling out, it would also keep the storms from coming in as I should find, should I have to spend a winter or two within its shelter. Besides, I had heard, that these felon-dungeons were constructed under the direction of the celebrated 'humane Howard,' therefore, they must be the very best for comfort as well as security, and, as I said before, I, from their day-light appearance, and these considerations thought well of my domicile. But, in those days, I always looked on things on their brightest side.

We turned in, and my door had not been many minutes closed ere I began to feel as if I were being smothered. My old complaint on the lungs had gone with me to this place, and though I constantly was cheerful, very stubborn fits of coughing had convinced me that I was far from being well. I now began to feel as if I was closed up in a coffin, and not a breath of air above and around me. How dreadful were my sensations! I can never forget them. My chest heaved for air, but the cooling life-giving stream came not, and I stood leaning on my bed, pumping and gasping, in the close suffocating den. I thought of the black-hole of Calcutta, and concluded that the fate of its sufferers would be mine. I thought of getting up to the air-hole, but it was above my reach, and there was not anything in the place I could put my feet upon, else I should have deemed it luxury to have stood inhaling the blessed fluid all night. Oh! humanity! humanity? I thought, what is the humanity which builds prisons on such plans as these? I endeavoured to tranquillize my mind for the sustainment of this trial, and I found the effort was not made in vain. I was now coughing, and had burst into a profuse perspiration, and sitting on my bed, I felt a breath of air waft coolly and gratefully on my dewy forehead. I then knelt on the bed, and being more on a level with the air hole, I thanked God for the relief afforded by a more plentiful supply of the heaven-breathed element. Soon after I got cooler, my coughing became less frequent, and I lay down on the bed with my clothes on, promising myself a sound repose during the remainder of the night. I had not dropped asleep, when the rattling of the keys was again heard; the outer door was unlocked; lights glanced in the lobby, and the names of Hunt and Knight were pronounced; bail had arrived for them; they were called from their cells, and Hunt bidding me 'good night,' and saying, he would be with us again in the morning, the door was banged to and locked – the light departed – and I was soon in a peaceful sleep. I afterwards, so long as I continued here slept in Hunt's cell, but it was no better than the others; all were exactly the same as to dimension, and the too great exclusion of air.

Chapter 52

Prison Regulations — Fare — Mode of Life — Visits of Friends — Other Matters — Sir Charles Wolseley — Indictments Cut, and found true — The Grand Jury — Magnanimous Trait of the same

THE doors were thrown open in good time the next morning, and after we all had washed at the pump, we were subjected to the prison rule of examination as to whether we were infected by cutaneous disease. Some of our party felt indignant at this, considering it a degradation; but I, who remembered the unpleasant discovery at Cold-bath-fields, approved of it, reflecting that it was impossible to keep the inmates of a large prison, in a clean and healthy state, without daily examination. Our breakfast consisted of milk, coffee, and bread and butter, and I may as well mention here, that the prison allowance of gruel, bread, potatoes, soup, and butcher's meat were henceforward regularly dealt out to us; a small quantity of butter – I think to each man – was also given us twice a week in common with the other prisoners, but half of this was afterwards disallowed and cheese substituted, by order of the visiting magistrates.

The daily routine of a pent-up life, such as we led, could not afford much variety of incident. We were all – now that Hunt and Knight were gone – young men, and full of life and spirits. We chatted, sung, told stories, had hopping and leaping matches, and walked in the yard; we sometimes also wrote letters, and when one arrived from a wife or a friend, the lucky wight would retire aside and read it by snatches and morsels, lest it should be too soon done; newspapers were also permitted to pass, and we received one or more daily. Hunt and Knight also came to the round-house the morning after they were bailed, and then set off for Manchester, to make preparations against the day on which we should have to plead.

Meantime we continued to make ourselves as easy as possible. The doctor came to see me and gave me a mixture, which did me some good; but I obtained the greatest relief at night by standing, or kneeling on my bed, and inhaling the stream of air as it flowed in. On some nights, when my cough was rather merciful, I found amusement in composing, as at Cold-bath-fields, bits of rude verse, like the following:

> *Here is no repining;*
> *Every heart is true and steady.*
> *Here is no declining;*
> *Still for England's service ready.*
> *Here is not a tear shed;*
> *Such a weakness, we disdain it.*
> *Here is not a bow'd head;*
> *Sign of sorrow, we refrain it.*
> *The more the cruel tyrants bind us,*
> *The more united they shall find us.*

This verse pleased my companions exceedingly; and it afterwards became of some celebrity amongst the reformers.

One day, James Murrey, who was so dreadfully beaten at the White Moss, and one Heiffor, a barber from Manchester, were introduced into our yard by one of the turnkeys. They came for the purpose of looking us over, and identifying any of us who might have been present at that outrage, but, fortunately, none of our party happened to be on the moss that morning; and none of us were ever sworn to as having been there – at least, neither of these two visitors swore to any of us. After viewing us some time, during which not a word was interchanged, they went away. We remarked that persons frequently came upon the round house and on the great tower to look at us; and as we knew some of them were not our friends, we afterwards made it a rule to walk into the day-room and shut the door, the moment we noticed any such observers. We also made it a rule to sing 'The Lancashire Hymn,' every evening before locking-up time. We closed the door of our day-room during this piece of devotion – for we always sung in the true spirit of devotion – and surprised, at first, our almost insensible turnkeys, by the awakening of tones of sublime and heart-stirring music.

We were sometimes taken out to pump water, and that was a little variation from our dull life, it afforded us opportunities for practical joking, and some laughter. We went to chapel on prayer days and Sundays; and were also pleased with a trip to the great tower, where our heights were taken by a standard measure, and a description of our hair, eyes, complexions, and external marks, was carefully noted down in a book, and may there, probably, be found to this day, should any of my learned and searching readers wish to consult it.

One morning Sir Charles Wolseley, Hunt, Mr Thomas Chapman, of Manchester, and other friends, called us down to the round house, and, after some congratulations, and hearty shakings of hands, they informed us that several bills of indictment which had been presented against certain individuals of the Manchester Yeomanry corps, had been thrown out by the grand jury, whilst all the indictments preferred against our party had been returned true bills. They also informed us that the yeomanry at Manchester, had caused a strongly indignant feeling throughout the nation; that the public press had very handsomely taken up the affair, and that we needed not to fear being deserted in our struggle, for friends were coming from all parts to give bail for us. Mr Hunt put into my hand a copy of the *London Times*, in which was set forth an account of my arrest at Middleton, as already quoted. Sir Charles had also seen my dear wife and child, and in compliment to the spirited conduct of the former, on the above occasion, he had made her a present of a one pound bank note, for which kindness I sincerely thanked him, and felt relieved from some apprehensions lest they might be distressed whilst I was at this place; indeed we were all tranquillized by an assurance that our families would be protected during our absence from home. This, if I recollect aright, was the first time I had ever exchanged a word with Sir Charles; and it seemed I was destined to know him only for his kindness, many instances of which he afterwards gave me, as will probably appear in the course of this my narrative. He was one of the few who dared to be honest in the worst of times! who marched with the van of freedom against English mis-rule! – may happiness attend his latest moments of consciousness, and may his name be ever cherished in many hearts as it is in mine!

Mr Harmer, solicitor, of London, with Mr Dennison, of Liverpool, also called to see us. Mr Pearson, who, as we understood, was to be our legal manager in the case, was frequently at the gate; and what with the attentions of friends, and our own resources, we contrived to lead a much more worldly-mannered life than might have been thought possible in such a place.

One day, the iron gate of the round-house was thrown open, and a number of gentlemen entered and walked up the yard into the day-room, where most of us were at the time; we were given to understand they were 'the grand jury,' the same men who had found the indictments true against us, and had cut those against the magistrates and yeomanry. They looked at the place and at us for some time, but mostly at us; we also eyed them pretty closely, but no civilities passed; in truth, we had none to spare; and it was quite as much as we could do to refrain from reproaching them in words. That, to be sure, would have been a sad breach of the irresponsibility which hedges our English juries, but it would have been quite natural, and might have come with a not monstrously bad grace from men in our situation, and treated as we had been. There was perhaps enough said in our looks; they gazed at us till I suppose they could guess what we would say, and then they went back, and in reply, they stopped half our butter! One of our young fellows – Swift, I think – was devouring a wedge of bread and butter when they entered, and, as he had not the manners, or the cunning, to put it aside, but kept biting and chewing, and anon looking most wolfishly towards their honours and worships, that circumstance perhaps suggested the propriety, and the expediency, and the 'high and imperative duty,' of 'stopping our butter.'

When the time comes that the grand jury system shall be abolished, or greatly modified in England, the conduct of these gentlemen in the bills affair – not the butter – will be quoted as one very strong authority for the change.

Chapter 53

Prisoners called to Plead — The Sweating Room — Scene in the Court — Amount of Recognizances — Sureties accepted — Prisoners Liberated

AT length the day came when we were to appear before the court, to plead to the indictments found against us. The turnkeys conducted us through the round-house, through another yard, through a part of the great tower and into a long room at the back, which at this time was lighted by a lamp or two, casting a pale but distinct gleam through the place. Here we were told to wait, and there being a bench or two in the place, we were at liberty to sit if we chose it. I however preferred looking about me, and soon espied a man not of our party, who was seated on one of the benches. This room, I should inform my reader, was, as I afterwards learned, termed 'the sweating room;' it was the room in which prisoners waited until called for trial, and to which they were, in the first instance, conducted after trial: it was therefore, indeed fitly named. How many hundreds of victims – some, doubtless, innocent – had there sweated until their hearts were sick? The one before me, was an example to the point; he sat near the light, and I remarked him well. His dress and general appearance were those of a respectable country shop-keeper, or small farmer. He seemed to be about forty years of age, his hair a little grey, and smoothed decently, but not affectedly, on his brow. His coat was drab and of the plain country cut; one of those good, but old-fashioned, purple and spotted silk handker-chiefs, was around his neck; and his shirt collar, which was turned down, looked so plain and white, that my imagination reverted to his comfortable country home. He sat with his hands clasped betwixt his knees, and his looks directed intensely, but calmly, towards a door in another part of the room. The sweat stood in big bright drops on his forehead; so big that they broke into each other and trickled down his face. Then he would wipe his brow, and soon again it would be clustered with the perspiration. He came from some country place near Bolton, and had just been tried for the then deathly crime of passing forged bank notes, and acquitted; another indictment, however, lay against him, and he was waiting to be again conducted into court.

'He is an old offender,' said our turnkey, 'and if it goes against him this second time, he may say his prayers – nothing can save him.'

'But surely,' I said, 'if he only escape this once more, he will never give you a chance of having him here again?'

'I rather think he will get off;' he said, 'the old judge seems not very fond of these things; but then he'll be here again – he's well known – he cannot keep out of it.'

'Has he ever been taken before?' I asked, 'No,' replied the turnkey, 'but they have had their eyes on him some time, and it's well known he's done a deal in the note line. He might as well go up and be cast now,' he continued, 'it will only give us trouble another time, we're sure to have him, when once they get properly into the note business, they never give over till it's too late.'

The door from the interior opened, a person entered, and speaking to our conductor we were motioned to go forward. We descended some steps and passed along a subteranean passage nearly dark; at the further end of which the light increased, and we could hear voices and a kind of confused hum above. In a few minutes, a man was handed down some steps into the passage, by another who held his arm; the former appeared to be in distress – they passed to the room from whence we had come, and our guide motioning us to advance, we mounted the steps, and found ourselves in a oblong box or compartment, mounted by iron spikes, in a large crowded place, lighted by numerous lamps and chandeliers, and with hundreds of eyes gazing upon us. The spectacle was certainly calculated to inspire us with awe and alarm; our sudden transition from our scene of gloom and wretchedness to one of light and splendour produced a momentary confusion of mind, a vacant wonder and uncertainty as to what all this could mean. One moment however, and a glance around, were sufficient to recall the mind to its duty; and then whilst the ear was listening, the eye was observing, and the memory receiving impressions which have never yet been erased.

In the box where we stood, were besides ourselves, several officers of the prison; the deputy governor, the young gentleman who received us at the gate, stood in a small space on one side; behind us, but separated from our box, was a packed mass of human beings; with javelin men in their liveries, and their glittering weapons. On our right was a large pew or compartment crowded with well-dressed persons; before us, and somewhat elevated, sat the judge, a man of venerable years, clothed in a long robe of bright scarlet and ermine, with a flowing white wig, and a countenance of rough, blunt mould; a look like that of a surly old lion, at once stern, wilful, and magnanimous; – this was the venerable Baron Wood. On the bench with him, were several gentlemen and ladies – probably the sheriff and his friends; all the space on the left was equally crammed, and the galleries on each side were crowded with elegantly attired females; who, I flattered myself, seemed generally to be pre-possessed in our favour. On the floor betwixt us and the judge, was a large table covered with green cloth, on which lamps were burning, and books, papers, and writing apparatus were confusedly distributed; around the table were a number of barristers in their costume; some writing, some conversing, and others observing us. Hunt, Moorhouse, Johnson, and Knight, were in the space near the table, on the judge's right. Sir Charles Wolseley, Mr Chapman, Mr Harmer, Mr Dennison, Mr Pearson, and a number of other friends, were near them; and every other inch of the floor was occupied. A number of reporters for the metropolitan and county press were also there, plying their ready pencils; and it is probable, that the description of this scene, which some of those gentlemen sketched on the spot, might, if now consulted, display a more correct and striking picture of the group, than the present one drawn from memory alone.

Mr Littledale, who on this occasion acted for the government, requested that the indictment might be read, and it was accordingly read by the clerk of the arraigns. It stated that the prisoners, being persons of a wicked and turbulent disposition, did on the first day of July, conspire and agree together, to excite tumult and disturbance; and that they did, on the sixteenth day of August, unlawfully, maliciously, and seditiously, assemble together, and cause others to assemble, to the number of 60,000, in a formidable and menacing manner, with sticks, clubs, and other offensive weapons; with banners, flags, colours, and placards, having diverse seditious and inflammatory inscriptions, and in martial array; and did, on the said sixteenth of August, make great tumult, riot, and disturbance; and for half an hour unlawfully and riotously, did continue assembled, making great tumult and disturbance, contrary to the peace of our Sovereign Lord, the King, &c. &c.

Each of us pleaded, 'not guilty,' and elected to traverse until the next assizes. The judge purposed naming the amount of our bail in a few days, but after being respectfully urged with sundry good reasons, for an immediate determination, he mentioned, ourselves in £200, and two sureties, each in £100, as the amount of recognizance which would be required on behalf of us, who were in custody. We were then re-conducted to our old quarters, and our fellow defendants on bail, departed into the town with their friends.

I may as well mention, that the poor fellow we had seen in the sweating-room was again put to the bar the same night, to answer an indictment for uttering another note of the same parcel as the one for which he had been acquitted belonged to, but in consequence of the strong observations of the worthy judge, who held this was a part of the transaction for which he had been already tried, the man again got off – I believe no evidence was tendered. If I am not mistaken in the person however, he was soon after apprehended for a like offence, and the predictions of the turnkey were verified.

On Tuesday, the seventeenth of September, we were again brought up to put in bail. Hunt, Knight, Johnson, and Moorhouse, were each bound in £400, and two sureties, in £200 each; and the conditions were that we should severally appear on the first day of next session of Oyer and Terminer, to answer the indictment which had been read. All the required forms having now been complied with, Sir Charles Wolseley and Mr Chapman becoming my sureties, we were discharged from custody; and after some show off, by Mr Hunt, without which indeed, he scarcely knew how to get out of any matter, we left the dock, and went with our friends to an inn in the town, where we took a frugal repast, and remained for the night.

One encouraging reflection will come in place before I close this chapter, it is this. The observant reader will have noted that we were sent from the New Bailey to Lancaster Castle, because we had not sureties ready to give bail with us. Now suppose a catastrophe like that of Saint Peter's Field was by any means to take place in Manchester in these days, does not the reader feel assured that no ten honest labouring men would be allowed to be dragged off for want of bail? I am of opinion that now, gentlemen in great numbers and of vast wealth, would come forward without the slightest appeal from the prisoners, and tender themselves as sureties for the fulfilment of the law. Such, if my view be correct, is the great change which has taken place since the year 1819; and should not this change, which is only one of many, that are and have been working vast alterations for the better, in men's thoughts and feelings, encourage us to hope that even without tumult, or violence, or destruction of property, or oppression of person, all that is requisite for the redemption of our native country, will in due time be ours if we can only have patience to rest upon reason, and eschew violence. Some are in the habit of shouting, 'no surrender,' but I say we should all surrender; we should surrender our passions, and our prejudices, and our uncharitableness towards others. We should seek to win as much as we can from the common humanity of our adversaries. The good and the wise will pursue this course, and they will succeed, whilst the treacherous, the arrogant, and the intolerant will dwindle far behind in the march, and will perish of self-contention, instead of coming up to win the laurels.

Chapter 54

Progress from Lancaster to Manchester — Preston — Blackburn — Bolton — Manchester — Hunt and Moorhouse — Vanity of Vanities — Home

IT had been arranged that we should all travel the country back from Lancaster in a four horse stage coach. One belonging to Moorhouse, which had conveyed some of our friends to Lancaster, was accordingly selected, and in it and upon it we left Lancaster on the morning after our liberation. Some very inflated and bombastic accounts of this progress, if I may so call it, appeared in several publications of those times, but, as it is not my wish either to give a reprint of exaggerations, or to detract from the real honour of our triumph by a wreath of tinsel, I must leave such statements as I find them in the prints of the day. The morning turned out to be as fine a one as any holiday-folks could wish. We were cheered by rather large crowds in the streets of Lancaster, breakfasted at Garstang, and on approaching Preston, we fell in with multitudes of people, numbers of whom carried handsome flags and banners, some with the words, 'Hunt and liberty,' and various other matters. From Preston to Blackburn, the crowds increased, and our passage through the latter town was more prolonged, and the shouts louder than before. From Blackburn to Bolton, we were, I believe, drawn the whole of the way, and the honest and simple-hearted country weavers seemed to think no labour, no distinction too great for the persecuted travellers. At Bolton we were similarly welcomed; Mr Hunt, and Mr Pearson each addressed a dense crowd from the windows of the Swan Inn. We stopped at Bolton all night, and went towards Manchester on the morning of Thursday, the ninth of September. On arriving at Pendleton, the crowds became immense, and we approached the town at a very slow pace. Several stand coaches containing friends who had come out to meet us, here joined the procession. The spectacle now, was calculated to produce feelings of surprise, and perhaps, of pleasure; but any feelings of that sort were saddened, in my breast, by seeing all this fine energy cast like flowers at the feet of one whom I now began to suspect, was excessively egotistical; and I almost doubted, whether he who loved himself so well, could ever really love his country for its own sake; whether one of such a nature could be expected to remain faithful, if, from any change of circumstances, his country no longer yielded the incense to his self love, for which his whole heart seemed to beat. But I was amused, as well as a little humiliated, by what was continually occurring near me. Hunt sat on the box seat; I sat immediately behind him, and the other defendants were disposed of as suited convenience. Moorhouse stood on the roof of the coach, holding by a rope, which was fastened to the irons at each side. He had kept that position all the way from Bolton, I am not quite certain whether or not from Blackburn. Hunt continually doffed his hat, – waved it lowly, – bowed gracefully, and now and then spoke a few kind words to the people; but if some five or ten minutes elapsed without an huzza or two, or the still more pleasing sounds, 'Hunt for ever,' – 'Hunt for ever,' – he would rise from his seat, turn round, and cursing poor Moorhouse, in limbs, soul, or eyes, he would say, 'Why don't you shout, man?' 'Why don't you shout?' 'Give them the hip' '—— you, don't you see they're fagging?' Moorhouse himself was fagging; he would however, wipe his forehead and face, which were as red as a kiln, and waving his hat, and raising his voice, now become perfectly hoarse, he would, 'hip,' 'hip,' and the third 'hip,' was generally drowned in a loud huzza, accompanied by the afore-mentioned exclamation, now become so grateful to the ears of our leader; he would then resume his seat, the bowing and hat-waving went on as before, we had a little calm, and advanced a short dist-ance, Moorhouse was again reminded, and the many-throated voice again yielded the words of acclamation. At times I had some diffi-culty to avoid laughing in Hunt's face; at times I was vexed at being a party in such a piece of little vanity; I contrasted all this glare and noise, with the useful results of calm, sober thought, and silent determination, and I made up my mind that, when once out of this, I would not in future be any party in such trumpery exhibitions; in the unworthy setting up of the instrument, instead of the prin-ciple of a great cause. To this resolution I have, I think, been faith-ful; and though I have been, and still may be blamed, it is not likely that I shall ever depart from the rule.

We arrived at Smedley, and were all hospitably received by Mr and Mrs Johnson. At length I got away, and with my wife on my arm, and my little girl holding my hand, I was once more happy in traversing by hedge-sides, with their autumnal hues, towards that lowly home, from which thirteen days before, I had departed under such different circumstances.

Chapter 55

Oldham Inquest — Reporters excluded — Peter Finnerty — Condy, Ross, and others — Author corresponds with the Press

I SHALL not pretend to enter into any thing like a general history of those times, but shall content myself with stating events which more or less affected my own concerns. The inquest on John Lees, at Oldham, commonly called the Oldham inquest, was the next transaction of importance, as connected with our unfortunate meeting. I was without work, and so I put a pencil and some paper into my pocket and went to Oldham, with a view to copy such parts of the evidence as, in my opinion might be useful in the ensuing trial in which I should have to take a share. The inquest was held in the large room of the Angel Inn. The reporters for several London journals had been put out of the room, for persisting in furnishing daily reports contrary to the coroners order, and a rather strict supervision was held over the other reporters, both for the London and Provincial press, lest they should trespass in like manner; a few reporters only, were therefore admitted, and I took my seat beside them, and noted down very expertly for a first effort, a good deal of the evidence which was given on that day. At one time there was a general clearing out amongst the reporters – several had got in, and were taking notes as usual, the coroner therefore ordered them out, and Mr Barnes, editor of the Times, Mr Ross, and Mr Condy, were expelled, as was also Mr Finnerty, of the Morning Chronicle. The coroner asked who I was? and on my explaining to him my motive for attending and taking notes, he said no more, and I remained, one of the privileged few. A short time before this, whilst perambulating the streets of Manchester in search of work, I was going down Bridgwater-place, when a gentleman threw up a window of the Bridgewater Inn, then the head Inn of the town, and called me by name. It was Mr Pearson, our attorney, and he, finding I was at liberty for a short time, asked me in introduced me to Mr Finnerty, who was stopping there; and thus I became personally known to that rather remarkable man. I had previously learned somewhat of his history from several passages in Cobbett's Register. He had suffered under the government of Castlereagh in Ireland; had been convicted of a libel in England, and had gone through a long imprisonment for it, in Lincoln Castle.

When I came out of the room at the inquest, Mr Finnerty, profiting by his accidental knowledge of me, asked me into a room, and with much ease, and perfect self-possession, in neither of which was he seldom deficient, he enquired what I had been doing at the inquest, and on my producing my notes, he slapped me on the shoulder, and continued, 'Ah! Bamford, my dear fellow; you must let me have the loan of those notes. You will I know – won't you now?' I said I could not spare them; they would be of service to me on my trial. 'Ah, and is it the thrial your dreaming about? niv'r disthress yourself on that account, man: you'll all be well taken care of. Why isn't there Harmer here, and Pearson, our friend, and Hunt, himself a host? Ah! my dear friend, you needn't be bothering your head about the thrial yit. You could let me have the notes, you know, and get them back in print – they'll do you honner, boy! and hear ye now, I'll pay you for your throuble.' I refused to part with my notes, to the evident chagrin and disappointment of my new friend, who eyed me with his peculiar owl-like squint, and paraded to and fro, in fretful mood. I however kept my writings, and went home; and in a day or two I received a note, requesting me to call on him at the Bridgewater Arms. I did so, and the result was, that I agreed to attend the inquest on his account; and to furnish him with notes and verbal communications for the Morning Chronicle. I accordingly attended at Oldham, during several days, and afterwards at the Star Inn, Manchester, until the proceedings were quashed on the alleged ground of an improper interference with the jury. And thus commenced my first correspondence with the public press.

Chapter 56

MR HUNT it would seem, had been taken with a horror of Lancashire juries and Lancashire jails. Nothing would satisfy him save a
removal of the trial to another county, and in accordance with his
pressing solicitations, myself and the other co-defendants, joined
him in an application for a removal; and after a hearing before the
judges, the application was acceded to, and the cause ordered for
trial at the next Spring Assizes at York.

Seeing, as I suppose, that I was pretty active with my pen, and
had besides, rather more than a mere countryman's share of ready
information, Mr Finnerty intimated that if I were in London, he
could procure an engagement for me at the Morning Chronicle
office. Mr Pearson approved of the idea, and was almost sure that
something for my advancement in society, would offer if I were only
at the metropolis. Sir Charles Wolseley entirely coincided, but,
whether I went to London or not, he should be glad at any rate, to
have me as his guest during a week or fortnight at Wolseley Bridge.
These flattering prospects determined me, and a day or two after
Mr Finnerty had left Manchester, I arrived by the coach at Wolseley
Arms Inn, Wolseley Bridge. During the supper, which the coach
passengers took together, a London reporter before-mentioned, and
a tradesman from Manchester, who shortly afterwards became
bankrupt, made as I thought, some too free allusions to the parts
which Sir Charles Wolseley, and Mr Finnerty, had been acting in
the Manchester affair, and to their political conduct generally. I
remained silent some time, until I perceived a look directed towards
me. I then said, it was a pity the two gentlemen they had been
making free with, were not present, but if they would stop whilst
a message was sent to the hall. I had no doubt they would soon
come over, and give the talkers whatever explanation they chose to
ask to their face. My sentiment was approved of by several at the
table, and especially by one gentlemanly-looking man, whom I
thought would have been with the other party. 'John,' I said to
the waiter, 'Yes, sir,' – 'Can you step to the hall, and, – 'coach,

gemmen,' – 'coach, coach,' said the driver at the door, and in a trice the two respectable back-biters had left the room, when I and several other of the passengers enjoyed a laugh at their expense.

The next morning I went over to the hall, and found Finnerty quite comfortably domiciled. Lady Wolseley was in the straw up stairs, so that Sir Charles had much of his own way below. Friend Finnerty, now that he had the run of a splendid suite of apartments, attendance of servants, and all hospitalities, was also somewhat changed in his manner. His place was in the parlour with Sir Charles; mine in the housekeepers room, with the occasional company of that amiable, respectable, and well-informed lady. I dined with her in the servants hall, and took my other meals in her apartment, in company with her, the lady's maid, a joking, smiling, and modest young girl, and a Monsieur something, the French cook, I lived pretty agreeably amongst my kind hearted new acquaintance, yet, at times, I could not prevent gloomy sensations from pressing on my mind. Finnerty had become quite condescending, for which I could not prevail on myself to feel thankful. Sir Charles was always kind and affable, without pretension, but still I could not but feel that in his house, I was, only a very humble guest. I had read how 'an Ayrshire ploughman,' had once been deemed good company for a Scottish duchess, but I found that the barriers of English rank were not to be moved by 'a Lancashire weaver,' though he could say, 'I also am a poet,' and, quite as much as the Scottish bard, a patriot also. I lodged at the Inn, and often on mornings, would I stroll out solitarily, to look at the deer on the moorlands. Those majestic and beautiful animals, would toss their proud antlers – gaze a moment in surprise, as if they also knew I was a stranger, – and,

> Stretching forward free and far,
> Seek the wild heaths.

Sometimes I rambled through the town of Rugely, but I knew not any one there, nor did any one know me, and my visits consequently yielded but little social intercourse. Often would I saunter through the secluded and quiet village of Colton, but I knew not then, that such a man as Walter Savage Landor existed, and if I had, I am not certain that I should have ventured to knock at his door. The little village of College, or Col-edge, with its church, the banks of the Trent, and the grounds about Wolseley Hall, were often the objects of a contemplation which was continually wandering to other scenes. Several times I went with Monsieur to shoot rabbits, but I killed none; and was more likely to be shot myself; twice I walked across my comrade's fire, and the pellets came peppering about my legs. I was thinking of other things. Wearied, but no ungrateful; out of place, and, 'out of geering,' as the mechanists would say, in one of my fitful moods, when in all that beautiful district, I could see but little that was beautiful, I sat down in the inn and wrote the following lines.

> Fair is the prospect to my view,
>   Altho' it be confin'd
> But oh! 'tis nothing like the scenes,
>   Which I have left behind.
>
> Yon' eminence but shews a farm,
>   With trees thick scatter'd round;
> My hills rip out the rushing storm,
>   And by the clouds are crown'd.
>
> And peaceful seems yon' group of cots,
>   With chimnies painted white;
> But there is one, though far away,
>   More pleasing to my sight.
>
> And College bells must sweeter ring,
>   Before they ring as sweet;
> As those which o'er Saint Leonard's hang
>   The Sunday morn to greet.
>
> And Trent too, loiters by the way,
>   As journeying to the main;
> My streams rush onward rapidly,
>   The briny flood to gain,
>
> Oh! there is something wanting here,
>   Which cannot be supplied;
> Save on those hills for ever dear,
>   Where once I did abide.

At length the glad morning came, when an end was to be put to this. I was to go with Finnerty to London, with a gig and horse, which Charles Pearson had left at Stafford, I think, on his way down to Lancashire. Sir Charles made me a present of two pounds; Finnerty took the whip, and bidding good morn to our worthy host, we drove slowly from Wolseley Hall.

Chapter 57

Rugely — Mavesyn Ridware — Appearance of the Country — The Old Mare and her Appeal — Litchfield — Birmingham — Finnerty's Mishap — Stratford on Avon — Shipston — Finnerty leaves for Oxford

WE passed through Rugely, Mavesyn Ridward, (Malvoisin, one of the heroes of Ivanhoe) and along a rural country of farm-steads, clustered cottages, and other sights of profitable industry. I soon thought Finnerty was but an indifferent driver, he could not get the mare to go; he kept lashing, stamping on the bottom of the gig, hissing, and calling 'go-'long,' but the tit did not quit the ground. She would trot a little down a slope or on a short level; but there was no speed nor any continuation. I often got out to ease her on the ascents, for I did not like to have my weight lashed out of her, but still there was little amendment; she could not get to a pace much more keep one; in fact she spoke by her manner, as plainly as a dumb beast could speak, 'I cannot do it gentlemen, – I would, freely if I could, but I have not the work in me – I am done – I am old!' I soon framed this address for her in my mind, and repeated it to my fellow-traveller, who said it was not so; she had been starved by some rascally hostler, and a warm mash or two would bring her round. He however withheld his whip rather more, until her pace became a creep, when again he would give her a cut or two, stamp, hiss, and lash again, and make up the lost lashes by as many imprecations against the 'scoundrelly hostlers.' I was right however; had she been fit for work, it is not likely that Charles Pearson would have left her.

I began to be amused by the manner of my fellow-traveller, and I thought better of him for laying the blame anywhere save on the dumb beast. I soon found that he wished me to be a useful companion on the road, that is, a kind of half cad, and half comrade;

and, as I really thought he had much goodness at heart, I felt disposed to humour him in all his bearable caprices.

At Lichfield, Finnerty spent an hour in looking at the cathedral, whilst I looked after the mare at the inn. At Birmingham, which we reached tardily, we dined, gave the mare a good feed, and after resting two hours, my friend, unexpectedly by me, gave the word to proceed, and, with reluctance on my part, for I thought the beast had done enough for that day, we went on to some road-side inn, about nine miles further, where we got down and the jaded thing was released and put into a warm stable. On looking over the luggage, it was discovered that a new silk umbrella, which Finnerty had brought at Manchester, was missing. He went into a passion, and stormed with all the wordiness and gesticulation for which his countrymen are remarkable; whilst I, sometimes provoked, sometimes amused, sat coolly and smoked a pipe until supper was ready. He laid all the blame on me; he expected I would have seen that the luggage was safe; he had trusted all to me, and was thus disappointed, like a fool as he was, for troubling himself about other people's welfare. He was sure it had been left at Birmingham, and it was my neglect in not putting it in the gig; and then again he repeated what it had cost him – two pounds, I think.

When I could get a word in, I reminded him of its being in his hand at a certain part of the road we had just come, on which he acknowledged that it was so; but he said he put it on my side, and I, no doubt, had suffered it to slip down by the apron. I was of the same opinion, that it had slipped out of the gig, but I defended myself from all blame as to its loss, proffering however to go back in the morning, and see if I could find it. This rather pacified him, and we got supper, but his philosophy had been too sorely tested, and when we parted for the night, he was in very bad humour. I got up early next morning, and went back on the road about four miles, looking at every rut by the way, but nothing could I see of the umbrella; as I returned I enquired at several places, but nothing could I hear of it. He was at breakfast when I got to the inn, and on making known the bad result of my search, the 'fat was in the fire,' again, and we yoked up, and went forward mutually dissatisfied.

At Stratford-on-Avon, he had come too a little, for I also had been knitting my brows. He went to see Shakespeare's monument, and I, the house in which the poet resided – a dilapidated place, the walls covered with the names of persons who had visited, and I added mine. An old chair, I think, and a lump of wood, called part of the stump of his mulberry tree, were the only moveables remaining.

At an ascent betwixt Stratford and Shipston, I must drive and Finnerty would walk, for the once. He got out encumbered with his top and box coats, and began to ascend a narrow track which I saw would lead him from the road, and not to it again; as he had not however, of late, paid much respect to my opinions, I thought, I might as well not obtrude them just at that moment, and so I kept moving forward, leaning on the gig-side, and keeping an eye towards my blusterous friend. He mounted to some height, when, looking up, he perceived his dilemma, and then, with a twist, and a jerk, expressive of impatience, he descended the way he had gone up. I laughed until tears came into my eyes, and had with difficulty composed myself, when, he having hallooed as loud as he could, and I having stopped, he came up puffing and perspiring, and so we went on.

At Shipston we learned that a coach would pass through the town that night for Oxford, and Finnerty took a sudden and to me a happy resolution, to proceed by it, leaving me to bring the horse and gig the day following, to the Mitre Inn, at Oxford. He intimated that he had a particular engagement to be there next morning; and thus, for the present, I lost the society of my troublesome, querulous, but sometimes amusing companion.

Chapter 58

Journey from Shipston to Oxford — Chapel House — Woodstock — Fair Rosamond — Blenheim — Aspect of the Country — Oxford — The Mitre — Mr Finnerty — Journey resumed

It was a fine morning when leaving Shipston, I urged the old tit gently on the road to the great seat of learning. Every nook, dell, and hill, was new to me; and the men, the women, the children, and the houses were objects for continual observation. The mare had it pretty much in her own way; her load was lighter, and she went trotting when she listed, and walked when she had a right to do, namely, up hill, and it was only when I detected her absolutely crawling that I touched her with the whip. At Chapel House, a large posting establishment, we both breakfasted, and then went on, through Eustone, Kiddington, and to Woodstock, the scene of the tale of Fair Rosamond, which had deeply interested me when a boy. At a respectable looking public-house where I stopped, I endeavoured to learn whether there was any tradition, as to the probable site of the famous bower of the unfortunate beauty, but the people knew nothing respecting it. I heard enough about Blenheim and its duke, but I should not feel justified in repeating what they said, and the less so, because the persons with whom I conversed were strangers to me, and neighbours to the nobleman, and therefore the more likely to remember his failings, and forget his commendable parts. The weather kept remarkably fine, and presented one of those sunny, balmy days, through which we English, so often look for the coming storms of winter. The country, especially near Woodstock, was all that heart could wish for: hill and dale, pasture, arable, and wood, appeared in continual succession.

> *A world of goodness spreads around,*
> *A heaven above doth bless me,*
> *But, man the foe of man is found,*
> *And laws unjust oppress me.*

On entering Oxford I was struck by the noble and venerable appearance of many of its buildings, which I concluded in my own mind, must be its churches and colleges. The streets were occupied by a numerous and very respectable-looking population, and I was not long in descrying, by the peculiarity of their dress, some of those fortunate and ingenious youths who, 'born with silver spoons in their mouths,' are, as we are taught to believe, 'designed by a wise providence,' and are certainly permitted by, a wise people (?) to spoon up, the riches and superfluities, which else, would by their very grossness, render said people dull of intellect, and sluggish in action; and yet I didn't think the young fellows looked like, 'spoonies.'

Having been directed to the Mitre Inn, I drove thither, and resigned the horse and gig to the hostler, with a charge to look well to the former. I then enquired at the bar for Mr Finnerty, and was shewn into a very smart room up stairs, where a plain featur'd lady beyond the bloom of life, with a bonnet on, dressed in a florid style, and with a deep pattern-shoe on one foot, was caressing a fine child that could run about. I paused and held back, the lady was surprised, – I apologized and said I understood Mr Finnerty was there. She said he was, and asked me to take a seat, he was in another room, and she would go for him, and she went out, taking the child with her. In a minute I heard my friend's voice as if something was wrong; he came in, shook my hand, and asked me to take refreshment. I took some tea, and meat, and gave him an account of my pleasant journey. Whilst we were talking, the same lady with another child, entered the room, and almost immediately went out again. He gave me to understand that the children were his, and that Mrs Finnerty, himself, and the children, would return to London together. He asked how I should go? and I told him that I should walk it. He asked when I should start? and I said I had no connections in Oxford, nor any business to transact, and I saw no reason why I should not set out that night, and had best be making my way. Of course, he said, if I preferred going, there could be no reason why I should not; he then gave me his address in London, and said I must be sure and call upon him, and he would, immediately on his arrival, have some conversation with Mr Perry, about me, and he doubted not that Mr Perry would put something in my way. I then got up, and taking me by the hand, he bade me good bye, and said I must be sure to see him in London. I said I would, and repeating his salutation, I came down stairs, and went into the street.

Chapter 59

Journey continued — A Country Public-house, its Company and Conversation — Morning — High Wycombe — Beaconsfield — Uxbridge — London

THE shades of evening were closing over the city, when I thus adventured to begin my journey. I had no luggage save a small bundle and an umbrella, which I threw over my shoulder, and a stout ashen plant in my hand. I knew not which way to set forth, but went along the street towards the left, until I saw some respectable-looking people, of whom I enquired the way to London; and they gave me such directions as enabled me soon to quit the town and strike into the open country. I continued to walk and it soon became dark, and when night had completely set in, I could scarcely trace the road before me. I walked however briskly, and went a long way without meeting any person, or hearing any thing save now and then, the tinkle of a sheep bell. At length, when I must have left Oxford four or five miles behind, I begun to hear noises at a distance on my right, and soon after I saw gleams like those of lights in the windows of a town. In a short time, there were lights before me, and I found they proceeded from a public-house, into which I went and asked for some ale, which was brought to me, and was of most excellent quality. On looking around, I liked the appearance of the house also, the rooms were neatly furnished and clean, the company was apparently respectable, and the people of the house obliging. I enquired how far it was to the next village, and how the road lay, and they all gave such an account as made me begin to think I had best remain where I was, the people of the house were of the same opinion, and so I took up my quarters there for the night.

Whilst we were chattering and enjoying ourselves comfortably with our pipes, some young fellows came into the next room, and called for ale. They were in high glee, and from their conversation, which we could not but hear, we learned that there had been a kind of battle-royal in the village, betwixt some of the lads of the place, and a party of collegians, and that the latter after fighting bravely, which they allowed them the merit of generally doing, had been soundly thrashed, and compelled to retreat. I concluded that it must have been the noise of this row, which had saluted my ears on the road. Some enquiries on my part, elicited an opinion from the company, as to the general conduct of the young gentlemen at college, and it certainly, like all other human emanations, had its dark side, as well as its bright one, only rather more of the former, than should be expected, considering they were to become examplers to, and directors of others.

They were represented as courageous fighters, generous remunerators, and profuse spenders; all of which most of the company allowed were good English gentlemanly qualities; but then, in their intercourse with those not of their class, they were represented as being arrogant, wilful, and capricious; and too prone to lay on hard, when they got the upper hand.

It was not to be wondered at – said an elderly person who sat on the other side of the room – it was not the young gentlemen's fault, but the fault of their 'Pa's' and 'Ma's' at home, and of the institutions of the country. If Will was schooled to be an officer in the army, would he not begin by trying to domineer over, and command all who would submit to him? If Dick was to have his father's broad acres, how could he better prepare for the enjoyment of them, as things went, than by learning to drink, gamble, and box; by picking up stable slang; and becoming a connoiseur in, 'dogs, horse-flesh, and women?' – as they had it – and by an early imitation of that reckless self-willedness, which he had seen practised by his class at home. If James is for the church, should he not learn to be combative when a boy; inasmuch as he would have to contend against 'the world, the flesh,' and, – another antagonist – and in favour of tithes, preferments, and fat livings? and if Jack was preparing for the navy, what so natural as that he should practise with a bamboo, instead of a rope's-end, on the heads and shoulders of the King's subjects? Great folks, he said, sent their sons to college, and they came there tainted with the vices of their order, and the follies of their parents: they were here planted thick together like young trees; the rank and worthless dragged the others up; the vicious overshadowed the virtuous, and when they had become noxious or morally withered, they went back into the world, as their fathers had done, to prepare a new race to succeed them. All allowed that the elderly gentleman's remarks were about the fact; I begged leave to drink his health, the company followed my example, and the conversation then becoming general, and chiefly on rural affairs, I went to bed.

I rose early; the morning again was as fine as could be desired, and I felt happy at travelling beside broad pastures, with the free wind blowing around me. I first traversed a level plain, and then went up a rather steep eminence, after which followed a road through woods a long way; all were new and interesting scenes to me. I walked some twelve or fourteen miles, and then made a hearty breakfast of bread, cheese, and ale, at a neat looking road-side public-house. From thence I went on, through High Wycombe, and Beaconsfield, where again I stopped a short time. I could not but admire the cleanness, and airiness of the town. Towards evening I arrived at Uxbridge, and rested, after which I went towards London, and had gone some miles in the dark and rain, when a stage coach overtook me, and I mounted, and was set down at the Bolt-in-Tun, Fleet-street, where, perhaps it is unnecessary to say, that I received very civil treatment, and stopped for the night.

Chapter 60

Mr Hunt and Family — Sir Richard Phillips — Author's Petitions to Parliament — Earl Grosvenor, and his House at Grosvenor Place

THE morning after my arrival I went to the warehouse of a friendly tradesman, in Cheapside, to look after some clothes, and other requisites, which I had directed to be sent after me, and I found all safe. I next went and took private lodgings, and then sought out Mr Hunt, who I found at the house of one Giles, a bread-baker, in Wyche-street, Strand. With him, was a certain tall, and personally fine-looking lady, whose history had excited much of my curiosity; and a gentle young being, a ward of his, as I understood, who was taking lessons in music, and preparing for the very arduous life of an actress. Whilst Mr Hunt and Mrs V. were briefly absent, she sung for me, and played on the piano forte; her tone and manner seemed tinged with melancholy, and when I thought of what trials she must surmount, or perish; what perils imminent, would continually beset her path; that Hunt only, was her guardian and protector, who did not protect his own; and especially when my thoughts reverted to my dear child at home, I became greatly interested in the fate of this gentle young creature. She sung for me, 'Scots wa hae wi' Wallace bled;' it was the first time I had heard the music, and I by no means thought it adapted to the words; I have heard it often since, and am still of the same opinion. Hunt and the two ladies, formed the whole of his family. They seemed to be living pretty comfortably together, that is, as comfortably as could be expected with one of his very unsteady temper. His caprice and violence, made the elder lady appear, at times, ill at ease; the younger meek and timid thing, would go to her music books, or take up sewing, or step into another room; the storm would be over in a minute, and all would be free and chatty again; but then, no one knew how soon the storm might return. The habits of the family were strictly economical, and nothing more. Hunt drank water or coffee, though beer (porter) or wine were not prohibited to the ladies, or guests; they seemed to have at their disposal, sufficient of worldly substance to ensure contentment, and were only wanting that, 'peace of mind, which the world cannot give,' and which never can exist except in the bonds of true tender love to each other, and the Creator. Hunt and Mrs V. had, in their early days, evidently been two of the finest of their species; they were as yet neither feeble nor bent, though somewhat marked by years. I compared them to a storm-beaten column, and a stately tree, from which the sun was already departing.

Hunt introduced me to Sir Richard Phillips, and I had, during my stay, many opportunities of conversing with that worthy gentleman and scholar. He was friendly towards Hunt, but did not like his overbearing manner. Once I recollect, when Hunt came, he ordered the footman to say he was not at home, and on observing probably, a degree of surprise in my look, he said Mr Hunt, was neither happy himself, nor would he let his friends be so. They must not only serve him, but they must do it at his own time, in his own manner, and to the extent he wished, or he would quarrel with them. His earnestness and vehemence, he carried with him everywhere, and exhibited on the most trifling occasions; in consequence, he became annoying and oppressive, and his best friends were sometimes compelled to defend themselves by not being at home. I knew there was too much truth in Sir Richard's representations, to blame him greatly for his conclusions, though I must own I did not like my friend Hunt, with all his faults, to be thus dealt with; but Sir Richard said there was no other mode, and he must either shut his door occasionally, or quarrel with him at once, and have done with him.

I gave Sir Richard, my account of the Manchester affair, and at his suggestion, and under his care, petitions to the houses of lords and commons, were drawn up on my behalf, praying an investigation into the whole of the transaction, and offering to prove the allegations of the petitions at the bar of each house. Both petitions were duly presented, and with the usual result, namely, both were 'laid upon the table.' How much more in character would it be if a shelf were put up in each house; the honoured applicant would then be understood when he said that his petition was 'shelfed.'

But, connected with my petition to the lords, an incident occurred, which, as it affords a glimpse as it were, of the outer court etiquette of the great in London, I will narrate.

Earl Grosvenor was the nobleman selected to present my petition to the house of lords, and Sir Richard went with me to his mansion in Grosvenor-place, I think it was. His lordship was not at home, and we were directed to call on a certain day. It happened that Sir

Richard was then engaged, and I went to his lordship myself. The great burly porter, who wore a rich livery trimmed with gold lace, would scarcely admit me within the door, when he found I had not a letter of introduction. I explained to him my business with his lordship, but it was of no use, he could not send my message up. A fine table, with pens and paper, was near the window of the hall, and in my simplicity I made a move towards it, saying, I could soon write a note to his lordship, but he said he could not allow me to write there; it was contrary to orders, and would cost him his place if the other servants saw me. I accordingly bundled out, and went to a tavern, and wrote a note, which I took back; the porter then took the note, and told me to come again in about twenty minutes, or half an hour. It was raining, and I had nowhere to go under cover, save the tavern, so I went there again, – not much liking however, this mode of noble housekeeping – and waited with impatience the time for the interview. I again went, and now the folding doors were thrown open, long before I arrived at the steps; the late surly porter received me with a respectful inclination, and a smile, saying my note had been sent up, and his lordship would see me. He then rang a bell, and a servant appeared, to whom the porter announced my name. The servant asked me to follow him, and he led me into a very grand room, where he led me, saying his lordship would be with me in a few minutes. I had never seen anything like the richness of this place before, every thing seemed almost too sumptuous, and too delicate for a human habitation, and to me it seemed a little museum of curious and costly things, arranged but to look at, and not to use. There were mirrors, and pictures, and cushions, and carpets glowing like silk; and delicate hangings, and curtains, as fine as gossamer in summer: then the tables shone like glass, and the chairs with their high cushions trussed up, quite tempted one to sit. Well, I stood looking about me some time, and no one appeared, and at last I thought 'I'll sit down at any rate; if his lordship should come in, he cannot be so greatly offended at one taking a seat in his house.' So I sat down, and was quite surprised; I almost sunk to my elbows in the soft downy cushion, and immediately jumped up again, thinking those seats could never really be meant for human bones to rest upon, and I would not for the world have been taken by his lordship, sitting there, with the cushion up to my elbows, like a puff of soap suds. I began to make the thing right again, and was so busied, when I heard a slight creaking noise; immediately I resumed my posture of attention, and a tall, gentlemanly-looking person, forty, or forty-five years of age, dressed in a blue coat with yellow buttons, undoubtedly of gold, entered and accosted me in a very courteous and affable manner, and immediately entered upon the business of my petition. I addressed him as 'my lord,' which indeed he was, and told him somewhat about the subject of my petition, which I now shewed him, and requested he would be so kind as present for me to the house of lords. He looked at it a few minutes, and said he would present it. He then questioned me about the state of the country, and particularly of my own neighbourhood, to each of which I gave him brief and true answers, according to the best of my ability. He then questioned me about our new rector, at Middleton, the Rev. John Haughton, and as I was bound in truth, though not at the time, over-partial to him. I gave his lordship a fair and honourable account of the worthy clergyman, whereat he seemed much pleased; soon after I made my final bow, and was myself bowed out by the porter, and so I took my leave of that grand mansion and its immensely rich owner.

Chapter 61

Sir Richard Phillips, his Advice — Alderman Waithman — Mr Finnerty, his Friendship — Author's Dilemma — Author's Sickness — Charles Pearson — Author assisted by the London Committee — Return Home

I FREQUENTLY called to see Sir Richard Phillips, who always advised me to cultivate literature and poetry, as two friends who would be ready to console me at all times, and under all circumstances. He wished me to write something in the metrical way, about the Manchester affair, but I never did; it never presented itself as it were, to me in the form of poetry; it was too overpowering, too brimful of affliction, to be measured in verse; I made several attempts that way, but it would not do, and I never sought to describe it in any other form until this present publication. I felt grateful to Sir Richard; he gave me much useful caution and advice as to other matters in London. He acted the part of a real friend, and was the only professed scholar and literary character, to whose acquaintance I can refer with entire satisfaction. He introduced me once to Alderman Waithman, at that time a dissatisfied, bilious looking man. He had recently experienced some provoking opposition in the city, and seemed as if both mind and manners were soured. I had no desire to meet him again, and I believe I never did.

I called several times at the office of the Morning Chronicle, to enquire if Mr Finnerty was in town, and at last learned that he was so. I accordingly made my way to a suburb, somewhere west of the town, and following my directions, I knocked at the door of one of a lot of recently constructed edifices, at the angle of a square. The same lady with the patten came to the door, and invited me to walk in, and shewed me into a small neatly furnished room on my right. Finnerty soon made his appearance, and after mutual compliments, he asked, when I arrived in town ? what I had been doing ? and such like, all of which I answered. He seemed, I thought, very mysterious and embarrassed in his manner; did not ask me to sit down, or take any thing, but at last said, would you like a walk round the square, Bamford ? I, thinking he wished for more private conversation, said I would, and we went out, and walked round a large square hollow, like to those laid down for the foundations of houses, with a fence of deal boards all around. We paced once round this place, chatting about indifferent matters, I expecting him to introduce my business with the Morning Chronicle, and at last, on my mentioning it, he did say he had not been able to see Mr Perry yet. We had then arrived at the angle from whence we set out, and were opposite his own door, when giving me his hand, he said, 'good morning, Bamford, I shall be seeing you in town some of these days;' and with that he went into the house, and shut the door. I was mute with astonishment; my first impulse was to send the pannel in with my foot, but then, I thought, neither the door nor its owner had done me harm, and at last consoling myself with the reflection that it was no place for a worthy honest man, and that I was better out of it than within it, I went away.

I should not have been much troubled at the sudden termination of this friendship, which I had for some time suspected to be all on my side; had I not, on returning into the city, weary, disappointed, and hungry, found that I must change my last shilling for my dinner. I had paid several sums on the road, for hostlers, baiting, and so forth, before Finnerty left me at Shipston; and I had also paid all the expenses of the journey from Shipston to Oxford, which Finnerty had undertaken to pay, and said he would re-imburse on my arrival at the latter place. I had quite forgotten to mention these matters at Oxford, but now forced by necessity I probably should have done so in a delicate way, had Finnerty, as I expected he would, asked me to take breakfast with him. But, as I said, they had quite slipped my memory, and friend Finnerty's too, as it seemed, and now I had the uncomfortable prospect before me of starvation, or a beggarly dependence on the hospitality of friends, neither of which conditions had I anticipated on leaving home.

Next morning I went to the house of Mr Pearson, in Aldersgate-street, and stated to him my willingness to try my hand at writing in his office, at terms previously mentioned by him, namely, a guinea a week. He immediately set me to work at copying, and thus by a word I was metamorphosed from a rude Lancashire rustic, into 'a limb of the law.' I worked hard until two o'clock, and then went out, not to dine, for I had not wherewith to purchase a dinner. At four I returned and wrote again until six, and then shut up, and went to my humble lodgings at London Wall. I did thus for three or four days, getting my breakfast and supper at my lodgings, and going without dinner. I began to feel unwell; I was cold, shivery, and nervous; I had never been quite well since the night I came drenched into London, and now, feverish as I was, the employment became intolerably irksome. At length I went to bed, and was so ill next morning I could not rise; I was in a fever, and the agitation of my mind, added to the indisposition of my body. My landlady was very kind, but I durst not ask her for anything beyond a little tea or gruel, lest she should want money, and I had none. I was scorching hot, and my tongue was baked like a crust. At length I got up, and went out, and pledged a silk handkerchief, and, thinking if I could get a mess of broth, such as I had used to have at home, they would make me well, I entered a eating house, and asked for a basin of broth, but they had not any of that sort. I then asked for a mess of stew, such as we had in the country, and explained to them what I meant, but they had not anything prepared in that way; they had very good ox-tail, and mock turtle soups, and a-la-mode beef, with plenty of soup to it, and on the recommendation of the waiter, I chose a plate of the latter. It looked very nice, and smelled well, and I promised myself a little savoury refection, but what was my surprise, when the first spoonful I took, I thought it must have parboiled my mouth. I had never tasted anything so hot before; I called the waiter, and told him how it was, adding that there certainly must be some mistake; he smiled – as did several persons who overheard me – and said it was right; a-la-mode beef was always so, and was allowed to be an excellent dish. I could not eat the beef, so I supped the broth, and went to my lodgings with my mouth and throat on fire, from the high seasoning of the soup. My head was now worse, my eyes were as heavy as lead, and I laid down, with some apprehensions lest I should die in that little dim back-room. I drank however, amazingly, of gruel and tea; soon after I was in a profuse perspiration, which continued all that day and until noon the day following, when I again got up, very weak, but the fever had left me. The next day I went to Mr Pearson, and told him that I had been ill, and hoped he would excuse me, but I could not bear to sit at the desk. He readily accepted my apology, and gave me a pound note for what I had done; he also invited me to come to his house that evening and take tea. I went and met him, his lady, a mild and beautiful young being, and a gentleman who was about to come out as 'a phenomenon' at the bar. The day after, I again went to Mr Pearson's by appointment, when he took me to Peel's coffee-house, and set me to take memoranda from the newspapers, of passages from the judges addresses to grand juries on several state prosecutions. I gave him my notes, and believe I did the work to his satisfaction.

In a day or two after this, I was informed that the London committee for the relief of the sufferers at the Manchester meeting, had determined on presenting each of the persons who had been apprehended and held to bail, with a sum of money – ten pounds, I believe, – as some compensation for their loss of time, and the inconvenience they had experienced. I, accordingly went to the counting house and manufactory of Mr Alexander Galloway, the treasurer, whose place was then near Holborn, and presented myself for the reception of what belonged to me. He was at his desk, writing, and I found him a cool, cautious methodical man of business. He was very affable, and mild; and I must say reasonable and convincing in his manner; he was about the middle height, forty-five years of age perhaps, a little stooping in the shoulders, with an appearance of industry about him, and very plainly dressed. On my stating who I was, and the nature of my visit, he said he was sorry he could not pay me then, as, never having to his knowledge seen me before, he could not be certain that I was the person I represented myself to be, and he wished me to bring some gentleman, or produce a note from some one whom he knew, that I was the same Samuel Bamford who had been arrested and committed to Lancaster Castle. I mentioned Mr Hunt, Mr Harmer, Mr Wooller, and Mr Pearson, who would instantly verify, could I get to see them, but the afternoon was far worn, and I might not be able to meet with them that night; I however, had a letter or two of Mr Hunt's, and one of Major Cartwright's which I offered to produce. Those, he said, would not do; they would not shew that I was the person to whom they were addressed. I must confess, I was now a little picqued, and disappointed, for I was in want of some money for immediate necessaries. He saw, I thought, that I was hurt, for he begged I would not deem him needlessly cautious, as I must perceive, on reflection, how necessary it was, in a great place like London, to be quite certain as to the persons with whom they transacted business. He shewed me, and he entirely conciliated me, by the earnestness with which he did it, that he could not possibly have any wish to withhold the money from the person for whom it was ordered, and all he sought to ascertain, was that I really was the person. I saw, and appreciated his motive, and his method of exactitude, and left him with the intention of obtaining a note from Mr Harmer, whose office in Hatton Garden, was the nearest place where I could expect to meet the requisite identification. Mr Harmer was not within, nor would he be that night, and I gave the matter up until next day, submitting to the rather familiar inconvenience of going to bed dinnerless and supperless. On the forenoon of the following day, I procured the necessary verification, and Mr Galloway paid me the money, which proved a great present relief as it enabled me to procure necessaries, and to pay off my lodging, and other small accounts. I afterwards called on Mr Galloway frequently, in a friendly manner, and at one of these visits, I saw Robert Owen, who was then exciting attention by his plans for the amelioration of the condition of mankind; at another visit Major Cochrane was there, an officer who was with the 15th hussars, on the field, at the great meeting at Manchester. Mr Galloway's counting house appeared to be frequently resorted to by literary and scientific men of all parties, and of all professions.

My petitions to parliament had been duly presented, and had appeared, thanks to my friend Sir Richard, in several of the London journals. They excited some attention, and the committee of the relief fund deemed it proper that similar petitions should be presented by others of the sufferers. I, accordingly, having now no further prospects, or business in London, returned to Lancashire, and besides being of some use to Messrs. Hall and Service, who were sent down to select proper objects for relief, I promoted the getting up of petitions praying for enquiry, and when that had been done to a sufficient extent, I found the time at hand when it was necessary that I should begin to look about for evidence, to produce at the approaching trial at York.

Chapter 62

Instructions for the Collection of Evidence — Other preparations for Trial — Meeting of Witnesses at Middleton — Journey on Foot to Leeds — Reception there

ON application to my attorney, Mr Pearson, I received a set of instructions for the collection of evidence, and as, to some of my readers, they may be a kind of legal curiosity, and to others in like emergency, should such occur, they may be of use, I here give them; they were as follows.

A. 1. – To prove that Mr Hunt arrived in Manchester in January – attended a meeting called by public advertisement. 2. – To produce the advertisement. 3. – To produce the resolutions. 4. – To prove that the meeting met and dispersed peaceably.

B. 1. – To produce the advertisement calling the meeting of the ninth of August. 2. – To produce the resolutions entered into by the magistrates prohibiting the meeting. 3. – To produce the posting bill of the reformers, acquiescing in the determination of the magistrates, and abandoning the intention of holding the meeting.

C. 1. – To prove the arrival of Mr Hunt in Manchester, previous to the ninth of August. 2. – To shew the peaceable conduct of the people assembled to greet his arrival, and also to prove Mr Hunt's peaceful demeanour, and the substance of his speech at St Michael's Church.

D. 1. – To produce the requisition calling the meeting of the sixteenth of August. 2. – To produce Mr Hunt's letter to the reformers. 3. – To produce a copy of the resolutions intended to have been passed.

E. 1. – To shew the preparations for attending the meeting on the sixteenth of August. 2. – That the assembling from different townships, did not take place from any previous concert between the defendants. 3. – To explain the origin, object, and character of the banners used in the procession. 4. – To prove the peaceful demeanour of the different parties from the various townships, in the approach to Manchester. 5. – To prove the proportion of those who carried sticks, – the description of such sticks as were carried, and the absence of all weapons of offence or defence. 6. – To prove the presence of numerous parties of women and children, some infants, at the meeting, and with the different columns of reformers, in evidence of the absence of all intention of mischief on their part. 7. – To prove the object of the music, and the use made of it, in playing national and loyal airs.

F. 1. – To shew the peaceable and quiet conduct of the persons at the meeting, before the military arrived. 2. – To prove the invitation to order, addressed to the meeting by Mr Hunt and others, before and after the arrival of the soldiers. 3. – To shew the violence and inhuman conduct of the magistrates in directing, and the yeomanry in effecting the dispersion of the meeting.

G. – To prove the state of the ground after the meeting.

H. – To produce evidence of the character of the prosecutor's witnesses.

I. – To produce particular evidence in favour of each of the defendants individually.

Such were the instructions furnished by our attorney, and perhaps, under the circumstances, better could not have been given. How far we acted up to them as a whole, will be seen whenever the report of the government short-hand writer is published, as it will be, I have no doubt, some day. For my part, I exerted myself to the utmost to make good my branch of the defence, which it will be observed, included many of the proceedings connected with the movements of the country parties. Acting under these instructions, I wrote down with my own hand, the examinations of about twenty-two witnesses, chiefly resident at Middleton, which examinations were copied literally by the clerk, and formed the basis of the defence relative to our proceedings. I next subpoened my witnesses, and they were requested to meet at the Dog and Partridge public-house, at Middleton, at six o'clock on the morning of Monday, the nineteenth of March, in order that we might all go in a body on foot to York. On the evening preceding we took supper together, and we were joined by a number of witnesses from Manchester, who preferred to walk with us rather than go by coach. On mustering, I think, we amounted to about three score, of whom, probably a dozen were women, who, in high glee, chose to take the road with their relatives and friends. I should state that Mr Pearson had placed in my hands a sum of money to pay the expenses, in which I was limited by my own discretion alone; all my plans had been laid before him at Manchester, and he entirely approved of them. We set forward therefore, with light hearts; and amid this crowd of faces beaming with hope and the excitement of novelty, I could discover two only which wore a cast of thought and sadness. My wife and child, were as they always wished to be, with me; they were going with us as far as Rochdale, whence they were to return; my faithful dog Mora also, went gambolling before us. I tried to be cheerful, with a view to promote the same feeling amongst all around me, and I could have succeeded, had I only been concerned; but when I caught my wife turning her head aside to conceal her emotion, and, looking down, met the tearful eye and enquiring look of my child, who held my hand, I could not but experience a pang that brought darkness and uncertainty to my heart, and which I endeavoured to conceal by smiles and consoling words.

At Rochdale, we breakfasted at the Angel Inn, in Blackwater-street, and were there joined by witnesses from Bury and other places, who augmented our numbers to about four score. After an affectionate parting, full of hope on my side, and of sadness on theirs, I left my wife and child to retrace their steps sorrowfully towards home, whilst I went forward, though somewhat thoughtful, amongst my joking, light-hearted companions. The ascent of Black-stone-edge, 'the back-bone of the English alps,' as it has been termed, tried the marching qualities of the women, and by the time we arrived at the top, two of them were fatigued, and went on with the mail coach, which overtook us there. Their journey by this convey-ance was a most unpleasant one; some 'gentlemen' (?) from Man-chester were also passengers, and they used coarse and abusive language towards the females. The coachman and guard were appealed to for protection, but they only laughed, and, to please 'the gemmen,' contributed their share of insult. The women, 'gave it them,' however, told them what they were, and when the coach arrived at Halifax, they got down, and refused to go any further with the unmanly beings. This conduct, we only learned on our arrival at Halifax, and I mention it to shew the strong and unworthy feeling which our opponents, even of the class commonly deemed respectable, were wont to indulge, in those days.

Mr Hunt, with Johnson and Chapman, followed us in a post-chaise, and they were detained a considerable time at Rochdale, in consequence of the land-lord at the Roe Buck Inn, one Marriott, refusing to supply them with fresh horses, on learning who they were. He was even uncivil to the travellers, but soon found that he was not likely to get anything by that mode of behaviour, and horses having been procured from another house, the journey was proceeded with.

At Bradford many of the tender-footed men were lame, and I gave them money to go on with as best they could. Most of the women also, had by this enough of walking that day, and they availed themselves of such modes of conveyance as were readily attainable; some however, held out, and walked with us every step of the road to Leeds, where we were hospitably received by the body of re-formers, and lodged for the night. The next morning we made a strong muster, being joined by numbers from Stockport, Hyde, Ashton, Staley-bridge, Saddleworth, and other places, and now I believe we mustered about one hundred and twenty persons: some of the women, and an equal proportion of the men, were too lame to walk, and were sent forward by carriage; the main body however, on foot, passed through Tadcaster, and arrived at York in a compact body, at night-fall, on Tuesday, the twentieth of March. We were lodged and boarded, at a large inn, the Elephant, I think, on this side the river Ouse.

Chapter 63

The morning of our Trial — Preparations in the Court — Its interior appearance — Witnesses — Hunt's Hat — The Jury — Counsel for the Prosecution — Arrangements for the Defendants

OUR long expected trial, which had excited a strong interest in the public mind, commenced on the morning of Thursday, the sixteenth day of March, 1820, before Mr Justice Bayley, and a special jury. At an early hour, the court was beset by persons waiting for admission. At a little before seven o'clock, the reporters for the London and Provincial press were admitted, and soon after several individuals, principally solicitors, and others connected with Provincial newspapers, were admitted into the gallery: a number of ladies also took possession of a box at the corner of the court, on the right hand of the bench. At eight o'clock, a more general admission of the public took place, and the front seats in the two galleries were instantly occupied. A vast number of persons immediately followed, till not one inch of either gallery was left unoccupied. The box which, the day before, was reserved for the attornies; was on this occasion, appropriated for the reception of magistrates, except the front seats which had become occupied by some London reporters. In the rush and confusion however, many had invaded the place who had no claim to seats there. These were forthwith informed by the officers of the court that they must retire. The mandate was reluctantly obeyed by some, but others obstinately retained their seats, until they were finally removed by order of the magistrates, when they arrived.

The number of witnesses put down for the prosecution, exceeded eighty; for the defence, one hundred and twenty.

At a quarter before nine, Hunt, Moorhouse, Saxton, Jones, Wild, and Healey, came into the court; soon afterwards, I and Swift came up and applied for entrance at the common door of the court. We were informed by the keeper that no more could be admitted, the place being quite full. We smiled at this, and said we must be admitted, and desired him to open the door; he stoutly refused, and we enjoyed the joke some time, and at last told him who we were, and that we should be wanted, and must take part in the trial.

The man then admitted us, but almost as a favour, and we made our way up an avenue towards the witness box. Hunt saw us coming, and beckoned us to step over the backs of the seats, which we did, and I was presently by his side.

I may here remark, that at Manchester, both before and after the meeting; at Lancaster, and London, Hunt had uniformly worn a white hat, and it had, in consequence become the radical badge; Johnson had also done the same, but here, before a judge, and a jury of their country, they deemed it proper to display the common black hat. I, however, who never thought it wrong to be the same always, and in all places; who saw not anything to be really ashamed of in the colour of my hat, and who would not just then, have discarded it, to please judge, jury, or king, threw it down innocently enough, amongst the lawyer's bags and papers, and other hats of a different colour; some of whom were the sombre ones of my co-defendants. There was some looking and smiling, at the presumptuous appearance of a radical hat. Others of our party, like myself, stuck to their white colours, declaring they would not change them under any circumstances. I only mention this incident to show a trait of what the world deems prudence, and its judicious exercise, by some of our leaders.

At nine o'clock, Justice Bayley took his seat on the bench, and immediately the cause of the king against Henry Hunt, Joseph Johnson, John Knight, James Moorhouse, Joseph Healey, John Thacker Saxton, Robert Jones, Samuel Bamford, George Swift, and Robert Wilde, was called on. The names of the persons summoned to act as special jurors were then read, and the following answered to their names. William Hall, Esqr, foreman, William Cheater, Esqr, James Barker, Esqr, John Hutton, Esqr, George Atkinson, junr. Esqr, Francis Robinson, Esqr, Timothy Hutton, Esqr, George Beswick, Esqr, John Chadwick, Esqr, and William Selby, Esqr. A tales was prayed, and Mr Septimus Bromley, of Sculcotes, Hull, and Mr George Addy, of Wakefield, were added to the jury. The latter individual wished to be excused from acting as a juryman, but on his stating, in answer to a question from the judge, that he had no particular reason, except that he did not like the business, he was ordered to remain.

At this time the court was most excessively crowded; all the bottom seats, and avenues, as well as every inch of standing ground, a passage for the witnesses excepted, were closely occupied. In each of the galleries, the people were packed like bees in a hive, and there was ground for apprehension that the fronts might be forced out. It was some time before order could be obtained, so eager were persons of all ranks to witness the commencement of this trial. The jury box had been partly filled by strangers, and had to be cleared, and several common jurymen, who happened to be in it, made a remonstrance to the judge, on the hardship of being turned, not only out of that box, but also out of the one which had always been assigned to the waiting jurymen. This circumstance was occasioned by the arrangements which the high sheriff, Henry Vansittart, Esqr, and his subordinate officers had made for the accommodation of the public. The box usually assigned to the magistrates of the county, was this day opened for the reception of the Manchester and Cheshire magistrates; the one usually reserved for attornies, was given up to the reporters for the public press, and the attornies being deprived of their usual place in court, went into the jury box, and filled it so entirely as to occasion the remonstrance just mentioned. Justice Bayley said he did not understand the arrangements of the court: the place was now full: if however, there was any situation to which the waiting jurymen had a right, he would order it to be cleared, and kept for their accommodation; the box was accordingly cleared.

The jury having been sworn, Mr Littledale opened the proceedings, and the indictment was read, the substance of which having been already given, I shall not now repeat. We of course, all pleaded 'not guilty,' except John Knight, who, since being bailed out of Lancaster Castle, had again been committed on a subsequent charge, for attending a meeting near Burnley.

Mr Scarlett, Mr Serjeant Hullock, Mr Serjeant Cross, and Mr Littledale, conducted the prosecution; Mr Holt was retained for Saxton, and Mr Barrow for Moorhouse and Jones. Hunt, Johnson, Wilde, Swift, Healey, and myself, conducted our several defences, and for that purpose we took our places at the barrister's table. Some conversation ensued respecting this arrangement, and Mr Hunt expressed his willingness to agree to any other, but the judge decided that every individual conducting his own defence should sit there; the others must take seats behind their counsel.

Mr Hunt said he had not been previously aware of the arrangements for the court, and he had therefore invited his co-defendants to the situations they occupied; room, however, would easily be found for them behind the bar, as he intended to move that all the witnesses on both sides, (and he knew many were in court) should be ordered out of it.

Justice Bayley accordingly ordered all the witnesses to withdraw from the court. Mr Barrow, added, 'And out of hearing also.'

The order was immediately complied with; and amongst those who retired were the Rev. W. R. Hay, the Rev. C. W. Ethelstone, Mr Hulton, Mr Sylvester, Mr R. Wright, and several other of the Manchester magistrates, together with a number of gentlemen and tradesmen who had been subpoened as witnesses. The defendants who had retained counsel also took their places behind them, on the seats usually allotted to attornies, and the very inconvenient pressure in the court was considerably mitigated.

Immediately under the judge, at the straight edge of the table, which was a half-round, sat the counsel for the prosecution, already named, with their attorneys. On the judge's left, and occupying the curved edge of the table, were George Swift, Mr Harmer, of London, (who kindly suggested various matters to us) next myself, then Mr Hunt, Mr. Pearson, Mr Wilde, Mr Barrow, Mr Holt, Mr Healey, and Mr Johnson, the two latter sitting near the witness box, and almost directly in front of the judge. The further side of the table, was occupied by attornies and others; a number of elegantly dressed females were upon the right and left of the judge, and occupying seats below, and standing on the floor; the large box behind us, at first assigned to magistrates, and which had been almost filled by those of Lancashire and Cheshire, who vacated it on the order being given for witnesses to retire, was now filled with a crowd of ladies and gentlemen, chiefly as we understood, residents in the county; many ladies had obtained seats in the body of the hall, and one was observed taking the likeness of the venerable judge as he sat in his robes.

Chapter 64

MR SCARLETT, after the opening by Mr Littledale, proceeded to address the jury, but as it would be entirely beyond the scope of this work to give the proceedings of the trial, which has no doubt, long since, been placed amongst the public records, I shall only touch on such passages as concern myself, and throw light on my conduct, both previously to, and during this important examination. I shall intersperse such observations with brief remarks upon, and descriptions of some things which occurred both in public court, and were privately known to ourselves, and shall be content to be judged, so far as my name may be concerned, by the facts which I now truthfully narrate. Mr Scarlett's description of us, should not however, be omitted; it was as follows:—

'Of Mr Hunt it was unnecessary that he should say anything, because his name had been so much of late connected with these transactions, as to leave no doubt on the mind of any man as to his character and avocations. The others were obscure; they were very little known, and he should therefore state who they were, premising that they were charged with assembling, and inciting others to assemble, to disturb the public peace. John Knight had formerly been in business; his occupation had latterly been that of an itinerant orator – Joseph Johnson, was a brush maker, residing near Manchester, and he believed he also was in the habit of attending public meetings. Of John Thacker Saxton, all the description which he had was that he was some way or other connected with the office of a newspaper called, the Manchester Observer. Joseph Healey was represented as an apothecary. James Moorhouse was a coach-master, residing at Stockport. George Swift was a shoe-maker at Manchester. Of Robert Wilde he knew nothing, save that he lived near Ashton-under-line. Samuel Bamford, and Robert Jones, were individuals in humble circumstances. The jury, he said, would find by unquestionable evidence, that these persons were connected in some secret design. He would be able to show the course which the parties took when he called his evidence, and therefore it was not necessary for him at that moment, to state the specific acts of each; it would be sufficient to give a general view of their proceedings.'

The learned counsel then indicated the line of accusation he should take against Mr Hunt especially. He commenced with the Spitalfields meeting at London, in the June previous, setting forth the resolutions, and describing them as illegal. Mr Hunt was next traced to Bullock Smithy; thence to Manchester, connecting him with the proposed meeting on the ninth of August. Then he described the drillings at White Moss, and the beating of Murrey, and his companions. He showed Mr Hunt to have been stopping at the house of Johnson, at Smedley, where he said he received the visits of Knight and others of the defendants. Next he represented the people as marching from all parts on the morning of the sixteenth of August. They were, he said, provided with banners and inscriptions, and they marched upon Manchester with all the regularity of an army. From Rochdale, from Middleton, from Oldham, from Lees, from Stockport, and many other places, parties might be seen marching towards Manchester. 'At Middleton, Mr Bamford was seen placing in marching order, a body of two thousand men; they were without uniforms, but he displayed sufficient talent to put them through their evolutions. He addressed them, and gave to each of them laurel leaf, that they might distinguish one another. The town of Manchester, was, in fact, surrounded by an immense force, who seemed as if they were going to invade it. Every road which approached the town was covered with parties marching in military manner, and amongst those who were marching to the town, some of the individuals who were seen training at White Moss were recognized. At eleven o'clock, Mr Hunt and his party were preparing to enter the town from the residence of Johnson. Mr Hunt was attended by a triumphant band; the Middleton and Rochdale force had united – they became his guards – and thus surrounded, he entered the town of Manchester.'

Next he commented on our banners, and some of his strictures may shew the difference betwixt the interpretation of the laws in those days and the present. I will give a short extract of that part of his address.

'On some of the flags they would find the words, "Equal Representation or Death." What could be the object of a sentiment such as this? He would ask the jury to lay their hands on their hearts, and say, what good object could those have in view who exhibited a flag bearing such a motto? They were not met there to discuss whether the present state of the house of commons was the best that could be imagined. Good and wise men differed on that point, but, whatever difference of opinion might be entertained on the subject, of this he was sure, that there was no man, who considered the question rightly, that would not stand by the law and the constitution of the country as they were now administered, and if threatened with violence, that would not resist to the uttermost, an attempt to make a forcible alteration of the system.

'Another banner bore the inscription "No Corn Laws." He came not before them to discuss whether the law on the subject of corn was good or otherwise; he had his opinions on the question, but it would not be decorous or proper to state them there. He knew that wise men might sometimes frame a mischievous law, but it was not to be removed by riot and violence. Would it not be a most dangerous thing to say to a mob of sixty thousand persons, for the purpose of getting rid of such a measure – particularly when the minds of the people were irritated and inflamed – would it not, he asked, be an appeal of a most inflammatory nature, to say to them, "We will have no Corn Laws; we will force the legislature to do as we please."

'Next came the inscription, "Annual Parliaments." There were no doubt respectable and honourable men in the kingdom, who thought annual parliaments would be very useful; but would any of those individuals say that such a proposition was to be carried by violence, as the *sine qua non* of their existence? Let the people meet to petition for reform – let them submit to parliament what they think expedient for the public good – and no man can complain. But was it the business of a public meeting to dictate to parliament, and to declare that it would effect a certain object, or would have nothing? The next inscription was "Universal Suffrage and Election by Ballot." These two points were the pretexts for calling this assembly; he felt considerable surprise that Mr Hunt did not perceive that those three terms, taken together, meant nothing but the subversion of the constitution, but as long as these questions were *sub judice*, what right had any man to say, "we will, in spite of all opposition, have these three things." To do so, was illegal; and it was most unfit that, on the subject of public grievances, the mob should be suffered to dictate to the legislature. Let them meet and petition; let the weavers, and shoemakers, and other artisans, in this kingdom, who are destined to earn their bread by the labour of their hands, inform the legislature of the best course to be pursued with respect to public affairs, if they have more wisdom than those by whom such affairs were conducted. The law enabled them to do this; but let not demagogues state to them that these three points were the only things which could be of service to them. Another inscription was, "Let us die like men, and not be sold like slaves." Who, he should like to know, had been selling the people of Oldham, of Rochdale, of Middleton, and of the other places, the inhabitants of which went to Manchester on that day? He never heard of any such sale; but some person, who did not, perhaps, choose to speak those words, thought fit to place them on a banner." '

Such were some of the constructions which the learned counsel attached to some of our banners and their inscriptions; constructions which if followed in these days, would place some of the chartist exhibitors in a rather perilous position.

Witnesses were now called, who traced Mr Hunt through Bullock Smithy, Stockport, Heaton Norris, and from Manchester, to Johnson's at Smedley. On the examination of a witness named John Chadwick, who swore that he saw Murrey at the White Moss, on the morning of the fifteenth, Mr Hunt objected to his evidence, because he had said he did not know any one who was there by name.

Mr Scarlett said, he wished to shew that some of the White Moss drillers had attended Mr Hunt.

Mr Hunt said it mattered not, unless some of those persons were among the accused.

Mr Scarlett hoped Mr Hunt would not be allowed to disturb the proceedings of the court.

Mr Justice Bayley. – Mr Hunt has a right to take the objection, and I am doubting whether this is evidence.

The witness was here sent out of court.

Mr Scarlett said, he was about to show that some of these persons who were training, and who assaulted Murrey, had attended the meeting of the sixteenth, and had also cheered opposite Murrey's house; he would shew that Mr Hunt and his party had done the same. This, he conceived, was perfectly regular.

Mr Justice Bayley. – When you have shewn that any of the persons of the White Moss party were at the meeting on the sixteenth, then it will be evidence, but I think you had better prove that first.

The witness was again called in and examined, and said the first person he saw at the meeting on the sixteenth, was a man whom he had seen at the White Moss, with a letter brought from Manchester. A person arrived at White Moss after witness had seen Murrey; the parties then formed into a square like four walls, and the man who was to read the letter was in the centre. The letter was not read, as they said there was no name to it, and they would have nothing to do with it; the man then joined them. The man who was to have read the letter, was the man who led up the Middleton and Rochdale parties on Monday. This man was drilling the men, and giving the word of command.

Such was the first link of the evidence, which by inference, connected me with the White Moss affair. Why that link was not broken will hereafter appear. For the present, Mr Pearson advised me to sit still, and not cross-examine the witness, – he would be sure, he said, to swear I was the man he saw at the Moss; he would swear right a-head, no doubt. It was for the witness to point me out, and not for me to offer myself to his notice – I accordingly kept my seat. This was the only evidence tendered on the first day of trial, which applied to me.

On the morning of the second day, the court was crowded soon after seven o'clock. The rush when the doors were open was excessive, and a number of ladies again encountered the pressure of the crowd; they were soon, however, accommodated with such places as could be spared near the bench, and in the magistrates' large box on the left. The defendants were assisted by Mr Harmer, and Mr Pearson, as on the previous day. Mr Justice Bayley took his seat at half-past nine. Many persons of rank in the county were present during the day.

William Morris, the first witness examined by Serjeant Cross, said: I am a weaver, residing five miles from Manchester. In the month of August last, I saw many groups of people near Middleton; Samuel Bamford used to be amongst them. Early on the morning of the sixteenth of August, I saw many hundreds of people put into regular form at Middleton, with two flags; and twenty-five men were in each section. I know not who formed them into sections, but there certainly was a large number collected – two or three thousand at least. They marched off four abreast, after being first drawn into the form of a square, in the inside of which was placed a chair, on which Bamford stood and said: – "Friends and neighbours,

I have a few words to relate; you will march off this place quietly, and not insult any one, but rather take an insult. I do not think there will be any disturbance, or anything to do; if there is, it will be after we come back – there is no fear, the day is our own." He got off the chair and spread laurel amongst the men who were to command the sections. They put it, some in their breasts, and some in their hats. Before they went away, a large number of people came arranged in form from Rochdale, with a band of music before them, and bearing two flags. Both bodies joined and went off together, each with a cap of liberty. The men had nothing in their hands but bits of switches, or small sticks. Before that day I saw the Middleton people forming and arranging, both in fields and highroads. Bamford was with them at different times. John Whitworth, who had been a private in the Sixth Regiment of Foot was drilling the men, but not on the sixteenth of August. John Heywood, who had been a private in the Sixth Dragoons, had also done the same.

In his cross-examination by me, the witness said: 'I heard you recommend them to be peaceable, and understood you wished them to continue so during the whole day. Many thousands went with the Middleton and Rochdale people who were not formed with them, as well as a good deal of women and children.'

Such was the evidence of this witness: it was, I dare say, as near the truth as he could recollect, and was, on the whole, strongly in my favour. I knew some points in his character which would have enabled me to put him through a severe cross-examination, but I forebore, not wishing to injure the testimony he had given on my behalf. Hunt, however, who could not miss an opportunity for display, took him up, and handled him most unmercifully; on which Serjeant Hullock remarked aside to one of his brother counsel, what a fool Hunt must be to destroy the man's credibility, he being to all intents and purposes *our* witness. The life of this man had been one of adventure and intrigue. He had been long in the army, and deserted from it whilst a sergeant on a foreign station, taking with him his arms and accoutrements. Soon after this trial he was apprehended for passing forged Bank of England notes, and was convicted, but, strong interest having been used to save his life, he was transported, and died abroad.

John Heaton being examined by Mr Littledale, said: 'I live at Middleton, and am a plumber and glazier. On the morning of the sixteenth of August, I saw many people assembled, and Samuel

Bamford among them, and in front. They had music, and two flags; the inscriptions were – "Liberty, strength, and unity," and something with a cap on a pole. Bamford had a bunch of laurel in his hand, and many others had a little of it in their hats.'

In my cross-examination, he said: 'I saw nothing but small sticks. I don't know your wife, but there were many women and children, three, four, and five abreast, who appeared to partake of the conviviality of the process. The people did not appear sulky; they had no angry looks, but were more, as it were, in joy. I have some little property, and had then, but I felt no occasion to go home and shut my doors when I saw this procession.'

On the third day, James Platt swore to having seen me on the hustings on St Peter's Field, and this finished the evidence against me; but the criminatory proceedings were not closed until the afternoon of the fourth day. The court continued to be crowded each day, from an early hour. The ladies seemed still as curious as at first, and their eagerness to witness the proceedings induced many of them to seek an entrance into the court through privileged avenues, so early as seven o'clock. At eight, the public gates were generally thrown open, and the galleries, and area, became speedily filled in the usual hurried manner, by a mixed throng, which rushed into every seat and corner of the court that was not defended by constables, for the use of magistrates, attornies, and jurors.

Chapter 65

On various matters

ON THE evening of the second day, Mr Harmer left us to attend the trial, if I mistake not, of Sir Francis Burdett, at Leicester. A Mr Bryant, who I understood to be a kind of chamber counsel at London, remained with Hunt and Pearson, and assisted the former in making his points and objections, but from him, I derived no benefit. The time was now approaching when I should be called on for my defence, yet I had never had one minute's private conversation with our attorney; he had never, according to my recollection, been at my inn, nor asked me to his; nor had he ever spoken to one of my witnesses, or given me any instructions – except those already noticed – for the collection of evidence; I was, in fact, entirely left to my own resources. Every night after the court had risen, he, Hunt, and Bryant, retired and spent the evening together, and remained unapproachable by, and invisible to, the other defendants. Indeed, excepting those who had counsel, Hunt alone, so far as I was enabled to judge, was the only one of the party who had the benefit of careful legal advice. During my cross-examinations of the witnesses against me, Mr Pearson would occasionally suggest a question, or advise the suppression of one, but, in other respects, I was left to seek counsel from my own judgment. I regret having to say this, but truth requires it. Every night Hunt retired with his friends, discussing the occurrences of the day, and preparing for the next; consequently, he came into court ready at all points, and like a loaded gun, he only required a sudden impulse, to make a grand discharge. Under these circumstances, it was no wonder that he performed so well; that he appeared to be so greatly talented, whilst his co-defendants had not credit for the little talent which some of them really possessed. This was just the position which Hunt wished himself and us to occupy. He would be all in all; and he could not endure that the humblest of us should come betwixt the public and himself; that the smallest shadow should intercept one ray of his luminous presence. This intense selfishness was constantly displayed in all his actions. I saw it and was astonished; I could not account for it except by condemning him; and that was not to be thought of; though the facts came oozing out like water-drops, I could not harbour an unkind thought of our leader; 'it was his way;' 'it was the way of great folks;' 'it was perhaps necessary that he should do so and so;' – anything, in fact, rather than allow the unwelcome truth to whisper, that in his weak points, Hunt was the weakest of men. I had recently some misgivings as to the integrity of his character, but they had speedily vanished; I could not endure an unworthy opinion of any of my comrades, still less of he who occupied the most prominent station before the public. This may be called simplicity; it was the simplicity of an uncorrupted mind. I deemed all reformers as good as myself, and I knew that I could answer for the sincerity and disinterestedness of my own intentions. It was not until years had elapsed, that observation and reflection enabled me to penetrate the mist which had so long enveloped me; then it was that I became aware of the real nature of past transactions, and of the character of some who had been my political friends, and fellow-workers in the cause of reform.

But during this important trial, circumstances arose which compelled us, at times, to forget all anxiety and seriousness. Healey, as before intimated, was one of the five defendants who had a seat at the barristers' table. On the second day, Mr Scarlett had a smelling bottle which he frequently used, and then laid on the table before him. Our friend the doctor was seated nearly opposite to the learned gentleman, and I observed him once or twice cast very desirous looks towards the phial whilst the barrister was using it. Mr Scarlett, however, did not, or affected not to notice our surgical friend, and at last, the patience of the latter being tried beyond control, he leaned across the table and very respectfully solicited the loan of the bottle, which was readily granted. 'Oh yes, doctor! by all means,' said Mr Scarlett, politely handing it to him, who immediately applied it to his nose, and evinced its pungency by very zestful sneezing, which obliged him to apply his handkerchief to his eyes. Of course there was some tittering around the table, and Mr Scarlett was declared to have 'taken the doctor fairly by the nose.' Hunt laughed till his eyes were brimful, whilst Healey sat quite unconscious and serious. Soon after the bottle was returned with compliments, and the trial claimed our attention. On the third day Mr Scarlett did not bring the smelling bottle, and the doctor seemed disappointed. On the fourth day, the doctor lugged a long square smelling bottle out of his pocket and laid it down before him. Mr Scarlett took no notice. The doctor smelled and laid it down. Mr Scarlett took no notice. The doctor smelled again. Mr Scarlett did not see him. At length, determined not to be outdone in generosity, the doctor thrust it towards Mr Scarlett with a bow, and a request that he would use it. Mr Scarlett coloured, but he good-humouredly took the phial, and having smelled, he politely returned it with thanks, which the doctor as politely acknowledged, the same ceremony was repeated once, if not oftener afterwards, and the doctor then perfectly satisfied, gave up the farce.

On the morning of Sunday, the 19th of March, I retired to my little back-room, at a cottage opposite the inn, for I boarded at the latter place, and lodged with a worthy couple across the street. I now read and compared my notes, and spent several hours in framing the heads of my speech for the day following. On the morning of Monday, Mr Chapman was sent by a committee of our

friends, who were carrying into effect arrangements for the subsistence of the witnesses: the latter had been boarded at our hotel, at
the rate, if I mistake not, of five shillings per head per day, and it was
found necessary to reduce the expenditure, else there would not be
funds to carry us through the trial. The witnesses were thenceforth
to provide for themselves, and would have an allowance of three
shillings per day for that purpose; all the money was to go into a
common fund for disbursements. I accordingly handed to him what
money I had remaining, and that cause of anxiety was removed from
my mind.

Chapter 66

Friendly Advice of Mr Hunt — A Nice Legal Distinction — Author's Address
to the Court — Summary of his Defence by Evidence

IT became apparent towards the noon of Monday, the fourth day
of the trial, that the prosecutors were about to close their case, and
that the defence must be commenced on the afternoon of that day.
Whilst we were talking of the matter, Hunt said, 'Bamford, you
will be called on to address the court the first of all the defendants.'
I said, I thought that scarcely probable, as we should most likely be
called in the order in which our names stood in the indictment.
Hunt said, he knew that was contemplated by the opposing counsel,
and particularly by Mr Scarlett, who wanted to bring him out in the
evening when he was exhausted, the court wearied, and the public
satiated and listless. But – with an oath – he said he was not to be
taken aback that way; he was too old a bird to be caught by such a
manoeuvre. He then opened to me his plans, and said that Messrs
Barrow and Holt, the counsel for Moorhouse, Jones, and Saxton,
would first address the court, then I should be called on, next
Healey, then Swift, and lastly Johnson. I asked him if he thought the
opposing parties would acquiesce in that arrangement? and he said
if Mr Scarlett objected, as he durst say he would, he himself, would
make a special application to the judge on the subject, or to adjourn
the trial until the following day. 'Now, Bamford, by ——' he said,
'I'll tell you what you must do if called this afternoon.' 'Well, what
should I do?' I inquired. 'You must talk against time,' he said.

'Talk against time?' I asked, 'what's that?' 'You must keep possession of the court an hour and an half at least,' he said; you must talk to put on time, in order to prevent them from calling on me, under any circumstances to-night. I know well that is what Scarlett is aiming at, and we must play our game so as to put it beyond his power.' 'But I am not prepared with matter for an hour and a half's speech,' I said; 'I should break down if I attempted it.' 'Don't mind that,' he replied, 'don't mind anything, only keep on.' 'I should make myself look like a fool, and they would be laughing at me, and stopping me,' I replied. 'Phsaw and suppose they did, you could listen, and when they had done, begin again.' 'But I should not know what to say,' 'Say! say anything, the d———est nonsense in the world, never mind what you say, only keep on until they cannot call me to-day.' Something like a glimmer of the naked truth flashed across my reluctant mind, and I replied, 'No; Mr Hunt, I will not do as you desire, I will not exhibit myself before this court as a fool; I will speak as long as I can speak, to the purpose, and with common sense. I would speak until dark if that would serve you, and I was prepared for the task; but I am not, and I won't make myself ridiculous.' 'Very well,' said Hunt, and looked another way, quite cool and distant.

I then shewed the manuscript of my address to Mr Pearson, and he advised the striking out of a passage wherein I alluded to the circumstance of my having slept at the house of my wife's uncle, on the night previous to Murrey being at White Moss, and to the fact of the servant girl having removed my shoes whilst cleaning the house after I went to bed, and my not being able to find them on the following morning, and her having to find them for me. He said that passage should be erased; it had not been proved that I was at White Moss, and the attempt to explain away what had not been proved, would rather strengthen the opinion, if such existed, that there was really some truth in the supposition of my having been on the Moss. I reminded him of what Chadwick had sworn, and of what Morris and Heaton had sworn, as to my leading up the people, but he said that was not sufficient to call on me for a replication; I had not been pointed out – not personally identified by Chadwick, and I had best not take any notice of that part of the evidence. I must confess, I did not see this distinction clearly, but I yielded to his advice, and the passage was struck out: the servant girl alluded to, also was not examined as to that point by me.

I think it was about three o'clock in the afternoon, when Michael Fitzpatrick, a reporter for the New Times, and the last witness for the prosecution, made his exit from the witness box. Mr Barrow and Mr Holt, then addressed the court on behalf of their several clients, and Mr Hunt made application to the judge, that I should next be heard, and the other defendants after me, in order that as an indulgence, his address might be deferred until the following morning. Mr Scarlett, I think, observed that such a course would be irregular, but did not strongly object to it, and the favour was granted. I accordingly addressed the court in the following terms:

'My lord, and gentlemen of the jury. – Before I enter into a detail of the evidence which I intend to produce in my defence, I think it necessary to notice some expressions made use of by the learned counsel for the prosecution, in the speech which he addressed to the court on the opening of these proceedings. I allude to that part of his address where he said that "Bamford was seen training a body of ten thousand men on the morning of the 16th." If the brief which the learned gentleman had before him, instructed him to make such an assertion, so much the better; and I sincerely wish, for his own honour, that it may be so. (Mr Scarlett intimated across the table that, such were his instructions.) But your lordship and the jury, cannot have failed to observe, that the testimony of Morris contains no such proof, and he alone has appeared against me with respect to the transactions that took place at Middleton, previous to our movement towards Manchester. Indeed, Morris states that he knew not who formed the people into section, division, and square; that they were so formed, but by whom he does not undertake to say. The learned gentleman also, in commenting upon some of the banners, and their inscriptions, described one as bearing the words "Annual Parliaments," and "Universal Suffrage," and insinuated that such were put forth as a demand, whence he inferred a design to subvert the constitution and government. Now the mottos on the banner so erroneously described, were nothing more than an avowal of what we considered, and do still consider, as our political right. There was no such thing as a demand about it; why should we demand that which we were going to Manchester to petition for?

'With respect to drilling, I have, in common with my neighbours heard much, seen some, and could have seen more; for it was, to use a common, though very memorable phrase, "as notorious as the

255

sun at noon-day." If it will not be trespassing too much on the time of the court, I will endeavour to give a brief account of its origin and intention. In the course of the last six years, Manchester has witnessed many public meetings, to all of which, with the exception of the last, great numbers of people from the surrounding towns and villages, proceeded in groups; and on those occasions, they were uniformly styled by the liberal and venal press of the place, mobs, riotous, tumultuous, and disorderly mobs; they were ridiculed as illiterate, dirty, and mean, having chapped hands, and greasy nightcaps.[1] They were scandalized as being drunken and disorderly; as being libellous and seditious, dividers of property, and destroyers of social order; and was it not then very natural that these poor, insulted, and vilified people should wish to rescue themselves from the unmerited imputations which were wantonly cast on their character? It certainly was natural that they should wish to give the lie to their enemies; and thereby shew to the nation and to the world, that they were not what they had been represented to be. They determined to give one example of peace and good order, such as should defy the most bitter of their enemies to criminate; and for this purpose, and this alone, was the drilling, so styled, instituted. Only one witness for the prosecution has sworn to having heard amongst the drillers, the word "fire," all the others swear only to their facing, and to their marching in file and in line, which evolutions were certainly most suited to familiarize them with that uniformity of motion, which would be necessary for the preservation of due order and decorum in their progress to the place of meeting. But as to these facts, I do not tender to your lordship and the jury, my own assertion only, I refer you to the papers laid before the house of commons, relative to the internal state of the country. The particular document to which I refer in those papers, is dated the fifth of August; only four days previous to the first proposed meeting at Manchester, which should have been on the ninth; so that if we suppose the drilling parties to have been in existence a week or a fortnight before the day on which the letter referred to is dated, the ground of my argument is strengthened. That military gentleman who did us the honour to stand so long before us on Saturday evening, and whose services, I trow, consisted in marching with Colonel Fletcher from Bolton to Manchester, and from Manchester to Bolton, talks of "midnight drillings," and of parties

[1] This was a phrase in one of Harrop's trashy journals.

coming to the meeting in "beautiful order," the former representation is not, I presume, legal evidence, and of course will not appear
on your lordship's notes. The latter confirms what I have said
respecting the wish of the people to preserve the strictest decorum.

'Your lordship and the jury will find by the evidence which I shall
produce, that by nine o'clock on the morning of the ever-memorable
sixteenth of August, numbers of persons assembled at Middleton;
that they were formed into a hollow square; and that whilst so
formed, I addressed them, earnestly cautioning them to be on their
guard against enemies, and representing the advantage which might
be taken of their numbers, to create a riot, by persons who might
be employed for that sole purpose; that I advised them not to insult
any person, but rather suffer an insult on that day, as their opponents would be glad of a pretext to accuse them of riot and disorder;
that I entreated them to bear towards every one a spirit of good-will,
in token of which I distributed amongst them branches of laurel,
emblems of purity and peace, as described by Morris and Heaton;
and having heard that if I went to the meeting, the police of Manchester would on its own responsibility arrest me, I cautioned the
people against offering any resistance, if such an attempt should be
made, as I preferred an appeal to the laws of my country, rather
than to force; that I insisted no sticks should be taken, and that in
consequence, several were left by the way; that we went in the
greatest hilarity and good humour, preceded by a band of music,
which played loyal and national airs; and that our fathers, our
mothers, our wives, our children, and our sweethearts were with us.
And this was the dreadful military array which the learned counsel
described as "one vast army, bearing from all parts to the invasion
of Manchester," – poor, forlorn, defenceless Manchester. – These
were, "the soldiers ready to fight for Mr Hunt;" with bare heads
and with arms locked, – a fighting posture forsooth – who terrified
that immortal author of given books, Mr Francis Phillips; and of
such persons, O dreadful to relate! was formed that "cordon,"
impenetrable to every thing, save the newly-ground sabres of the
Manchester yeomanry cavalry.'

At this time the judge arose hastily and motioned me to cease
speaking; the blood had gushed from his nose on the cushion before
him, and he retired, with the High Sheriff, and one or two gentlemen that were near him. In a short time his lordship returned, and
I merely added some conversations on the conduct of a magistrate

who had detained papers of mine, which being a manuscript of one of Hoyle's games at draughts, the zealous functionary suspected it might possibly be the plan of a plot in cypher. I also said I should leave my share of the general defence to Mr Hunt, whose superior knowledge and eloquence would, no doubt, obtain for us full justice, which was all we wanted.

In confirmation of this speech, I adduced evidence which shewed that I inculcated peace and good order to the Middleton party before we left Barrowfields; that there was not to be any opposition to the police, should they come to arrest me or any other person; that the people were to keep themselves select, and return with their banners, and not to stop in the town drinking, nor loitering in the streets; that no sticks were allowed in the procession except to aged persons, and that several were resigned on the ground, or left by the way; that the wives of several of the party accompanied their husbands, and that there were many young females and children with the procession; that we seemed quite cheerful on the road; that there were no symptoms of alarm in Middleton or on the road; and that the drillings were public and in open day. In short, all that I had advanced in my speech was fully confirmed by my evidence.

After me, Swift, Healey, and Johnson got up in succession. Healey had for a day or two appeared to be labouring under a cold with hoarseness. He sat opposite the judge, with a handkerchief thrown over his head, the corners drooping on his shoulders, exactly as the flaps of his lordship's wig drooped upon his. He frequently looked up towards the glass dome above him, as if a stream of air came from thence and he was affected by it; but he did not attempt to move to another seat, which he probably would have done, had he experienced illness from that cause. Whether this was the case or not, it is a fact that he had a speech to read which had been written by a friend at Lees, and he could not read it. He then had a cold, became hoarse, and the clerk of the court read the speech for him. This official was a well-fed, red-faced, snub-nosed, personage; with spectacles on his nose, and a wig of legal cut on his head. He held the document at a considerable altitude, as if he were looking over his spectacles instead of through them, and he read the speech in a monotonous, half-speaking, half-singing tone, much as a school-boy, some twenty years ago would have droned out his lesson. The doctor stood at his elbow, his looks evincing surprise and disappointment, that his document should have fallen into such incapable hands; next he became impatient, as was manifest by his varying attitudes, and sharp gesticulations, by which he meant to supply the want of modulation and emphasis in the reader. An artist was in court sketching at the time, and if he took this pair of originals, his portfolio may some day turn out one singular illustration of nature.

Chapter 67

Hunt's Address to the Court — He denounces Carlile

HUNT had thus obtained what he so ardently desired, a night for consultation, reflection, and repose, and a crowded morning audience for his grand exhibition. I shall not dwell upon his defence, except to notice one passage relative to Richard Carlile. In the commencement of his address he said, 'I am not only charged in the opening speech of the learned counsel with having attempted to overthrow the constituted authorities of my country, but also to extinguish in the flame of infidelity, the altar of our holy religion. It has been industriously promulgated that I was connected with Mr Carlile; it has been promulgated that I am a man of his principles, – where is the proof? Without it why should the imputation have been cast? I shall not advert to the conduct of that man, because the law has imposed its punishment upon him, and he is now enduring the reward of his temerity. It would therefore be improper, and imprudent, and unjust, for me in open court to touch upon such a subject, but why was the topic introduced? I will tell you, gentlemen; to connect our cause with that of irreligion, and to identify the cause of the reformers with that of Mr Carlile.' 'I profess to be a reformer, but not a leveller; I profess to be a lover of liberty, but not of licentiousness; sweet, lovely liberty, gentlemen, is pure and amiable as sacred truth; licentiousness is as disgraceful as darkness and falsehood.' And then in a subsequent passage, he said, 'You have heard the miserable attempt to fix upon me an irreligious connection with Carlile. I have known the man, and if I do not say what I think of him, it is because he is now suffering the sentence of the law, and therefore is not a fit subject for any body's animadversion. Of him

I shall say nothing now, but I shall say, that none of the principles, professions or doctrines, he is said to have espoused, were ever, at any moment of my life, imbibed by, or believed in by me. In the face of God! and my country! I most solemnly declare, that I never read one line of the theological works of Carlile, until Doctor Stoddart's libel upon me, first put them into my hands in the following manner. – Mr Scarlett was then employed, as he is now, against me, in the court of King's bench. Carlile's trial was going on, mine was the very next, and I was bound to watch it, or else expose myself to the consequences of being absent when called on, to a verdict for the defendant. Such was my unfortunate case, or else I should not have been in London, much less in court, when Carlile's trial was pending. I here further declare, in the face of heaven, that among the reformers, rich or poor, I never recollect to have seen one line of the theological works of Thomas Paine; why then identify the reformers with such doctrines.' 'Good God! was it not enough to charge us with crimes against our fellow-men, but that also we must be designated as infidels against our religion, and our God.'

Whilst Hunt uttered those last sentences, the tears trickled down his face. 'Good God!' I also mentally exclaimed, 'is it possible? are not my ears deceiving me.' Carlile, the reader will recollect, was one of those who went with Hunt in the carriage from Johnson's to the meeting on the morning of the sixteenth. He was so fortunate as to escape from the field, and had since been tried, found guilty, and sentenced to imprisonment for a theological work, if I mistake not; and was at the moment Hunt thus denounced and renounced him in prison. No human power, nor dread of human power, should have been able to compel Hunt to make use of such language at that time, and under those circumstances. Whatever Carlile was, good or bad, religious or the contrary, the law had for the present done its work with him, and that is seldom part done; and, above all other moments, that was not the one to aim a clumsy and treacherous blow at a late comrade, now bound and fettered. 'Can this,' thought I, 'be also one of the fashionable levities of great folks?' 'if it be, it is requisite that I should be more guarded, and more self-governed in future.' And so I was; I continued to respect Hunt for his good points, but I was no longer entirely blinded to his faults. I never could forget this scene.

Chapter 68

Another Chapter of Varieties

WE will now suppose the trial to be proceeding, and Hunt and the other defendants examining their witnesses. Meantime I will endeavour to amuse the reader by a few anecdotes of a more individual character, than any traits which could be found in the general investigation which is supposed to be in progress.

It was about the second or third day of the trial, that in cross-examination, I put what was considered a leading question. One of the counsel immediately called it back, and said that was not the proper way to put it. I apologized on account of my ignorance of the forms of examination, when Sergeant Hullock, nodding his head, said, 'a pretty apt scholar however, I think.'

One morning I observed that Mr Scarlett was reading some verses of mine (The Lancashire Hymn) in a Manchester Observer newspaper. In the evening, when I was passing along the corridor from the court, I accidently joined Mr Scarlett and Mr Maule, the solicitor for the government. They both recognized me respectfully, and I returned the salute. Mr Scarlett said he had seen some verses of mine which were certainly open to comment by the prosecution, but he should not make any use of them to my prejudice. He also said, he understood I had published a small poetical work, called 'The Weaver Boy.' I said I had. He then said, if it should so happen that I should have to come to London in consequence of the trial, he could wish me to bring him a copy. I said I would do so with pleasure, and if I did not come up, I would forward one to him. Mr Maule said, 'and let me have a copy also,' I said I would take care he had one, and so with mutual civilities we parted.

After the defence was closed, and when Mr Scarlett was making his speech in reply, I certainly felt more surprised than flattered by the distinction which he thought proper to make in my favour. 'Bamford,' he said, 'and when he mentioned the name of that defendant, he could not but express his regret at the situation in which he saw him now placed; he (Mr Scarlett) admired his talents, and the respectful manner in which he had conducted his defence;

and probably others as well as himself (Mr Scarlett) were sorry that he was not found in better company.'

One day I had done something which pleased Hunt mightily, and when the court broke up, and we were in the yard, Hunt said, 'come Bamford, take my arm; you are my right-hand man.' I took his arm, and we walked down the street, with a great crowd at our heels, shouting 'Hunt for ever!' 'Hunt for ever!' and huzzaing. Looking back, I saw the judges carriage with his lordship in, and the horses restive in consequence of the noise, and I put out my hand and desired the crowd to be silent. Hunt heard what I said, and giving me a sudden jerk, began cursing in his usual wont when in a passion, and asked who ordered me to stop the people from shouting? I pointed to the carriage then in the midst of us, the horses still prancing; but that did not pacify my shout-loving friend, and he continued his maledictions until I turned to go to my lodgings. A similar cause of displeasure was given by Moorhouse on another night when the mail-coach was passing, and was in danger of being upset. Moorhouse received his reprimand at Hunt's apartments, and was then invited to walk out of the room. He wept with mortification! I laughed! as I have often done since, when thinking of the circumstance.

One day a female witness from Middleton, a married woman, gave very important evidence in a most impressive manner, and was to return home the following morning. Before going she wished to see Mr Hunt, in order to have the honour of saying, she had shaken hands with the great man. I offered to introduce her, and we went to Hunt's apartments, but he was not there, and we were referred to a tavern, the Black Swan, I think, in Coney-street. We found there that Hunt, Bryant, and several others were up stairs, and I sent in my name, and after standing in the bar a short time, the waiter said, 'Mr Hunt could not be seen, he was engaged.' I thought there must be some mistake, and requested the man to give my compliments to Mr Hunt, and say I should be glad to see him for a minute. The man did so, and came down again with the same result. I was ashamed and offended at receiving such a slight; but, determined that he should not have any ground to plead a mis-understanding, I desired the waiter to go up once more, and say, a lady who was going into Lancashire wished to bid him good-bye. The servant very obligingly went up again, and returned as before, 'Mr Hunt could not be seen.' The next morning I took my seat at a distance from him in the court, and it was not until repeated over-tures on his part, and many fervent expressions of regret, that I resumed conversation with him. But I could scarcely have justified myself if I had suffered any personal offence to alienate me from him during the trial. I considered the cause too great, too holy, to suffer injury in the least by any circumstance affecting one so humble as myself. I was, in fact, too simple-minded, too sincere, and too generous for the situation in which I was placed; and it was not until multiplied acts of deception and ingratitude had been practised upon me, that I learned (if I have yet done so) to value mankind according to their real worth. I narrate the above as a specimen of the intercourse and confidence which existed among us at York. The same really contemptible feeling of class-ism, the curse of England and Englishmen, and of Englishwomen also, existed in too great a degree amongst the witnesses. There were 'the broad cloth' and 'the narrow cloth' ones – the rich and the poor; and the former seldom sought opportunities for inter-communication with the latter, but rather shunned them. This 'pride that licks the dust,' – for it is nothing else – has begot a counteraction as wrong as itself. It has filled the working classes with a fierce contempt and hatred of every one wearing a decent coat. This latter is being as mad as the other is being mean. The proper course of those who feel and contemn this distinction, is, first of all, to respect themselves; next to invite a respectful equality by unoffending manners; and thirdly, to assert their right position in society by withholding the smallest deference to mere assumption. This would be quite sufficient, without rudeness or noise, to restore the natural balance of society.

Chapter 69

The Judge's charge to the Jury relative to the Author — Verdict of the Jury —
Their names

WHEN the judge came to read over the evidence, the following passage occurred: – 'The next evidence (for the prosecution) was that which related to Bamford, and it only shewed that he recommended peace and order; still he was identified with the placards if they thought them illegal. If a meeting for considering a reform in parliament be illegal, he is an offender, but it was his (the judge's) duty to tell them that it was not. There was no illegality in carrying sticks unless they were for an unlawful purpose – nor banners, unless their tenor was such as to excite suspicion of the objects of those who carried them, or concurred in bringing them with an evil intention. As to numbers, they alone did not make a meeting illegal, unless attended with such circumstances as did actually excite terror, or were reasonably calculated to excite terror; such circumstances were forbidden by the law. They had truly heard that where there was no law there was no transgression; if the meeting was innocently intended, then the law was not violated. We next come,' observed his lordship, 'to Healey's admonitory remark to me, to take care, and not, in any thing I say, prejudice your minds against him. If I do, gentlemen, discard any expression of mind, having such a tendency, altogether from your minds. I mean to do my duty with integrity, to the best of my poor judgment. If I err, and err with intention, then, gentlemen, there is that power to which I am awfully responsible. Between the crown on one hand, and my country on the other, I shall do, I hope, equal justice. The defendants, I trust, shall suffer no undue prejudice at my hands – my conscience will uphold me in what I have to say to you; and He who will sit in judgment on all our poor acts, will have to determine what motive dictated them. I have now closed my observations upon the evidence for the prosecution, and before I sum up that for the defence, I wish to state that I have made a summary of it, which will bring its leading points with less fatigue to your minds. If, however, I omit anything material to any of the defendants, or, as I go on, shall miss one fact in their favour; then it will be only necessary to remind me of the omission, and I will read in detail the part to which my attention is called.'

Mr Hunt: Probably you will allow us, my lord, to avail ourselves of your kind permission, as you go on, without deeming our interruption obtrusive?

Justice Bayley: Yes, Mr Hunt, I not only allow you, but I desire you promptly, as I go on, to call my attention as you please.

The learned judge resumed his charge, and said that, 'with respect to Bamford, all that had been proved in his speech, was a recommendation to peace and order. There were no sticks in his group, save a few common walking sticks, carried by old men. There were women and children in the throng, and it was for the jury to consider whether Bamford and these people, carrying their wives and daughters with them to such a crowd, meant to create, on that day, riot, tumult, and disorder? With such an intention, nothing was less likely than that they would carry to the scene those who were the dearest objects of their affection. According to the evidence for Bamford, the people in his party so far from being tumultuous, were peaceable and joyful, and the drilling, as it was called, so far from being illegal and nocturnal, was open and innocent; the only object of it being merely to enable the people to attend the meeting, as conveniently for each other and the public as it was possible.' The learned judge then enumerated the names of the witnesses who swore that the Middleton party, on the sixteenth of August, went to the meeting in the utmost peace, and conducted themselves whilst there with equal tranquillity. 'There was no act of violence' said his lordship, 'according to these witnesses, committed by them, no violation of peace, which would bring them under the reprehension of the law; and so far in favour of Bamford. And again, whilst commenting on the various flags, his lordship said, 'with respect to Bamford, who went with the Middleton flags, nothing could be more decent than his conduct throughout the day. If the account given by the witnesses he adduced be a correct description, he every where recommended peace and order.'

At a quarter past twelve, the learned judge closed his charge, and the jury retired. Shortly before five, they returned into court, and the foreman read their verdict as follows:—

'Moorhouse, Jones, Wilde, Swift, and Saxton, not guilty. – Henry Hunt, Joseph Johnson, John Knight, Joseph Healey, and (to the astonishment of the judge, the bar, and the audience) Samuel Bamford, guilty of assembling with unlawful banners, an unlawful assembly, for the purpose of moving and inciting the liege subjects of our sovereign lord the king, to contempt and hatred of the government and constitution of the realm, as by law established, and attending at the same.'

Mr Justice Bayley: Do you mean that they themselves intended to incite?

The Foreman: Yes.

Mr Justice Bayley: Let the verdict be so recorded. You find, gentlemen, on such counts as the words of your verdict are applicable to. Do you find that they created terror? or incited it in the liege subjects of the king?

The Foreman: We mean, my lord, to find on the first count, omitting a few words.

The learned judge then requested they would retire and look over the counts of the indictment again, and say to which count they meant to apply their verdict.

The jury withdrew, and in a few minutes returned with a verdict of guilty generally, on the fourth count, and not guilty, on the remaining counts.

Mr Justice Bayley: I take it for granted the defendants are still under recognizance?

Mr Hunt: We are, my lord.

Mr Justice Bayley: Then let them now additionally, in court, enter into their own recognizances to keep the peace, and be of good behaviour for six months, Mr Hunt in the sum of two thousand pounds, Mr Johnson in one thousand, and Bamford and Healey in five hundred each.

The parties immediately gave their several recognizances.

His lordship addressing the jury, said they had his best thanks for the patient attention they had bestowed on this arduous trial. He was very much obliged to them. Then facing the body of the court, his lordship added, 'I very much approve of the conduct of the court at the time the verdict was given in,' – alluding as was understood, to the universal silence which prevailed at the time.

The reader will perhaps not think that I speak too strongly, when I say that the infamy of the verdict against myself, has seldom been surpassed. And lest the names of the jurymen who were the instruments of so great an injustice, should sink into premature oblivion. I again here record them. They were William Hall, Esq, foreman, William Chaytor, Esq, Thomas Parker, Esq, John Hutton, Esq, George Atkinson, junr., Esq, Thomas Robson, Esq, Timothy Hutton, Esq, George Beswicke, Esq, John Chadwick, Esq, William Selby, Esq, with Septimus Bromley, and George Addy, as tales.

During the whole of the ten days' investigation, I did not observe that any one of the jury took a single note of the evidence, or that they indicated by the action of a single muscle of countenance, that any impression was made on their minds. They sat motionless, and like men who were asleep with their eyes open; and it was clear, from the bungling form in which they presented their first verdict, that they had agreed upon it from a vague recollection of some points in evidence, and a clumsy misapplication of the counts in the indictment.

In a short time after we had left the court, I was somewhat surprised by the information that Hunt, Pearson, and Bryant, were about to leave York that night. I therefore hastened to Mr Pearson, and represented to him that I had not any money whatever to pay my lodging and tavern bills, every farthing I had having been given up to Mr Chapman. Mr Pearson advanced me two pounds, and I went and discharged what I owed. The next morning the generous-hearted Moorhouse yoked up his coach and dragged a full load of witnesses and defendants to Huddersfield, where we stopped for the night. The following morning (Wednesday) Moorhouse found that, in consequence of the heavy load, he should want a pair of leaders to help him over the hills, and he applied at several places, but in vain; no horse-keeper in Huddersfield would furnish us a pair for love or money; and the radicals of the place, indignant at the paltry annoyance, harnessed themselves to the vehicle, and drew it over the steep hills, as far as Blackmoor Bottom. At Oldham, our faithful and kind friends, – alas, that so few of them remain! – met us, and conducted us to a good substantial dinner, at the White Horse Inn. Here I was met by my dear wife and child, and our present joy was only saddened by the reflection that, ere long, there must be another parting. We were soon again in tender conversation by the hedge-rows and green fields; and I arrived at Middleton, 'poor in gear,' but rich in the satisfaction of having performed my duty well; in having, though condemned, largely contributed towards the vindication of the conduct of the reformers on the sixteenth of August – in having created a feeling of respect in my enemies, and a favourable impression in the upright judge who tried us, – in having disclosed to a great assemblage of wealth and aristocracy, as well as to the nation at large, that somewhat of moral and intellectual respectability had been attained by the artisans of Lancashire, whom on this occasion I represented. From that time they advanced a step in the grade of society; they were contemplated with a mingled feeling of curiosity and deference, and they were no longer considered as 'the swinish multitude,' 'the base unwashed helots,' nor denounced as the 'dividers of property, and destroyers of social order.'

If I did this, or any part of it, for my working fellow-countrymen,

I was entitled to their gratitude. We shall see, ere long, how that just claim was discharged; how they remembered one, who, whilst pleading his own cause, had never forgotten theirs.

Chapter 70

Opinions with respect to the Trial at York — Reflections on Public Characters

THE following remarks in an article of the Times newspaper, of Tuesday, March 30th, so fully and so clearly express the general feeling of the nation, as to the facts elicited during this important trial, and the real nature of the transactions at Manchester, that I need not apologize for their introduction into this work; and especially, as but very few of my readers will have seen the remarks, and still fewer will have recollected their tenor.

'It has become the painful duty (says the Times) of an impartial journalist to recall, and republish the statements made by certain members of his majesty's cabinet, and of the House of Commons, respecting the proceedings at Manchester on the sixteenth of August, and to contrast those statements and assertions with real facts, as they have been sworn and proved in open court.

'But we must here guard ourselves *in limine* against the imputation of using improper language. When in these remarks we say that a thing is false, or untrue, we must be understood as only noticing its absolute contrariety to fact; we would on no account be thought to imply an intention to deceive, on the part of those eminent persons from whose speeches we shall introduce extracts: they must, indeed, be agonized with shame, on finding how they have been deceived. In the above modified sense, therefore, it is now perfectly clear to all the world, that every thing that was stated in the House of Commons respecting the riotous character of the Manchester meeting, by Lord Castlereagh, the Solicitor-General, and other honourable members, was totally and absolutely false; it was directly opposed to truth: it does not appear to have had versimilitude or probability in its favour. It is no more descriptive of the proceedings at Manchester, on the part of the military, the magistrates, and the mob, than it is descriptive of the proceedings at Runnymede, in

King John's time, further than there were magistrates, military, and a mob, at Manchester. The actions of all three are wholly misrepresented.

'We shall begin to show our impartiality with the statement of Lord Stanley, a gentleman who generally votes with the opposition:–

' "In the rear of that column of cavalry," said Lord Stanley, "the people closed in; and stones and sticks were thrown at the cavalry, who then turned round, and some wounds were inflicted." '

It is almost needless to observe that this statement is derived from Mr Hulton's evidence, which, being unsupported, was supposed by the learned judge to have proceeded from a terrified imagination, and a bad position for seeing; it is, in fact, disproved by every witness who was examined on the subject.

From Lord Stanley we pass to ministers themselves, or persons connected with the ministry. God knows what an inclination to be deceived there must have been in men who so easily suffered themselves to be so deceived.

The Solicitor-General: – 'Nadin, the officer, saw the meeting, and found that it would be impossible to execute the warrant by the civil power alone.' * * 'The yeomanry troops, before they had attempted to strike a blow, were attacked by the crowd, some of them unhorsed, and their horses thrown.'

These statements are not only proved to be false by the evidence, but the first of them was invalidated by the judge himself, who informed the jury, before summing up, that 'there was no evidence of Nadin's inability to execute the warrant,' whilst the man was in York, to have proved such inability, if he dared to have sworn to so atrocious an untruth.

Mr Canning was abroad when these events took place, and therefore the needless effrontery with which he took up and repeated the enormous falsehoods first conveyed to others, is truly miraculous. But as they derive no credit from the repetition of an absent man, they need no refutation as coming from him.

Mr Wilbraham Bootle declares that 'not a blow was struck till the yeomanry were assailed with stones, brick-bats, and other missiles, brought to the spot for that express purpose.'

It is not sufficient to say of this and all similar assertions, that their falsehood was proved by more numerous and respectable witnesses than were ever before brought to prove a fact in a court of justice. But it must also be added, that not one creature was produced, of any description whatever, to prop or sustain the credibility of such statements. The authors of the falsehoods shrunk from owning them at York, as an unnatural father does from acknowledging his offspring.

But we now come to the greatest dupe. It is needless to copy here all that Lord Castlereagh has said, and, we believe, would have sworn, if he might, with respect to the Manchester meeting; such was the credit which his eager simplicity reposed in the basest, falsest, and most perfidious of informers.

'The truth was,' he said, 'that the magistrates did not determine upon dispersing the meeting until it had assumed the character of tumult and sedition. * * As soon as the character of the meeting had declared itself, the magistrates put the warrants into the hands of the constables, and it was not until they had declared their inability to execute them, that a military force was employed at all.'

All this is totally false. More than twenty witnesses swore at the trial, and none contradicted them, that the meeting never assumed the character of tumultuous.

Observe, reader, the simple tone of narrative which the following extract assumes; not one word of which, it is now proved, has the slightest foundation in, or approximation to truth. The riot act! gracious heaven! Is it even mentioned at the trial? The reader of it too! But he is no more, poor fellow! He was trampled under foot in that fatal fray. Could he have but lived, and gone to York, he would have specially enlightened the court and jury as to the manner in which his elocution was rewarded. Yet his brethren were present at York. Why did they not come forward and relate his sufferings, and vindicate his fame?

'The magistrates determined,' said Lord Castlereagh, 'to disperse the meeting, and to disperse it in the most mild and gentle manner. At the time the riot act was first read, it was from the window of the house in which the magistrates had assembled; it was represented that this method of reading it was not such as was contemplated by the act; another magistrate was therefore sent into the crowd, and, whilst attempting to read it, was trampled under foot; they then sent a third magistrate to read it at the hustings, in order that no man might remain in ignorance of the fact of its being read.' (Cries of 'hear,' 'hear,' from all parts of the house.)

But the following, from the noble lord's speech, exceeds all credibility of human invention; and we are convinced, that if we had confined our labours to the production of this single extract, its matchless, its boundless, its inconceivable falsehood, must have obliged him who, with a degree of inconsideration bordering closely on criminality, has adopted it, to drag forth the guilty author. Indeed, the general opinion now is, that the conduct of the magistrates must be immediately investigated by some tribunal or other.

'This unarmed multitude,' said his lordship, 'though the place had only the day before been cleared of all the stones that were calculated to hurt a human being, assailed the military with so many that the next day, two cart loads were found upon the ground, ("hear, hear";) so that it was clear that the parties had come with stones in their pockets; it was also evident that there were men amongst them armed with pistols, for, from the house behind the hustings, pistols were fired upon the troops. (hear.) * * *

But to return to the point from which we started: we must here observe, that if a liberal construction will readily exempt the persons above quoted from the fraudulent intention of deceiving the house and the country, they never can be acquitted of the charge of great levity and indiscretion, in thus accrediting and obtruding statements as true, which the first breath of enquiry has dissipated, and which the slightest examination or consideration would have proved to be false. Who, we ask, are the real authors of the monstrous untruths above quoted? The dupes, the victims, must now bring these before the public. The too easy, unsuspecting son of guiltlessness, the solicitor-general, will tell us who seduced his innocent mind into the preposterous belief and assertion that, 'the yeomanry were first attacked and unhorsed by the crowd.'

The cart load of stones! Oh, for the love of laughter, let us hear who showered them down, not on Saint Peter's Field, but upon the unhappy, unsuspecting head of Lord Castlereagh; and that too, without breaking it. Whose waggons carried them off when the battle was ended? Where are they now deposited? Oh, preserve them! preserve them carefully! they may form a barrow for this illustrious victim of credulity, when his eloquence shall cease to charm, and they may help to hand his fame down to after times. Yet – to be serious on a subject so grave – nature is said, in a homely phraseology, to 'adapt the back to the burden;' and she may therefore strengthen the nerves, and bronze the countenances, of those who have to sustain this lamentable detection. But the character of the age in which we live is affected by occurrences of this kind. The future student must read the transactions of the present period. If then he take up the parliamentary history, he will find in the speeches of the ministers, readings of riot acts, – magistrates trampled on, – yeomanry assaulted, – hooted, unhorsed, – cart loads of stones, – forests of bludgeons! – not one tittle or which has any existence or place in the state trial, to which he will naturally turn, in order to observe the issue of atrocities so horrible. What will ministers do? Their station in the realm has unfortunately snatched them from obscurity; they must, therefore, either destroy every record of their speeches, or cancel every publication of the late trial, by which all their statements are dissipated and reduced to nothing; or else, (comes the last lamentable clause of the disjunctive) they will stand recorded for ever as having solemnly averred in the house of legislature, that which was found in a court of justice, to be totally untrue.'

To this severe, though just exposition, the leading journal might have added, that Lord Stanley was foreman of the grand jury, who, at Lancaster, found true bills of indictment against the reformers, and cut those against the magistrates and yeomanry. Mr Wilbraham Bootle also was one of the said high functionaries. Their deeds, any more than their words, must not be suffered to escape entirely from our recollection. Posterity must know these things, in order that when they point to the tombs of these noblemen, they may not confound them with those of their family, who had not any such words or deeds to answer for.

Chapter 71

How the Author was assisted when he wanted it — The Emptiness of Popular Applause — Author's departure from Middleton — His Child — Farewell to his Wife

THE terms of our recognizances were, that we should appear in the Court of King's Bench, on the first day of the ensuing Easter term, and not depart therefrom without the permission of the court. On the approach of that time, I therefore became anxious about the means whereby I should get to London. I should have been miserable if from any circumstance I had incurred a risk of not being in court when called, and had thereby, forfeited the bail which my friends had given with me. My radical acquaintances, however, never asked me when, or how, I was going, and I felt too much what was due to myself, and my situation, to throw out the least hint about the matter. One or two of the most sordid and ungrateful of my acquaintance, and God knows I had too many such, even told me, that I needed not expect any assistance from them, even if I went to prison. I smiled in contempt, and replied that it would be time to deny me their assistance when I asked for it. Others there were, who no doubt, would have acted with an honourable considerateness, had I made known to them my total want of funds for the journey, but I deemed it their place to ask me, and not mine to ask them. I could not but feel that I was about to be victimized on their account; I knew what was my duty, and was prepared to do it, but I would not condescend to remind them of theirs.

One day I was at Manchester, and in conversation about these matters, I asked Mr Evans, the editor of The Observer, if there were any funds in the town which would be available in assisting the convicted parties to London? He said he had some money in hand belonging to the relief fund, and asked me how much I should want? I said I should think three pounds would be sufficient. He said I should have it, and if I would call on him a day or two before I set off, he would pay it me. I called on him the week following, and he gave me three pounds. I purchased a pair of strong shoes, a pair of two of hose, and some other necessary articles, and then I went home, and prepared in other respects for the journey.

It would be of no use to dwell on the hours of care, thoughtfulness, and anxiety on my part, nor of the regrets and tears which I tried to soothe and to suppress, on behalf of my wife and child. Previous to my departure, every one with a heart susceptible of our common human emotions, will understand and appreciate their feelings and mine; suffice it to say, that when the last moment had been spent on my hearth, I started to my feet, threw my stick and bundle over my shoulder, locked the door, gave my wife the key, and with her on my arm, and my little girl by the hand, I took my way down Middleton and towards Manchester. I could not but reflect that when I went that way on the sixteenth of August, there were ten thousand with me ready to shout, sing, or do whatever I requested; now, as if they were afraid I should want something from them, not a soul came forth to say 'God be with you.' One or two whom I saw on the road did, as they passed ask if I was 'going off,' to which I replied by a nod. The words stuck in my throat, I was ashamed both for myself and them; ashamed of my past folly, and of their present faithlessness. At the bottom of the town we parted from our dear child, telling her to go to a certain neighbour's (as had been previously arranged), and be a good girl, and her mother would bring her something from Manchester. She looked at us alternately, in tears, and then said, 'And when will you come, father?' I stooped, kissed her, and said I would come soon, and, dashing the drops from my eyes, I gave my arm to her mother, and we ascended the hill in silence.

We stopped at Harpurhey, and whilst there, a Middleton man, a weaver, came into the place, and said he understood I was going to London; I told him I was, and he urged me to accept a shilling, as he understood I had come away with but little, if any money. I thanked him, but refused to accept of it, alleging that I was better able to struggle with my difficulties than he was to spare a shilling from the wants of his large family. He then said that as he was coming through Middleton, John Ogden, a shopkeeper, and a neighbour whom I well knew, told him I was before him, and he would probably overtake me; that I had gone away without asking for, or receiving a farthing, and that if he overtook me he was to give me the shilling (which he put into his hand) and request me to accept it from him. I said that altered the case; John Ogden was able to spare a shilling; I would therefore accept it, and he must give my thanks to the donor for his good and kind consideration. My neighbour then took a glass of ale and smoked a whiff or two of his pipe, and hurried to the warehouse at Manchester; and reader, that shilling was the only Middleton coin which I had in my pocket when I started for London to receive judgment.

So much for the shouting, huzzaing, and the empty applause of multitudes. A young aspirant to public notoriety, may be excused if he feel a little tickled with the shouts of adulation, but whenever I see a grey-headed orator courting such acclamations, I set him down as being either a very shallow, or a very designing person. I have no patience with such hollow trumpery – with the fools who offer it, or the questionable ones who accept it.

We stopped at the house of a relative that night, and the next morning I left Manchester in company with my wife, and my friend and late co-defendant, Thacker Saxton. At Stockport, Saxton remained with some radical friends whom he found there. My wife still lingered with me, after having often stopped and gone on again. At last we arrived at Stockport Moor; the afternoon was advanced, and the sun was descending;

> *I saw the tear from her young eyes*
> *Affectionately starting,*

as my friend Spencer Hall has so beautifully expressed it; and here was a final pause and a parting – that is, I left her standing with her looks bent towards me, and there she remained till distance closed the view.

Chapter 72

Fellow-Travellers — Friends at Macclesfield — Country Scene — Leek — Its Manufactures

I NOW walked on at a quick pace, and had not gone many miles before I overtook a young man and his wife, whom I soon learned were going to Macclesfield that night. I said I was going to that place, and somewhat further; and when I told them of my destination, and that I intended to walk the journey, they were quite glad of my company, and we agreed to travel together. I soon learned they were going from Preston, in Lancashire, to Loughborough, where they intended to settle amongst the woman's relations. They were a very good-looking couple, he a stout florid young fellow, and she a tall handsome-featured woman; she was also a good walker, which he was not, being already foot-sore.

On our arrival at Macclesfield my companions rested at a public-house, whilst I went in search of some honest radicals, to whom Saxton had given me letters of introduction. They were chiefly working men; some of them were in pretty good circumstances, being master weavers. I soon found them, and they took myself and fellow-travellers to a decent inn, where we got refreshment, and spent a very agreeable evening. In the morning, when our bill was called for, there was no charge against me, the kind friends who were with us the night before having settled everything which stood to my account.

We set off from Macclesfield, about six o'clock on a lovely morning, and soon were in a finely variegated and wooded country, as any one will allow who has travelled betwixt Macclesfield and Leek. After walking some four or five miles, we began to talk about breakfast, and my male companion said, he would have cheese and bread and ale, whilst I anticipated a good breakfast of tea, with a couple of eggs, if they were to be had. Soon after the man stopped, and his wife said as we went forward, she was glad I preferred tea for breakfast. I asked her why? and she said her husband was a very hardworking man, and a good husband on the whole, but he was a little too greedy, and expected her to fare as he did on the road, instead of letting her have a few indulgences, such as tea and coffee. It was not from want of money, she said, for he had enough with him, nor was it want of kindness to her – it was over-carefulness alone which made him so. But now, as I was for having tea, he would hardly for shame deny her having some also. I promised, if it was necessary, to put a word in for her, and she thanked me. Having travelled a little further we came to a neat little tap-house, on the descent of a valley, where the cool shadow of trees made the air grateful and refreshing, and a tiny wimpling rill ran like melted pearls over dark gravel, beneath young-leafed hazels, and by green-swarded margins. Here we agreed to stop and take what the house afforded. The smart-handed landlady soon placed a nice repast of tea, bread and butter, and a couple of eggs before me, whilst a jug of ale, with bread and cheese, were presented to my fellow-travellers. The woman said she could not eat, and I asked her to come and join me at tea, adding, very likely the cost would be little more for tea than for the breakfast they had before them. On hearing this opinion, her husband told her to get some tea, and then with great pleasure the woman came to my table and made a hearty breakfast.

We rested awhile at this pleasant little hostel; the man and I (I might as well call him John at once) each smoked our pipe, with the window thrown up, and the cool breeze wafting around us. It was delicious to breakfast as we had done, and then to repose after a fine, health-creating morning's walk. John however, I soon found, had not many conversational matters at his command. He was a plain, honest bricksetter; knew something of the value of work in his line, could make out an estimate of the expense of buildings and such things, and those were the most of what he understood. Not so his wife, she was a sensible, well-informed woman for her station, and it was evident that on most subjects (except the purse-keeping) she was his superior, and exercised much influence over him. She had been, as she afterwards informed me, a servant at an inn at Loughborough, where the young bricksetter, then on tramp, fell in love with and married her. They went down to Preston to settle amongst his friends; he was very wild and reckless, and one day he fell from some scaffolding, and was shockingly maimed, so that he could never be so stout again as he had been. Latterly he had been more steady, and had saved a trifle of money, and as they had no children, she had prevailed on him to return with her, and live amongst her relations, and that was the cause of their journey.

At Leek we rested again during an hour, took some refreshment, and then resumed our journey towards Ashbourne. In passing through the streets of Leek, we noticed a number of weavers at their looms, and obtained permission to go into the weaving places and see them. The rooms where they worked were on the upper floors of the houses; they were in general very clean; the work was all in the silk smallware line, and many of the weavers were young girls – some of them good-looking, most of them very neatly attired, and many with costly combs, ear-rings, and other ornaments of value, showing that they earned a sufficiency of wages, and had imbibed a taste for the refinements of dress. The sight of these young females, sitting at their elegant employment, producing rich borderings and trimmings, in good, well-aired, and well-finished apartments – some of them approached by stairs with carpets and oil cloths on them – the girls also being dressed in a style which two hundred years before would have been deemed rich for a squire's daughter, was to me very gratifying; whilst to my travelling companions it was equally surprising, and they expressed their feelings by sundry exclamations of astonishment.

The afternoon was very hot, and we walked slowly, – that is, I and the woman did, – for poor John was sadly hobbled with his sore feet, and we had to keep sitting down and waiting on the road for him to come up. At length we gave him an hour's respite, by stopping at a public-house about four miles from Ashbourne. It was almost dark when we entered that very clean and pleasant little town. At the first inn we went into we found accommodation, and after partaking a good warm supper, with some hearty draughts of old ale, and pipes for a dessert, we sought that repose which had now become necessary.

The next morning we were up again early, and continued my plan of travelling, namely, to walk a good stretch before breakfast. We sat down after walking about six miles; our meal was as good as we could wish, coffee and eggs for the woman and myself, and ale, cheese, and bread, for friend John. We were now in a right farming country, where large stacks, barns, and cattle sheds were quite common on the road-sides. The roads were broad and in good condition, and there were very often wide slips of good land on each side, apparently much trodden by cattle. Occasionally we came to a neat, homely-looking cottage, with perhaps a large garden, and a potato ground attached, and with rose shrubs and honey-bines clustering around the door. These were specimens of our real English homes; there was no mistaking them; in no other country do such exist; and he or she who leaves this land expecting to meet with like homes in foreign ones, will be miserably disappointed. In England alone, is the term home, with all its domestic comforts and associations, properly understood. May it long continue the home of the brave! and eventually become the home of the really free.

We stopped but a short time at Derby; I visited, however, the grave of Jeremiah Brandreth, in Saint Cuthbert's church-yard, and paid to the remains of that deluded victim, a tribute of heart-felt emotion. I then joined my comrades, and we hastened on as well as John's feet would allow him, towards Shardlow. There he got into a cart, and the female and I walked on, promising to wait at Kegworth till the cart arrived. Some rain had fallen a few days before; the Trent had been flooded, and of all the verdant pastures I have ever beheld, none have surpassed the rich, vivid green of the meadows between Shardlow and Kegworth. It was refreshing to look upon them, and as the sweet air came across them, cooling one's dewy brows, one almost felt tempted to stop and seek an abiding place in that delicious valley.

During our walk we had a very agreeable chat; I entered into some particulars of my early life, and into matters always interesting to females, namely, the histories of some tender attachments which I had formed, but which had lapsed, either through my own indifference, or, as I was pleased to suppose, the faithlessness of the objects I loved. This seemed to touch a tender chord in my companion, she was all attention, and when I paused, she put questions which compelled me to resume my narrative. I spoke of the noble and exalted pleasures of true affection, and pictured the sickening pangs of love betrayed, and the unhappiness which must eventually haunt the betrayer, whether man or woman. I repeated some verses of poetry, which heightened the picture, and at last, on looking aside, I found that her cheeks were glistening with tears. She now became more communicative, and informed me that she had somewhat to accuse herself of, with respect to a young man, the first indeed whose addresses she had encouraged: that she now often thought she behaved coldly towards him, without any just cause, and that, in consequence, the lad enlisted, and joined his regiment before his friends knew what had become of him; that she soon afterwards was married, and he was killed in battle. Weeping freely, she added that, at times she accused herself of having been the cause of his death. I consoled her as well as I could, by the reflection that her conduct appeared to have arisen more from youthful carelessness than want of feeling. She said she was an only child, and his mother was still living, and she thought if she could get settled down beside the old woman, it would afford her some consolation to assist her, and be a child to her in her old age. I approved of this with all my heart; and now being at Kegworth, we stepped into a public-house and waited the arrival of the cart which soon came up, and, after a cup or two of ale betwixt John and myself, and a whiff of tobacco, we set forward, and a short journey through a pleasant neighbourhood brought us to Loughborough.

Chapter 73

The Family Meeting — The Welcome Home — Another Meeting — Friendship instead of Love

NOTHING would satisfy my fellow-travellers, but my accompanying them to the house of the old folks, as they called them. I was not much averse to going with them, especially as I knew that I must stop somewhere in the town all night. I accordingly accompanied them along several streets and turnings, until we were in a humble but decent-looking thoroughfare, when, knocking at the door, the woman in a whisper told me her parents lived there. A tall, venerable-looking dame opened the door, and in a moment our female traveller was locked in her arms. A cheerful, clear-complexioned old man at the same time got up from his chair and shook John heartily by the hand, and on John mentioning me as a fellow-traveller, he gave me a like frank reception. He then embraced his daughter, and when the first emotions of tenderness were over, we sat down to a very comfortable but homely refection, and the family party became quite cheerful and communicative. Meantime, the news had got abroad amongst the neighbours, several came in, and in a short time we were joined by a fine-looking girl, a younger daughter of the old folks, who had been at work in one of the manufactories. In short, we had a joyful family and neighbourly meeting; liquor was sent for; a young fellow tuned up his fiddle, and the old couple led off a dance, which was followed by others; liquor was brought in abundance, and the hours flew uncounted.

John and I, and the old man, were seated in a corner smoking and conversing, when I observed the younger sister come in somewhat fluttered. She took the old mother and her sister aside, and by the expression of their countenances, and the motion of her hands, I perceived that something troublesome and mysterious had occurred. In fact, she was explaining to them, as I afterwards learned, that in going to the public-house for more liquor, she had to pass a stage coach which was stopped, and that on looking up, she saw a young soldier getting off the coach, with his knapsack slung on one shoulder, and a foraging cap pulled over his face, but she saw enough to convince her that he was Robert – the same who once courted her sister and whom they had heard was killed in battle. This news, as may be imagined, was soon known in the house, and caused a great sensation, particularly amongst the women. We had just learned the cause of their whisperings, when the door opened, and a young fellow, pale, slender, and well formed, wearing regimentals, and an undress cap, and with a knapsack properly adjusted, stepped respectfully into the room, and seeing the old woman, he put out his hand and took hers, and spoke to her affectionately, calling her mother. She gazed a moment on his face, as if incredulous of what she beheld. The company had drawn in a half circle at a distance around them; John, myself, and the old man, kept our seats; the younger sister stood beside her mother, and the married one was on a low seat behind her.

'I scarcely know what to say to you Robert,' said the old woman. 'I am glad to see you have escaped death for your mother's sake, but I almost wish you had not called here to-night.'

'And why not mother?' 'my *other* mother,' he said, trying to force a smile, – 'Why not call at a house where I left friends, and mayhap a little of something more than friendship?'

'Nothing beyond friendship now Robert,' said the mother, endeavouring to appear cool.

'Why, where is Margaret?' he said, 'I hope nothing has befallen her?'

'Margaret is your friend,' said the old woman, 'but she is nothing more now. Yonder sits her husband,' pointing to John.

John advanced towards the young man and took his hand, and looking towards Margaret, said he believed she had been his wife about two years.

The soldier trembled, and staggered to a seat.

Margaret got up and gave her hand to the young soldier, saying she welcomed him home with all the regard of a sister. She was now married as he had heard, and was about to settle in Loughborough, and if he had never returned, his old mother should not have wanted the tender offices of a child whilst she lived.

'Thank you Margaret,' he said; 'that is some consolation; you wouldn't neglect my old mother I know.' He put his hand over his eyes and burst into tears.

'I would not Robert,' she said, 'and if in former times I did not value you, as perhaps you deserved, I was willing to make the only atonement I could, by cheering the drooping years of your supposed childless parent.'

'That is very good!' – 'very fair! on both sides!' – 'very handsome!' said a number of voices. Neither of the interested parties spoke – they were both deeply affected.

The old woman and youngest daughter then conducted Margaret into another room. The old man shook hands with the soldier, and endeavoured to cheer him. Meantime, information had been conveyed to Robert's mother, and she now entered the room, shaking and leaning on a stick. The meeting was most tender; it was such as could only take place betwixt a parent and child equally affectionate. The dancing had, at first been given up; a warm substantial supper was in a short time spread on the board, Robert and his mother took some of the refreshment, and then went home; Margaret did not make her appearance. Shortly after supper, I was conducted to lodgings at an Inn, and spent most of the night in confused dreams of the strange scenes which, like those of a romance, had passed before me.

The following morning I breakfasted at the old folks, according to promise. I asked not any question, nor did I hear anything further. Margaret's eyes appeared as if she had been weeping. John was attentive to her, and she seemed as if she valued his attentions; but could not entirely cast the weight from her heart. I left the family to pursue my way, and John accompanied me as far as Quorn, where we parted, and I never saw him afterwards.

Chapter 74

Journey pursued — Leicester — Northampton — How to get lodgings

I MERELY walked through Mountsorrel, and leaving Rothley on my right, where many Knights Templars lie interred – I pushed on to Leicester, where having spent the remainder of the day in looking at various antiquities – particularly the chamber in which Richard the Third slept on the night previous to the battle of Bosworth, and the bridge over which his dead body was thrown on its return, – I took up my abode for the night at a respectable-looking little pot-house. Here I met with excellent accommodation, and enjoyed the lively conversation of some stocking weavers, who, when they learned from whence I came, and the share I had borne in Lancashire politics, would almost have carried me in their arms.

The following morning I pursued my journey, and passing through a fine country consisting of sheep-pastures, and arable land I dined at Market Harborough, and in the afternoon went on to Northampton.

I scarcely knew where to apply for lodgings; there were so many snug-looking public-houses, that I was spoiled with choice. At length I entered one of the said neat-looking places, and asked a decent elderly woman if I could have lodgings there. She frankly said at once that I could not, they were full of soldiers; and in fact, I had seen a large number on parade, as I came through the town. I asked if she could direct me to a place? and she pointed to a respectable-looking house a little higher in the street. I went there, but received the same reply; they were 'full of soldiers,' and I learned that the latter were but just come into the town, and were on their march to Liverpool, for Ireland. I now was directed to a public-house where coachmen and guards stopped, and where many travellers were in the habit of resting. It was getting late and almost dark, and I determined not to be shuffled out of this next place by any pretence. I entered a rather handsome bar parlour, where a numerous company was sitting, apparently farmers, who were taking their pipes and glass, after the fair or market. I asked the landlady, a smart, but unassuming woman, if I could have a bed for the night. From the moment I entered she had been eyeing me over and seeing, as I suppose, my shoes all dust, and myself a brown, and not a very polished-looking customer, she said she was very sorry, but there was not a bed to spare in the house; so many soldiers had brought billets that they were quite full. I drew my hand across my brows, looked at my feet, rather feelingly, and requesting she would serve me with a pint of ale, I sat down. The ale was brought, and I gave it a hearty pull, and then asked for a pipe and tobacco, which were placed before me. My next order was for something to eat, intimating that a chop or a steak, with a hot potato, would be preferred. Meantime, I drank up my ale and called for another pint, and sat smoking, and chatting with the farmers, quite in a comfortable way. When they heard I came from Lancashire, they made many inquiries as to late events, and present prospects, and I told them all they required, so far as my information went, and as candidly and fairly as my judgment enabled me, and we became very agreeable company. When my supper was brought in, I despatched it with a hearty relish, and then having ordered some brandy and water, I called the landlady to receive my shot, observing that it was time I should look out for lodgings – for I wished to try what fair means would do first. 'Oh!' she said, 'make yourself comfortable, young man; you seem very good company, and we'll make you a bed somehow or other, you shall see.' 'Another glass, sir, did you say?' asked the maid, who stood at her mistress's elbow. I nodded assent, and thus got installed for the night, and had a most excellent lodging.

I have been the more circumstantial in narrating this transaction, inasmuch as it contains a useful intimation to foot travellers. I have never since, save on two occasions, tried the experiment of getting lodgings at a public-house in the way I put the question on this night and on those occasions I took the plan more from curiosity than any other motive. A foot traveller, if he is really desirous to obtain lodgings, should never stand asking about them. He should walk into a good room, – never into the common tap-room, – put his dusty feet under a table, – ring the bell pretty smartly, and order something to eat and drink, and not speak in the humblest of tones. He will be served quickly and respectfully, that is, if those two things happen to be understood at the house. After his repast, he should take his pipe or cigar if he be a smoker, and whether he be or not, he should drink, chat, and make himself quite at ease until bed-time; when all he has to do, will be to call the chamber-maid, and ask her to light him to bed. That will be done as a matter of course, and he will probably have saved himself a tramp round the town in search of lodgings, and probably, after all, the making of his own bed under a manger or in a hay-loft.

Chapter 75

Stoke Goldington — An important Functionary — A betrayed One — A Country Alehouse — An Alarm — A Sudden Departure — A Magistrate and his Clerk — An Acquittal — A Wedding

AT six o'clock the following morning – the weather still delightful – I left Northampton. With feelings of veneration, I stopped to admire the fine old cross, as it is called, erected on the spot where the body of Eleanor, Queen of Edward the First, rested on its way to London. Near this place, as I was informed by a finger-post, the road to Needwood Forest diverged, and I longed for an opportunity to range through those interesting haunts of our English yeomen of old, but my imaginative wanderings were soon checked by the information which a countryman gave me, that the forest lands were nearly all inclosed.

At a little quiet, retired public-house on the Northampton side of

Stoke Goldington, I stopped for breakfast. I chose to halt here for two reasons, the first, because I wished to pay my respects to a worthy old couple, if they were still living, and the second because I had walked about eleven miles, and was hungry. When in my nineteenth year, I was absconding from a ship at London, weary, exhausted, and anxious lest I should be pressed, I called at night-fall at this public-house, then kept by a decent elderly man and his wife with several children. I was in my sailor's dress, with but little money in my pocket, and I told the good folks my situation. They could not find me a bed in the house, but they took pity on me, and shook me down some good clean straw in an out-building, where with the ducks for my companions in one corner, and the fowls in the other, I spent a night of sleep that might have blessed a king. The kind people also gave me a breakfast of milk and bread in the morning, and when very gratefully, and willingly, I offered payment, they refused to receive anything. I could not therefore pass their door without calling to thank them, but I found them not there, they were both, I believe, dead, and the people now at the house, knew nothing about the circumstance which had made me a debtor to their predecessors.

Whilst I sat enjoying my repast, a portly country-looking personage, with an air of some authority, came into the kitchen where several others were. He was followed by a neatly and plainly attired young woman, who sat down at a respectful distance, and seemed to shun observation. I soon learned from the tenor of his conversation with the landlord, that he was a kind of deputy constable, in some of the neighbouring townships, and that the young woman was going with him before a magistrate, on a charge which would send her to prison, for having become a mother without producing a legitimate father for her offspring. This was enough to interest me on behalf of the girl, even had not the coarse jokes of the constable, and one or two others, excited my disgust and strong aversion. I once or twice put in a word of a civil and rather exculpatory tendency, for which I almost got laughed at by the men, but was repaid by the modest and grateful looks of the poor girl. The son of the squire's coachmen, had, as I understood, been courting the damsel two or three years, but when she was in a way for bringing a charge upon him, he had nearly ceased visiting her, and had entirely given over talking about marriage. These circumstances, which, to the young woman must be matters of deep affliction and shame, were to the country boors, subjects for scornful and bitter joking, all of which she bore very meekly, and what made me think better of her, with a good sense, and self-respectful manner, which prevented her from making the least reply. She sat with her head, not entirely downcast, but with an air of shame, indignation, and repentance, whilst blushes, paleness, and tears, were alternately visible on her cheeks. I ardently wished for an opportunity for getting her out of the hands of these ruffians, and particularly of the one who had charge of her, and as I had learned the constable and she were going my way, I determined to avail myself of any chance for that purpose. I therefore fell to cultivating a good opinion with the functionary; I gave him some tobacco, and my glass to drink from, and in a short time he was telling about the numerous perils he had gone through in his apprehensions of thieves, poachers, and trespassers; on the sound judgment his office required, and the courage and activity he had on sundry occasions displayed, whilst I wondered how so rare a constable could have remained so long in a humble country situation. At length he must go, and as he said he should be glad of my company as far as we went, we all three left the public-house.

We had not gone far ere a young fellow, apparently a farm labourer, climbed over a stile from the fields and joined us. He was going to a doctor, he said, having had his face, some weeks before, injured by a young colt kicking him. His head and features were bandaged so that none of them were visible save his eyes and part of his nose. He walked with us, saying very little, but occasionally sighing, as it were from pain; I observed the young woman glancing rather doubtingly towards him once or twice, but neither she nor the constable seemed to know him. After walking some distance, the constable said he had to turn off across the fields to a village. He said I might as well go that way, as the foot-road led into the highway again, and was as short, and there was an excellent tap at the alehouse, where we could have a glass after his business was done. I agreed, for I wanted to see something more of this affair, and so I stepped with him, his prisoner, and the young man, into the meadow path, – for the doctor also lived in the same village. We soon arrived at the little hamlet, and the constable inquired of a servant in livery if 'his worship was at home?' He said he was, and would be down stairs in half an hour, and if he called at that time, he would see him. We stepped into the public-house, where we ordered some ale, and having found it very good, we began to smoke, having agreed, very philosophically, that it was the wisest course to 'take thing easy in this world.' We had sat thus, blowing clouds for some time, and going on our second jug, when the young fellow came suddenly into the room, and gazing wildly, said a person was killed just above, and the doctor had sent him for a constable, as they could not remove the body until one arrived. Our active officer then, potent with ale and authority, laid down his pipe, pulled out his staff, took a huge draught, and charging me with the custody of the young woman until he returned, he hurried out of the house. As soon as he had disappeared, 'here,' I said to the girl, 'take that shilling, and run for thy life.' The young fellow at the same time pulled his bandages from his face; a scream burst from the girl, he laid hold of her arm, I turned to light my pipe, and the next instant they had disappeared.

I then hastened up the lane in search of my active coadjutor, and met him coming down swearing and brandishing his truncheon. 'Where are they?' I said, for I thought I would be first to speak. 'Where are who,' he asked. 'Why the young Jezabel and that fellow with the broken face?' 'Where are they?' he repeated, glaring on me with his two eyes, as if they would have started from his head. 'Where are they indeed?' 'You should know where one is at least.' I then told him, in a somewhat deprecatory tone, that I only turned to the fire to light my pipe, and when I looked again, both the prisoner and the young fellow were gone. 'But you are not gone, at any rate, he replied, 'nor shall you go until you have been before the justice to answer for this. Come along,' he said, 'come this way,' and, laying hold of my arm, he reconducted me to the public-house. 'Heigh ho!' I said, 'there's nothing like taking things easy in this world.' 'D—— you and your easiness too,' he retorted, quite in a rage. 'John,' he said to the hostler, 'go and see if his worship is astir yet.' John went, and soon returned with the tidings that his worship was ready. My conductor and I then went into the house of the worthy magistrate, and were met at the yard door by a set of very cross pointers and cock-dogs, who made a general assault, as if they would have worried us, and myself in particular, for they seemed to have barked at my companion before. We were conducted into a neat carpetted room, where his worship and his clerk sat at a table covered with a green cloth, and with a number of papers and writing materials before them. 'Well Andrew!' said the clerk, a thin, sallow, suspicious-eyed person, 'where is the girl you were to bring?' 'Lord bless his honour's worship,' said Andrew, 'I left her in the custody of this here man, and he's let her run away.' 'How's that?' asked his worship, lifting his eyes from a game act which he had been perusing. 'How did you come to leave her in this man's charge? I thought you had been an older officer, and had known better than that,' said his worship. 'May it please your honour's worship,' said the constable, 'I, and the girl, and this said prisoner, that now is, were awaiting your honour's pleasure in the public-house, when in comes a scurvy knave as was awaiting o' the doctor, and said there was a person killed, and I must go and take charge of the corpse; so I 'livered my prisoner into this man's charge, and away I went arter the corpse, and when I had ran up and down 'o the village, I couldn't hear o' no corpse, and the people all, sir, a laughing at me.

The clerk gave a dark and bitter frown, the magistrate burst out a laughing heartily – I laughed too; in fact, I had been doing so in my mind during the last half hour. When the clerk saw the magistrate laugh, he was suddenly taken with a like cheerful sensation, and we all three laughed at Andrew, the constable.

'Well,' said the magistrate, composing himself, 'but what has this to do with the loss of your prisoner?' 'Please you honour,' said the constable, 'before I went a seeking the corpse I left the girl in charge of this man – whom I believe is no better than he should be – and when I came back, he tells me the girl had run away whilst he was a lighting of his pipe?'

'How was it?' asked the magistrate, addressing me. I gave him the same account I had given the constable, on which he first, and then the clerk, burst again into a hearty fit of laughter, to the apparently sore puzzlement of the constable, who seemed to think it a subject of too grave a nature for such light entertainment.

'What do you wish his worship to do in this case, Andrew?' asked the clerk.

'I wish his honour would send this here man to jail, instead of the girl,' was the reply.

'Can we do that?' asked the magistrate, half serious, half joking.

'We can hold him in sureties, if Andrew undertakes to prefer a bill at the assizes,' was the reply, in the same strain.

'Let it be done then,' said his worship. 'Andrew you will be bound in a bond of fifty pounds to prosecute this charge at the next assizes?'

'Please your honour's worship, I'd rather be excused,' said Andrew – looking alarmed – 'Who's to pay expenses?'

'I rather think the prisoner won't pay at any rate,' said his worship – 'those who prosecute will have the first chance of that.'

'Then I couldn't do it,' said the constable, – 'I'd rather not have any hand in the affair.'

'Is the man to be discharged then?' asked the magistrate.

'Yes 'Yes, if your honour pleases,' said the constable. 'I don't like them ere bonds.'

The magistrate then asked me what I was, and where I came from? and I told him I was a weaver, and came from Lancashire.

He asked me where I was going to? and for what purpose? and I told him I was on my way to London in expectation of getting a place.

Had I relatives in London? and what sort of a place did I expect to obtain? I said I had not any relatives in London, but I had some good friends, and I had little doubt of getting a situation under government.

'Under government,' said he, with surprise – the clerk also elevated his eyebrows.

Yes sir, said I, half laughing, I'm going up in expectation of a government place.

The man is *non compos*, said the magistrate in an under tone.

'Very likely sir,' replied the clerk.

'You are discharged then,' said the magistrate, 'We can't do anything with you, unless there be an undertaking to prosecute.'

I bowed respectfully to his worship; gave the clerk a questionable smile, and quitting the room, I made the best of my way to the public-house, where I had left my bundle and stick.

Another person had come in whilst we were away, and the landlady had told him about the girl running off, and my being taken prisoner. This person was an attorney's clerk, and he took up my cause earnestly and advised me to prosecute the constable for a false imprisonment. He was giving me that advice when the constable returned. I pretended to entertain the project, and when the official became aware of the subject on which we were deliberating, he became very uneasy, and seemed almost willing to make any compromise rather than be under the clutches of the other 'limb of the law.' At length, after I had sufficiently tormented him, I agreed to a settlement, the terms of which were that he should pay for a quantity of ale, I and the attorney's clerk, whom I found to be a queer ironical fellow, agreeing to pay for as much to come in, after his was drank.

We had sat here a rather considerable time, and had got into high good humour with each other and the liquor, when the sounds of voices and a fiddle were heard approaching the house, and in a minute after in walked the girl we had prisoner in the morning, arm in arm with a young fellow, who by his speech and dress we recognized as the one with the patched face; in short, they were the two runaways, followed by some half a dozen young men, two young women, and an elderly person fiddling. They had been at church, and had got wed, the banns having been published there some months before. They were now all ready for dancing, singing and, mirth; I scarcely ever saw a set of happier-looking countenances; the lad was in raptures; the bride seemed to have more self-command than any in the place. She thanked me most gratefully for the kindly feelings I had evinced; her husband joined her, and I found it of no use offering to break up from the wedding party. The constable was quite reconciled, as the charge, he said, would be taken off the township, and the ratepayers would deem it no bad day's work of his. The attorney offered his friendly services in reconciling the squire's coachman to the match, and the landlady brought in a posset of spiced ale for the wedding feast. The fiddler rosin'd his bow afresh, and played up a jig that set all the lads a capering. In short, we ate, and drank, and danced, the afternoon away – evening followed – night came, and then the noon of night; and the last scenes I committed to memory, were the fiddler falling from his chair, and smashing his viol, and the attorney painting the constable's face delicately with a blacking brush, whilst the latter person was fast asleep.

Chapter 76

Newport Pagnel — Woburn — An Aristocratic Alehouse — Redburn — Ancient Superstition — St Alban's — Interesting Objects — Barnet — London

THE next morning I was at Newport Pagnel at an early hour. The place had a most romantic appearance as I approached it. There must have been heavy rains upwards, for the Ouse had overflowed its banks, and numerous cattle were grazing on small green islets surrounded by the flood. The weather continued all that a foot traveller could wish, and I walked on leisurely, enjoying the cooling breeze, the odour of flowers, and the music of birds, some six or eight miles, until I arrived at the celebrated village of Woburn, where I stepped into the first public-house I came to on the left hand side. – I think it was the sign of the Bedford Arms. The place seemed very fine, and the people I saw moving about, looked, I thought, in a strange supercilious way at me; none of them stopped to ask what I wanted. At length I desired a woman to bring me a glass of ale, intending it as a preliminary to breakfast. She did not pause a moment to receive my order, but looking down, swept past me. 'Bless us,' I thought, 'what sort of a public-house have I got into now.' No one attended to me, and soon after I asked again for a glass of ale; this servant also went away without speaking, but in a short time a female of a superior appearance came and said they did not entertain foot travellers. I expressed my surprise at that, and assured her I was both able and willing to pay for whatever I called for. She said she did not doubt it, but it was an invariable rule of the house, not to serve persons travelling on foot, and the rule could not be departed from. Could I not have a draught of ale? I asked. No, foot travellers could not have anything there. I accordingly rose, and replacing my bundle on my shoulder, I begged her to inform her employer that the rule of the house might bring trouble and humiliation sometime, inasmuch as if other engagements did not press me, I would go before the nearest magistrate, or the Duke of Bedford himself, and prefer a complaint against the occupier, for refusing to entertain a traveller without, sufficient cause. She smiled at my law (as well she might, having scanned my appearance, and thence formed an opinion of my purse), and said there were other places in the village, where I might have whatever refreshment I wanted; and then, probably thinking she had wasted time enough on me, she turned and walked off, and I came out of that inhospitable, and pride-infected place. At another inn I met with a reception the very reverse of the first, the people, both landlord and servants, were very obliging and attentive. I made a good breakfast, rested, chatted, and received an invitation to call there again if I came that way.

I wonder whether the people of the Duke's Arms are yet in

business ? and if they are, whether, like scores of their arrogant brotherhood, they have not been so far humbled by those great levellers, the railways, that if a wayfaring man now enters their house, he can have a cup of ale for money ?

I walked to Redburn to dinner, which consisted of a plain but delicious repast, at a very humble pot-house. Here I remarked a horse-shoe nailed inside the weather board of the door, and on my pretending ignorance of its purpose, and asking what it was for ? an old wrinkled dame, seemingly the mother of the household, told me with perfect seriousness, that it was to keep all witches, and bewitched persons and things out of the place, and that so long as it remained there, nothing under the influence of witchcraft could enter.

At St Alban's I walked amid the ruins of the old Abbey, having previously passed a fragment of a wall in the meadows below, undoubtedly a part of the remains of the British city of Verulam. I lingered rather long with these scenes, and it was getting dark when I passed the Obelisk at Barnet, where the famous battle was fought in the wars of the roses. Every step I had advanced to-day, the people, their houses, and their manners, became more London-ish; and it will not then appear surprising, that at the first public-house I went into, I was made welcome to comfortable quarters, and so remained there during the night. The next morning I walked into London, and took my breakfast at a coffee-house.

Chapter 77

A Cruise amongst the Booksellers — Visit to Mr Hunt — London Politicians and Jury Reform — A Painful Discovery

MY next business now was to examine the state of my purse, which was speedily done, and found scarcely able to make a jink, however shaken. My next consideration was, how to set about replenishing it. I had, in contemplation of some such a dilemma as the present, brought with me from Lancashire some manuscript poems, which I felt pretty confident of being able to sell for a decent sum, should I be in want of money during my stay in London. I was already in want of it, or about to be, and I was thus driven to my last resource the first day of my arrival. I wished to raise some money immediately in order that I might be enabled to redeem some things which I had directed to be sent by the carrier, and be thereby enabled to appear before my friends in a respectable garb.

I therefore inquired my way to Ave-Maria-lane, and went into a great publishing establishment there; but, without waiting to see my productions, they told me they could not do anything with poetry. At another place, in Paternoster-row, I could not see the great man, because I had not a letter of introduction. I went down Ludgate, and into the shop of William Hone, but he was out of town. At a shop in the Strand, the brown paper enclosure of my effusions was first opened, a glance given at the contents, myself scanned over, and the writings returned, with an assurance that 'It wouldn't take.' At a grand place in Oxford-street, the shopmen stood laughing at me, as I verily believed, under pretence of being diverted by my Lancashire rhymes; and at a similar establishment in one of the wide streets beyond Charing-cross, I received the comfortable advice to return home, and remain at my loom. Alas! I thought, I wish I could return home.

I had now enough of the poet's trade, at least for one day: of

The rich man's scorn, the proud man's contumely,

and, wearied and disappointed, I turned my footsteps towards the lodgings of my friend Hunt, at Mr Giles's, in Wych-street. To be sure the booksellers were not entirely blameable; my appearance was, no doubt, somewhat against me. My clothes and shoes were covered with dust, my linen soiled, and my features brown and weathered like leather; which circumstances, in consideration with my stature, and gaunt appearance, made me an object not of the most agreeable or poetical cast. Still, I thought these booksellers must be very owls at mid-day not to conceive the possibility of finding good ore under a rude exterior like mine. And then I bethought me – and comforted myself therewith, inasmuch as others had trodden the same weary road before me – of Otway, and Savage, and Chatterton, and of the great son of learning, as ungainly as myself – Samuel, the lexicographer – and, I might have added, of Crabbe, and others of later date, but their names had not then caught my ear. And thus, musing as I went, and chewing bitters until they almost became sweets, I once more found myself in the shop of Mr Giles, the bread baker, in Whych-street.

I asked for the good old man, and a plump, short-statured lady, in mourning, advanced from an inner room. I saw in a moment that she was Mrs Giles, and, smitten with a saddening thought, I ventured to ask for her husband. She informed me civilly, but not in that friendly tone I had been accustomed to there, that Mr Giles was dead, that she was keeping the business on, and that Mr Hunt and his family had removed to an address which she gave me, in Charlotte-street, Oxford-street.

The afternoon was far advanced, when, after traversing a part of the town I had never seen before, I knocked at the door of a very respectable-looking house, and asked for Mr Hunt, and on sending up my name, was instantly admitted. Mr Hunt and, Mrs V., and the young lady, his ward, were each glad to see me; and I had not been long in the house before a very acceptable respast of bread, butter, and a beverage made from roasted corn, was set before me, and I partook of it with a relish, though I was never very fond of his 'corn coffee;' but as we all know, 'hunger is the best sauce.' Many questions of course were asked on both sides, and matters were discussed, and after conversing about an hour, as night was setting in, I took up my bundle and stick – received a hearty shake of the hand, with an invitation to 'come to-morrow,' – 'come any time.' And so, bidding my friend and his family good evening, I left the house and turned into the street, to go, I knew not whither.

'This is not the way,' thought I, 'in which I treat my friends from a distance, when they call upon me in Lancashire. I should not have let Mr Hunt leave my dwelling, humble as it is, without knowing whither he was going, and how he was to be entertained.' But then came the old excuse, 'It is the way of great folks,' – 'one of the peculiarities of London,' and so forth; and cogitating on this and various other matters, I retraced my steps, as well as I could find my way, to Mrs Giles's, in Wych-street.

I thought the widow seemed more friendly after I had expressed disappointment at my visit to Mr Hunt. I asked her if there was a decent tavern in her neighbourhood which she could recommend as a comfortable place for lodging. She expressed entire ignorance of any of them, but said one of the journeymen could possibly inform me; and she called one, who recommended a house in Newcastle-street, close by, as a suitable and likely place for stopping at. She sent him to inquire if they could lodge a person from the country, and in a short time he returned, saying I could have a very good bed there if I chose. I accordingly went with the man, who showed me the house, and I entered the public room, and, taking my seat at a table opposite the boxes, I ordered a pint of beer, as they call it, and bread and cheese for my supper.

I had finished my repast, and sat smoking, when three or four persons entered the room, and commenced a conversation which became animated. They were, as I soon learned, some of the London politicians of the working class, and the subject was the English jury system. It was, if I mistake not, the approaching trial of Thistlewood and his companions, which led to this discussion. One party would have it that the English jury was one of the most complete inventions which human wisdom could have accomplished, and they lauded it as fervently, and with about as much sense, as a certain class of politicians are in the habit of lauding our 'glorious constitution,' a thing which exists in imagination only. Another party thought that the system was faulty, and instanced the packing of juries, and a third party thought the verdict should go according to the majority. I sat listening attentively, but did not interfere, until at last, one of the speakers asked my opinion of the subject in dispute.

I frankly confessed that I differed from the whole of them, and thought the English jury one of the most bungling pieces of judicial machinery which could have been put together, and I noticed several instances of its clumsy and imperfect operation within my own knowledge, not however mentioning the later trial at York. I asked how it could be otherwise, seeing the manner in which jurymen were selected. In the county I came from I said they were generally men who had just the brute instinct of beavers to, scrape a little substance together, and to keep it; but who for all other purposes, were far behind their neighbours; and infinitely so in qualifications necessary for deciding betwixt right and wrong, guilt and innocence. A time would come, as I ventured to suppose, when that piece of old trumpery would be done away with altogether; meanwhile I would, had I the power, endeavour to render it more useful by ordering, in a legal way, that all jurymen should be elected by ballot, in each township – that their appointment should be annulled at the will of those who appointed them – that property should not qualify, – that five, seven, or nine should be the number, and a majority should carry a verdict – that all juries, whether grand juries, coroner's juries, or leet juries, should be taken from this body,

295

and that they should be paid from county or other rates, independent of the crown. This plan was generally approved of, and I should have been honoured with a speech or two in compliment, but happily the girl came with the chamber candle, and so bidding my London patriots good-night, I retired from their company.

After ascending several heights of stairs, I demurred, and asked the girl how much further upwards we must go? She begged pardon, and said the bed intended for me was on the second floor, and had been occupied by a lodger during a fortnight; he had gone away and they did not expect him that week, but he had suddenly returned, and claimed his old bed. Against this I could not adduce any argument, especially as it was too late to go out that night, and so following my guide, I climbed to the upper-most floor of the house. I looked at the apartment, which did not please me very well; it was of no use however beginning then to be very nice, and so I threw down my bundle and stick, whilst the girl with the candle in her hand, remainded me that it was customary for strangers to pay before going to bed. 'Oh! very well,' I said, 'how much is it?' – not thinking the charge would be more than sixpence at most. 'Eighteen-pence if you please sir,' said the girl. I put my hand hastily into my pocket, and pulling out all the money I had, I counted it, and found it to be just a penny short of the demand, namely, one shilling and five-pence. 'Well lass,' I said, 'this is all the money I have in the world, and it is a penny too little,' and I looked, as much as to say, 'will it do?' 'Never mind, sir,' she replied, 'you will be calling some day, in going past, and you can give the penny to master or mistress.' I said I would do so; and the girl then bidding me good-night, left the room.

Chapter 78

An uncomfortable situation — A Saint-like Sinner — A Walk before Breakfast — Forgetfulness of Friends — A Poor Prisoner — A Friend indeed

I HAD never slept on so mean a bed as was presented on my turning down the clothes. I had slept for weeks on old sails in the half-deck of a ship, or in the cable tier, and slept comfortably, but I had never lain on anything that looked and smelled so filthy, as the narrow, hard couch now before me. I, however, threw myself upon it, and wooed forgetfulness, in order to escape from disgust; but there was such a racket on the other side of the partitions, as, for a long time, forbade all repose, and convinced me that I had got into a not very respectable house. When at last all was still, and I was beginning to sleep, the peaceful charm was broken by the entrance of a drunken soldier, who rolled into another bed, and kept me awake by narrating various sprees, as he called them, in which he had been engaged during the day. At length he also became oblivious, and his very welcome snore, informed me that I was at liberty to sleep if I could. The 'sweet restorer soon came,' and when I awoke in the morning, my noisy companion was gone, probably to attend an early parade.

I was not long in dressing, as may be supposed. I merely coaxed the holes in my stockings a little lower, and turned my neck-kerchief the cleaner side out, and my embellishments were finished. There was no water or towel in the room, and I would not make free with soldier Jack's blacking, as I had nothing to satisfy his demand, should he return and make one, I therefore slipped on my shoes and clothes, dusty and soiled as they were the night before, and grasping my trusty cudgel, and my bundle, I sallied from the room, wishful to get a breath of sweet air, if there were any such in London. As I passed along a kind of landing, a door opened just before me, and out stepped, as quietly as an old hen off her perch in a morning, as demure a looking piece of purity as the world ever exhibited. As she turned to go down the stairs, I caught a glance of her face. She was almost forty years of age, with rather agreeable features; modest and humble looks, as if she had been at prayers, and was dressed in second mourning, of the most devout cut. 'A mother in Israel,' indeed, would that frail dame have passed for. As I followed her towards the door, I really felt in a degree ashamed at being seen coming out with her. I involuntarily turned towards the lady as she went away, and at that moment she gave me a look which spoke as plainly as a look could speak, what was her unfortunate vocation.

I sauntered down into the Strand, and turned towards Charing-cross, not that I had any business in that direction, but I thought a man without money might as well go one way as another in London. I was half-inclined to believe also, that the people I met seemed as if they knew I was pennyless. After wandering an hour or so, looking in at the shop windows, and gazing at whatever was new, I retraced my steps on the other side of the street, with the view of calling at the office of 'The Black Dwarf,' and a faint hope of receiving an invitation to breakfast. Mr S. was very glad to see me, and was very civil, but he did not seem to have any thought about breakfasting, and so after a short conversation standing, I went once more into the street. At Mr West's, the wire-worker, I was not more fortunate, and my friend, Sir Richard Phillips, at whose shop I had called the day before, would not be at home for several days. I consequently had no abiding place, save the street, and I 'maunder'd about,' as we say in Lancashire, devising new expedients, and conjuring up hope almost against despair. I had become quite wolfish, and the sight of good substantial meats, and delicate viands in the windows of the eating-houses, all of that which in my road I stopped before, and contemplated, tended to increase the pangs of hunger, which were no ways allayed by the savoury fumes arising from the cooking cellars. At last I wandered round Fleet Market, and coming to the prison, I found a poor debtor begging at the gate.

'Please to bestow a trifle on a poor prisoner,' he said.

'God help thee lad,' I replied, 'I am more poor than thyself,'

'How is that?' he asked.

'Why,' I said, 'thou has a room to retire to, and a bed to repose upon, but I have neither home nor lodging, nor food, nor a farthing of money towards procuring them!'

'Why then God help *thee!*' he said, 'thou art indeed worse off than myself, except as to liberty.'

'And that I may not have long,' I said.

He asked me what I meant; and I told him that I was come up from the country to, receive judgment for attending the Manchester meeting.

'If that be the case,' he said, 'come back in an hour, and if I get as much as threepence or sixpence, thou shall have it.'

I thanked him sincerely and gratefully, and promised I would come back if no better fortune befell me and so pleased that I had found one friend in the course of the morning, though a poor one. I bade him good-bye, and went on towards Bridge-street.

At sight of the bridge I recollected a gentleman on the other side of the river, who had behaved very kindly to me the last time I was in London, and I thought I might as well call upon him, for at all events I could not be more disappointed than I had been. I therefore passed over the bridge, and soon found the shop of my friend in the main thoroughfare, called Surrey-road, I think. Several young men were busy in the shop, and I asked one of them if Mr Gibb was within?

'Oh yes,' he said, 'Is that you, Mr Bamford? Walk forward, he's in the sitting-room at breakfast; he'll be glad to see you; step in.'

I thought that was like a lucky beginning, at any rate, and, without a second invitation, I entered the room.

A glance of one moment brought the gentleman to his feet. He took my hand and made me sit down, and rang the bell, and ordered another cup, and more butter and toast, and eggs and ham. 'You have not breakfasted, I suppose?' he said.

I replied that I had not, it was just what I had been wanting to do during the last hour and a half.

'Bamford,' he said, as we went on with our repast, 'What's the matter with you? you don't seem as you did the last time you were in London.'

'How am I changed,' I enquired.

'Why the last time you were up,' he said, 'you were all life and cheerfulness when I saw you, and now you seem quite thoughtful. Are you afraid of being sent to prison?'

'No,' I said, 'I was not.'

'What's the reason you are so serious,' he asked.

I said 'I could not help being so.'

'What's the cause,' he said, 'Tell me the reason of this great change?'

'Well then, to tell you God's truth,' I said, 'I have not a farthing in the world, and I could not have had a breakfast if I had not come here.'

'Oh! if that's all, man,' he said, 'make yourself easy again. Come! take some more, and make a good breakfast,' and I took him at his word, I did make a good breakfast.

When we had finished, he took me to his dressing-room, where were water and towels to wash. He also ordered the servant to clean my shoes, and found me a clean neck-kerchief, and a pair of stockings. When I returned to the sitting-room, I was quite smart, comparatively.

'Now, Bamford,' he said, 'This is my breakfast hour; at one we dine, at five take tea, and supper at eight; and so long as you are in London, my table is yours, if you will attend at meals. Take this one pound note, (putting one into my hand,) and if there is not a change in your circumstances for the better when that is done, come for another.'

I thanked him most sincerely. I never was more affected by an act of kindness in my life. He was in truth, 'a friend in need, a friend indeed.'

Chapter 79

A Change in my Situation — Proceedings in the Court of King's Bench

I NOW went to the warehouse in Cheapside, where my luggage had been directed to be left, and found it had arrived. I took it to a tavern, and put on a change of linen and articles of outer apparel, and then I went and engaged lodgings, to which I removed my things. I was now decent in appearance, and more comfortable in mind. I visited my friend Mr Gibb, and did not forget the poor fellow in the prison. In the afternoon I again called upon Hunt, who received me very cordially, and I took some more of the 'roasted' with him. The day following, Healey and Johnson arrived in London, and on the twenty-seventh of April, we all made our appearance in the Court of King's Bench, when Mr Hunt moved for a rule to shew cause why the verdict returned at York should not be set aside, and a verdict of not guilty entered on the record, or why a new trial should not be granted.

The Lord Chief Justice Abbot asked if the application was for Mr Hunt and the other defendants?

Mr Hunt said it was so made.

The Lord Chief Justice: Now state on what ground it is that you make this motion.

Mr Hunt: The first ground, my lord is a misapprehension of the learned judge who tried the case, in rejecting evidence as to the acts of aggression of cutting, maiming, and killing by the yeomanry cavalry, and other military, upon the persons of those who attended at the Manchester meeting. The next point is the learned judge's admittance of evidence as to certain resolutions of a meeting held in Smithfield, and the admission of evidence as to certain trainings and drillings, at a place called White Moss. The third point is the misdirection of the judge, in consequence of such rejections and admissions; and the fourth ground is, that the jury gave a verdict contrary to the evidence.

The Lord Chief Justice: – Have you any other ground?

Mr Hunt: – Yes, I have a fifth and last ground, which is, that the jury gave a verdict contrary to the direction of the learned judge.

The judges not having before them the notes of the trial, the deterimination as to the points urged by Mr Hunt, was postponed until Monday, the first of May, when we were ordered again to be in attendance. We were accordingly in court at the time appointed, with our solicitor Mr Pearson, but the judges did not pronounce their determination, and we were directed to appear on the eighth of the same month; the court was each day crowded to excess.

On the eighth of May, the judges delivered their opinion, unanimously refusing the rule applied for by us. The Attorney-General then urged that judgment should be immediately pronounced; but Mr Hunt requested that time should be allowed us to prepare. I was as fully prepared on the first day, as I was on the last: but coincided, through courtesy, in Mr Hunt's various expedients, to put off the evil day to the uttermost. The request now made by him was granted by the court, and we were ordered to come up again on Saturday, the thirteenth of May, for judgment.

On that day, Hunt, Healey, and myself, appeared before the judges, and Johnson came shortly after. Mr Hunt stated that certain affidavits which he had sent for from Manchester had not arrived, and he craved the indulgence of the court until he was enabled to procure them, which he expected every hour. This was accordingly granted, and we retired once more. Soon after two o'clock, we again went into court, and Hunt tendered an affidavit, telling forth that the person who had been despatched to Manchester for the affidavits had not arrived, nor had any letter been received from him. Mr Hunt next stated that since the above affidavit was sworn, a letter had been received by Mr Pearson, wherein it was alleged, that the writer had been unable to procure the affidavits by the time appointed, but there was no doubt they would arrive in the course of Sunday.

The Lord Chief Justice then ordered the case to stand over until Monday morning.

Chapter 80

THIS being the day appointed for pronouncing judgment, the court and the hall were crowded at an early hour by spectators, and hardly on any former occasion did public curiosity appear to be more excited. Several persons of distinction were present in court during the greater part of the day. Among others, we observed Lord Binning, Lord Apsley, and Mr Tierney.

About half past eleven o'clock, the Attorney-General having prayed the judgment, we all came into court. We were accompanied by Mr Pearson, the solicitor, Mr Wooler, and other friends. The whole of the proceedings occupied the attention of the court from the hour above-mentioned, until past six o'clock in the evening.

Several affidavits were put in by Hunt, Johnson, and Healey. I did not tender any affidavit; indeed I had not been a willing party to these fruitless procrastinations.

The Chief Justice asked the Attorney-General whether he meant to put in affidavits on the part of the crown?

The Attorney-General. – Not at present; it will depend, my lord, on the contents of the affidavits now put in.

The first affidavit read was that of Mr Hunt, which entered into a history of the transactions that took place in Manchester on the sixteenth of August.

The joint affidavit of William Brundret, Dwarris Hart, Joseph Holland, Richard Sheridan, Samuel M'Cabe, George Burney, William Hunt, William Gregory, John Riley, Henry Barrett, William Mackelroy, and Alexander Anderson, all of them persons who had signed the requisition for calling the meeting, was next put in and read. These persons described themselves as housekeepers, at Manchester and its neighbourhood, and weavers, &c. by trade. They described the dreadful state of depression and poverty to which they had been subjected, as the motive for calling the meeting, in order thereby to obtain, by legal means, a redress of their grievances. They stated, that with the utmost industry, working fourteen hours a day, they could not earn more than eight shillings per week.

The affidavit of Ann Jones, a married woman, occupying a house which commanded a view of all that took place at the meeting, was next put in. She deposed that the meeting was quiet and perfectly harmonious, until the yeomanry cavalry broke in upon the unresisting crowd, who were cut down and trampled upon with merciless fury. Her house afterwards became the refuge of the wounded and dying, to whom she administered such relief as her means would afford. She likened her house to an hospital after a military slaughter.

The affidavit of Nicholas Whitworth, stated that after the sanguinary transactions of the sixteenth of August, he had made it his business to enquire into the extent of the mischief, and he had seen and spoke with near four hundred persons who had been wounded by the military. Some of these persons were injured from sabre cuts, and others by gun-shot wounds.

Part of the affidavit, which merely spoke to the deponent's information and belief as to other circumstances connected with the transactions of that day, was rejected as not admissible.

The affidavit of Robert Willis Hall stated, that the deponent had seen and spoken with three hundred persons; men, women, and children, who had been injured by gun-shot and sabre wounds, received from the military on the sixteenth of August.

The affidavit of Joseph Rayner stated, that deponent had seen and conversed with three hundred and eight persons, injured from the like causes.

Mr Hunt said that before the other defendants and himself proceeded to offer any observations in mitigation of punishment, he must entreat their lordships to confine their attention solely to the fourth count of the indictment, upon which the conviction was founded, In order to this, it was necessary that their lordship's should distinguish the evidence which supported that count, from that which was adduced to sustain the others, of which the defendants were acquitted, but which embraced much more heinous charges. This caution was the more necessary, not only because it would be the height of injustice, that, by blending all the evidence together, they should be punished for offences of which they had been acquitted, but, because one of their lordships (Mr Justice Best) had misconceived many parts of the evidence, and had made comments upon them with that warmth which was natural to him, and which could not but have a prejudicial effect upon the minds of the other judges, in meting out the punishment they were called upon to award. He therefore prayed that the learned judge, who tried the case, would read such parts of the evidence as applied to the fourth count only, so that the court might see upon what foundation their sentence was to proceed. He, however, would leave this matter entirely to the discretion of their lordships.

The court assured us that in awarding the punishment, they should confine their attention solely to that part of the evidence which was applicable to the count on which the jury found their verdict.

Mr Hunt then prayed, as matter of indulgence, that the other defendants might have the priority of him in addressing the court in mitigation of punishment.

The court said, they saw no reason for departing from the ordinary course of their proceedings. Mr Hunt's name stood first on the record, and therefore he would begin.

Mr Hunt then addressed the court in a long speech during which he was several times stopped by the judges for irrelevant matter, and once by Justice Bayley, who, as at York, requested that he would forbear to use complimentary language. Mr Johnson followed in a speech more condensed and to the point. Whilst, when Healey's turn came, he produced a speech ready written by his friend at Lees. It was all to no use however, – the doctor could not make out the polysyllabic words without spelling, and I who stood behind him had to look over his shoulder and read for him, whilst my cheeks burned, and my ears tingled with mortification, amid the suppressed titters of the gentlemen of the long robe, and the spectators. When he was fast, and I was not attentive, he would look over his shoulder supplicatingly, and say in an under tone. 'Prompt, Bamford! prompt,' and then I set him going again. At last this was beyond endurance, and I said – 'Throw that confounded paper down man, and speak off-hand.' He accordingly wrapped the paper up, and went on very fluently, arguing that the inscription, 'Universal Suffrage or Death,' which was on the black banner from Lees, was only meant as the expression of an opinion, and was not a demand, with death as the alternative. 'Suppose,' he said, 'that one of your lordships had a bad leg.' The gentlemen of the long robe looked aghast, wondering what sould come next; for it was well known that Justice Best, who was on the bench, had two of the worst legs in England.

'Suppose,' said our imperturbable friend, 'that one of your lordships had a bad leg, and I, amongst other medical and surgical gentlemen was called in. Well, we hold a consultation, and we pronounce it to be a bad case – a case of gangrene, my lords; and my opinion as to the mode of treatment is asked, my lords? I say, amputation or death! my lords, amputation or death!' And so he went on to argue that bribery and corruption having produced a political gangrene in the state, there must be amputation of the corrupting influence, or political death would ensue.

Hunt sat on a low seat behind Healey, and when this scene was passing, I, half-diverted, half-ashamed, looked down at him, and saw him nearly suffocated with his efforts to refrain from laughing outright.

I spoke somewhat as follows: –

My lords, – I understand that the evidence upon which I was convicted, relates to the motto, 'Unity and Strength.' I must, however, confess myself at a loss to understand how guilt can be implied thereon. If we examine that part of the evidence for the crown which applied more immediately to my case, we shall find that the unity and strength which I inculcated, and which was also expressed upon the banner from Middleton, was of a quite contrary description to that imputed to me by the verdict. Morris, in repeating, or attempting to do so, my address to the people upon the Barrow-fields, says that I made use of the following expressions: – 'Friends and neighbours, I have a few words to relate; you will march off this ground quietly, not to insult any one, but rather take an insult.' Heaton declares that 'the people did not seem sullen and sulky. They had no angry look, but were more, as it were, in joy'. Now, my lords, herein you will perceive a full comment upon this short text. Here is the 'Unity and Strength' of which our banner spoke. But if we go further on to read the evidence of Dyson, who was one of my witnesses, we shall see the utility of this motto still further exemplified. Dyson says that I made use of the following words in my speech to the people, previous to their departure from Middleton: – 'Friends and neighbours, those of you who wish to join in the procession, will endeavour to conduct yourselves orderly and peaceably, so that you may go as comfortably as possible. If any persons insult your or give you offence, take no notice of them. I make no doubt, but there will be persons who will make it their business to go about in order to disturb the peace of the meeting. If you meet with any such, endeavour to keep them as quiet as possible, and if they strike you, don't strike again, for it would serve as a pretext for dispersing the meeting.' Before proceeding further, I solemnly and firmly assure your lordships that I never again will advise my countrymen to exercise that degree of patience which I here did, until every drop of blood shed on that day has been amply and deeply atoned for. Never again will I recommend forbearance, until the perpetrators of all the horrid murders which I then witnessed, and from which I miraculously escaped, have been brought to condign punishment. My lords, I speak this not from a spirit of vindictiveness, or from a wish for indiscriminate vengeance, but from a high sense of the wrongs and injuries inflicted on my country, and from an indignant feeling that justice has been denied. Dyson proceeds – 'If the peace officers come to arrest me, or an other person, offer them no resistance, but suffer them to do their duty. When you get to the meeting, endeavour to keep yourselves as select as possible, with your banners in your centre, so that if any of you should straggle away, you will know where to find each other by your banners: and when the meeting is over, keep close to your banners, and leave the town as soon as possible, for if you should stay drinking or loitering in the streets, your enemies might take advantage of it, and if they could raise a disturbance, you would be taken to the New Bailey.' Now, my lords, this is the kind of 'Unity and Strength' which I recommended to the people, accompanied by a degree of patience, which, as I before said, I will never again recommend, until justice be obtained. This is surely not a criminal Unity – this is surely not a Strength, calculated to overawe the authorities, and to fill 'his Majesty's liege subjects with terror and alarm'. This is only that 'Unity and Strength' which is the foundation of liberty and the security of property. How often since my arrival in London, for the purpose of waiting upon this honourable court have I heard boastings about the liberties of Englishmen – but if such a thing does really exist, how can it be secured without a moral 'Strength' on the part of the people, for its maintenance; and where shall we find strength without 'Unity?' This unity and strength, therefore, is nothing more or less than the foundation of all the glory and happiness which we enjoy; and shall it be said, then, that in this enlightened age, an Englishman shall be persecuted and punished for inculcating those maxims, upon which the glory of his country depends. If such must be the case, the era is every way worthy of the deed. Another instance of this unity and strength may be adduced in the situation of Middleton, which is a considerable manufacturing town, and situated in a populous district, and yet to secure its peace and tranquillity there are only two constables annually sworn in, and not a soldier quartered upon us; yet we have had no breaches of the peace, either on the part of the people or the authorities. It was, indeed, at one time, deemed expedient by some individuals to raise a posse of special constables. This measure, however, I most strenuously opposed, and happy am I to inform your lordships that the good sense of the people prevailed, and the affair was dropped. Now, here again is that 'Unity and Strength' exhibited, to which our motto so aptly alluded. Surely if any persons had a right to such a motto, it was the inhabitants of that place, whose conduct had beautifully illustrated it. I concluded my speech, of which the foregoing is only an extract, by assuring their lordships that I appealed not to their humanity, not to their commiseration, but to their justice. Humble as was my situation in society, I would not condescend to beg the boon of mercy from any man or set of men, however exalted their situation. I would disdain to receive that from their pity to which justice entitled me.

The Attorney-General spoke at considerable length in aggravation of punishment, and contended that the conduct pursued by the defendants in this last stage of the proceedings, was an aggravation of their guilt. The only topic fairly addressed to the court in mitigation of punishment was the hardships which the defendants had suffered, after they had been apprehended; but those sufferings were the natural consequences of their own crimes, which he still thought approached as near as possible to the offence of high treason. There could be no doubt of the illegality of the defendants' conduct in every part, and for the sake of the public welfare he called upon the court to pronounce such a sentence on the defendants as would, through their example, teach others to abstain from pursuing conduct equally criminal and dangerous to the peace of society and, the security of government.

The Solicitor-General declined offering anything on the same side, but left his learned friend, Mr Scarlett, who was present at the trial, to say what occurred to him on the subject.

Mr Scarlett rose principally to correct a mistake under which Mr Hunt seemed to labour, namely, that he (Mr S.) was selected to conduct the prosecution. There could not be a greater misapprehension. It was purely matter of accident, from the circumstance of his situation at the bar, and the absence of his senior, that he was employed in the case. As to any resentment he might be supposed to entertain towards Mr Hunt, nothing could be more erroneous. He never entertained any towards that individual, of whom he knew nothing but what he happened to read of him in the public papers, and to suppose that he was selected to conduct the prosecution on account of this resentment, was really absurd. If such a selection could have taken place on such an account, he could only have treated it as a personal insult towards him on the part of the Attorney-General. Adverting to the case under consideration, he entertained no doubt of the illegality of the defendant's conduct, who, he said, endeavoured to divert the attention of the court and the public by introducing matters which had nothing whatever to do with the offence for which they were called upon to answer. He insisted, that whatever might have been the conduct of the magistracy and yeomanry of Manchester, it was wholly irrelevant to the question of the defendants' guilt or innocence of the crime imputed by the indictment.

Mr Sergeant Cross followed on the same side.

The court having deliberated upon their judgment for nearly half an hour.

Mr Justice Bayley proceeded to pass sentence, and in doing so he entered into a long commentary upon the case. The case had been fully submitted to the jury, and the court having no reason to be dissatisfied with their verdict, were pronouncing such a judgment as would satisfy the justice of the case between the public and the defendants. Taking all the circumstances of the case into consideration, and giving the defendants the benefit of such mitigatory suggestions as had been urged, the sentence was, – That Henry Hunt be imprisoned in his Majesty's gaol at Ilchester, in and for the county of Somerset, for the term of two years and six months, and at the end of that time to enter into security for his good behaviour for five years, himself in 1000*l.* and two sureties in 500*l.* each; and that the other defendants, Healey, Johnson, and Bamford, be severally imprisoned in his Majesty's gaol of Lincoln for one year, and that they do severally enter into securities for their good behaviour for five years, themselves in 200*l.* and two sureties in 100*l.* each.

Mr Hunt. – I hope, my lord, the confinement is not to be solitary?

Mr Justice Bayley. – We make no order on the subject. I make no doubt that the persons to whose custody the defendants will be committed, will shew them every indulgence consistent with their safety. Their duty will be performed under the inspection of the magistracy, and we take it for granted, that every thing will be done to avoid aggravating the inconvenience of imprisonment.

We were then taken into custody, and when we reached the hall, we were greeted with the acclamations of the assembled multitude.

Chapter 81

Healey's Outfit for London — Generous Aid of the Relief Committee — Arthur Thistlewood, and his Companions — Hunt's Envy and Detraction — His base Slander — Execution of Thistlewood and his Party — Trait of Disinterested Friendship — Other Acknowledgments

IT IS now requisite that my narrative should return, as it were, and trace some events and occurrences parallel in time to those already recounted, from my entrance into London, until the last scene in the high court at Westminster. The narrative will then merge into one channel, and will so continue.

It is perhaps almost unnecessary to say, that I made no more attempts for the present, in the publishing line. My friend, Sir Richard Phillips, whom I frequently called upon, advised me to drop the idea, as a volume of poetry, unless of an astonishing kind, would be quite unsaleable.

I received a letter from my wife, informing me that a number of friends came from Oldham, expecting to see me the Sunday after I set off from London; that they were quite grieved when they learned I had gone away unprovided for, they having very promptly, and liberally got up a subscription, whereby they put a handsome sum into Healey's pocket to come up with.

In a day or two I saw Healey, and he told me how he had managed matters. He had heard about my poor departure, but he determined to try another plan. He got a number of small circulars printed, informing his friends that 'Joseph Healey, would be under the necessity of taking his departure for London on such a day, to receive judgment in the court of King's Bench; and as he was entirely without funds to carry him up, he would thankfully receive whatever sums the friends of reform contributed for that purpose,' or words to such effect. The consequence was, that a number of the Oldham and Lees radicals took the matter in hand, and went round collecting, and the following morning he had fifteen pounds given him at Oldham, besides which, he collected money at Hollinwood, Failsworth, and Newton, where he severally made calls; and was surrounded by friends who contributed handsomely. From his account it appeared probable that, at the time he arrived at New-cross, he would have twenty pounds in his pocket.

Such was the difference betwixt his departure for London and mine. But then the means were different. Had I begged it must have been from the generosity of strangers, and not from those who were indebted to me.

Mr Johnson was in respectable lodgings, in the Strand, I think. Healey lodged with Mr Chapman, of Manchester, who had come up, at a cousin of the latters, in some street on the other side of Smith-field, whilst I got a cheap and cleanly, but humble domicile at, 'The One Bell' tavern in Fleet-street.

When Healey had been a few days in London, he wrote to his friends in Lancashire, giving an account of the heavy expenses he had necessarily incurred, and stating that he had only ten-pence left. I had not quite expended the pound which my friend Gibb had presented to me.

One morning I recollect, when the pound was done, and I was daring to entertain the question, whether or not I should take my friend at his word, and ask for another, I stumbled upon Healey in the street, who pulled some money out of his pocket, and wanted to know if I had got mine. I did not understand the question, and told him so, on which he informed me, that the relief fund committee had awarded to each of us defendants ten pounds; that he had drawn his the day before, and I should get mine on applying to Mr Gallo-way. I accordingly lost no time in seeking the counting-house of that gentleman, Healey went with me, and I received the money. Thus, by the very kind and considerate attention of the committee, all further anxiety as to the ways and means of existence for the present, was done away with.

We now indulged ourselves with a trip by water to Richmond; that is, Healey, I and Chapman, but there was either nothing very extraordinary in the landscape, or I was in no humour for appreciat-ing it: I thought nothing of it. A walk through the Tower was more attractive, and I paused long beside the helmets and cuirasses and weapons from the field of Waterloo, all hacked and crushed, and still rusted in gore. At the Waterloo Museum in Pall Mall, I doffed my hat before that of Napoleon, and I reverently touched the sword of Ney, and the truncheon of Murat. At the British Museum I wondered and admired, but nothing interested my feelings as did the mementos of the brave and unfortunate of our own days.

The detection of Arthur Thistlewood and his companions, took place, if I mistake not, during our trial at York; it caused a great sensation at the time, and the conviction of the same misguided men occurred soon after our arrival in London. It was the subject of general conversation, and particularly the intrepid bearing of the prisoners during their trial. Mrs Thistlewood had an asylum with the family of our friend West, the wire-worker in the Strand, and I frequently saw the unfortunate woman there. She was rather low in stature; with handsome regular features, of the Grecian cast; very pale, and with hair, eyes, and eye-brows as black as night. Still she was not what may be called interesting; she had a coldness of manner, which was almost repulsive. She seemed as if she had no natural sensibilities, or as if affliction had benumbed them. She wore her hair very long, and when she went to visit her husband, which she did with devoted attention, she was strictly examined, and, amongst other precautions her long hair was unbound and combed out. Hunt frequently indulged in imprecations against Thistlewood and his party. He aspersed their courage, the fame of which seemed to have hurt him. But the worst thing I ever knew him do, was his slandering of Mrs Thistlewood, whom he represented as carrying on a criminal intimacy with West, during her husband's incarceration. A baser, more unfounded, or more improbable slander, was never uttered. Its atrocity was its antidote. In fact, he would have said anything of any one, against whom he entertained a pique. My blind adherence to Hunt, could not but be much shaken by such oft-repeated instances of an ignoble mind.

On the morning of the execution of the conspirators, I remained in my room, earnestly praying God to sustain them in their last hour; for though they professed not to believe in a future existence, I did, and could, therefore, sincerely say, 'Father, forgive them! they knew not what they did.' At noon, when all was over, I came down stairs. The execution was the subject of conversation in every place, and I soon heard, as perforce I must, the particulars of the disgusting transaction. When I met Healey, he told me that he and Johnson had been to see it, and had paid a rather heavy price for places, at a window nearly opposite the scaffold. I said he was welcome to the gratification such a scene could afford; for my part, I would not have gone on any account; and such places were the very last at which persons of our description should be seen. He put it off by saying he merely went from curiosity, to see how such things were done. The executioner, he said, bungled in severing one of the heads: he could not hit the joint of the vertebrae, and when at last, the knife touched it, the head went off in an instant.

The day before we received sentence, I called on my friend Gibb, and he not being at home, I enclosed in a letter of thanks, a bank note for the one I had received from him. A day or two after my arrival at Lincoln Castle, a letter came to hand from my kind friend, enclosing the same note, and making me welcome to it. Such traits of generosity ought not to be forgotten.

My grateful acknowledgments are also due to others. To Messrs Hodgson and Raw, of Cheapside; to Mr Galloway, his amiable lady and family; to Sir Richard Phillips; to Mr and Mrs Dolby, of the Strand; to Mr West, and his lady; to the ladies of Mr Hunt's family; and, though last, not least of all, to our venerable co-patriot, Major Cartwright, whose friendship traced us to our prison.

We were conducted from the court to a small, and rather darkish room at Bellamy's coffee-house, where Hunt expressed himself in strong terms respecting the sentence on himself. We endeavoured to console him, as did also Mr Pearson, but he continued giving fitful vent to his feelings, until our conductors again invited us to take their arms. They ushered us into a couple of stand coaches, and we were driven to the King's Bench prison, where Hunt engaged two rooms at the tavern, which is within the prison. Johnson, Healey, and myself got lodgings in the wards of the building; and thus, reader, was I domiciled in the fifth place of my confinement.

Chapter 82

IF THE verdict of the jury at York may be termed infamous, how
shall the sentence upon me of twelve months' imprisonment be
described? As infamous also, no doubt. The former circumstance
can be attributed to political fanaticism only; it was contrary to the
evidence, and the oath which the jury had taken; the latter circumstance may, I think, be fairly imputed to that quite uncalled-for
passage in my address to the court, where I said, I would never
again recommend so great a degree of forbearance as I had done,
until the blood shed at Manchester had been atoned for. That
sentence, I should have acted quite wisely and patriotically enough
in withholding: it was a declaration which my situation did not
require, and which my fellow-radicals had no right to expect. I
should have been advised against any extravagance of the sort; but
as at York, I had no counsel save my own discretion, and here it
failed me. But then, where was the justice of imprisoning me, not
for a crime committed, but for a speech delivered? Yet so it was, I
am sincerely of opinion. I believe, and not without reason, that
Judge Bayley did all he could to prevent that sentence being passed
on me; but there were four judges on the bench, and the majority
govern, and three being probably against me, he would be necess-
itated to deliver the sentence in which the three concurred.

The same evening Sir Charles Wolseley entered the prison, he
having been sentenced to eighteen months's imprisonment in
Abingdon jail, with heavy recognizances at the expiration of his
confinement, for attending a reform meeting at Stockport. I met Sir
Charles on the flags, and with him a gentleman whom he introduced
to me as Colonel ——, of the Guards. Both the colonel and Sir
Charles complimented me on my address to the judges.

It was a curious place which I had got into this time. It seemed to
be an epitome of the great world we had left, only there were not any
spinning or weaving going on here, nor rushing of horses, nor
rattling of chariots, but all the degrees of luxury and want, of careless

pleasure and thoughtful woe, were presented: all the extremes and contrarieties of our English condition might here be observed.

No sooner had we stepped inside the gate, than we were accosted by several men who offered to let us apartments entire, or lodgings, or shares of apartments, but we declined making any immediate engagements, preferring to look round, and get some information from those who knew the place.

A crowd was collected near the gate, some waiting the arrival of prisoners like ourselves; some taking leave of friends, or creditors, or attornies, or members of their families, returning into the great city; and others whose acquantance was perhaps now but slight with the world, would be standing there smoking and, sharing, mayhap, by sympathy, in the painful or pleasurable emotions of their fellows. A number of young and athletic men were stripped and playing at racket against the high walls of the prison, whilst numerous lookers-on sat smoking and drinking, blaming or applauding the players, and betting on the games. Some were hanging out dingy, half-washed linen to dry near their windows; the cobbler's hammer was at work; the barber had stuck out his pole, and displayed his pomatum, tooth powders, and perukes, as if people that had nothing to care about save cosmetics and curls. The broken-down starved dandy, stalked gaunt as a winter's wolf; the ruined gamester; the over-speculative stock-jobber; the player in his last act; the honourable tradesman ruined; the spend-thrift with nothing to spend; the fox-hunter, hunted at last to his earth; all were here. The warrior found bars of vulgar iron too strong for his polished steel; the miser, in his living rags, hutched beside the priest in his lawn; the banker was here bankrupt; the statesman without estate. The senator in vain called 'order, order,' each man was thinking, acting, reading, resting, singing, praying, eating, drinking, weeping, or smiling for himself, and his own concerns, just as in the wide world outside. But here all of human reason and passion, of pleasure and pain, of hope and despair, were pent up like the rolling, tossing, boiling wave of a volcano, that comes not up to the brim.

The day after our committal to this prison, a son of Mr Cobbett came to visit Johnson, but if I recollect aright, he was not introduced to any of the other political prisoners. His father, since his return to England, had been at variance with Hunt, and he had suffered his personal feeling so far to estrange him from the common cause, as to neutralize his powerful pen on the subject of the Manchester meeting, and the extraordinary proceedings at York. In fact, Cobbett was jealous of Hunt's popularity, just as Hunt was jealous of Thistlewood's fame; the same unworthy and unseemly spirit had now possession of both our great leaders; and the result was that they hated each other with a most sincere hatred. Not so the worthy Major Cartwright; he was always the same. The day after our sentence I found him in the coffee-room, promising Healey to write to some of the magistrates of Lincolnshire on our behalf, should our condition when there require it. He questioned me as to the mode in which I purposed spending my time in prison, and on my expressing a desire to learn something of the Spanish language, he promised to send me some books on the subject, and he kept his promise; but I never made any advance in the study – my wishes were greater than my endeavours.

We were visited by Dolby, the publisher, by Wooller, of the Black Dwarf, by Mr Pearson, our, or rather Hunt's attorney, and by one or two others, but somehow or other, most of our London friends seemed to have forgotten that we were yet in the land of the living. They never came to ask for us any more than if the prison had been our tomb. Alas! how many unfortunates in that place have made the same reflection. How many, on coming forth, have found that not a friend was left to welcome them back to the world.

The day after my arrival, I announced my situation to my wife, in a letter, containing the following lines:

TO JEMIMA

I never will forget thee, love !
  Tho' in a prison far I be;
I never will forget thee love !
  And thou wilt still remember me.

I never will forget thee, love !
  When wakes on me the morning light;
And thou shalt ever present be,
  When cometh down the cloud of night.

I never will forget thee, love,
  When summer sheds the sultry ray;
And thou shalt be my comforter,
  Amid the winter's cheerless day.

Oh! they may bind, but cannot break,
This heart so, fondly full of thee;
That liveth only for thy sake,
And the high cause of libertie.

On the morning of Wednesday, the seventeenth of May, Mr
Hunt was sent off in custody, to the Jail of Ilchester, pursuant to his
sentence, and on the following morning, myself, Healey, and Johnson were called into the lodge preparatory to our removal to Lincoln. Here was a number of turnkeys and other officers, and the first
movement was the unclasping of some handcuffs, for the purpose of
fastening us before we set out. Healey and Johnson demurred
strongly, and showed a disposition to resist, seeming to consider it
a great affront and degradation. I said the degradation was with those
who offered the insult, and not with those who were compelled to
receive it. We were then hand-chained, and ushered to the door of
the prison, where we expected a coach would have been in waiting,
but there was not any, and we were informed we should have to
walk to the booking-office. Here was another demur, my fellow-
prisoners expressing a strong repugnance to walking the streets of
London hand-cuffed. The person who seemed to have the super-
intendence of this transaction, said we should have had a coach, but
there was not any on the stands at that early hour. So we set off,
and I endeavoured to soothe the spirit of repining, by observing
that an iron manacle, worn in a just and righteous cause, was more
honourable than golden links worn by a tyrant or his minion.

But few people were in the streets, and without encountering
much observation, we arrived at the Saracen's Head, on Snow Hill,
where we entered a four-horse stage coach, and were soon, to my
great satisfaction, dashing along a broad highway, past meadows,
corn-fields, and trees in all the verdure of spring.

Chapter 83

Our Conductors — Occurrence at Newark — Approach to Lincoln — Entry
into the castle

I DO NOT recollect having ever noticed two worse-looking fellows,
than the twain, now our conductors. One was a middle-aged man,

with a villainous physiognomy, and features as immovable as if chiselled in stone. I looked, and looked, and looked again, but he appeared always the same trained, and inscrutable being. He seemed to have just learned how to do a turn churlishlly in open day, but would be more at home in lending a hand in a lonely place at midnight. I never, to the best of my recollection, so thoroughly disliked a man for his looks and manners. His comrade was younger, and somewhat more urbane, and better-looking, but there was a restlessness, and a lurking distrust in his every glance and action, which indicated an acquaintance with, if not the habitual practise of wily and unrelenting scoundrelism. I never, before or since, set my heart so against two strangers – God forgive me if I was wrong in my estimate of their characters, – and I thought I shouldn't at all wonder if something occurred that would lead me to defy them before we got to Lincoln. These fellows sat outside the coach, – we were inside – they seldom opened their lips to us, nor, I believe, to any one else. I could perceive that they were armed with pistols. Our fellow-traveller inside, was a gentlemanly-looking personage. He rode a considerable distance before any conversation ensued. When he understood who we were, and what was the cause of our being chained, he became quite chatty and agreeable, but nothing occurred which claimed a place in my recollection. When we stopped for refreshment, our conductors, like two mutes, were always with us; the hand-chains were removed, and replaced before we set out again. And thus we travelled through a rather wet day, and all night, and at dawn on the following morning, the coach stopped at Newark, and we had to take a fresh conveyance.

We were now only sixteen miles from the place of our destination, and I proposed that we should wash ourselves, and adjust our dress before we made our appearance at the jail. This favour, was after some hesitation, granted, and we were not long in finishing our toilette. The elder fellow then approached me with the clasps ready for my wrists, but I said I would not have them on any more. He looked surprised, and moved as if he would compel me; but I bade him keep back, for no force he could command should induce me to submit.

Healey and Johnson expressed a similar determination, and the two fellows asked the reason for so sudden a resolve?

I said it was not a sudden resolve on my part, for I never intended to enter Lincoln with the chains on. I cared but little how I appeared in London or the country through which we had passed, and where I was, as I should probably remain, a perfect stranger; but I knew the consequence of a first appearance in a seemingly degraded state, before persons with whom we must remain twelve months. There was no necessity for the handcuffs, I said; he might put them in his pocket. I would give him the word of an honest man that I would go with him peaceably, without the shackles, but I would not go at all with them.

Healey and Johnson gave a similar pledge, and expressed a similar determination; and the fellows seeing the point was not to be carried by force, gave it up; and a post-chaise being waiting at the door, we stepped into it with one of our conductors, the other riding on the seat, and in this form we passed through a fine level country, and approached the ancient city of Lincoln, the cathedral and castle looming in the distance, long before we could distinctly see their outlines.

At length we were upon a pavement, and soon entered a street which we passed along, and then begun to ascend the hill on which the upper-town stands. Our nags dragged hardly and slowly for some time, until having got on a level, we went forward more rapidly, and in a minute we stopped before a huge gate, which, after the application of a heavy knocker, was soon opened, and we drove into a fine broad yard, and alighted at a strong nailed door, which we passed, and were conducted into the governor's apartments, where the warrant for our detention was read, and we were received formally into his custody.

Chapter 84

Our Governor — Our Apartments — Interview with the Magistrates — Sketch of the Prison — A singular Museum

OUR new governor came from his chamber in his morning gown to receive us. I thought there seemed to be a little aim at effect in this. His voice was clear, his utterance rapid but distinct, and accompanied by considerable action. His complexion was brown, his features rather attenuated, his eyes quick, clear, and deep-seated, his forehead capacious, his hair rather thin, and a little grey, his age forty-five or fifty, his stature about the middle size, and his motions very lively. Such was John Merryweather, the governor of his majesty's castle of Lincoln, as the impression of his appearance on the morning of Friday, the nineteenth of May, remains on my recollection.

After our disagreeable conductors had retired, our governor showed us the apartments we were to occupy. We mounted two heights of stone steps, and our rooms were the first two on the right hand. Our day room was a very good apartment, with fire-place, table, chairs, and every requisite; lofty over head, a smooth floor of hardened mortar or composition, and a sash window, with a strong grating of iron before it. Our bed-room was the next to it, and of the same dimensions. In it were two good clean beds, a table, some chairs, and I think, a cupboard or two, for clothes or other articles. The rooms were remarkably clean, airy, and agreeable, and we expressed more than satisfaction, thankfulness, for the indulgent feeling which had assigned us such comfortable quarters. Mr Merryweather gave us some general directions as to the manner in which we were required to comport ourselves towards the other prisoners, and then retired; but was quickly followed by the turn-key, a stout active man, named Tuxford, who after some further explanatory chat, went down and sent to us the woman who made the beds, and attended on the debtors, by going errands for them into the town. With her assistance, we soon had materials for a good breakfast and dinner; a fire was burning in the place on our arrival, and whatever cooking utensils, or eating vessels we required, were quickly procured. And thus, friend reader, thou seest me located in the famous castle of Lincoln, the sixth place of my confinement for alleged, or suspected, political offences.

We had scarcely set our breakfast things aside, when after a knock at the door, the governor again entered, accompanied by about half a dozen gentlemen, one or two of whom seemed to be clergymen. They were, he informed us, magistrates of the county, who had business to transact in the adjoining court, and had taken the opportunity to visit us on our arrival. They asked if we were satisfied with our accommodations, and we assured them we were perfectly so, and quite grateful for their attention to our comfort.

The Rev. Caley Illingworth, chairman of the bench of magistrates, expressed a desire for himself and the others, to afford us every indulgence compatible with our situation, and their duty to the executive, provided our conduct was such as justified them in pursuing that course towards us. The only restraint they wished us at present to observe, was, the avoidance of the company of the debtors, the holding of conversations with them on religious or political subjects, and the circulation of publications, containing opinions of which they (the magistrates) could not approve. They also required that we should not receive the visits of any persons without the knowledge of the governor.

We promised obedience to their injunctions, and after many assurances of good feelings on their part, and suitable acknowledgments on ours, the gentlemen withdrew, leaving us still more pleased than before, with the situation we had fallen into.

The worthy guardians of the peace and morals of the county, were evidently apprehensive lest our presumed opinions should contaminate those of the other prisoners; but when they saw, after many weeks trial, that we acted with good faith, avoiding the debtors, and not seeking opportunities to speak on unpleasant topics, the injunction was no longer held in force; and, when in time, the governor saw us take part in the sports of the place, he expressed his satisfaction; and afterwards there was little distinction betwixt us and the debtors.

It would be foreign to the nature of this work to give a description of this prison. It will, no doubt, be found in the history of the county, and to that I must refer the reader. The present jail is a modern structure of brick and stone, consisting of a centre and two wings, or projections. It stands on the left, in advance, as we enter the yard, and nearly the first half of it, with the exception of the upper rooms, was, at the time I am writing about, occupied by the governor. Then came the front door, a lobby and steps leading to the debtors sleeping rooms; and opposite the front door, was a grated iron gate, leading to the cells of the felon prisoners, through the bars of which, was seen a dolorous array of bolts, manacles, and chains, calculated to strike terror into the minds of the guilty who entered there. On the other side of this front lobby, were the passages leading into the debtors's day-rooms, four in number; each apartment having one or more sash windows, with strong gratings outside. All the rooms, like those we occupied, were kept in a clean and airy state.

Considerable alterations were in progress; a new tower on the left of the gate was in the course of being built; the archway of the inner gate was of recent erection, and I was surprised when the governor informed me that the castle was a fief of the Duchy of Lancaster, and pointed out the arms of John O'Gaunt, cut in stone, on each side of the gate; so that, as he said, though we were at Lincoln, we were still within the duchy of our own county.

The porter's lodge was also a recent building of stone, it stood on the left of the gate as we entered. On the other side of the entrance was another building to match it, and here were the apartments assigned to female debtors, when there were any. At present they were occupied by a gamekeeper of some great gentleman, who was under a charge of manslaughter, for shooting a poacher.

The outer turnkey, was a merry, loquacious, little fellow, about seventy years of age. He proved to be very obliging, fond of money, and somewhat singular in his way. He kept a kind of curiosity shop, consisting of instruments of murder, or murderous assault, such as hedge-stakes, splintered with breaking skulls, poles broken and bloody, hatchets, bars, and bludgeons. Then he had an arrangement of the skulls of murderers, male and female, and highwaymen; and, next, halters, each ticketted with the name of the man or woman who had suffered in it. This impressive exhibition he displayed with apparent satisfaction, especially when the visitor slipped a piece of silver into his hand.

All around the prison building, I have thus sketched, arose high stone walls, some parts of them, appearing to be of a great age. They comprised, as I was informed, an area of about eight acres, one part of which was a large green in front of the jail, on which the prisoners for debt took exercise; in the centre of this green was a shrubbery, and the green was bordered on three sides by a long slip of garden ground, embracing the foot of the wall, appropriated to the use of the governor, and cultivated by the more orderly of the felons. On the wall opposite the governor's apartments was a round tower, on which executions took place; and an ancient keep, called Lucy's tower, in the rear of the jail – part of the original fortification – was now kept locked, and was tenanted only by owls and an immense number of shell-snails, which completely formed its floor. In a hollow at the foot of this tower, were seen the green heaps above the graves of felons who had died within the prison, and of criminals who had been executed; and on a more level plot behind the Town Hall (which building fronted the gates at the extremity of the yard), was the place of interment for debtors, some with stones and inscriptions, and other with only the green mantle of their mother earth lapping over them.

> *And these had once been lov'd full well,*
> *Though some might hate or fear them;*
> *But now they slept in narrow cell,*
> *Nor wife, nor child lay near them.*

High above the gates and prison walls, at a short distance outside rose the towers of the venerable and magnificent cathedral. The lady tower contained a peal of bells which were only rung twice a year; on Lady and Michaelmas days. They were the sweetest-toned bells I have ever heard. One of the towers was cracked, and men were employed in boring through it to brace it with iron. This was the tower of the great bell Old Tom, which boomed forth the hours to us, as they too slowly joined the eternity of the past.

Such is the sketch of the place we were at present consigned to, as correctly described as my recollection enables me to give it. Since then, I have heard, that alterations have been made for the worse, as it regards the debtors. Of the exact nature of the alterations, I am not informed, and I should be sorry to find them such as intimated, were I to revisit the prison.

Chapter 85

Jabez Bunting — Hurtful Interference — Our Governor and His Housekeeper — Various Matters

As I was walking in the yard the day after my arrival, several gentlemen in clerical garb entered the gates, apparently on a visit of curiosity to the place. As they approached my line of walk, I noticed the Rev. Jabez Bunting, Wesleyan preacher, a native of Manchester, amongst them. Recognitions were given and received, and I mentioned to him the circumstance of having often sat under his ministry, at Middleton, when he was but a young man, and I a boy. I called to mind also the names of some of his old friends at that place, who were relatives of mine; and I thought I somewhat interested him, when stating a fact of which he seemed not to be apprised, namely that my grandfather, Daniel Bamford, was the first who opened a door to the preachers of his sect at Middleton; and that John and Charles Wesley, George Whitfield, John Nelson, Samuel Taylor, and others of the old band, were frequent expounders under that humble roof. The gentlemen soon departed, and I mention the circumstance only, because it gave rise, after they were gone, to a series of very pleasant recollections of my young days, which served during half an hour to dispel gloomy thoughts, and lead me back to 'sweet that morning time' when,

> *With hymns we went praising*
> *By rindles and bowers;*
> *Or, sheltered, sat gazing*
> *At rainbows, in showers.*

One thing, however, struck me as a falling off from the good old apostolic customs of the preachers in my younger days. The reverend gentleman went away with his company without vouchsafing a blessing or a word of advice to me – not that I cared much about it – but I thought old John Gaulter, or little Jonathan Barker, would not have done so.

We had not been long here before we had reason to expect that we had either some very insidious foe, or some very indiscreet friend in the neighbourhood. One morning, Tuxford came and requested to be allowed to examine the paper we used in our letters. There seemed to be something mysterious in his manner, but we readily shewed him all we had, and allowed him to take away a sheet of each sort. Soon after he returned with the governor, who explained the reason for the proceeding, when to our astonishment it appeared that Lord Sidmouth had received an anonymous threatening letter, bearing the Lincoln post mark. The letter was sent to the governor, with a request that he would examine into the matter so far as he was able, and with the view of ascertaining whether the letter was written on the sort of paper we used.

We, of course, as in truth we must, entirely disclaimed all knowledge of the document or its writer, and strongly condemned the feeling which could lead to the writing of anonymous letters, under any circumstances. The governor expressed himself as perfectly satisfied with the examination, so far as we were concerned. He then similarly examined the debtors, but no clue was obtained towards connecting any one in the castle with the infamous document, and the only result was, that thenceforth we stood better in the governor's opinion, as well as that of the visiting magristrates.

Our governor was a genius in his way; he was not an educated man, but he had the reputation of being an adept in astronomy. He had a handsome-mounted telescope, and frequently spent whole nights in star-gazing – a very proper employment, I thought, for the governor of a prison. One or two desperate attempts at escape had been promptly foiled by his vigilance, and that of his sub-officer.

The story of Elizabeth Barton, his housekeeper – for he was a bachelor – was rather a romantic one. She was now about fifty years of age, a clean and industrious woman, and withal, was very tender hearted to the prisoners. She was now rather infirm, but had been an uncommonly handsome woman, and in the prime of her charms she was the wife of a man of desperate habits, who initiated her into the business of passing forged bank notes. She was taken in a transaction of that sort at Lincoln, and committed for trial, at that time almost equivalent to death; whilst her husband was equally unfortunate at York. Both were convicted, and the husband was executed, but the situation of the youthful widow, now resigned to her fate, excited a commisseration so lively, that strong means were used to have her life spared, and it was so, on condition of a long confinement. This she spent in a manner which obtained for her the good opinion of her superiors, and the good wishes of her fellow-prisoners; and she had ever since been the manager of the governor's household.

When we went, our doctor became her medical adviser. He gave her physic, and a lotion, or something of that sort, for her legs. But there must have been a mistake this time, for she soon dispensed with his attendance, complaining that his medicine made her very ill, and his lotion burned the stockings off her feet.

Every morning the servant from a public-house near, attended at the gate, and served the debtors with ale. Each debtor, was allowed to purchase a quart per day, but many went without, and others took it in their stead, and kept it for sale at the price of a shilling a bottle, thereby gaining fourpence. Pipes and tobacco, and indeed ale, might be had to any reasonable extent, provided the money was forthcoming. Spirituous liquors were prohibited: I did hear that such articles might be obtained secretly, but I never saw anything of the kind during my twelvemonth's stay in the place.

After I was sentenced, a number of my friends at Middleton bestirred themselves, and besides making a present collection, they put down their names for a regular monthly contribution so long as I remained in prison, and thenceforward I received from them one pound per month. Without this aid I should have been sadly put to my wits as to the means of living, for I never would have asked them for a farthing, or made known my situation. However I accepted it as tendered, in good-will, and the most friendly relations continued betwixt us. Healey complained that he had not the means for supporting himself and paying for his room and bed, and on making a representation to that effect to the governor, a room above was assigned him with a bed, free of any charge; together with the county allowance to prisoners, consisting of three loaves a week, one pound of butcher's meat, and a quantity of coals.

Soon afterwards it was understood that Mrs Johnson was in a critical state of health, and was about to come to Lincoln to visit her husband. On that occasion I wished to give up my share of the apartments Johnson and I held, in order that he and his wife might be more comfortable during her stay. I accordingly mentioned the circumstance to Mr Merryweather, and intimated that I should, for the present, be willing to take a part of Healey's room. Mr Merryweather assented in a moment, as he always did to whatever was reasonable, and I had a bed put up for me in the room above; which room was the identical one previously occupied by my late friend Finnerty, when he was confined here on a charge of libel. It was a very pleasant room, with a fire-grate, cupboards for victuals, and places to put coals, potatoes, or other matters in. We both had iron bedsteads, and very comfortably I slept, considering circumstances, and very grateful I was for the accommodation I experienced.

I was in the habit of receiving a considerable number of letters, newspapers, and pamphlets – perhaps four or five where Healey received one. Letters of a general nature I read to him, those of a private nature I of course did not. Letters containing money for myself I sometimes read to him, and sometimes did not, as I judged most proper; those with money for both of us were open to both, and when I divided the money, I always took his receipt for it, giving him mine when he had to pay. The circumstances of so many letters coming to me I soon found excited envy and jealousy in his breast. He suspected that I did not disclose to him all the letters that contained money on our joint account. This was, perhaps, his most weak point, and it was not long ere I discovered that an influence was at work with him, which at length entirely put a stop to all confidence and friendly feeling betwixt us, and rendered me during the remainder of my imprisonment, a stranger to the society of my two fellow-prisoners. This, to be sure, was no great loss, and as such I treated it; but my equanimity was assailed by the means taken to annoy me, and to lower me in the estimation of my friends.

It is not my intention to enter into a detail of these things. Such a proceeding would embrace too much of what was personal to myself, and not interesting to the public, especially after the lapse of time since they occurred. It would be foreign to my purpose also, and would disfigure this work, hitherto, I hope, useful and interesting. I shall not, therefore, embody such matters at present, at least, and if ever an exposition comes from my pen, it must appear in a distinct publication. Should it become more needful than it now seems to be, it may appear; if not, those wrongs also may be forgotten, as they have long been forgiven. One or two circumstances, I must however, mention, in due course, and until then I proceed.

Chapter 86

A Letter — Visitors — An Examination — The Doctor Perplexed — A Scene — A Trait in Nature

I WAS soon, as may be supposed, in active correspondence with some of the most distinguished reformers. Hunt and Sir Charles Wolseley each wrote to me about once a fortnight; the latter also furnished me with a daily newspaper: his letters breathed, as in fact they always did, an exuberance of spirits. Hunt's were of a different expression. His first letter to me, which was a singularity in its way, was a good specimen of his style of writing, and in its abrupt transitions, quite characteristic of his personal character: it was in letter and word as follows: –

Ilchester, Wednesday Morning,
May 24th, 1820.

My dear Bamford,
    I have this moment received your favour and it gives me great

pleasure to hear that you are so comfortably situated, indeed your time will pass pleasantly away; it is a mere nominal imprisonment, not so with me; although I have the best apartments in this Gaol, yet, bad is the best, it is true I have a very good Bed Room, and a very good sitting Room, but then I have only a Yard about ten paces square surrounded with High Walls and not a green grass plat to cheer the Eye or meet the Foot, mine is *literally solitary confinement* at present. I have one of the prisoners sent in, in the Goal livery to attend on me as my servant by day, but my society is thank God, derived from my own mind, and if I were situated ten thousand times worse than I am, the Cowards could neither take from me the conscious feeling of an Honest man nor the present reflection that every act of my public life was instigated by a sincere desire to promote the general happiness and prosperity of Mankind, and the welfare of my poor fellow Countrymen in Particular; I can now lay down and enjoy the sweetest repose in a dungeon with the conscientious satisfaction of knowing that I have not been disappointed in any selfish private views of my own which I never wished to gratify. I have never thought of SELF and if I could only be sure of obtaining happiness and *justice* for my suffering poor insulted fellow creatures they might lock me up in a Dungeon for life, and I would laugh with scorn at all their malevolent and impotent attempts to punish me.

I shall be always delighted to hear that you *all three* are well, and that you continue to enjoy every comfort while you are in confinement and every blessing when you are at *liberty*. Your time of probation is short, very short when compared to my horrid sentence – But I would not for the world change situations with one, nay the *honestest* of my persecutors. I am, thank God in the highest Health and in the best Spirits and my time is fully occupied, as I began last night to write the History of *my own life* which I intend to come out on the first of every month and as mine has been a most active laborious public life, interspersed with events of some importance in a political sense, I think it will be read with interest and I trust to some advantage by the Reformers. I heard that you were treated most infamously by the Tipstaves of the King's Bench when you left that receptacle of infamy and vice. Altho' this is the worst Jail in England yet I would rather suffer all its inconveniences than be doomed to be an eye witness of the daily profligate drunken scenes perpetrated by the inmates of the King's Bench. *   * I will take care not to loose a moment while I am here I go to Bed at eleven, and rise every morning at five and I hope I shall not sleep sound if I suffer one day to pass over my Head without doing *something* to expose the infamy of our persecutors. – However I believe the unfeelingness of their intended destruction of me by such lingering means, is like the rebounding of a blow that has fallen heaviest upon their own Heads. Remember me kindly to Johnson and Healey and believe me dear Bamford

Your sincere friend and well-wisher

H HUNT.

Remember me also kindly to your wife and all the brave wives and sisters and sweethearts of the Reformers in her neighbourhood – Now let us see what the Lancashire and Yorkshire Reformers will do – What will Saxton do – Wooller has behaved well – What a melancholy thing that Cobbett should suffer his envy to destroy his character – how pitiful does he appear now as compared to Wooller, I understand he (Cobbett) came into the King's Bench to see and spend the day with Johnson – Did you see him and if so did you not call him to account for either his *cowardice,* his *supineness,* or his *treachery,* in neglecting the cause of those that he so long pretended to advocate. If he is offended with me because I am become acquainted with his character, yet there is yourself and his friend Johnson there is the cause – how did he account to Johnson for his worse than neglect in not noticing the trial at York – Does he not know that what he said was well watched by the tools of the system our persecutors – He blamed Sir F. Burdett for coolly looking on and silently encouraging the Ministers to pass the Suspension Act in 1817. What then is to be said of his conduct now? Adieu –

The letter was directed,

> Mr Samuel Bamford,
> > The Lancashire Poet and Reformer,
> > > in His Majesty's Jail, Lincoln.

Countersigned near the Seal,

Richard Pike, T. K.

Mr Swan, member for Grampound, who was in the King's Bench, for bribery at the election, wrote to me, enquiring about the treatment we experienced on leaving the prison. The Honourable Robert Bligh, brother to the Earl of Darnley, did the same as follows:—

Dear sir,

I am desired by very particular friends of yours, to write to you for the particulars of the very unworthy treatment you are said to have met with upon your leaving the prison this morning; and whether it is true that you were hand-cuffed, that a proper statement of it may be laid before the House of Commons. Believe me,

Yours most faithfully,
ROBT. BLIGH.

Direct to me, King's Bench
Prison.

The reader will thus perceive though condemned and in prison, we were not entirely disregarded by some who had influence in high places.

One day, as I was lounging in the yard, the Rev. Mr Nelson, one of the prebendaries of the cathedral, and a county magistrate, accompanied by a gentleman whom I did not know, came up to me. Mr Nelson introduced the gentleman as Sir Montague Cholmley, a member of parliament for the county, and a magistrate. Mr Nelson said he wished to ask me a question in the presence of Sir Montague, and he hoped I would answer him in all sincerity and truth. I promised him I would, if it appeared to me a proper question, and I did not suppose that he would require an answer to one that was not so. He said he certainly would not. The question was, whether or not I was satisfied with my treatment at that place? My instantaneous reply was, 'perfectly so.' Was there nothing then, in the conduct of the governor, or the regulations I was subject to, of which I had to complain? My reply was, 'nothing whatever.' Then I never had complained, either verbally or in writing? 'Never! such a thing never entered my mind; on the contrary, I was most grateful for the indulgence I received.' – 'Did I suppose,' asked Mr Nelson, 'that I was as well-treated there as I should have been, if confined at Lancaster?' 'Yes,' I said, 'and a great deal better, I was of opinion. In my own county I should probably have been put in the worst dungeon the magistrates could have found.'

Was I aware of any grounds of complaint on the part of either of my fellow-prisoners, I was next asked. I was not aware of any such cause, I answered. Sir Montague then informed me that a letter had been sent from Lincoln to a gentleman in London, whose name I have forgotten, containing allegations of great cruelty, on the part of the governor towards us, and of most uncalled-for treatment generally, and he was come down purposely, he said, to ascertain the truth or falsehood of the charge. I said that so far as I and my two fellow-prisoners were concerned, the charge was most false, and I was certain they would bear me out in my statement. But, I added, 'your worships can see them, and let them speak for themselves.' They assented, and I led up to the room occupied by Healey and myself; and opening the door, walked in, inviting the gentlemen to follow. I could not see the doctor at first, and thought he must have gone out, but a kind of splashing noise directed my looks to the door, and there he was behind it, as it stood open. 'Here is Doctor Healey, gentlemen,' I said, as they advanced into the room. I never saw a look of greater mortification and embarrassment than the doctor exhibited at that moment, as the gentlemen bowed to him, and smiled at each other. The doctor was busy washing his shirt, and was actually up to his elbows in suds, which he vainly tried to conceal, first by holding his hands behind him, and when he saw that posture did not avail, by wiping the suds off, and rolling down his sleeves. After a moment or two spent in civil enquiries as to his health, and so forth, the same questions were put to him which had been to me, and nearly the same replies were elicited, whereupon the gentlemen expressed themselves quite satisfied, and left the castle.

We had a regular scene after they were gone. I dearly liked a harmless joke, and had many opportunities for seeing my comrade exhibit himself in his various moods. 'Well,' said I, 'I never knew such a thing in my life.' 'Such a thing as what,' asked the doctor, who rather sulkily was preparing to go back to his suds – 'Why, such a thing as that a learned doctor should be caught up to his elbows in suds, and washing his shirt' – and I laughed until my sides almost cracked. The doctor looked fiercely, and giving me a hearty malediction, said I had no right to bring them up; I brought them purposely, and he knew it; I had done it to lower his respectability. I laughed louder than ever, pretending great sorrow that so celebrated a character should have been caught in the suds, – laying emphasis on the latter words. The sense of humiliation I suppose, now recurred with double force, and in his passion he caught up the mug and offered to throw the suds upon me, but I stepped out of the door that moment, and the doctor's foot slipping in the wet, he came down on the floor, and smashing the earthen vessel, all the suds were soon floating around the room. I then thought it time to retreat, and stepping down stairs I escaped into the yard, doubled up with laughter. The doctor ever afterwards took care not to be surprised washing his shirt.

I may here mention a trait in the natural instinct of the feathered tribe. The governor had a splendid peacock, with a hen, and a young one which had the run of the grounds. One fine clear day, the cock and hen were beside the shrubbery, and as it happened, I and some other persons were at the time near the place. The hen suddenly turned her head, side upwards, and uttered a kind of cry, in which the cock joined, and the chick was instantly close to her wing. I looked up but could not see anything, and the two birds keeping their heads aside, turning them as if following a moving object with their eyes, I was convinced there must be a bird of prey within the ken of their vision. I again looked in the direction they seemed to be doing, and at length descried a small black spot at an immense height over head. It seemed to move in a circle; and in some time I could perceive that it was gradually descending. It came lower and lower, the fowls still keeping a steady eye on it, and the young one being under wing, and at last it came so near that we made it out to be a fine glead hawk. He took a few circles around the castle, as if he intended to make a stoop, but, probably seeing too many of the wrong sort, he at length gave a wheel, and swept out of sight.

Chapter 87

THE worthy Major Cartwright, faithful to his promise, did not forget to use his influence with some gentlemen of the county in our favour. Happily, we had no need of that, – though he was not to be thanked the less – for the magistrates evinced every disposition to be kind towards us, and the governor and his subordinates, though naturally a little fond of power, never gave us reason to suppose that they wished to increase the small portion of restraint we necessarily experienced. The governor, I must say, – like the magistrates who directed him – never hesitated about doing us a good turn. I had hitherto paid him a sum per month for the use of a bed and bedding which he found me, but immediately on my application to be allowed to find my own bed, – which a worthy old lady offered to provide for me – the application was granted, and the county allowance was also given me on a subsequent application.

We were frequently visited by respectable inhabitants of the town, and of other places, and the governor, never to my knowledge, or belief, prevented any one from seeing us. The Rev. James Hawks, a unitarian minister, and one Bedford, a tailor and draper, retired from business, were visitors of Johnson and Healey, but they never changed a word with me; whilst my best and firmest friend was the above venerable lady, – the wife of a blind and aged minister of the church, who was living at Lincoln on a small allowance. This good old woman was like a mother to me, reproving me when blameable; advising me in difficulty, – for she was a sensible, strong-minded woman – consoling me amid vexation and ingratitude, and defending and encouraging me in the right. I sometimes thought that if spirits of the departed were really permitted to return to the earth, it was not improbable that the spirit of my departed mother might be the animating principle of the good being whose benign influence watched over me. I shall ever love a good old woman for the sake of Mrs Stainton – she was to me what my own mother would have been had she lived.

It was scarcely to be expected that two men so entirely dissimilar in person and mind as Healey and myself, should long remain together, without having cavillings, differences, and ultimately, dislikes. It is all very well to have a ramble through a countryside with a man, or to be in company once or twice a week, but to have to endure the company daily of one we cannot thoroughly esteem, is rather too much for human patience; at all events, it was often too much for mine. Nothing sooner tried me than an exhibition of duplicity, and false pretension, and of these God knows I had enough. I was surfeited to disgust. But I forbear.

The room which Healey and I occupied, opened into a lobby

where there was a back window looking down into the condemned ward, and over a great extent of country even to Belvoir castle, the flag-staff of which we could see with a glass on a clear day. This lobby, in consequence of the view, was often visited by strangers, particularly on Sundays, and it was my wish and endeavour to keep it in a state of neatness and order. This very proper desire, was however, often thwarted by Healey, who would put his offal, and the scrapings of his dishes, on the window sill, and his potatoes with their peelings on the floor, near the door, and in sight of every one who came up. One Sunday, on his doing this, I remonstrated with him in terms which led to warm words on both sides, in which I upbraided him with his mean jealousy on account of the letters received, and of being perfidious under the guise of friendship; and I concluded by likening him to the viper which stung the bosom of its benefactor. This enraged him beyond endurance, and he came at me with a two-handed blow with the poker. I caught the weapon in my hand, and in trying to wrest it from him, he having a very tenacious grasp, I lifted him off his feet, and laid him, with but little violence, on the floor, and tore the thing out of his hands by main force. I then held the heel of my shoe over him, and said, if he was not so utterly contemptible, I would stamp the breath out of his body. I then flung the poker under the grate and went out of the room, and on returning I found him on his feet, pretending to spit blood from his lungs, which he said I had injured by crushing him. The fact was that his lip was a little swollen and cracked, having probably come in contact with his own knuckle, or mine, during the scuffle, and that was whence the pretended blood from the lungs came. I will not repeat the terms of reproach which I flung away upon him. He went down stairs and brought up the turnkey, and accused me of having knocked him down, beaten him with the poker, dragged him on the floor, and stamped on his breast, and concluded by spitting out streaks of blood as before. I then gave a true version of the affair, – showing the turnkey the state in which the lobby and window were, and requested him to examine Healey's lip and see if that was not bleeding inside. He did so, and found it bruised, and blood oozing from it. He then told the doctor he did not believe a word he said; that he had found him in falsehoods before, and that if he were not more circumspect in his conduct, he would report his behaviour to the governor, and have him removed to the other side of the prison. Healey thus took nothing by his motion, whilst I took only the resolution to get out of his company as soon as possible.

But it was not at Lincoln alone that I was doomed to be annoyed. The grossest slanders were propagated at Middleton, and other parts of Lancashire, and in some cases, they were but too coldly combated by those who called themselves my friends, but who alas! knew little of that 'generous friendship,' which,

> *No cold medium knows;*
> *Burns with one love, with one resentment glows.*

One hoary-headed slanderer, who hated me because I had prevented him from imposing on the relief fund, and obtaining money to which he had no right, circulated a report that I was actually a government spy; that I had sold the Middleton blue banner to the authorities at Manchester for twelve pounds, and that if the banner were sought for, it would be traced to the police office at the said town. The fellow actually went about the town swearing most confidently that such was the case. A committee was appointed to investigate the charge, and a deputation waited upon my wife, who opened a chest, and pulling out the banner, displayed it; and yet the scoundrel afterwards went up and down persisting in what he had said.

Chapter 88

Kindness of the Magistrates — New Quarters — Arrival of my Wife at Lincoln — A Strange sort of Civility

IT MAY readily be supposed, that the fine yard the prisoners had access to, would induce them to take much out-of-door exercise. This was the case, and I in particular of our party, frequently joined in the running, leaping, and football matches which took place. I generally entered with ardour into the game, and being a good footman, was not considered a mean auxiliary to any party. Often, however, when the game was over, and I was quite warm with the exercise, would I fling myself down on the grass, and perhaps take a nap until some fresh sport called me again into action. By such unthinking conduct I took many colds, and neglecting to diet myself, or take medicine, the colds struck to my weak part, the lungs, and in time I began to have my old tightness at the breast, and my night cough, as at Lancaster, only much worse, attended by profuse perspirations and other weakening symptoms.

It was about the beginning of August that my dear wife, hearing of the state of my health, expressed her wish, in a letter, to come over and see me, and I gladly assented, provided the necessary means could be obtained. I had, at Hunt's request, written a piece called 'The Song of the Slaughter,' which first appeared, I think, in his memoirs, and was afterwards published at the Observer Office, Manchester; and with three pounds, accruing from the sale of it, and one pound which my wife borrowed, she was speedily in a condition to join me, and announced her intention of doing so.

About this time the Rev. Mr Nelson, and another magistrate, came to the castle on business, and before they went, I took an opportunity of stating to them my wife's intention of coming over, and requesting the use of a room to ourselves during her stay. They asked if there was one anywhere unoccupied? and I said that fortunately there was one, the very next to that I was now in. They directly went into the turnkey's lodge, taking me with them, and sending for Tuxford, they ordered him to get the room I had mentioned coloured and cleaned, and to put up a bedstead, and give me the key of the place, that being my apartment during my wife's visit. Then, turning to me, Mr Nelson said, 'We (meaning himself and the other magistrates,) do not approve of all that the Manchester magistrates have done, any more than of some of your proceedings, but we consider you to be here as prisoners under peculiar circumstances, and we should be sorry to be the means of depriving you of any little indulgence compatible with your safe custody, especially, so long as you comport yourselves as you have hitherto done. There is one thing, however,' Mr Nelson added, after a pause, 'which we must enjoin upon you, and that is, that you do not make any public statement as to this matter; that you do not mention it to the newspapers, or make a noise about it. It is an indulgence, and at variance with the rules we ourselves laid down for the governance of the prison, but, as I said, under the peculiar circumstances of yourself and your fellow-prisoners, we will do all we can to make you comfortable so long as, by your conduct, you enable us to be kind towards you.'

I expressed my unfeigned gratitude to the worthy magistrates, and promised to obey their injunction. The place was immediately white-washed and cleaned, and the day following, to my very great comfort, I removed to that welcome domicile, with thankfulness of heart to those who had been so kind, and with extreme satisfaction at being thus left alone, and to my own thoughts.

It was on the eighteenth of September, that my wife was to arrive. I looked for her coming impatiently. I walked long in the yard, pacing the flags to and fro betwixt the door and the gates. Knock after knock came, but it was not her. No trunk, no band-box, the sure forerunner of a female traveller, came to bless my sight. At length, wearied, and somewhat agitated, I went to my room, mended the fire, filled the kettle, put some tea in the pot, and made other preparations for breakfast; and whilst thus endeavouring to wile away the laggard moments, footsteps were heard, and the turnkey's daughter conducting a porter, laden with a trunk, and the long-looked-for band-box, entered. 'Mrs Bamford is coming,' she said, 'Mr Johnson was shewing her up the steps.' I was hastening to meet her, but on hearing that he also was coming, I remained. I wondered what he could have to say, as since Mrs Johnson's arrival, we had scarcely exchanged a word. I continued pacing the room – I thought my wife was a long time in coming, and at length I sent the girl to shew her up. At that moment she came along the passage alone, and apparently much grieved. Johnson, she told me, had met her on the flags, just as she entered the inner gate, and accosting her in a tone of friendship, he returned with her towards the prison, as if to conduct her to my room, which she, of course, expected he would do; instead of which, he took her into his own room, where his wife was at breakfast, and – would any man, any husband, or wife believe it? – without one word of explanation, they asked her to sit down THERE and take coffee with THEM. My wife expected seeing me, and wondered I did not appear. They kept pressing her to sit down and take something. She was astonished and afflicted, and requested to be shewn where her husband was; at length she burst into tears, and declared she would not take anything except with me, and quitting the room, determined to find me herself; Johnson then followed her, and pointed the way up the steps to my ward.

Our meeting was both mournful and tender. The sight of my features, so much altered for the worse, and of my pale and wasted hands, renewed her tears, and it was not till after a fit of downright crying on her part, during which I let her feelings have uninterrupted vent, that she became more calm, and we unburdened our minds of whatever lay heaviest, and most painful there. And of such matters, what with the falsehood or apathy of friends, and the open or insidious detraction of enemies, God knows, we had enough.

Chapter 89

The Patriots of Oldham — A Comforter in Prison — Story of a Robbery —
A Melancholy Spectacle

AMONGST the best and truest supporters of persecuted radicals, and the radical cause, were a small but firm band of patriots at Oldham. Their like never, to my recollection, existed previously in Lancashire, nor has it ever since. To them I owe an especial acknowledgment, and if a grateful remembrance of the men and their good deeds, and a public recognition of their good works, through a medium so humble as this, be any equivalent for their kindness, they have it. Some of the best have long since been called to the reward of 'the good and faithful servant.' Some still remain, but scattered, and bowed by the storms of life. A few winter's gales, and we shall all be gone! to, I hope, 'where the wicked cease from troubling, and where the weary are at rest.'

It may easily be conceived that the society of my wife was a great solacement. I had now always one true friend to converse with, and though the replenishment of my 'basket and my store,' was somewhat more frequently required, we did not regret on that account; since, if there were plenty we partook it, and if not, with Milton, we could sit down to our 'herbs and our other country messes,' and be thankful for them. Our greatest cause of anxiety now was, the absence of our child; but as she had been left with her uncle and aunt, in whom we had unlimited confidence, we were the more easily reconciled to her having stayed at home. My wife certainly saved something by going to market herself. She could go out and return without a single question at the gate – without any rude hand examining her basket; and then, when at night I was locked up, it was in company with the one most fitted to administer to my wounded mind. One who with me could retrace the hours and days from childhood, and leading me to bright recollections, could wile me from present ill, to past happiness, until the present also at times became tinged with brightness.

Afar it faintly shone !
As might some star alone,

Which rode amid the storm, when all the rest were gone.

One melancholy spectacle took place here, during my wife's stay, and as it was the first of the sort I had ever witnessed, I will record it, together with the most probable report as to its cause which I could obtain.

Some forty or fifty years back, a pedlar from Astley Bridge, near Bolton, was robbed and murdered at a lonely farm-house in the fens of Lincolnshire. The murderers were never brought to justice, and the property, of which there was supposed to be rather a heavy amount, was never recovered. The people at the farm afterwards advanced in prosperity rapidly, but all soon died except the wife, who lived to be a rich old widow, keeping her many thousands of sheep, and hundreds of cattle on the said lone farm. It was a custom, when we were at Lincoln, and had been during many years, for harvest-men to go from Lancashire to Lincolnshire – a 'cowkin' as they called it – and a party of these from the above village of Astley Bridge had, for some years, been in the habit of doing the harvest work at the identical farm above-mentioned. The murder and robbery were almost forgotten, and were seldom mentioned, except by the old people of the district where it occurred. The widow was now a most antique-looking personage, short, dumpy, and active for her years, and wearing a gown and bonnet which all the women agreed could not have been made during the last half century – it was intimated, in fact, that they were new soon after the catastrophe of the poor pedlar above-mentioned. During the harvest previous to our arrival at Lincoln, a plan to rob the old widow was laid by her own shepherd, and the men from Astley Bridge, accompanied by two from Manchester, and the time was to be fixed by the shepherd, who was to send a letter to one of the men near Bolton. The shepherd, who was a married man with a family, and lived at some distance from his mistress, wrote; and the robbers arrived, and entered the house with their faces masked and disguised as mummers. The old woman, with one man and one woman servant only, were at home, and the man was deaf and dumb. The mummers danced on the floor when they first came in – the deaf and dumb man sat jabbering and making grimaces in a corner, and it was not until the robbers began to break open drawers, and to use the women roughly, that he seemed to comprehend their purpose and his duty. He then sprung up, and snatched an axe which lay on the wood-heap, and aimed with it a blow at one of the ruffians, which, however, was avoided, and he, the next moment, was disarmed and wounded, and then cruelly maltreated. The robbers next tied the inmates fast, and plundered the house of about nine hundred pounds worth of plate, money, and notes, and having done that, they leisurely de-camped.

The report of the robbery, of course, made a great noise in the country. The officers of justice were indefatigable in their endeavours to get a clue to this mysterious outrage; and amongst the servants and neighbours, none were more assiduous in offering suggestions and probabilities than the shepherd above-mentioned – the oldest and most confidential servant on the farm. The hounds of the law, however, soon laid on a true scent, and set off for Lancashire with the speed, but not the noise, of bloodhounds. The two Manchester men (Unsworths) had left the country – supposed for America – and could nowhere be found. The two from Astley Bridge were taken, and on one of them was found the letter from the shepherd appointing the time for the robbery. Of course the two men were brought into Lincolnshire. The shepherd was taken, and confessed everything; he also delivered up a tea-pot full of guineas – his share of the plunder – which he had concealed in his garden hedge. One of the men from Astley was admitted evidence, and the shepherd and the other were left for execution; and that was the spectacle I have now to describe.

It was rather a cloudy and gusty morning when, getting up to my window, I beheld the gallows fixed, and two halters ready noosed, swinging in the wind. To me this first sight of the instrument of death was both melancholy and awful, and I retired from the win-dow in a spirit deeply regretting the imperfection of our human means for the protection of right and the punishment of wrong.

The debtors were kept locked up all morning, but we were allowed the range of the yard, which, as all respectable visitors were ad-mitted, soon became crowded; there was a very great crowd, as I was informed, outside the walls. At about eleven o'clock, the prisoners were ready to leave their ward, and the great bell at the cathedral began to toll. I thought I would do the violence to my feelings for once, of watching the passage of human nature from life to a violent death. I placed myself on the rampart leading to the round tower, on which stood the gallows, and had a full view of the criminals as they approached across the green. First came the governor, bearing a white wand; then some halberdiers and other sheriff's men; then the deputy sheriff; next came the criminals, the chaplain of the jail, the turnkey, executioner, and assistant; and the mournful procession was closed by other javelin men. The shepherd appeared to have his eyes fixed on the apparatus of death from the moment he came in view of it: he walked with a steady military air, for he had been a soldier, and had a good pension; but as he drew near where I stood, his eyes still fixed on the gallows, seemed glazed, and insensible to any object. He appeared faint, and required assistance to mount the ascent. The other, who was a short, stiff, curly-browed fellow, in a blue coat, was more dogged in his manner. He held his head a little on one side, gave a glance at the gallows, spat out some white froth, and, at the word to advance, he went on again without help. The governor motioned me to go up with them, but I respectfully declined. In the round tower, the funeral service was read, and the man in the blue coat, conducted by the executioner, soon was seen ascending the steps to the drop, – the shepherd followed. The halters were quickly round their necks, and the caps over their faces, and, in less time than I have occupied in stating it, the drop fell, and the sufferers were in the agonies of death. The shepherd struggled very little, and seemed to be dead in a minute. The other vibrated some time, and kept raising his hand by jerks, as if he was aiming to get hold of the noose and release his neck; but ere the hand was high enough, it began to drop gradually, and soon they were both hanging, piteous and helpless spectacles. When they hung an hour or so, the bodies were removed on the backs of men to the Town Hall, and were laid side by side on the floor.

The gallows remained some time after, and one of the young genteel ruffians of the country, a Sir Harry Goodricke, mounted the platform with some companions, and, as a specimen of gentlemanly taste, he stood looking on the people outside, and steadying himself by laying hold of the halters still pendant from the gallows.

Chapter 90

My Indisposition — Advice and Remedies — Friends in London — Hunt's kind Professions — Remedies applied — Favourable Crisis — A Reverend Calumniator Detected

IN THE beginning of October, my wife returned into Lancashire. Our parting was fraught with saddening anticipations. I still kept up appearances as well as I could, and partook of active exercise, but my health was no better, and the means I took to restore it were just the opposite of what my case required. The same carelessness which caused my disorder served to aggravate it. I continued to eat and drink as usual, – neglected all dietary rules, – and eschewed all medicine, not liking to own that I was ill, and still less to call in the doctor. I thought the disorder would go away of itself, as other slight ailments had done before. And so I kept coughing, and sweating, and getting weaker. My wife wanted to send for the surgeon, but I would not; instead of him, I sent for a bottle of wine, and took a glass or two of that every day, to mend my weakness, but it only made me worse. And in this state I was when we parted. I had begun to have some apprehensions that this disorder would be rather troublesome to get rid of – it might bring me very low – possibly it might conquer me at last, – but this latter contingency I viewed as very uncertain, and at all events too distant to call for immediate seriousness; and thus, like all careless young fellows, I continued to neglect.

My wife, however, had deeper apprehensions, and on her arrival at home, she communicated her fears to my sister and some friends, and the result was, that I soon received a package, containing, amongst other sundry matters, some medicine, a box of sodaic powders, and a letter of advice from Mr Hanson, surgeon, Bridge-street, Manchester; and a large warming plaster for my breast from a friendly surgeon at Middleton. I took the powders because they were pleasant and refreshing, but the other things I suffered to lie for the present, contenting myself with the hope that a stricter regimen, which I had now adopted, would set all to rights, and so I continued getting paler and weaker – without fear, generally serene in mind, and at times even cheerful.

It happened about this time, that I had to pay Healey some money, which had come in a letter, and I sent for him to my room, (for I continued to occupy the one set apart for me,) in order that I might take his receipt in my book for it. The medicine, the plaster, and the box of sodaic powders, with Mr Hanson's address on the lid, were lying in the window-bottom, and I observed during the transaction, that Healey cast his eyes on the box, and seemed to read the inscription. He, however, went away without making any observation, and I thought no more of the matter.

I was not forgotten by my kind friends in the city of London. They made a subscription, and sent me money; and with a view of assisting me in the study of French, they also sent me a number of elementary books on that language. A teacher came, who resided in Lincoln, and he gave lessons to Johnson and I twice a week, but I never could make anything of it; his mode of instruction was not, I think, very intelligible, and I finally gave up, little better than when I began. This took place in the earliest part of my imprisonment, and before I was so very unwell.

No sooner was my wife gone, than Hunt wrote to me, regretting her departure, and wishing to know the cause of her leaving me; and when I replied that 'circumstances prevented her from staying with me,' he said in one of his letters:—

'What circumstance do you allude to that prevented your Jemima from staying with you *longer*? I hope it was not the want of a few pounds, if it were, you have not treated me like a friend not to write and say so. By G—— she shall go and see you again if this be the only cause.' And in a subsequent letter he said, 'I will remit you one pound per month, as long as she is with you. Recollect that I do not promise more than I am prepared to perform; I shall send her two pounds to pay her coach-hire to Lincoln and back; and with the sum we get from —— I will pay her, or you for her, one pound per month, as long as she is with you, always provided *that she stays with you till your day of deliverance.*' * * * 'I have made up my mind to this, and by G—— you shall be together, you do not know how much it will add to my happiness to know that I have been instrumental to the accomplishment of that which will make such a pair happy.'

Well, the two pounds which were to carry my wife back to Lincoln were never received by her. Of course she did not start, and the debt account which was to furnish her one pound a month, was met in part by a set-off by the party, which gave it a *quietus* for the present. He afterwards wrote as follows:—

'Our good friend, Sir Charles Wolseley, has promised me that he will join me in the scheme of having your Jemima with you at Lincoln. He and I between us, will allow her ten shillings a week so long as she is with you.' – Thus stood things in the month of January, 1821.

Meantime I had been very ill of the disorder heretofore mentioned. My old mother, Mrs Stainton, said it was time something should be done, or it would be too late. Accident, however, did that for me which a course of medicine would perhaps have failed in accomplishing. Seeing the warming plaster which had been sent to me from Middleton lying in the window bottom, I thought I might as well wear it – it could do me no harm, and might possibly do me good; so I put it on my breast, and felt very comfortable with it at first. In about three weeks my cough began to be less troublesome; I slept better at night, and the sweats had very much diminished. I found, however, that I was covered with an outbreak of watery pustules, and wondered where I could have got that troublesome skin distemper, the itch, which I believed this was. I now thought I should become as scabbed as a mangy dog, if I did not send for the doctor, and so I wrote him a note, requesting he would visit me. He came the same day, and after examining me, asked me what I had been doing? and what medicine I had been taking? I told him then all about my illness, and the powders and pills I had taken. He asked me if there was nothing more I had to mention? and I said there was nothing more, except that I had put a plaster on my breast about three weeks previously, and it had made me very sore. He looked at my breast – now raw – and said that was the thing. I had worn the plaster longer than it was intended I should do, and it had flayed me on the part, and caused the eruption which I mistook for the itch.

I must keep my room strictly, he said, until I saw him again, and take some medicine which he would send. It was a severe erysipelas which I had got – it would cure my cough, and restore my health, if it took a good turn, and if not it would kill me very suddenly. I must keep my room, he said, and observe his instructions punctually, or I should quickly have done with the doctors.

I followed his advice strictly; I kept my room about a week, and took his medicines – the watery humours dried up – my skin became rough, and it rubbed off in scales – the cough entirely left me – rest returned – the perspiration ceased to be excessive, and, though still low and weak, I was soon entirely free from every symptom of the perilous disorder. Had not the erysipelas attacked me the doctor said I should have inevitably been consumptive.

In January, 1821, my wife at length came to Lincoln, in accordance with my earnest wish, and the repeated solicitation of Hunt, who still professed in this matter to have *our* happiness entirely at heart. Amongst other things of which she then informed me, none surprised me so much as a circumstance made known to her by Mr Hanson, the surgeon at Manchester, before-mentioned. He said that at dusk on the evening of the fifteenth of that month (January), a stranger entered his shop, and asked him if his name was Hanson? – Mr Hanson said it was. The stranger asked if he knew one Samuel Bamford, a prisoner in the castle at Lincoln? – Mr Hanson said he did know such a person. The stranger asked if Mr Hanson had not 'sent medicine to that prisoner?' and Mr Hanson said he had. 'My name is Hawks,' said the stranger; 'I am a clergyman residing at Lincoln, and my motive for calling is to inform you that Bamford has imposed on you, for he neither is unwell, nor has he ever been so, at Lincoln.' 'Mr Bamford never imposed upon me,' said Mr Hanson, 'he never applied to me for medicine; I sent it voluntarily and without his application. Pray what could induce you thus to attempt to injure Mr Bamford?' 'I thought,' said the fellow, now somewhat ashamed, 'that his conduct might perhaps prevent you from assisting others really in need.' And he added something about having seen me lately playing at foot-ball.

'Were you ever in Mr Bamford's company?' asked my friend Hanson, 'I never was,' said the stranger.

'Had you ever any conversation with him, on any account?' was the next question. 'I never exchanged a word with him,' was the reply.

'Then how do you know he had not been unwell?' was asked. 'I heard him say he was very well,' was the reply.

'Really, I think Mr Bamford has been used badly; and your mission hither does you no credit, though you are a clergyman. I must take the liberty to say that I don't believe you,' said my friend Hanson. 'You may go, sir,' he added, and the reverend rascal sneaked out of the shop.

Mark, reader, this was what my wife told me.

The very day after, as I was walking on the flags, this same 'clergyman' entered the gates, to pay one of his usual visits to my two fellow-prisoners.

Looking him sternly in the face, I said, 'Pray is not your name Hawks?'

'My name is Hawks,' he said.

'Will you have the goodness to inform me what could be your motive for waiting on Mr Hanson, a druggist, at Manchester; stating to him that I was an impostor, for that I neither was unwell, nor had I ever been so at Lincoln?'

The detected and confronted slanderer hung down his head, and shuffled, and stammered, till he got to the steps leading to his friend's apartment, when, as he ascended, he turned and said, – 'My motive was, that such persons as you should be better known;' and with that he mounted the steps quickly and disappeared,

I continued walking on the flags until near dark, and when he at length made his appearance I accompanied him to the gate, much to his annoyance and apprehension; for he kept a pretty sharp look-out, as if he expected a salute from my wooden clog. I told him in no very complimentary strain, that it was only a thorough contempt for himself, and a deference for the regulations of the prison, that prevented me from driving his ribs through the bars, and so bidding him go home, like a detected scoundrel as he was, I left him to chew the cud of bitter reflection, whilst I returned to my prison-room, now made happy by the society of my wife.

Afterwards, on perusing a piously worded epistle from this same Hawks, in 'Drakerd's Stamford News,' where he spoke of 'Christian benevolence,' and 'a heavenly-descended religion;' – I exposed the whole of the above transaction, in a temperate, but impressive letter to the editor, which I requested him to insert. He, from good motives no doubt, declined it, although he was so weak as to communicate its contents to my mean calumniator.

I was disgusted. – I was sick and beyond the power of reasoning with the villainy which I met with at every step – I could not enter into such ungenerous warfare, nor lower myself to the rascally weapons used against me. The still unobtrusive voice of truth was not heard, and I was too often condemned. This was one of the most painful passages of my life. Envy, and its sure attendant – detraction, haunted me within the prison and without – I never think of that time without horror – the boroughmongers had incarcerated my body, but the reformers wounded my soul. How I preserved a manly bearing, none can know save HE who sustained me – and that I have lived to forgive – to wipe from my heart the foul drops which these things generated there, – I have to bless the same Creator, whose wisdom and beneficence is extended beyond the perishable animosities of perishable men.

> *To God my thanks ascend,*
> *Who doth my steps attend:*
> *For he hath ever been to me,*
>   *A mighty friend.*

> *His wing hath been my shield,*
> *His hand hath been my stay,*
> *As, through a dark and stormy world*
>   *I sought my way.*

Chapter 91

Ridiculous Scene at Ilchester — Sir Charles Wolseley's Generosity — My Friend Hunt — His Plan Developed — His Disappointment — His Last Letter

SAXTON, our late co-defendant, waited on Hunt in Ilchester jail, with an adulatory memorial, subscribed by many thousands of names, put on the paper much in the same way that certain chartist petitions have been bolstered up of late. Hunt's tom-foolery excited my contempt. – He actually, for aught he knew, instituted an order of knighthood; the order of 'Saint Henry of Ilchester.' The first knight was himself, Saxton having dubbed him, and the second knight was the said Saxton, Hunt having dubbed him in return. The dubbing, I think, was done with a fire-poker, swords not being allowed in Ilchester prison. Saxton himself afterwards laughed at the affair, and amused his confidants by telling how he flammed Hunt. The latter, however, was quite serious, and felt flattered when any of the prominent radicals accepted the ridiculous distinction. I, Sir Charles Wolseley, Lewis, and others, escaped the poker-ing, being in prison, but we were to have it when we came out. Hunt at that time must have been deranged, – his vanity – his egotism were irrepressible, and I had now, and for ever after, done with his judgment. I also honestly criticized his memoirs, as he desired me to do, and I got the certain reward – his displeasure.

My friend, Sir Charles, only obeyed the promptings of his own generous heart in his conduct towards me and my wife. His was not a friendship of words only. He supplied me, unasked, with money, for I never troubled any of my friends in that respect. Nay, on one occasion, when they wrote to me from Nottingham saying, that if I was in actual want of cash, a one-pound note was at my disposal; I thanked them, and declined it, stating at the same time that I had no doubt it would be acceptable to John Knight at Lancaster Castle, and it was sent to him. But as I have found, old John would have seen me boiling the stones of the castle wall for dinner sooner than he would have done me, or any one else, a like turn.

As for my friend Hunt, no sooner had my wife become settled the second time at Lincoln, than his motive for helping her there became apparent. He wanted me to make affidavit of the fact of her being allowed to live and lodge with me, in order that he could exhibit it as a precedent for a like indulgence to the lady he co-habited with; and when, in accordance to the pledge I had given the magistrates, I refused to do this, he sent me a letter full of reproach. On the twenty-seventh of January he wrote as follows.

'ONE PART of your letter has staggered me a good deal – It is what I did not, I own, expect from you.' – 'If you at any time mention that my wife is here, you need not go so far as to say she sleeps here, because that is an indulgence which in no other prison in England would have been granted, &c. &c. &c. If —— or —— or —— had written thus I should not have been surprised, but that you should have been so selfish I am surprised indeed. Sir Charles Wolseley has been urging me to publish his indulgencies, which are more liberal and extensive than yours. I, really as you have such a short time to stay, was about to request you to make an affidavit of the full extent of your accommodations, to have exhibited them as a contrast to mine.'

And then he went on with a strain of egotistical rant, and continued – 'But no more of this – I find I have been a fool – I have been undergoing every privation here because I would not truckle to the villains, and because I wished to do a service to all who are imprisoned.' * * * 'You must be mistaken about your magistrates; they would be pleased to be praised, and I think while you consider yourself you have done them an injustice in wishing to withhold the praise due to them.' *   *   * 'Do you know that I am excessively hurt and mortified at hearing such a sentiment from you, because you are the last man I should expect it from' – and so forth.

I could not but be sensible – though Hunt's self-love, – which he was constantly disclaiming – blinded him to it – of the difference betwixt a man being indulged with the company of his own wife, and being indulged with the company of another man's wife. There was no parallel in the two cases, and I felt indignant that he should attempt to construe one. I, however, wrote to him a temperate but firm letter, which seemed to have non-plussed him, for it was not until the twelfth of March, that he wrote his last letter, containing the following passages:—

Ilchester Bastile March 18th, 1821

Dear Bamford,
    I have taken up my pen several times with the intention of Answering the Castigation I received from you, in your letter of the 6th ultimo, but I always felt a sort of petty indignation arising in my Breast, at your ungenerous expressions, which I was anxious to suppress, and very loth to communicate you, therefore while I was labouring under such temporary irritation I was determined not to Write – You will say, and say earnestly, that I have taken plenty of time to cool, and I assure you I have divested myself of every particle of such a feeling, but I find that this delay has created other sensations in my mind which are much more difficult to eradicate, being that of sincere sorrow and regret that I should have experienced such unkindness from one, that I had never intentionally given offence, and one whose good opinion and friendship I had long cherished.' *   *

    Well, we will let these things pass, this is a strange World we live in, and after all we must learn to *bear and forbear* and we shall get on I see – Pray remember me to your Jemima and assure her that nothing will please me more than to hear that you are both Well and happy together – If I were a rich man you should not want for any comfort that money would purchase while you are in Gaol, as it is, I beg her acceptance of what I can afford,
    I am dear Bamford your sincere friend
H. HUNT.

My heart rose to the gorge, and I would have sent the remittance –
it was a one-pound note – back, but it happened that we were
destitute at the time, and had been so during several days; and as
there was no plan save that of accepting the note, or asking some
of the debtors, or the turnkey, for a loan – which I could not frame
to do – the note was appropriated.

It was only the money I received from him, towards the fulfilment of his promise to see my wife provided for at Lincoln. Sir
Charles Wolseley – who made no professions – did all that Hunt
should have done in that respect. I wrote a cool letter of acknowledgment to Hunt, and we never corresponded afterwards.

I had seen a little through the veil with which devotion had covered my eyes. I would not be any longer a passive instrument for
his will, and so, as I no longer suited his purpose, he had done with
me, and I gained the loss of his friendship.

Chapter 92

A Mother's Farewell — My Friends at Home — Kindness of Magistrates
again — Scene in the County Court — Moral

I was witness about this time, to a very affecting incident which
took place at the prison. A young, good-looking countryman, had
narrowly escaped being hung for an atrocious case of housebreaking.
He was sentenced to transportation for life, and had sent for his
mother to come and take leave of him before he went off. She was
a little neat-looking woman, pale, and rather browned, and attired
in a plain but very cleanly habit. She stood before the barred gate
leading to the dungeons, and when she heard the clank of chains
coming along the dim passage, she started, clasped her hands con-
vulsively, and listened. Her son soon made his appearance, dragging
his chain. He extended his arms towards her, and she rushed into
the gloomy passage, and to his bosom – uttered his name – and
fainted. They rubbed her temples, and tried to give her water, but
in vain. Her teeth were fast set, her colour deathly pale, and she
continued thus long – he standing weeping over her and uttering
words of endearment. 'Mother! Mother! – Dear Mother! – Oh!

tnat I should have brought you to this!' – Many eyes unwont to melt, were also in tears, but no one, save the son, spoke. At length they motioned him to return, but he broke away, and kneeling, caught his mother in his arms, and pouring tears fast on her face, he reverently kissed her wan forehead and her cheeks, and resigning her to the attendants, he said, 'Now let me go! I've killed my poor mother! – I've broken her heart!' – and they led him away. They then carried her out, for air, and when, after some time, her senses returned, she cast a look around, and peered down the passage. 'He is gone,' said one of the bye-standers, on which she sighed, and departed slowly out at the castle-gate, weeping.

I was indebted, this spring, to Mr Berry, one of my late sureties, residing at Failsworth, and some other friends, for a suit of new clothes, which I had begun to be in need of. They sent me a sum of money, with a request that I would fit myself out decently, to come home, and I obeyed their directions, by which I lost some friends, as will shortly appear.

Mrs Johnson, the wife of my fellow-prisoner, never recovered from her indisposition. She kept declining in health, and returned home to die. I mention this painful circumstance, because I am desirous to render that testimony to the conduct of the magistrates and governor, which it so truly merited.

I believe it was the wish of Mrs Johnson that her husband should, if possible, come to see her before she died; and an application was made to Lord Sidmouth, by him, for that purpose, but without effect. The visiting magistrates, and the Rev. Mr Nelson in particular, then took up the affair, and memorialized his lordship, but with no better result than before. The magistrates of the county next got up an urgent but respectful memorial, which was presented to his lordship by the county members, but without effect: Lord Sidmouth assigning as a reason for his refusal, that if he conceded the point in this case, he did not know on what grounds he could refuse it in others which might occur, and that the practice would lead to endless confusion and evasions of the law. Mr Johnson did not therefore see his wife – though it was not the fault of the magistrates that he did not; and when they could not do anything more, they gave him the entire range of the grounds within the walls – every indulgence, in fact, excepting walking out of the castle gates. Most of his time, when out of doors, was thereafter spent in the gardens, apart from the other prisoners. I was frequently asked why I did not claim the same privilege; and I replied by reminding the interrogators that my case was different – I had the society of one whose companionship was a greater blessing than the range of any length or breadth of land could bestow. His privilege was not necessary to my happiness – I was content with what I had – and, moreover, whilst a claim of that sort would not benefit me, it might injure him, by causing his confinement to our common bounds. I therefore never interfered; and I should have acted a very selfish part if I had.

The expiration of my imprisonment was now fast approaching, and I and my wife often amused ourselves by conjectures as to how we should get home. It was soon decided, however, that we must walk it, and she, laughing, boasted what a light step she would lead me when we were on the road. Some perplexities as to the means for travelling, whether on foot or otherwise, were happily dissipated by the same beneficent friends who had smoothed our path at London. Healey, entirely unknown to me, had written to Mr Galloway on the subject – with respect to himself – which I have alluded to, and the result, to my great surprise, was a letter from that gentleman, directed to me at Lincoln, which set all our apprehensions at rest on that score.

Two of my friends in Lancashire, namely, the afore-mentioned Mr Berry, of Failsworth, and Mr Mark Smith, of Heywood, became my sureties for five years, in one hundred pounds each, and it now only remained for me to give my recognizances in two hundred pounds, previous to my liberation.

It was a very fine morning, I recollect; there was a large meeting of magistrates in the county hall, and many of the debtors were in court, for it was held for their relief also.

My wife took my arm, and we entered the court, and were shown to a seat opposite the chairman, Dr Caley Illingworth. The Rev. Mr Nelson was also there, and several other magistrates, whom I knew from their frequent visits to the castle.

'Joseph Johnson,' was soon afterwards called, but he did not answer. 'Joseph Healey,' was next called, but neither did he appear. I was then called, and, standing up, was invited to go across the table near the chairman. I did so, and entered into my own recognizances in the usual terms, after which I returned and sat by my wife. Healey and Johnson, shortly afterwards came into the court, and when some business had been disposed of, they were each directed to pass over the table as I had done, and then they severally went through the same form and took seats below the chairman.

Dr Illingworth then called our names, and we stood up, whilst he congratulated us on the near termination of our imprisonment – thanked us for our good behaviour, which had enabled the magistrates and the governor to afford us some indulgencies which we otherwise could not have had – and hoped that, in future, the reflections which must have presented themselves in prison, would, during the remainder of our lives, produce a line of conduct which would render unnecessary any further visitations of the law – or words to that effect.

I looked at my two fellow-prisoners, expecting that something would be said by them, and especially by Johnson, who had experienced so largely the best endeavours of the magistrates on his behalf; but neither of them spoke – they both sat down.

I, remaining on my feet, then thanked the magistrates and the governor for their kind behaviour towards me, and towards my wife, during my imprisonment. I could not, I said, suffer that opportunity to escape without expressing to them how unfeignedly grateful we were for all they had done on our behalf. Their kindness was such as I did not expect when I came to that place, and was certainly such as I should not have experienced in my own county. It had made a deep impression on both our hearts; and for myself I must say, that if any course could wean a man from error, by creating a grateful feeling in his mind, it was a course such as I had experienced at that prison. It would have an effect more powerful with me, than the harshest measures that could have been adopted. I again thanked them most sincerely and gratefully. I should remem-remember their kindness, I said, to the last day of my existence.

I then sat down, thinking, that now, at any rate, my two fellow-prisoners could not avoid following so proper an example. They, however, kept their seats, and spoke not one word. Then, in a few minutes, Johnson got up and walked over the table, out of the court; and the moment after Healey followed him.

I need not intimate what impression this scene created on the minds of all present, nor repeat the observations it gave rise to. I will only say, that I the next day left the castle with the good opinion and good wishes of all who had known me, whether rich landowners, or reverend magistrates, or poor prisoners. The governor spoke well of me, and ordered that I should be admitted to the castle on any day, so long as I stopped in Lincoln. But my most welcome applauder was my own conscience, which told me that whilst I had, in a becoming manner, submitted to the authorities of the country. I had also deserved their esteem – had disarmed, perhaps, some animosities – had done some good to the cause of reform – and had, by my conduct, made one more appeal for those of the class in life to which I belonged.

When I came to settle with the 'Old Daddy,' – the turnkey at the gate – which prisoners generally did by making him a present before leaving, – he begged I would give him my wooden shoes – for so he called my Lancashire clogs, which I wore in the winter. I gave them to him, and he expressed great delight, saying he would place them in his collection of curiosities, for it seemed that clogs had been but very rarely, if ever, seen previously in Lincoln.

Chapter 93

Objects at Lincoln — Tom Otter — Barton Ferry — Great Markham — A Scrupulous Landlady

WE stopped a day or two in Lincoln, at our friend Stainton's, and having sent our luggage to the carriers, we examined many of the venerable ruins of the place, particularly the fine Roman arch called 'The Stone Bow' – one of the most perfect specimens of Roman architecture in England. The splendid and venerable cathedral also attracted our particular notice, and we could not but lament the ruthless and insensate havoc made amongst the images and statues by the soldiers of the stern Cromwell.

It was on the afternoon of Wednesday, a fine day, that we bade adieu to Lincoln, and passing over the race-ground, we stopped at the 'Eel-pie House,' where we partook of their celebrated dish, 'collared eel,' and had our parting glass with some friends who accompanied us. Proceeding thence, we passed Saxmundham on our right, and at Dringey-nook, we came in sight of the gibbet of Tom Otter, who in the dark shady lane in which he then hung, murdered his sweetheart by beating out her brains with a hedge stake. We stopped at a very decent inn, at a short distance from the gibbet, and from thence

353

continued our journey through a level country, full of woods and plantations, till the broad waters of the Trent suddenly appeared before us. A shout and a signal brought the ferryman over, and after some persuasion, with fear and trembling, my wife at length went on board, and we were ferried over, and landed in the county of Nottingham. A short and very agreeable walk, through a rural country, with pretty English cottages embowered in gardens and fruit trees, brought us to the village of Great Markham, where we entered a snug little public-house, and took up our quarters.

We sat chatting over our tea, until it was nearly bed time, and when I requested that we should be shewn to our room, the landlady gave an enquiring and dubious glance at us, and retired, evidently to take a second thought upon the subject. The servant woman next came into the room, pretending to fetch something, but once or twice I observed her taking side-looks at us; and as I perceived there were misgivings of some sort, I ordered a glass of liquor and a pipe, resolved to amuse myself by watching the shifts and manoeuvres of these simple country-folks.

The mistress brought the glass, and the girl brought the pipe, and each gave a scrutinizing glance, which we seemed not to notice. We were both ready to burst into laughter, only my wife was a little apprehensive lest we should be turned out of doors. I thee'd and thou'd her in their presence, as a man might do his wife – and talked to her in my ordinary careless way; and at last the landlady came, and, begging we would not be offended, asked if the young woman was my wife? I now laughed outright, and my wife could not refrain, though she covered her face.

I assured the good woman that my companion had been my wife many years.

Nay, she had no ill opinion of her, she said, only she looked so young.

But young as she appears, she reckons to be my age within about three weeks, I said; and she was mother to a fine girl, now in the ninth year of her age.

Oh! she was sorry to have mistaken us, she said, we should have a comfortable bed ready in a few minutes.

And so saying, she left the room, satisfied no doubt, with the explanation which had set at rest her troublesome qualms of conscience.

We had most excellent lodgings; and in the morning we rose early, and commenced our journey, by lanes and shady foot-paths, – sweet with the breath of flowers, and echoing the music of birds.

Chapter 94

A neat Hostel — A Hint for Invalids — Worksop Ale — Sheffield — Startled by a Trifle — A Mountain Journey — A Prospect — A Discovery — The Spirit of Life visible — How others may see it

ELKSLEY. – What associations in a name! – The ley – the pasture-land – the lair of the elk. Where was now the elk? – Where the wide wold – with its 'gre wolf?' – and the elk stalking, the dimly-seen monarch of a misty land? All had disappeared – the elk, the wolf, were no more; and the dun moor, and black moss had become laden with pastures, and fields of grain, and garlanded with orchard blossoms, and dotted with cottages as white as lillies on a garden bed.

Here we breakfasted with the landlady, a tidy little body, and a delicate looking young girl, who had come from Nottingham, to stop here for her health. We found this a most agreeable resting-place; everything was fastidiously clean; the tea, the sugar, the bread, were of the best quality, whilst the butter, – if I may be allowed a new compound, – was most butter-fully rich. We, of course, much enjoyed our breakfast, for

> *We together far had come,*
> *Among the dews that morning.*[1]

And I believe our hearty eating made the poor lass from Nottingham quite hungry. She said she had not taken such a breakfast for a long time.

From hence we travelled a long way, nine miles, I think, chiefly through woods and plantations belonging to the Duke of Newcastle. We seldom saw a house, and the solitude was unbroken for long distances, except by the whirring of the pheasant or partridge across the road, or the bounding of the hare. At Shireoaks, we passed

[1] Spencer T. Hall, the poet of Sherwood.

a large mansion, and some substantial homesteads, and entering Worksop, with its ruined abbey on the right, we again rested, and partook some excellent ale. At South Aston, we entered Yorkshire; and near Aston, crossed the Rother river; and successively passing Handsworth, Darnal, and Attercliffe, (Qy. why not Ottercliffe? or Addercliffe?) we entered Sheffield when near night-fall, and having been directed to 'The Axe' public-house, or 'Hammer and Axe,' I forget which, we soon found the place, on our left, as we entered the town and there took our quarters for the night.

We intended to stop a day here, to look about us, and survey the curiosities of this great city of Vulcan, and well should we have been repaid for the delay, no doubt, but as important events not only frequently arise from small causes, but are baffled by them, our dreams of all the shining jewels of this wondrous cave, – shrouded in smoke and sulphur, and glaring red fire – were quickly annihilated by a very insignificant object. As I sat up in bed, I was almost startled by a sudden exclamation of my wife, who discovered one of those noisome flat insects, so common in the beds of towns and crowded places, crawling up my shirt. This determined her. 'She would not stop in that place,' she said, 'for the world – she could not eat in it – and we must set off directly;' and suiting the action to the word, she was dressed in quick time, and fidgetting to be gone – to get out 'into the green lanes,' and to 'breathe the sweet country air.' I rather thought, however, that the wish to see her child affected her; perhaps she had been dreaming of her; at all events, I am sure the anticipated pleasure of embracing my dear little girl once more, had considerable influence in my acquiescence to quit the town thus suddenly.

Well, we soon paid the shot, and were on our way out of the town. We got, however, on the wrong route, and, before we were aware of that, we found ourselves climbing the foot of the great hills which divide Yorkshire from Derbyshire. For several miles we continued to ascend, and every where we came to a small flat, and hoped we had surmounted all, a few paces discovered to us another eminence. I wondered how my little woman stood it, but she this morning shewed me her light foot indeed, and with all cheerfulness we breasted the hill, anon looking back, to see how far we had travelled towards home. At length we entered on a broad wild moor, where for miles and miles towards Yorkshire, all was a scene of dun heath and shelterless plain; whilst downwards, over Derbyshire and Cheshire, the eye commanded what seemed an almost illimitable expanse of mountain land.

> But where the vision began to fail
> There seemed to be hills of a cloudy pale.

In the valley we had left – now as we could discover of a beautifully undulating surface, and gaily green in the sun, – lay the town of Sheffield, shrouded in its furnace clouds. On our right and left were the wild and boundless districts I have mentioned, and before us was the wrinkled front of Mam Tor, frowning like an eld, in witch-land.

We walked to the height of Hattersage-Grange, and there stopped to survey the vast, solitary, yet pleasing scenes. My wife was seated on a grassy knoll, whilst I stood beside her with my stick and bundle over my shoulder, my back towards the sun – whose beams were somewhat mitigated by light clouds – and my looks directed over the wold towards the Yorkshire border.

'Well, I am convinced now,' I said, breaking a long silence, 'that Burke was not so far wide of the truth after all.'

'What did Burke say?' she asked; 'for my part I never heard him say much of either truth or falsehood.'

She thought I was alluding to one of the simplest of my radical comrades, whom we had nick-named 'Burke.'

'Pho! its Edmund Burke, the great orator and political apostate, that I mean.'

'And what did he say?' she asked.

'Say? He called the people "the swinish multitude"; and I am convinced he was right, for I have discovered I am one of them.'

'What do you mean?' she again asked, now more interested.

'I can see the wind,' I said, 'and that's a sure sign I'm one of the swinish herd.'

'See the wind! And what's it like?' asked she, looking up and laughing.

'It's the most beautiful thing I ever saw,' I said, 'and if thou'll come here, thou shall see it also.'

I will suppose that the curiosity natural to the sex was excited, for she instantly was at my side.

'Now look over the top of the brown heath with a steady eye, and see if thou canst discern a remarkably bright substance, brighter than glass or pearly water – deeply clear and lucid – swimming, not like a stream, but like a quick spirit, up and down, and forward, as if hurrying to be gone.'

'Nonsense!' she said, 'there is not anything.'

'Look again, steady, for a moment,' I said, 'I still behold it.'

'There is,' she said, 'there is; I see it! Oh! what a beautiful thing.'

I gave her a kiss, and said I loved her better than ever. She was the first woman who, I believed, had ever seen the vital element, the life-fraught wind.

'Is that the wind?' she asked.

'That is the wind of heaven,' I said, 'now sweeping over the earth, and visible. It is the great element of vitality – water quickened by fire – the spirit of life!'

I know not whether I was quite right in my philosophy, but we bowed our hearts, and adored the Creator; and in that, we were both right, I hope.

We stood gazing in wonder and admiration; for still, like a spirit-stream, it kept hurrying past – or as a messenger in haste; and so we left it glittering and sweeping away. This was on the morning of the nineteenth day of May, 1821.

And reader, I dare be bound with thee, that if having a good pair of eyes, thou wilt at the same season of the year, and on a day like ours, – with a mild sun, and a quick breeze out of Yorkshire – if thou, at such season, and on such day, climb to the top of Hather-sage-Grange, and stand with thy back to the sun – Mam Tor visible on thy left hand – then, also, shalt thou see the beautiful apparition – the spirit of life – which we saw. It will repay thy trouble well, I assure thee. Neither I nor mine can ever forget it, whilst memory is ours.

Chapter 95

Another good Hostel — Little John — The Blacksmith at Hope — The Winnits — Chapel-on-the-Frith — Stockport — Home

AT Hathersage, we heard the sound of a shuttle, and my wife re-marked that we were getting near home. Fortunately we stepped into a little public-house, never exceeded in neatness and comfort, except by the one at Elksley. Our breakfast was all that could be desired, and we did justice to it, having walked our ten or eleven miles, and over such a country.

At this place, in the church-yard, are shewn two small stones, marking, as people say, the grave of Little John, the faithful companion of the bold Robin Hood. A picturesque low cottage, situated in a garden, and overgrown with ivy and other creepers, is still shown as the one in which the broken-down outlaw took refuge after the dispersion of his band; and where he also died. Both objects are worthy the attention of the travelling antiquary. Such a place would be a likely shelter to a proscribed man; whilst the moors and the forest glades – then but little known, and seldom penetrated – would yield plenty of game to a good bow, and no one be the wiser of the trespass.

At Hope, where we called at the house of the village blacksmith, to ask for a draught of water, it being a warm day, we were, with old English hospitality, presented with a jug of good brown ale; and also pressed to sit down and partake the family dinner, of hot potato pie; but, with all gratitude, we declined the latter, and went forward, not stopping at Castleton, for we had now fairly set our hearts on getting home.

In climbing up the Winnits (Wind-Yates) we sat down to rest, and to view the rocky scenery around and above us. A spring of clear water was trickling near, and with that health-giving beverage we quenched our thirst. A fine hawk was circling over head, and a couple of ravens disturbed the death-like silence with their croak. The place was mysterious, and had an air of savage grandeur. The imagination might easily expand in such a vast and darksome gorge. Were it indeed the portal – the palace gates of the wind? Of the wild, and beautiful, and powerful existence which we had seen that morning? And if so, whither did it lead? We mounted to the top, and found ourselves again entering on a wide dun moor. Mam Tor, with her bold, storm-channelled front, on our right; the sun, in his mid-height above us, and a long and weary waste, with swampy bottoms, and grey grass waving in the wind, before us.

Not wearily, but cheerfully and lightsomely, along this desert track we went: and having gone a far way, we began to descend, and eventually rested again at a public-house in the pleasant little town of Chapel-on-the-Frith.

Here I was certainly taken to be a fellow who was running away with some old woman's daughter. The landlady could not, at first, believe that my wife was my wife; and when I told her, as I did the good woman at Great Markham, that she had been a mother nine years, she called John, her husband, to partake in her amazement, and 'wonderfully strange,' to our great amusement, they both deemed the case to be.

We stopped not at Whaley Bridge, for the sun was getting low, but hastened to Disley, and after a brief rest there, we again started, though neither I nor my fellow-traveller were so alert as in the morning. In fact our feet began to be worse for our two days travel, and when we got upon the paved causeway betwixt Bullock Smithy and Stockport, it was like treading on red-hot stones. Thus, long after night-fall, we went limping arm-in-arm into Stockport. We found the dwelling of our friend Moorhouse at the lower end of the town, and knocking at the door, were received with every hospitality.

My friend and his wife bustled about, and did all they could to make us comfortable. We got a supper of good refreshing tea, and then essayed to go to rest, but my poor little companion had to mount the stairs on her knees, – she would not be carried up – and when her stockings were removed, her feet were found covered with blood-red blisters. I got some hot water and soap, – washed her feet well, – wiped them carefully, till quite dry, – wrapped them in her flannel petticoat, and put her to bed. I then washed my own feet, for they were not much better than hers, and committing ourselves to divine care, we were soon oblivious of all weariness and anxiety, and on awaking the next morning, our feet were as sound, for anything we felt, as they were when we set out from Lincoln.

Our walk to Manchester the next morning was a mere pleasure trip. We scarcely stopped there, but hastening onwards, we entered Middleton in the afternoon, and were met in the street by our dear child, who came running, wild with delight, to our arms. We soon made ourselves comfortable in our own humble dwelling; the fire was lighted, the hearth was clean swept, friends came to welcome us, and we were once more at home.

> *Be it ever so humble,*
> *There's no place like home.*

Chapter 96

Of the Author and his Book

AND now friend reader, thou hast seen me, at last, through all the places of my imprisonment, and back to my home. Have I not led thee a somewhat strange and painful, yet not altogether unpleasing pilgrimage? whilst the consciousness that thou wast all this time treading the ground of reality – of this earthly world – must have rendered thy sojourn more strange. Even so it is; reality is always romantic, though the romantic is not always real.

Having written of myself and others, it may not appear unseemly if I give a short history of the origin and progress of the present work, and conclude with some general, but I trust not unimportant observations on the present condition of the country – the fallacious views of parties – and the means to be adopted for our safe transition to an approaching state of society.

I make no excuse about the 'partiality of friends' having induced me to take the step of publication. I have not any friends who, in that respect, either could influence me, or would attempt it. They would know it was not necessary to do so; they would have the confidence in me to feel assured that I should produce a book which, whilst it interested the reader, would form a tablet of facts, a group of characters, which otherwise would have passed into oblivion; and that it would, so far, be useful to the future historian of the days recorded. In the performance of this task however, I have sought counsel only of myself. A long train of fruitless exertions, – of disappointed hopes, – of harassments of body and mind, – of young days and years wasted and flung away for nothing, – except to find selfishness, ingratitude, and detraction, where I should have met every generous and manly virtue, – could not have weighed on any heart, as they did on mine, without producing a will of its own – a purpose beyond the ordinary motives of human nature; therefore impervious to them, and, in some respects, also above them.

I had friends, however, and I am proud to acknowledge them, who, when my purpose became known, lent me every assistance in furtherance of my object; but their friendship was not of that cast which – though some of them were public men – sought its reward in the public emblazonment of their names; therefore, on that point, I am silent. They expected something better from me, and they have had it, – the sincere though unpretending gratitude of my heart. Still, I may say, they are not great men, in the ordinary sense of the word; nor rich men, in the golden hue of richness; nor poor men, from a penurious craving spirit; nor high men on the stilts of gaudy pride; nor low men, degenerate through ignorance and vice. Some of them are poets, and of imperishable name too; others are encouragers and admirers of literature, of the genuine uneducated, as well as the educated stamp. Some are men 'well to do in the world;' some are humble, but trustworthy servants; and others in more distinguished situations: but all are of that class which is privileged to

> Hear the muses in a ring,
> Aye, round about Jove's altar sing.

Such are they who enabled me to bring my memoir before the public. Without their aid, I might have written – as indeed I should – for posterity; to the pecuniary benefit, mayhap, of some thankless 'next of kin,' or the emolument of that very respectable set of tradesmen, who are said to 'drink wine out of authors' skulls.'

But there were others, besides friends, whom I had to encounter, to smile upon, when I was full of sadness, to look up unto when my hopes were drooping; for in a case like mine where a purpose of novel execution had to be prosecuted like a piece of market business, we must try all, likely and unlikely, and spare none, shun none, on account of their looks, or creeds, or of our own suppositions. How many bitter disappointments, then, fell to the lot of him who travelled the great world, with nothing to exchange for its bread save the unperishing food of the mind – the etherial for the substantial, the spirit for the body! But why do I expatiate?

One of that class, about the education of which so much is now being said, – a self-taught writer, – produces a book which is certainly not to be despised on account of its morals, its politics, or its religion. He waits on some of the richest of those who profess to be friends to the working classes, and to them he respectfully presents his humble production, when, what is the reception he and his book experience? One 'never buys books; he has not time to look at them.' Another has 'hundreds of volumes, chests full he has never read.' One says, 'the book won't suit him;' another, 'never reads such

362

things;' and another superciliously walks away, he 'is not in that line, that morning.'

But I will not give way to the language which waits for utterance when I recur to these things. I will turn rather to the consolatory view, and recollect how indifference at the office of one rich man was more than atoned for by a courteous reception at that of another, – how rudeness at one place was followed by encouraging attention at the next, – how to the bustle and importance of the warehouse succeeded calm and respectful discussion, – how ignorant superciliousness was rebuked by thanks for my attention – how, in short, many received me with civility, many with kindness, – many heard me with patience, – many wished me success, – and gave me earnest of their wish, – many recommended me to friends, – many referred me to others, – several led me to their hospitable boards, and some who declined my work laid me under an obligation by the manner in which they did so.

The booksellers were certainly the most amusing class I had dealings with. One wrote to me for the work whilst publishing in parts, and sold it well for me. Another, whose windows were crowded with old tomes, and his counters with the numbers of Humphrey's Clock, Jack Shephard, Nicholas Nickleby, and such like serials, (a house of long standing in the trade,) looked at the volume, – looked at the title, – turned the book over, and gave it back, declining to sell it on any account; – another objected to a word in the title, – it 'would'nt do for his customers;' one, wrote to me from London, offering to become my agent, at forty-five per cent. of course, – and another London house, 'begged leave to decline the publishing of it at all.'

Amidst such variety of quickly succeeding incidents, some pleasing, others discouraging, some of them ups in the world, others decided downs, but with more the latter than the former, how could a man, struggling to rise, comport himself? it would be difficult; but old John Bunyan has a verse which answers the question.

> *There's no discouragement,*
> *Shall make him once repent,*
> *His first avowed intent,*
> *To be a pilgrim.*
>
> *Whoso besets him round*
> *With dismal stories;*

Do but themselves confound,
His strength the more is.

Nor lions can him fright,
He'll with the giants' (tyrants) fight,
And he shall have his right,
To be a pilgrim.

Chapter 97

Of matters relative to the Nation

TO THE effect which this, and other small works of mine have produced, I think I may refer to with some degree of certainty and
satisfaction. The publication of my small poem – or rather versifi-
cation of Berenger's 'La Lyonnaise,' – with its accompanying notes
and postscript, was quickly followed by that most important
assemblage of the trading and working classes, the operative anti-
corn-law banquet, at Manchester; a decided step, and one too,
'in the right direction.' That was the first time the two classes had
come together to shake hands, and look manfully in each other's
faces. A few more such meetings, and the occupation of the incen-
diary demagogue – the real 'divider and destroyer,' had ceased. Its
moral influence was greater than that of a hundred bazaars, or con-
ferences.

Since the publication of the present work, the question of the
education of the working classes has seemed to have received a
fresh impulse, and the agitation on that subject still forms an en-
grossing topic of discussion. A minister of the established church at
Manchester has thought the matter of sufficient importance to claim
the advocacy of his pen, and he has given it in a most excellent spirit.

A gentleman of Salford, heretofore of conservative principles,
also put forth a tract on the necessity of uniting the middle and
working classes; and just latterly, Mr Sturge, of Birmingham, who,
if I mistake not, has had one of my books in hand, has come forth
an advocate for 'complete suffrage.' – The ruthless tone of chartism
has been softened, and I know that some of the leaders have had my

books. – The more rational and honest have become loosened from the violent and unprincipled; and as, ultimately, the latter must wither of their own madness, so the former may be expected to adhere to realities only, dropping the extremes of things, until all the practical good has been obtained, wisely applied, and permanently adopted. If I may not claim to have been the pioneer in some of these, and other salutary movements, I may certainly, at any rate, take my place in the advanced guard; and it is some reward to find one-self so honourably stationed.

Still, much remains to be done, and I am ready to do my share, in my own way, and for – THE NATION! – That is the only party I will serve; though, if all things were finely balanced, even my country has only a step-mother's claim to my services, – I have given more to her than I have received – and far more than many of her most favoured sons had either the heart, or the brains, to contribute. But enough of this, I am willing still to lend a hand to the old lady, unkind though she has been. Let us then inquire how she is situated?

Behold the crown without influence, and the sport of faction; the factions themselves strong enough to enact evil, but too weak to effect much good. The aristocracy blindly clutching their rents, whilst their very acres are in jeopardy, as if they could not perceive, and would not be made to comprehend, until too late, that cheap bread for the people, means also, all they seem to care about, cheap pride; cheap pomp; cheap distinction for themselves.

Next are the priesthood, scrambling for worldly gain, and squabbling as to which sect or party shall have most hand in moulding the young brains of the rising generation; as if they had something else in view besides making them into good men and women; as if there were a precept, known only to themselves, and superior to that. 'Do unto others as ye would they should do unto you.'

Then there are the land-tillers, blind and blundering serfs to the landowners, though the latter knock them about like the clods of their own fields, and for the same purpose too, to make them yield rent.

Next come the manufacturers, working at the wrong end, and trying to make a pitiable impression on the heads and hearts of a class that never, since the days of Cromwell, was pervious to anything at variance with its own will, save a battle-axe, or a bullet. There they are, striving for cheap bread, as if it were present salvation, and forgetting what all history is constantly proclaiming, that nothing human is fixed: that crowns, sceptres, dominions, institutions, establishments, and monopolies, ever changing, ever departing from their old seats, springing up anew in other places, and leaving deserts where they formerly flourished. Tyre, Sidon, Carthage, Greece, Rome! – all the departed nations of the world, warn us of this; and still we remain as if we were unconscious that our time must come, is coming, – nay is almost at the threshold.

What, then, 'shall we do to be saved?' We must look our difficulties in the face like men. The times which have been, never will return; we cannot recall that which has departed, and is still going; – we cannot, any more than we can still the ocean, prevent our manufactures from being set up in other nations. We have read them too profound a lesson for that. We have exhibited the spectacle of a small community combatting the world, and buying, or beating it all round. We have shewn the secret of our strength, of all our warlike strength – and they will act upon it. We have shewn them how our manufactures produced commerce – which produced wealth – which created credit – which supplied taxes and loans illimitable, and enabled us to wield, with tremendous effect, all the resources of our vast navy, and our numerous armies; beating those we encountered, and subsidizing the remainder, until we either had time to beat them ourselves, or could get others to beat them.

And will not the nations lay hold of this wonderful power, and try to render it available to their own interests? Most certainly they will. The novelty of the thing itself would be a great temptation; and though no one nation may manufacture to the extent that we have done, they may manufacture for themselves, and they will do so. America, with its cotton-fields, and its teeming population, will spin its own yarn, and weave its own cloth, whether we will or no; and the nations of the continent will do, are doing, the same. They have nothing else to do in peace, nor can anything be more natural than that they should do so. We cannot, must not, always be spinners and weavers for the world; and if we could, I do not see that it is desirable we should. Let these truths be impressed on our minds, and let us, like a community of sensible men, calculate all our disadvantages, and prepare for the worst.

Whether or not we shall be prepared, depends on the exertions of the wise and good of all classes. If preparations are made, we may be a suffering family, but we shall be an united one, and half our evils will be obviated. Those we must endure will be borne in a noble spirit; whilst those we surmount, and they may be many, will be subjects for our common triumph.

Let all the sufferers then, of whatever class or description, – all who love their country, – all who would promote the happiness of posterity and of mankind, unite to procure by peaceful means, – a suffrage coextensive with direct taxation – an annual accountability of members to their constituents. – Cheap food for the hungry, – cheap clothing for the naked – cheap labour for the industrious, – (we must cut a straight-forward swathe, – we cannot turn aside to leave nooks and corners for classes) cheap rents for the cottager, – cheap rents for the farmer, – cheap education for every one, – cheap law in our courts, – cheap justice on the bench, and real justice too; – cheap religion, and freedom with it, – a cheap, money-despising, vanity-shunning, priesthood, – a cheap, noble-minded, open-handed aristocracy, – elder brothers and fathers of the people, – and lastly, or firstly if you will, a cheap government, and a cheap but firm executive.

I would not, like the O'Connorites, insist on having the whole of these things, or nothing; I would take any part, and think well of it, and get the others as soon as I could.

A bond of union like this, entered into and prosecuted without noise, without agitation or frothy declamation (with which the ears of the people are dinned now-a-days, and which is but the pumping out of so much energy to the winds), would put down all demagoguism, – all trading agitation, – all jealousies, – all dissensions, – all recriminations. It would bring together good men and true of all grades, and would create a brotherhood, which whilst it directed the masses would also prepare them for whatever vicissitude was at hand. Like the veterans of an army it would show its comrades how to bear as well as to dare.

But the whole extent of the evil must be steadily scanned: there must not be any half-measures; any exemptions for this or that interest; for this or that portion of the community. During fifty years, the English nation has been engaged in a gluttonous scramble for wealth, and now the time is coming when there must be a disgorging from the highest to the lowest. We shall be never the worse for it, after all, but better, more long-lived, both as individuals and as a nation, provided we get the crisis over pretty smoothly, and that depends upon ourselves. Our weaver lads must put up as their grand-fathers did, with jannocks and barley bread, and barm dumplings, and brown ale, – our farmers' 'ladies,' as the daughters of farmers are commonly called, – must don their clogs, and milk their own cows, and make their butter, and darn their own stockings. ——'The Mrs' may ride behind Robin, instead of taking out her gig; whilst the manufacturer's lady must not deem it beneath her to sit basting a good Yorkshire pudding, without a fire screen, instead of perching on a screw stool thrumming a piano. We must all take our share in the humiliation, and be thankful it is no worse. We must work like a willing crew or the ship will be lost.

Yes, the change must be prepared for in our towns, our villages, our homes, our manufactories, and our seaports, as well as at the seat of government. The evil does not all lie there. Our present condition is the consequence of our folly as a nation, and of the natural course of events. Our grandfathers and fathers were all mad for war with the French, and the most wise and popular government that could have been established would have gone mad too, with a mad people under it. The wars which plunged us into irredeemable debt, were the acts of the nation, and the nation must submit to its own infliction.

The very same cause which removed the silk manufacture from Spitalfields into Lancashire, – namely, cheapness – is now taking our manufactures into other countries. So that even the repeal of the bread tax, desirable as it is, would not save our trade, unaccompanied by such other measures as would cut down all other taxes to the very core, and place our expenditure on a most rigid scale of econ-omy. We must all be prepared to make sacrifices. We must deter-mine to deserve redemption; the nation must act as one man, or at least the influential portion of it must, and the sooner it is set about the better.

If we honestly lay our shoulders to the wheel, and lift all together, with a long pull, and a strong pull, and a sober and noiseless one, we shall get over the slough, upon firmer land, and into better ways. If not, and we stick fast, and begin to sink, how inglorious it will be to be reminded by the gods that we are perishing because we did not perform our whole duty.

Reader, consider these things seriously; and FARE-THEE-WELL.

July 27th, 1842.

COSIMO CLASSICS

COSIMO is an innovative publisher of books and publications that inspire, inform and engage readers worldwide. Our titles are drawn from a range of subjects including health, business, philosophy, history, science and sacred texts. We specialize in using print-on-demand technology (POD), making it possible to publish books for both general and specialized audiences and to keep books in print indefinitely. With POD technology new titles can reach their audiences faster and more efficiently than with traditional publishing.

> ➢ **Permanent Availability:** Our books & publications never go out-of-print.

> ➢ **Global Availability:** Our books are always available online at popular retailers and can be ordered from your favorite local bookstore.

COSIMO CLASSICS brings to life unique, rare, out-of-print classics representing subjects as diverse as *Alternative Health, Business and Economics, Eastern Philosophy, Personal Growth, Mythology, Philosophy, Sacred Texts, Science, Spirituality* and much more!

COSIMO-on-DEMAND publishes your books, publications and reports. If you are an Author, part of an Organization, or a Benefactor with a publishing project and would like to bring books back into print, publish new books fast and effectively, would like your publications, books, training guides, and conference reports to be made available to your members and wider audiences around the world, we can assist you with your publishing needs.

Visit our website at www.cosimobooks.com to learn more about Cosimo, browse our catalog, take part in surveys or campaigns, and sign-up for our newsletter.

And if you wish please drop us a line at info@cosimobooks.com. We look forward to hearing from you.

LaVergne, TN USA
17 December 2009
167406LV00001B/1/A